FIFTH EDITION

UNDERSTANDING READING

A Psycholinguistic Analysis of Reading and Learning to Read

BOOKS BY FRANK SMITH

The Genesis of Language (edited, with George A. Miller)
Understanding Reading (five editions)
Psycholinguistics and Reading
Comprehension and Learning
Writing and the Writer (two editions)
Reading Without Nonsense ("Reading" in UK—two editions)
Essays Into Literacy
Awakening to Literacy (edited, with Hillel Goelman and Antoinette A.
    Oberg)
Insult to Intelligence
Joining the Literacy Club
to think
Whose Language? What Power?

FIFTH EDITION

UNDERSTANDING READING

A Psycholinguistic Analysis of
Reading and Learning to Read

FRANK SMITH

1994

LAWRENCE ERLBAUM ASSOCIATES, PUBLISHERS
Hillsdale, New Jersey   Hove, UK

Lawrence Erlbaum Associates, Inc., Publishers
365 Broadway
Hillsdale, New Jersey 07642

Library of Congress Cataloging-in-Publication Data

Smith, Frank, 1928-
    Understanding reading / Frank Smith. -- 5th ed.
        p.   cm.
    ISBN 0-8058-1419-1 (hardcover) -- ISBN 0-8058-1420-5 (pbk).
    1. Reading. 2. Learning, Psychology of. 3 Written
communication.   I. Title.
    LB1050.S574   1994
    428.4--dc20   94-6097
                                                CIP

Books published by Lawrence Erlbaum Associates are printed
on acid-free paper, and their bindings are chosen
for strength and durability.

Printed in the United States of America

10 9 8 7 6 5 4 3 2 1

Contents

Preface to the Fifth Edition

Preparing a new edition of a book first published over 20 years ago is a chastening experience. My excursions through mountains of relevant literature reveal that little of substance has changed since the first edition of *Understanding Reading* was published in 1971. The main controversies persist (what it means to be a reader, how written words are recognized, and how reading should be taught). The basic theoretical positions are unchanged, and even some of the major protagonists are the same, such as Goodman (1967, 1992/1993) and Chall (1967, 1992/1993). Forests have been sacrificed to publish conflicting research results and theoretical arguments, but the only consequence seems to be a hardening of positions. It is unnerving to discover that what were once seen as fresh approaches are now ancient dogmas, adopted or rejected by waves of new champions, sometimes with immoderate enthusiasm or intemperate scorn. No wonder teachers and students can be confused, if they expect either side of controversies to be proved right or to admit to being wrong.

This is clearly not a matter of "facts." There is more evidence than anyone knows what to do with, but it comes into educational theorizing and policy as raw material, to be processed in different ways for different purposes. What matters is how facts are gathered, which facts are considered relevant, and how they are interpreted—all subject to personal predilection. There are no "pure facts"—their place in any theory is always determined by broader theoretical and political intentions.

Focusing on Issues

A major change in the present edition is that while continuing to accommodate recent developments in research, theory, and my own ideas, I introduce
a new section at the end of each chapter to outline the more persistent and
contentious issues that surround particular topics.

I do not attempt to resolve these issues—that would just be a matter of
reiterating the arguments of one point of view against others—but simply
underline what the major disagreements are. In the final chapter, I discuss
why I conclude that none of the advocates of the major positions will ever be
proved right or admit to being wrong, because they are divided by fundamental convictions about learning, teaching, language, and education.

In acknowledging alternative points of view, I have not concealed my own
position, and I certainly cannot claim to give opposing beliefs a comprehensive hearing in this book (although there are plenty of other books around
that do that). But when it comes to the point, teachers and students must make
up their own minds, which is something I said way back in the first edition, and
I would like to make clear what they must make up their minds about.

We all live and learn in a world where no final answers are guaranteed and
must make profound decisions for ourselves (even if our only decision is to
rely unquestioningly upon the opinions or decisions of someone else).
Throughout their professional lives, teachers are confronted by conflicting
points of view, frequently urged with compelling authority and conviction,
and they must be able to take a position. The first responsibility and right of
all teachers and students must be to exercise independent thought—though
in their own education they are often denied the opportunity with rational-
izations that they "aren't ready," "shouldn't be confused," or "lack thinking
experience" (Smith, 1990, 1993).

Computers and Brains

The preface to the fourth edition referred to the growing influence of
cognitive science, a discipline primarily concerned with abstract theories
related to the organization of knowledge, especially through language, in
humans and in computers. This influence has continued to grow—not, I think,
because cognitive science has anything significantly new to say about education, but because it has become the dominant force in contemporary psychology (although it embraces contending points of view on particular issues).
Cognitive science is influential because it is so intimately tied to the dominant
technology of the day, and it also claims to be authoritative because it asserts
that its technological methodology is the only valid one. But because of its
insistence on particular conceptualizations and procedures, cognitive science

is also narrow. Cognitive science looks at reading, and also reading instruction, from a limited "knowledge and skills" perspective.

Although I say that little of substance has changed in reading theory in recent decades, I do not mean that new concepts and theories do not make a difference. They do. New concepts are new ways of talking, and they encourage a focus on certain matters rather than on others. With the growth of cognitive science, for example, a profusion of new terms has been introduced for old concepts, such as "metacognition" (for "reflection" or "introspection") and "phonological awareness" (for "listening to the sounds of words"). People who would have no trouble understanding the old terms can be overly impressed and even confused by the terms that supersede them. An unwarranted aura of infallibility may surround the "experts" who use the new terms with facility, especially if they claim special insight.

I have chosen in the present edition to highlight at some length the ideological clash between whole language and direct instruction, partly at the expense of two giants who figured prominently in earlier editions, the linguist Noam Chomsky and the behaviorist psychologist B. F. Skinner. This book is not a history, and the names of Chomsky and Skinner have almost completely dropped out of current discussions of reading, despite the indelible marks that both made. Chomsky has become more deeply involved in recondite technical areas of linguistics and broader areas of political criticism, though his liberating mentalistic spirit pervades the whole language movement, and Skinner's reductionist dislike of mentalism lives on in the direct instruction point of view.

Within cognitive science, two new and mutually contradictory theories related to language learning have become influential—both claiming to be based on structures in the brain, but in fact only in a metaphorical way, and equally reminiscent of computer structures. One is called modular theory and the other connectionism. Both are discussed in this book, together with a closer look at other metaphors currently employed in psychological and educational theorizing—including my own.

I have added about 200 new references from the late 1980s and early 1990s (having scrutinized perhaps ten times that number) and removed about a third of the older references. But I have refrained from replacing the old with the new just for the sake of "updating." We all stand on the shoulders of forebears to raise our own flags. Where earlier studies remain unique or may have been copied but not improved upon, I have let them stand—indeed, I regard them as having stood the test of time. I would not want to support any idea that the "latest" research is always the most significant or the most reliable. Often it simply reflects current enthusiasms, special interests, and the predilections of funding sources.

I have not found it necessary to alter the order of chapters or the general thrust of the discussion. Most of the major changes have been to the Notes rather than to the chapters. I have tried to resist the tendency of books to put on weight with successive editions, and the final product is a few thousand words slimmer than its predecessor.

Further details of differences between the fourth and fifth editions of this book are given at the beginning of the Notes.

AIMS

My aim in this fifth edition of *Understanding Reading* continues to be what it was when the first edition was published, to attempt to shed light on fundamental aspects of the complex human act of reading—linguistic, physiological, psychological, and social—and on what is involved in learning to read. One topic, inseparable from reading, that has not perhaps been covered to the extent that it warrants, is writing. The neglect is primarily because I discuss the subject at length in a companion volume, *Writing and the Writer*, which is also appearing in a new edition (Smith, 1994).

There is no comparison of instructional methods nor any effort to promote one instructional program at the expense of another. My early researches persuaded me that learning to read resulted from practical and meaningful interactions between teachers and students, rather than from exercises and drills. Consequent experience with many hundreds of teachers and classrooms and the research of a growing band of "ethnographic" researchers has confirmed for me that the essential element in literacy instruction is the teacher. Literacy is not accomplished through the external controls of prescribed programs and formalized tests but through sensitive teachers who understand what they teach and who also understand the students for whose learning they are responsible.

Reading cannot be understood without consideration of perceptual, cognitive, linguistic, and social factors, not just in reading but in thinking and learning in general. Reading defies a simplistic analysis, just as teaching reading confounds simplistic solutions. Reading is complex, but so also are walking, talking, and making sense of the world in general—and children are capable of achieving all of these provided the environmental circumstances are appropriate. What is difficult to describe is not necessarily difficult to learn. One consideration that this book emphasizes is that children are not as helpless in the face of learning to read as often is thought.

Because an understanding of reading requires acquaintance with research in a variety of disciplines, more than half of the book is devoted to such general topics as language, memory, learning, the development of spoken language ability, and the physiology of the eye and brain. The aim is to make these topics comprehensible, with the assumption that many readers will have neither the time nor the experience to undertake deep or specialized study in these areas. At the risk of offending specialists, diverse subject areas have been covered only to the extent that they are relevant to reading. For those who wish to pursue any topic further, some introductory sources are listed in the Notes. In general, this book is designed to serve as a handbook for language arts teachers, a college text for a basic course on the psychology of reading, a guide to relevant research literature on reading, and an introduction to reading as an aspect of thinking and learning.

I have tried to provide an integrated discussion of reading, a coherent theoretical position, rather than a compendium of research. I have not attempted to cover all contemporary research and theorizing into literacy, but I have tried to indicate at least one specific source of evidence for every assertion I make and for alternative points of view. In general, I have tried to postpone multiple citations and detailed discussions until the extensive Notes section at the end of the book, where general references for further reading on major topics are also found.

Some of the Notes consist of extensive discussions which might be considered more appropriately placed in the main text, such as the examination of the whole-language/direct-instruction controversy in the Notes to Chapter 12. I am aware that not all readers automatically consult Notes that are mentioned in the text, and that few probably go on to plough through the mass of Notes at the end. But I have preferred to keep the main part of the book compact and coherent, without lengthy diversions or digressions. The Notes remain supplementary resources, and the longer sections have been written so that they might be read independently of the text.

The manner in which I have interpreted the evidence and tried to construct a coherent picture reflects basically my own thinking. My guide in all my excursions into the vast and shadowy forests of research into language, thought, and learning continues to be the insights I have gained from the pioneers to whom this book is dedicated—the teachers and learners of literacy.

Frank Smith

Introduction

There is nothing special about reading, apart from everything that reading enables us to do. The power that reading provides is enormous, not only in giving access to people far distant and possibly long dead but also in allowing entry into worlds which might otherwise not be experienced, which might otherwise not exist. Reading enables us to manipulate time itself, to involve ourselves in ideas or events at a rate and in a sequence of our own choosing, quite independently of the manner in which the text was produced or printed. We do not have such power when we listen to speech or watch a movie.

But there is nothing special about reading in terms of what a reader has to do. Reading does not make any exclusive or esoteric demands on the brain. There are no unique kinds of movements that the eyes must make in reading that they do not make when we examine a picture or glance around a room. No particular kind or degree of visual ability is required to discriminate among printed letters or words. And there is nothing exceptional about the language that we read either. Written language is not the same as speech; each has its own characteristics and conventions. But there is nothing the brain must do to make sense of written language that it doesn't do to comprehend speech. There is nothing distinctive about learning to read. Reading requires no special talent or unique brain development. Any child who can see well enough to distinguish one face from another in a photograph and who can understand the familiar language of family and friends has the ability to learn to read.

The difficulty some children experience in learning to read often is attributed to some kind of minimal and undetectable brain damage, but there is no convincing evidence that a particular part of the brain is uniquely

1

responsible for reading. It is, of course, possible—though by no means as common as some reading authorities would suggest—for an occasional child to have a brain injury that would affect language ability, but such an injury would not interfere with reading yet leave the comprehension of speech untouched. Children can obviously have visual defects that will interfere with reading, but these are problems that would show up in other visual activities as well. None of this is to say that it is impossible for a child to fail to learn to read despite perfectly adequate vision and spoken language ability; there are enough counter-examples in our schools. But there are many other possible reasons for reading difficulty apart from hypothetical brain disorders. Personal, social, or cultural conflicts can interfere critically with a child's motivation or ability to learn to read, and it is also possible for something to go wrong during instruction. Children can develop reading habits that make comprehension impossible.

All of the assertions made so far are reflections of the theoretical perspective of this book. There are other points of view. There is, for example, a traditional belief that reading is simply a matter of "decoding" the letters of written words into the sounds of speech, that it is basically a mechanical process, and that teaching children to read must involve drilling them in the recognition and blending of the sounds of letters. But analysis of the relationships between print and speech shows that the "rules" relating spelling to the sounds of speech in English are inordinately complicated and unreliable and also that they are largely irrelevant to reading in any language. Reading is less a matter of extracting sound from print than of bringing meaning to print. The sounds that are supposed to reveal the meaning of sequences of letters cannot in fact be produced unless a probable meaning can be determined in advance. It is a universal fact of reading rather than a defect of English spelling that the effort to read through decoding is largely futile and unnecessary.

The point of view of this book is that reading and learning to read are essentially meaningful activities; that they are not passive and mechanical but purposeful and rational, dependent on the prior knowledge and expectations of the reader (or learner). Reading is a matter of making sense of written language rather than decoding print to sound.

PERSPECTIVE

If I were to retitle this book, I would probably call it *Reading and the Reader*—partly to indicate the relationship to its companion volume *Writing and the Writer* but primarily to underline that one cannot understand reading without understanding readers. Theories which regard reading merely as a "process" or "skill" that can be examined without reference to the purposes of the person engaging in the activity may be as inconsequential as discussions of eating would be without reference to what is being eaten and the occasion on which the eating takes place.

It is a question of who is in charge. From the decoding point of view, the reader is under the control of the text and must mechanically identify every letter and word in front of the eyes. But the meaningful perspective holds that what goes on behind the eyes is the critical factor. Reading is seen as a creative and constructive activity having four distinctive and fundamental characteristics—it is *purposeful, selective, anticipatory,* and based on *comprehension*, all matters where the reader must clearly exercise control.

The purposeful nature of reading is central, not simply because one normally reads for a reason, whether to find a telephone number or to enjoy a novel, but because the understanding which a reader must bring to reading can only be manifested through the reader's own intentions. A person who has no purpose in reading can bring nothing to the reading, and the activity is bound to be meaningless. Reading is selective because we normally only attend to what is relevant to our purposes. To read any kind of text without discrimination, whether a novel or a set of instructions, is as pointless as reading every number in the telephone directory when we are looking for only one. Reading is anticipatory because although text is always ambiguous or incomplete, we are rarely surprised by what we read—our purposes define our expectations. And reading is based on comprehension because despite the ever-present possibility of ambiguity, the act (if not the content) rarely leaves us confused. Understanding is the basis not the consequence of reading.

The only circumstances in which most individuals are likely to "read" in the absence of a personally determined purpose, discrimination, anticipation, and comprehension is when they are receiving certain types of reading instruction or participating in the kind of laboratory-based reading research that is often termed "scientific."

These matters also serve to underline that there is far more to reading than meets the eye. In fact, because of certain fundamental characteristics of the human visual system and of language, fluent reading depends on the ability to use the eyes as little as possible. Such an ability is not taught. It is acquired by children as they employ perceptual and cognitive skills common to many everyday aspects of making sense of the visual world.

PREVIEW

Because reading should not be regarded as a special kind of activity but rather one that involves far broader aspects of human thought and behavior, an understanding of reading cannot be achieved without consideration of the nature of language and of various operating characteristics of the human brain. Consequently, the first half of this book is devoted to such topics as comprehension, knowledge, language, vision, and memory. These opening chapters are by no means intended to be comprehensive or even balanced disquisitions on the subjects covered; this is not a book about physiology, linguistics, or cognitive psychology. Instead, the chapters offer the minimum of background fact and theory that is necessary and relevant for an analysis of reading. A few suggestions are made in the Notes at the end of the book to set interested readers on the trail of more detailed sources.

Such a broadly based approach to reading has some incidental advantages. The more that is said about general topics at the beginning, the less there remains to be added when a detailed analysis of reading begins in the second half of this book, at which point much of the basic ground will have been covered. Questions related to learning and to how reading should be taught are left to the final chapters, partly because the pedagogical emphasis of this book is on enabling teachers to make informed decisions rather than on telling them what to do and partly because inferences about how reading should be taught become clearer as reading itself becomes more fully understood. The main instructional implication of the analysis of this book is that children learn to read by reading and by being read to. Drills, exercises, and rote learning play little part in learning to read and in fact may interfere with comprehension and provide a distorted idea of the nature of reading. The function of teachers is not so much to *teach* reading as to help children read. How this can be done—and the resolution of the paradox that children must read in order to learn to read—must of course eventually be faced. But for the moment it is more appropriate to postpone the ultimate issues and to look at the route by which the concluding portions of the book are reached.

Chapter 1, "Knowledge and Comprehension," examines the nature and organization of the knowledge we all possess and the manner in which it is used to comprehend the world, whether through language or more directly.

Chapter 2, "Language: Spoken and Written," considers the special demands that language in all its aspects makes on listeners and readers and the rather subtle differences that exist between speech and print.

Chapter 3, "Information and Experience," shows how information aspects of reading (and other forms of language) can be conceptualized technically and even measured. But there is much more to reading than the acquisition of information, which plays only a small and even incidental role in many kinds of reading, for "pleasure" or for experience.

Chapter 4, "Between Eye and Brain," goes behind the eyes to discuss the major contribution that "prior knowledge" already possessed by the reader must make to reading. There are also limitations on how the brain can cope with what is going on in the world beyond the eyes, with the result that reading must be fast, selective, and anticipatory.

Chapter 5, "Bottlenecks of Memory," is concerned with another major source of the brain's strengths but also of its limitations, again emphasizing the critical importance in reading of what the reader knows in advance about the text being read.

Chapter 6, "Letter Identification," is the first of four chapters that make a detailed theoretical analysis of reading, based on the preceding discussions. For ease of exposition, the topics of these four chapters start with letters and end with meaning, which is the reverse of the order in which reading is normally accomplished or learned. Readers usually focus their attention on meaning and become concerned with individual words, occasionally letters, only when understanding fails. But an analysis of letter identification demonstrates the possible mechanism by which words and even complex meanings can be ascertained.

Chapter 7, "Word Identification," shows how words can be identified "as wholes," without the prior identification of individual letters. The chapter also demonstrates how it is more economical, and generally essential, to recognize entire words "immediately" as perceptual units rather than to construct them out of individual letters.

Chapter 8, "Phonics and Mediated Word Identification," is concerned with the alternatives that are available when words cannot be recognized as wholes. "Phonics"—a system supposed to construct the identification of words from the sounds of individual letters—is shown to be cumbersome and unreliable. There are more productive alternatives available to readers when words cannot be identified immediately.

Chapter 9, "The Identification of Meaning," is directed to the ultimate purpose of reading—the understanding of the text in ways relevant to the reader's purposes in reading in the first place. It shows how "meanings" can be identified without the prior identification of individual words, just as words can be identified without the identification of component letters.

Chapter 10, "Reading, Writing, and Thinking," brings together the entire picture, summarizing and elaborating upon the act of reading and also discussing the relationships between reading and writing. Reading and writing are both "thinking activities," and thinking is a complex topic in its own right. The chapter concludes with a brief attempt to relate reading and writing to more general aspects of thinking.

Chapter 11, "Learning about the World and about Language," outlines some basic principles of learning, because children do not need—nor can they lack—unique abilities for learning how to read. Rather they must use quite fundamental approaches to learning to solve the particular problems that literacy presents. The chapter emphasizes the social nature of learning.

Chapter 12, "Learning to Use Written Language," reviews the conditions under which children learn to become literate (once again, reading and writing cannot be separated) and includes a brief discussion of the relevance of different kinds of instruction, by teachers and by computers.

ISSUES

Some people argue against the proposition that there is nothing special about reading. They assert that reading is an "unnatural" activity that cannot be learned in the same self-directed way that speech is learned. The different points of view are almost always fueled by "practical" considerations of how reading should be taught and by ideological convictions about whether individual teachers or specialist authorities should make instructional decisions. It is also sometimes argued that there *are* specific reading disabilities that must be attributed to absence of a special intellectual or visual capacity for reading. Such a position, of course, is not compatible with the view that reading is an unnatural activity that no one could be innately equipped for.

Notes to the Preface and Introduction begin on page 221, covering
Psycholinguistics and cognitive science
Research
On not being eclectic
Changes in the fifth edition
Acknowledgment

1 Knowledge and Comprehension

Understanding, or *comprehension*, is the basis of reading and of learning to read. What is the point of any activity if there is no understanding? Comprehension may be regarded as relating relevant aspects of the world around us—written language in the case of reading—to the knowledge, intentions, and expectations we already have in our heads. And learning can be considered as the modification of what we already know as a consequence of our interactions with the world around us. We learn to read, and we learn through reading, by adding to what we know already. Thus, comprehension and learning are fundamentally the same, relating the new to the already known. To understand all this, we must begin by considering what it is that "we already have in our heads" that enables us to make sense of the world. We must begin by comprehending comprehension.

COGNITIVE STRUCTURE

There are several terms that can be used to refer to the knowledge we carry around with us all the time. I speak of the *prior knowledge* or *nonvisual information* that enables us to make sense of the *visual information* that comes through the eyes when we read. I shall examine *long-term memory*, our permanent source of understanding of the world. But the different terms do not refer to different things; they are synonymous. The knowledge that we must already possess in order to understand written language (like the knowledge we need for the understanding of speech) must be part of our long-term memory. And remembrance of the sense we have made of past experience is the foundation of all new understanding of language and the world. In more general contexts, this basis of understanding is also referred to by psychologists as *cognitive structure*. The term is apt because "cognitive" means "knowledge" and "structure" implies organization, and that indeed is what we possess—an organization of knowledge.

Certainly, it would be simplistic to suggest that what we carry around in our heads is just "memories." The brain is not filled with an assortment of snapshots, videos, and tape recordings of bits of the past. At the very least we would have to say that all our memories have a meaning; they are related to everything else that we know. Cognitive structure is more like a summary of our past experience. I do not want to remember that on 16 July I sat on a chair, and that on 17 July I sat on a chair, and on 18 July I sat on a chair. I want to remember that chairs are for sitting on, a summary of my experience. We remember specific events only when they are exceptions to our summary rules or when they have some particularly dramatic or powerful or emotional significance. And even then our memories, when we "recall" them, turn out to be highly colored by our present intentions and perspectives about the world (Bartlett, 1932). Specific memories that cannot be related to our summary, to our present general understanding, will make little sense, which may be the reason we can recall so little of our childhood.

But it would also be an oversimplification to suggest that our heads are filled with an accumulation of facts and rules. The brain is not like a library where useful facts and procedures are filed away under appropriate headings for possible future reference. And it is certainly not like a bank in which we save nuggets of information deposited by teachers and textbooks. Instead, the knowledge we possess is organized into an intricate and internally consistent working model of the world, built up through our imagination and our interactions with the world, and integrated into a coherent whole. We know far more than we were ever taught.

THEORIES OF THE WORLD

Everything that we know and believe is organized into a *theory* of what the world is like, a theory that is the basis of all our perceptions and understanding of the world, the root of all learning, the source of hopes and fears, motives and expectancies, reasoning and creativity. And this theory is all we have. If we can make sense of the world at all, it is by interpreting our interactions with the world in the light of our theory. The theory is our shield against bewilderment.

As I look around my world, I distinguish a multiplicity of meaningful objects that have all kinds of complicated relationships with each other and with me. But neither these objects nor their interrelations are self-evident. A chair does not announce itself to me as a chair; I have to recognize it as such. Chairs are a part of my theory. I recognize a chair when I decide that a chair is what I am looking at. A chair does not tell me that I can sit on it, or put my coat or books or feet on it, or stand on it to reach a high shelf, or wedge it against a door that I do not wish to be opened. All this is also part of my theory. I can only make sense of the world in terms of what I know already. All of the order and complexity that I perceive in the world around me must reflect an order and complexity in my own mind. Anything I cannot relate to my theory of the world will not make sense to me. I am bewildered.

The fact that bewilderment is an unusual state for most of us despite the complexity of our lives is a clear indication that our theory of the world is very efficient. The reason we are usually not aware of the theory is that it works so well. Just as we take the air we breathe for granted until deprived of it, so we become aware of our dependence on our theory only when it proves inadequate, and the world fails to make sense. That we can occasionally be bewildered only serves to demonstrate how efficiently our theory usually functions. When were you last bewildered by something that you heard or read? Our theory of the world seems ready even to make sense of almost everything we are likely to experience in spoken and written language—a powerful theory indeed.

And yet, when was the last time you saw a bewildered baby? Infants have theories of the world too, not as complex as those of adults, but then children have not had as much time to make their theories complex. But children's theories seem to work very well for their needs. Even the smallest children seem able most of the time to make sense of their world in their own terms; they rarely appear confused or uncertain. The first time many children run into a situation that they cannot possibly relate to anything they know already is when they arrive at school, a time when they may be consistently bewildered if they are confronted by circumstances that make no sense to them. Children are often denied credit for knowing very much. But, in fact, most of our knowledge of the world—of the kinds of objects it contains and the way they can be related—and most of our knowledge of language has been organized before we arrive at school. At age five or six the framework is there, and the rest is mainly a matter of filling in the details.

For the remainder of this chapter, I shall talk a little more about how this theory is organized and then discuss how it is used so that we can comprehend the world.

Comprehension is more than understanding the circumstances we are in; it is the way in which we learn. This is the reason I have put the topic of comprehension first in this book and left learning until the end. This may be the reverse of the situation that often exists in school, where children often are expected to learn in order to understand. But learning is more a result of comprehension than its cause. Learning to read is literally a matter of "understanding reading."

THE STRUCTURE OF KNOWLEDGE

The system of knowledge that is our theory of the world may be regarded as a structure just like any other theory or system of organizing information, such as a library. Information systems have three basic components—a set of categories, some rules for specifying membership of the categories, and a network of interrelations among the categories. I briefly examine each component in turn.

Categories

To categorize means to treat some objects or events as the same yet as different from other objects or events. All human beings categorize, instinctively, starting at birth. There is nothing remarkable about this innate propensity to categorize, because living organisms could not survive if they did not in fact treat some objects or events as the same yet as different from other objects and events.

No living organism could survive if it treated everything in its experience as the same; there would be no basis for differentiation and therefore no basis for learning. There would be no possibility of being systematic. Just as a librarian cannot treat all books as the same when putting them on the shelves, so all human beings must differentiate throughout their lives. In our culture at least, everyone is expected to be able to distinguish dogs from cats, tables from chairs, and the letter *A* from the letter *B*.

But similarly, no living organism could survive if it treated everything in its experience as different. If there is no basis for similarity, there is still no basis for learning. Thus the librarian must treat some books as the same in some senses—so that all chemistry books are stacked in the same area—even though these books may differ in size, color, and author's name. In the same way everyone, in our culture at least, is expected to ignore many differences in order to treat all dogs as the same, all cats as the same, and many different shapes like A, *A*, ə, a, *a* as the letter *a*.

In other words, the basis of survival and of learning is the ability to ignore many potential differences so that certain objects[1] will be treated as the same yet as different from other objects. All objects that belong to one category are

---

[1]From this point on, I refrain from the cumbersome practice of talking all the time about "objects or events." But every reference to "objects" applies in general to "events" as well.

treated as the same yet as different from objects belonging to other categories.

The categories that we all observe, which are part of our theories of the world, are quite arbitrary; they are not generally imposed on us by the world itself. The world does not force us to categorize animals into dogs and cats and so forth—we could divide them up in other ways, for example treating all green-eyed animals as the same, in contrast to those with other eye colors, or differentiating those over 15 inches in height from those under 15 inches. The librarian could very neatly organize books on the basis of the color of their covers, or their size, or the number of pages. But we cannot usually invent categories for ourselves—hence the qualification "in our culture at least" in previous paragraphs. The reason we divide animals on a cat and dog basis and not on the basis of size or eye color is that the categories we have are part of our culture. Categories are *conventions*. In part, to share a culture means to share the same categorical basis for organizing experience. Language reflects the way a culture organizes experience, which is why many of the words in our language are a clue to the categories in our shared theories of the world. We have the words *dog* and *cat* but not a word for animals with green eyes or less than 15 inches in height. When we have to learn new categories, the existence of a name in the language tends often to be the first clue that a category exists.

Not that words are essential prerequisites for the establishment of categories. Quite the reverse—categories can exist for which we have no names. I can easily distinguish certain mottled brown and gray birds that come to my garden every morning, but I do not know a name for them. To know a name without an understanding of the category that it labels is meaningless. In fact, the existence of a category is a prerequisite for learning how to use words, because words label categories rather than specific objects. What we call a dog is any individual animal that we put in the category with the name *dog*.

The category system that is part of our theory of the world is essential for making sense of the world. Any situation that we cannot relate to a category does not make sense; we are bewildered. Our categories, in other words, are the basis of our perception of the world. Perception must be regarded as decision-making. We "see" what the brain decides we are looking at, which means the category to which visual information is allocated. If I see a chair in front of me, then I must have a category for chairs in my theory of the world, and I must have decided that what I am looking at belongs to that category. If I can see the word cat when I read, then I must have a category for that word quite independent of my knowledge of its name or possible meanings, just as I must have categories for the letters *c*, *a*, and *t*, if I can distinguish those in the word. Interestingly, we cannot see things in more than one category at a time; it is not possible to see the letters *c*, *a*, and *t* and the word *cat* simultaneously in the visual configuration *cat*, which is why children may find learning to read more difficult if they are required to concentrate on the individual letters in

FIG. 1.1. Ambiguous visual information.

words. Usually you only see what you are looking for and remain quite unaware of other possibilities. If I ask you to read the address 4IO LION STREET, you will probably not notice that the numerals IO in 4IO are the same characters as the letters IO in LION. When you look for the category of numerals you see numerals, and when you look for the category of letters you see letters. Even now that you are aware of what I am doing, you cannot look at IO and see both letters and numerals simultaneously, any more than you can see the faces and the vase simultaneously in the ambiguous illustration of Figure 1.1. We can make decisions about only one category at a time in relation to a single visual configuration (although we could see the face and vase in Figure 1.1 simultaneously if they did not share a common contour). And if there is no category to which we can relate an object to which we are exposed, we can make no decision at all; the world will not make sense to us. We must have categories in order to make decisions, categories that embrace not only sights and sounds but also tastes, odors, feelings, and sensations as well as many kinds of events, patterns, and relationships.

Rules for Category Membership

Categories in themselves are not enough. The category "chemistry books" is useless if a librarian has no way of recognizing a chemistry book when confronted by one, just as a child can make no use of the information that there are cats and dogs in the world without some notion of how to distinguish one from the other. A child who can recite the alphabet has established a set of 26 categories but may not be able to recognize a single letter. For every category that we employ there must be at least one way of recognizing members of that category. Every category must have at least one set of rules, a specification, that determines whether an object belongs in that category. Sometimes a single category may have more than one set of rules—we can distinguish an object as an onion by its appearance, feel, smell, and taste. We can recognize the letter *a* in a number of different guises. But just as we must have a category for every object we can distinguish in the world, so we must have at least one set of rules—a list of significant attributes or *distinctive features*—for allocating that object to a particular category. These are not usually rules that we can put into words. Knowledge of this kind is *implicit*— we can only infer that we have the categories or rules by the fact that we can make use of them.

The question of what constitutes the rules that differentiate the various categories that we employ in reading and language generally demands a good deal of attention in later chapters—especially when we see that "teaching" is often little more than telling children that a category exists, leaving them to discover for themselves what the rules are.

Category Interrelations

Rules permit the categories in a system to be used, but they do not ensure that the system makes sense. A library does not make sense simply because all the chemistry books are stacked in one place and all the poetry books in another. What makes a library a system is the way in which the various categories are related to each other, and this is the way our systems of knowledge make sense as well.

It is not possible to list all the different interrelations among the categories in our theory of the world. To do so would be to document the complexity of the world as we perceive it. Everything that we know is directly or indirectly related to everything else, and any attempt to illustrate these relationships risks becoming interminable.

For example, consider an onion. We know what that particular object is called—in more than one language perhaps—and also the names of several kinds of onion. All these are relations of the particular object to language. We also know what an onion looks, feels, smells, and tastes like, again perhaps in more than one way. We know where an onion comes from—how it is grown— and we probably have a good idea about how it gets to the place where we can buy one. We know roughly what we have to pay to buy one. We know how an onion can be used in cooking and probably some other uses as well. We may know half a dozen different ways of cooking onions (with different names), and we certainly know a number of things that can be eaten with onions. We know a number of instruments for dealing with onions—knives, graters, and blenders, for example. We not only know what we can do with onions, we also know what onions can do to us. We know people who love onions and people who hate them; people who can cook them and people who cannot. We may even know something about the role of onions in history. One enormous ramification of our knowledge of onions is related to the fact that we can call them by more than one name. An onion can also be called a vegetable, which means that everything we know about vegetables in general applies to onions in particular. Indeed, every time we relate an onion to something else—to a knife, a frying pan, or a particular person—then we discover that what we know about onions is part of what we know about knives, frying pans, and people. There is no end.

Many cognitive interrelations pertain to the system of language that is such an important part of everyone's theory of the world. One complex set of interrelations is called *syntax* and describes how elements of language should be related to each other in speech and writing. Syntax enables us to put words together in ways that are "grammatical" (although people whose language is often characterized as "ungrammatical" do not normally lack syntactic knowledge; they observe different conventions). Another set of interrelations is called *semantics*, concerned with the way language is related to the world at large or rather, to our perception of the world. The semantic richness of words determines to some extent the complexity we perceive in the world (Whorf, 1956) or at least how easily we can talk about it (Hunt & Agnoli, 1991). Knowledge of language must also include extensive understanding of the conventional ways in which language and other systems of communication are used on particular occasions, sometimes referred to as *pragmatics* or as *semiotics*. And a good deal of our knowledge of the world is actually held in the form of language, in verbal *descriptions* of things that we know. Our heads can also contain a host of *propositions*, ranging from simple facts (Paris is the capital of France, two times two is four), through proverbs and other compact bundles of ideas or common sense, to complex verbal formulas and even entire segments of prose or poetry. All of this verbal prior knowledge can become available to us at relevant times to help us to comprehend and even to bring about particular sets of circumstances.

Schemes, Scenarios, and Stories

Many important sets of cognitive relations relate to places and scenes with which we are familiar. We know the spatial organization of familiar landscapes and locations—the beach where we played as children, the family living room, or our first classroom. We are quickly aware if something in a familiar setting has changed (even if we cannot immediately determine what exactly is different). In addition, our theory also contains many more symbolic representations, such as maps (which is the primary way most of us understand the geography of the world and of familiar countries and cities) and diagrams, some of which we may have constructed without ever seeing or putting them on paper.

Our theories also contain (or can construct) extensive representations of more general patterns or regularities that occur in our experience. These representations are metaphorically called *schemes* (or occasionally *schemas* or *schemata*). Most of us have a complex generic scheme for what classrooms are like, for example. We can recognize and make sense of classrooms we have never been in before, just because they contain familiar arrangements of familiar elements. Our cognitive structures similarly include schemes of department stores and restaurants, for example, which enable us to make sense of new experiences and to behave appropriately. Many experiments have demonstrated that our ability to recognize scenes and to remember them depends on the extent to which they conform to our expectations of what such scenes should be like, to the schemes that we already possess.

Readers develop and require a large number of spatially organized schemes related to the way in which books and other kinds of written texts are organized. Among such schemes are those of specific *genres*—newspapers are not set out in the way that magazines, novels, or textbooks are. All of these schemes, or specifications for various kinds of text, are conventional. The appearance and organization of a book or a newspaper can vary considerably from one community or culture to another, and their schemes have to be known to us if we are to make sense of them. Other conventional rules of written *discourse structure* include organization into paragraphs, chapters, or sections, with titles and other kinds of heading, which readers as well as writers have to observe and expect.

The examples of schemes I have so far given have all been spatial, the way things are laid out, primarily for comprehension visually. But we also possess innumerable schemes for other sense modalities—for arrangements of sounds, tastes, smells, and a variety of tactile sensations, many of them closely related to each other and to patterns of events in the visual world.

Many of our most important schemes are laid out in time; they have a serial or temporal organization. Time and change are essential aspects of the way we perceive the world—how otherwise could we understand language, music, or even a football game? Schemes that have a temporal as well as a spatial basis are often referred to by the metaphors of *scenarios* or *scripts*. A department store script sets out expected and conventional patterns of behavior for ourselves and for others when we go out to shop, even when we are purchasing unfamiliar items in stores we have never been to before. An absence or mismatch of scripts can result in confusion, embarrassment, and misunderstanding. Collectively, scripts, scenarios, and schemes are sometimes referred to as *event knowledge* (Nelson, 1986).

Knowledge of relevant schemes is obviously essential if we are to read any kind of text with comprehension. A child who does not have a scenario about farming is unlikely to understand a story about farming or a reference to farming in a textbook. But there are special kinds of language schemes that readers particularly require. If we are readers, or if we hope to become readers, our theories of the world must include *story schemes*, specifications of how stories are organized and how they unfold. We must know that stories comprise particular kinds of plots, characters, and episodes. How well a story is understood and remembered depends on how well it conforms to conventional schemes for stories and on how well the reader is familiar with those schemes.

The complexity of cognitive structure is indeed astounding. Our prior knowledge resists all efforts to catalog it or to reduce it to a few simple categories. Attempts to "simplify" its organization or operation can only mislead, especially if made the basis of instructional or diagnostic practices in education. The enormous cognitive power of every individual is frequently overlooked if there is an emphasis on "needs" or "disabilities." Think for a moment of the complexity of the world in which we all live; of the multitude of individuals with different personalities, roles, and patterns of behavior; of the multitude of animate and inanimate objects in the world; and of all the multifarious ways in which these people and objects can be related to each other. Any circumstance or situation to which we cannot bring a relevant cognitive structure—including categories, sets of distinctive features, and a multiplicity of spatial, temporal, and other cognitive relations—will confuse or bewilder us. Our ability to make sense of the world, like our ability to remember events, to act appropriately, and to predict the future, is determined by the complexity of the knowledge we already possess.

My emphasis in this book is on the many kinds of things everyone does well. One of these superb but commonplace abilities is the accumulation of vast amounts of useful knowledge, of potential understanding, as a result both of experience and creative imagination. Another powerful yet everyday constant achievement is to make use of all this prior knowledge, the topic to which I now turn.

THE DYNAMICS OF COGNITIVE STRUCTURE

Cognitive structure, our personal theory of the world, may so far have seemed rather a crowded and static place, not very different in essence from a collection of facts and procedures. But the theory is *dynamic*, and not just in the sense that it is constantly being added to and changed, particularly during that lively period of intense exploration and learning we call childhood. We can do much more with the theory of the world than make sense of the world and interact with it. We can *live* in the theory, in worlds that exist only in the imagination. Within the theory we can imagine and create, testing provisional solutions to problems and examining the consequences of possible behaviors. We can explore new worlds of our own and can be led into other worlds by writers and artists.

But the aspect of imagination with which we will be most concerned is more mundane, although at first encounter it may sound quite exotic. We can use the theory of the world to predict the future. This ability to predict is both pervasive and profound, because it is the basis of our comprehension of the world, including our understanding of spoken and written language. Reading depends on prediction.

The Pervasiveness of Prediction

Everyone predicts—including children—all the time. Our lives would be impossible, we would be reluctant even to leave our beds in the morning, if we had no expectation about what the day will bring. We would never go through a door if we had no idea of what might be on the other side. And all our expectations, our predictions, can be derived from only one source, our theory of the world.

We are generally unaware of our constant state of anticipation for the simple reason once again that our theory of the world works so well. Our theory is so efficient that when our predictions fail, we are surprised. We do not go through life predicting that anything might happen—indeed, that would be contrary to prediction, and in that case nothing could surprise us. The fact that something always could rhinoceros take us by surprise—like the word *rhinoceros* a few words ago—is evidence that indeed we always predict and that our predictions are usually accurate. It is always possible that we could be surprised, yet our predictions are usually so appropriate that surprise is a very rare occurrence. When was the last time you were surprised?

We drive through a town we have never visited before, and nothing we see surprises us. There is nothing surprising about the buses and cars and pedestrians in the main street; they are predictable. But we do not predict that we might see anything—we would be surprised to see camels or submarines in the main street. Not that there is anything very surprising or unpredictable about camels or submarines in themselves—we would not be surprised to see camels if we were visiting a zoo or to see submarines at a naval base. In other words, our predictions are very specific to situations. We do not predict that anything will happen, nor do we predict that something is *bound* to happen if it is only *likely* to happen (we are no more surprised by the absence of a bus than we are by the presence of one), and we predict that many things are unlikely to happen. Our predictions are remarkably accurate—and so are those of children. It is rare to see a child who is surprised.

The Need for Prediction

Why should we predict? Why not expect that anything could happen all the time, and thus free ourselves from any possibility of surprise? I can think of three reasons. The first reason is that our position in the world in which we live changes constantly, and we are usually far more concerned with what is likely to happen in the near and distant future than we are with what is actually happening right now. An important difference between a skilled driver and a learner is that the skilled driver is able to project the car into the future and the learner's mind is more closely anchored to where the car is now—when it is usually too late to avoid accidents. The same difference tends to distinguish skilled readers from beginners, or from anyone having difficulty with a particular piece of reading. In fluent reading aloud, the eye is always ahead of the voice, checking for possible obstacles to a particular understanding. Readers concerned with the word directly in front of their nose will have trouble predicting, and they will have trouble comprehending.

The second reason for prediction is that there is too much ambiguity in the world; there are too many ways of interpreting just about anything that confronts us. Unless we exclude some alternatives in advance, we are likely to be overwhelmed with possibilities. Of the many things I know about onions, I do not want to be concerned with the fact that they are pulled from the ground or that they bring my cousin George out in spots if all I want is garnish for a hamburger. What I see is related to what I am looking for, not to all possible interpretations. Words have many meanings—*table* can be several kinds of verb as well as several kinds of noun—but there is only one meaning that I am concerned with, that I predict, if someone tells me to put my books on the table. All the everyday words of our language have many meanings and often several grammatical functions—*table, chair, house, shoe, time, walk, open, narrow*—but by predicting the range of possibilities that a word is likely to be, we are just not aware of the potential ambiguities.

The final reason for prediction is that there would otherwise be far too many alternatives from which to choose. It takes time to make decisions about what the eyes are looking at, and the time that is required depends on the number of alternatives. We take longer to decide that we are looking at the letter *A* when it could be any one of the 26 letters of the alphabet than when we know that it is a vowel. We take longer to identify a word in isolation compared with a word in a meaningful sentence. The fewer the alternatives, the quicker the recognition. If there are too many alternatives confronting the eyes, then it is much harder to see or to comprehend.

Prediction is the core of reading. All of our schemes, scripts, and scenarios—our prior knowledge of places and situations, of written discourse, genres, and stories—enable us to predict when we read and thus to comprehend, experience, and enjoy what we read. Prediction brings potential meaning to texts, reducing ambiguity and eliminating in advance irrelevant alternatives. Thus, we are able to generate comprehensible experience from inert pages of print.

Prediction is not reckless guessing, nor does it involve taking chances by betting everything on the most likely outcome. We do not go through life saying "Round the next corner I shall see a bus," or "The next word I read will be *rhinoceros*." We predict by opening our minds to the probable and by disregarding the unlikely. Here is a formal definition: *Prediction is the prior elimination of unlikely alternatives*. It is the projection of possibilities. We predict to reduce our uncertainty and therefore to reduce the amount of external information that we require. Our theory of the world tells us the most probable occurrences, and we decide among those remaining alternatives until uncertainty is reduced to zero. And we are so good at predicting only the most likely alternatives that we are rarely surprised.

Put more informally, prediction is a matter of asking specific questions. We do not ask "What is that object over there?" but "Is that something I can put my books on?" or whatever we want to do. We do not look at a page of print with no expectation about what we shall read next, instead we ask "What is the hero going to do?" "Where is the villain going to hide?" And "Will there be an explosion when liquid A is mixed with powder B?" And provided the answer lies within the expected range of alternatives—which it usually does if we are reading with comprehension—then we are not aware of any doubt or ambiguity. We are neither bewildered nor surprised.

Prediction and Comprehension Related

Now at last prediction and comprehension can be tied together. Prediction means asking questions, and comprehension means being able to get some of the questions answered. Comprehension, basically, is the absence of confusion. As we read, as we listen to someone talking, as we go through life, we are constantly asking questions, and if we are able to find answers to those questions, then we comprehend. The person who does not comprehend how to repair a bicycle is the one who cannot ask and find answers to such questions as "Which of these nuts and bolts goes where?" at appropriate times. And the person who does not comprehend a book or newspaper article is the one who cannot find relevant questions and answers concerning the next part of the text. There is a *flow* to comprehension, with new questions constantly being generated from the answers that are sought.

Such a view of comprehension differs from the way the word is often used in school. So-called comprehension tests in school are usually given after a book has been read and as a consequence are more like tests of memory. (And because the effort to memorize can drastically interfere with comprehension, the test may finish up by destroying what it sets out to measure.) If I say that I comprehended a certain book, it does not make sense to give me a test and argue that I did not understand it, though I may have understood it differently from the test-constructor. And a high score on a test certainly would not convince me that I had really understood a book or a speaker if my feeling is that I did not.

The very notion that comprehension is relative, that it depends on the questions that an individual happens to ask, is not one that all educators find easy to accept. Some want to argue that you may not have understood a book even if you have no unanswered questions at the end. They will ask, "But did you understand that the spy's failure to steal the secret plans was really a symbol of humanity's ineluctable helplessness in the face of manifest destiny?" And if you say "No, I just thought it was a jolly good story," they will tell you that you did not *really* comprehend what the story was about. But basically what they are saying is that you were not asking the kind of questions they think you should have asked.

THINKING AND "META-THINKING"

A comprehensive analysis of thinking would require a separate book and the critical discussion of a mountain of recent research, uncovering, perhaps, more mysteries and controversies than it could unravel. On the other hand, the topic cannot be completely ignored because thinking has become a focus of attention for many educators recently (see Smith, 1990).

In part, this concentration of interest has been generated by cognitive scientists trying to develop models of thought that might serve in the development of "thinking computers" and also by cognitive psychologists involved with human thinking who nevertheless want to simulate or test their theories on computers. As a result, thinking has tended to be fragmented into distinct clusters of "information-processing" procedures, more appropriate to the programmed sequential operations of electronic technology than to humans whose thought and actions are based primarily on their intentions, interests, and values.

It could also be argued that another reason for the sudden concern about thinking is the tendency to fragment reading and reading instruction into packages of decontextualized "basic skills," none of which particularly engage thinking.

Yet, reading cannot be separated from thinking. Reading is a thought-full activity. There is no difference between reading and any other kind of thought, except that with reading, thought focuses on a written text. Reading might be defined as thought that is stimulated and directed by written language. This entire book could be considered to be a disquisition on thinking, from a reading point of view.

Particular characteristics of the thinking ideally engaged in by readers must be separated into two categories, not always clearly recognized. The first is the thinking involved in the *act* of reading—such as drawing appropriate inferences in order to comprehend—and the other is thinking which is a *consequence* of reading, that might transpire in subsequent reflection. Reading involves no special kind of thought that is not already displayed by readers in other aspects of mental life.

Thinking should not be regarded as a set of specialized processes that are superimposed upon the organization of knowledge, our theory of the world discussed earlier in this chapter. Thinking is not a distinct faculty or set of skills, different from comprehension, prediction, or imagination; rather it is our theory of the world in action. The theory of the world is dynamic, constantly modifying itself in relation to our current concerns and state of affairs. Thinking is the normal operation of our dynamic theory of the world. The flow of thought is powered by our intentions and expectations, guided by the consequent experience. It is creative and constructive, not passive and reactive.

All of the aspects of thought that language distinguishes can be seen as the manipulation of cognitive relationships. *Reasoning* usually refers to relationships within a series of statements or states of affairs; the way one thing follows another. *Inference* involves relationships between particular statements or states of affairs and some more general circumstances, and *problem solving* relates existing states of affairs to desired states. *Classification, categorization, concept formation*, and other manifestations of what are sometimes called *higher order* or *abstract* thinking all impose and examine relationships among statements or states of affairs. The terms I have italicized are just *words*, not different kinds of thinking. We are not doing different things when we reason, draw inferences, or solve problems; they only appear different because of the context in which they are done or the consequences of doing them. They are not measurable.

We are constantly engaged in relational activities, in our everyday transactions of comprehending and learning about the world around us. What differs among individuals is not so much the general ability to think as the possibility of demonstrating aspects of thought on particular occasions. Three constraints bear on how well individuals can appear to think on particular occasions, none of them dependent on the acquisition of specialized or exotic skills. All of us on occasion find ourselves in situations in which we are unable to think—especially in "educational" contexts—but this need not be because no one has taught us specific "thinking skills."

Constraints on Thinking

The first constraint on thinking is *prior knowledge*. Like language, thought always has a subject. And just as we cannot talk or write competently if we do not know what we are talking about, so it is not possible to demonstrate thought in any way if we do not understand what we are expected or trying to think about. If I have difficulty understanding an article on nuclear physics, it is not because I am unable to draw conclusions, make inferences, follow arguments, or solve problems, but because I do not know enough about nuclear physics. And good nuclear physicists are not necessarily good writers, chess players, or automobile mechanics.

The second constraint on thinking is *disposition*. Philosopher John McPeck (1981), for example, asserts that the "judicious suspension of belief," which is his definition of critical thinking, is a disposition rather than a skill. Whether or not we take something for granted, whether we will challenge other people's assertions or question our own opinions in the light of new evidence, depends on individual propensities to behave in those ways, not on the acquisition of abilities that can be developed through instruction or even practice. Dispositions can be innate, aspects of personality we are born with, or they can be the result of experience—"once bitten, twice shy."

And finally, whether or not anyone will exercise thought, particularly of the critical variety, depends on possession of the *authority* to do so. Challenging conventional thought or other people's opinions, or even drawing one's own conclusions, is not something everyone is in a position to do, certainly not in every situation. In many institutions and in many patterns of personal relations, the authority for engaging in thought of a significant nature (as opposed to accepting or providing "right answers") is not distributed equally. Thinking can upset applecarts.

Metacognition

One other topic related to thinking that is receiving considerable attention from educational researchers is *metacognition*—literally "cognition about cognition" or thought about our own thought. *Metacognitive processes* are presumed to take place when we think about our own thinking, for example, when we reflect upon whether we know something, whether we are learning, or whether we have made a mistake.

Some researchers are inclined to regard metacognitive processes as yet another special set of skills which have to be learned. On the other hand, children learn many things, including talking and much of literacy, without awareness of learning. And we are usually aware when we do not understand something (in the sense of being confused) or when we do not know something at a time when some knowledge is personally relevant and important to us. Metacognition could be regarded as a newfangled label for the old-fashioned concept of "reflection."

ISSUES

There is a widespread assumption that thinking can be broken down into sets of skills that people must be taught, rather than that it is a basic human capacity. This is the instructional issue again, with proponents of the skills point of view arguing that children will not be able to think without specific instruction. Their opponents argue that children (and adults) may simply need experience of seeing others exercising thought in various circumstances and opportunity to do the same themselves. The role of prediction in reading has also been disputed (see Notes).

The metaphorical nature of terms like scheme and script is often overlooked. The use of computers as an analogy for the brain in educational theorizing has led to a belief that schemes, scripts, and cognitive structure itself are "data" which people must "acquire" through instruction. The alternative view is that the distillation of experience into forms that might be conceptualized as schemes or scripts is natural for humans of any age.

SUMMARY

(Terms printed in **bold type** in the Summaries are key terms that can be found in the Glossary.)

Nonvisual information, long-term memory, and **prior knowledge** are alternative terms for describing **cognitive structure,** each individual's theory of the world. The theory includes **schemes,** or generalized representations of familiar settings and situations, essential in all understanding and remembering. The theory of the world is the source of **comprehension,** as we continually generate and examine possibilities about situations in real and imaginary worlds. The basis of comprehension is **prediction,** the prior elimination of unlikely alternatives. Predictions are questions that we ask the world, and comprehension is receiving relevant answers to those questions. If we cannot predict, we are confused. If our predictions fail, we are surprised. And if we have nothing to predict because we have no interest or uncertainty, we are bored. **Thinking**—including **metacognition,** or "thinking about thinking"—is not a special set of skills but constant reflective activity, subject only to constraints of individual prior knowledge, disposition, and authority.

Notes to Chapter 1 begin on page 226 covering
Theories of comprehension
Prediction
Categories
Schemes
The ubiquity of metaphors
The narrative basis of thought
Thinking

2 Language: Spoken and Written

Language constitutes a substantial part of any person's theory of the world and obviously plays a central role in reading. The present chapter is concerned with language from a number of perspectives, including the relationships between the sounds (and printed marks) of language and their meaning, between productive aspects of language (talking and writing) and receptive aspects (listening and reading), and between spoken and written language. The chapter also refers briefly to grammar and to many other conventions of language.

All of these aspects of language are relevant to an understanding of reading; yet all are complex areas of study in their own right. Obviously it will not be possible to study any topic to the same theoretical depth as the professional linguist or psychologist—but fortunately such detail is also not necessary. The handful of basic insights that a student of reading must grasp are relatively easy to explain and to demonstrate. These insights, however, are not always part of the general awareness of educators in the field of reading; they are widely disregarded in many instructional programs and materials and in a good deal of reading research, so that they may appear to be new and even unfamiliar ideas. For example, one basic but neglected insight is that actual instances of language—the statements that people utter or write—do not convey meaning in any simple fashion. Meaning is not contained within the sounds of speech or the printed marks of writing, conveniently waiting to be discovered or decoded, but rather must be provided by the listener or reader. As a consequence, an understanding of reading requires a more complex theory of comprehension than one that simplistically assumes that meaning will take care of itself provided a reader can identify individual words correctly. Most of this chapter is concerned with the fundamental issue of how language is comprehended.

TWO ASPECTS OF LANGUAGE

Surface Structure and Deep Structure

There are two quite different ways of talking about language, whether spoken or written. On the one hand, you can talk about its physical aspect, about characteristics that can be measured, such as the loudness or duration or pitch of the sounds of speech, or the number, size, or contrast of the printed marks of writing. All of these observable characteristics of language that exist in the world around us may be called *surface structure*. They are the part of language accessible through the ears and eyes. Surface structure is a useful term because it is not restricted to a particular form of language, either spoken or written. Surface structure is the "visual information" of written language— the source of information that is lost to the reader when the lights go out—but it is also a part of spoken language—the part that is lost when a telephone connection is broken.

On the other hand, there is a part of language that can neither be directly observed nor measured, and that is meaning. In contrast to surface structure, the meaning of language, whether spoken or written, can be referred to as *deep structure*. The term is apt. Meanings do not lie at the surface of language but far more profoundly in the users of language: in the *intentions* of the speaker or writer and in the *interpretations* of the listener or reader.

These two different aspects of language, the physical surface structure and the meaningful deep structure, can in fact be completely separated in the sense that it is quite possible to talk about one without reference to the other. We can say that someone is talking loudly or softly, or fast or slowly, without reference to what is being said. We can say that a line of print is five inches wide, or has eight characters to the inch, without fear that someone will contradict us by saying that we have not understood the meaning of the text. Conversely, meaning is not directly affected by the form of the surface structure. If we are told that Paris will host the next Olympic Games, we cannot reply that it depends on whether the speaker's source of information was spoken or written. The truth of an utterance is not related to its loudness or the number of repetitions.

All of this may seem very obvious, trite even, but the distinction between the surface and the deep structure of language is crucial for an understanding of reading for one simple reason: The two aspects of language are separated by a chasm. Surface and deep structures are not opposite sides of the same coin; they are not mirror reflections of each other. They are not directly and unambiguously related. Put into technical terms, *there is no one-to-one correspondence between the surface structure of language and meaning.* Meaning lies beyond the mere sounds or printed marks of language and cannot be derived from surface structure by any simple or mechanistic process.

One way of exemplifying this absence of a one-to-one relationship between the two aspects of language is by showing that differences can occur in surface structure that make no difference to meaning and that there can be differences in meaning that are not represented in surface structure (Miller, 1965). For example, here are some radically different surface structures that do not correspond to radical differences in meaning: (a) *the cat is chasing a bird;* (b) *a bird is chased by the cat;* (c) *a warm-blooded feathered vertebrate is pursued by the domesticated feline quadruped;* (d) *le chat chasse un oiseau.* Four quite different sequences of marks on paper, but all represent (in general terms at least) the same meaning. When we try to say what words mean, all we can do is offer other words (a synonym or a paraphrase) that reflect the same meaning. The actual meaning always lies beyond words. It makes sense to say that *bachelor* means (or more accurately, conveys the same meaning as) *unmarried man*, but it does not make sense to ask what the meaning is that *bachelor* and *unmarried man* have in common. Alternative verbal definitions or descriptions simply compound the problem. They are additional surface structures.

On the other hand, it is not difficult to find individual surface structures which have at least two possible meanings or interpretations. For example: *flying planes can be dangerous; visiting professors may be tedious; the shooting of the principal was terrible; the chickens were too hot to eat; she runs through the spray and waves; he enjoys talking with old men and women (all women?); Cleopatra was rarely prone to talk (and Mark Anthony was not inclined to argue).*

The examples just quoted represent a particular kind of ambiguity, namely puns. But often puns are difficult to comprehend at once—you may not have seen the alternative meanings in all of the previous examples immediately—and there lies an important theoretical issue: Why are we so rarely aware of the potential ambiguity of language? It is not just puns but every possible sequence of words in our language, and just about every individual word for that matter, that is a source of potential misinterpretation. To understand why we are so rarely aware of the multiple meanings that might be attributed to surface structure of our language, we must look at a more basic question. If there is this chasm between surface structure and deep structure, how then is language comprehended in the first place? The question is of considerable relevance to reading, because if meaning is not immediately and unambiguously given by the surface structure of speech, then there is no point in expecting a reader to "decode" written language to speech in order for comprehension to occur. Speech itself needs to be comprehended, and print cannot be read aloud in a comprehensible way unless it is comprehended in the first place. Written language does not require decoding to sound in order to be comprehended; the manner in which we bring meaning to print is just as direct as the manner in which we understand speech. Language comprehension is the same for all surface structures.

Spoken language is not comprehended by "decoding" sounds but by bringing meaning to them. Reading aloud is not a matter of decoding from the surface structure of print to the surface structure of speech but must also be mediated through meaning. And for silent reading, attempts to understand through subvocal speech may be unnecessary as well as disabling, because meaning can be brought to print directly. Oral reading is more complex and difficult than silent reading.

The Trouble with Words

How then is language understood, whether spoken or written? The answer is not that we put together the meaning of individual words and thereby understand entire sentences. For a start, it seems very doubtful whether words can be said to exist in spoken language at all. Scientific instruments cannot isolate the beginning and ending of many sounds—or even words—that we hear as quite separate. The actual flow of speech is relatively continuous and smoothly changing, and the segmentation into distinct sounds and words is largely something that listeners contribute. You can get some indication of this by uttering the two words *west end* and repeating them while listening very carefully to what you are saying. You will probably find that if you introduce any pause at all in the utterance, it will be between the /s/ and the /t/—that actually you are saying *wes tend* rather than *west end*. Of course, English speakers would never think that you really said *wes tend*. But only because they speak the language and are able to work out—and hear—the sounds you *thought* you were producing. The fact that you need to *know* a language in order to be able to *hear* it properly becomes apparent when you listen to a foreign language. Not only can you not distinguish what the distinctive sounds of the language are, you cannot even distinguish the number of words in an utterance. Speakers of other languages—and children—have exactly the same trouble with English.

The very existence of words may be an artifact of the writing system. At least in writing we can provide a definition of a word—as something with a space on either side. Children learning to talk either produce groups of words that they use as one long word—*allgone, drinkamilk, gowalk*—or else single words that they use as entire sentences—*drink, tired, no*. Beginning readers often cannot say how many words are in a sentence, either spoken or written. They need to be experienced readers to understand the question.

Words and Meanings

Another reason why it is difficult to argue that the meanings of sentences are made up of the meanings of words is that it would appear that words often get meaning as a virtue of occurring in sentences. In fact, it is very difficult to see what meaning a word in isolation can have. Even nouns, which might seem the easiest class of words to account for, present difficulties. It is certainly far from true that every object has one name and every word one meaning. Every object has more than one name. The family pet, for example, can be called a canine, a dog, a boxer, "Rover," an animal, and a variety of other titles including, of course, "family pet" and "that slavering brute." What is the "real name" of the animal? There is not one. The appropriate name for the speaker to use depends on the listener and the extent of the listener's uncertainty. In talking to a member of the family, the name "Rover" is adequate or simply "the dog"; on other occasions no single word would be adequate, and the name would have to be qualified as "that brown dog over there" or "the large boxer." Everything depends on the knowledge of the listener or reader and the alternatives from among which Rover has to be distinguished. The same animal will be described in different ways to the same person depending on the characteristics of other dogs that are around. What then does a word like *dog* mean? The dictionary tells us that it is "any of a large and varied group of domesticated animals related to the fox, wolf, and jackal." But that surely is not the meaning of dog in the sentence "Beware of the dog," let alone such expressions as hot dog, top dog, putting on the dog, dirty dog, dog tired, or going to the dogs.

All the common words of our language have a multiplicity of meanings, with the most common words being the most ambiguous. To test this assertion, just look up a few words in the dictionary. Words that come most immediately to mind—the everyday words like *table, chair, shoe, sock, dog, field, file, take, look, go, run, raise, narrow*—require many inches and even columns of "definition." Less familiar words like *osmosis, gossamer,* or *tergiversation* are disposed of in a crisp line or two. Prepositions, which are among the commonest words of our language, have so many different senses that they are sometimes maligned as having "function" rather than "content." But it makes a difference whether something is in the box rather than on the box; prepositions have meanings—in great number. The linguist Fries (1945), for example, located in the Oxford Dictionary no fewer than 39 separate senses for *at* and *by*, 40 each for *in* and *with*, and 63 for *of*. You would surely have no difficulty in understanding the statement *I found the book by Charles*

Dickens by the tree by chance; I shall return it by mail by Friday—but it would be very difficult for you to tell me the meaning (or meanings) of the word *by* on all or any of its five occurrences. Prepositions in context seem full of meaning, but in isolation it is impossible to say what the meaning might be. That is why it is so difficult to translate prepositions from one language to another.

It is not necessary to pursue the argument about the nature of words or their meaning, because it is quite clear that sentences are not understood by trying to put together meanings of individual words. *The man ate the fish* and *The fish ate the man* contain exactly the same words, yet they have quite different meanings. A *Maltese cross* is not the same as a *cross Maltese*, any more than a *Venetian blind* is a *blind Venetian*. A house that is *pretty ugly* is not exactly ugly but is certainly not pretty. Obviously, the words in all these examples do not combine in any simple fashion to form the meaning of the whole sentence; in fact, the meaning of many of the individual words in the sentence would appear to be quite different from the meaning we might say they have in isolation.

Perhaps then word order is the key—the word *cross* has one meaning before *Maltese* and another meaning after. But words in the same position can represent different meanings—compare the final words of *She went down the drive* and *She went for a drive*—and words in different positions in a sentence may reflect the same meaning. Words that often seem to have a similar meaning, such as *look*, *view*, and *see* may suddenly acquire quite different meanings when an identical prefix is added, as in *overlook*, *overview*, and *oversee*, and words that may seem opposite in meaning, such as *up* and *down*, may occasionally lose their distinctiveness, as in *slow up* and *slow down*.

A common explanation is that grammar makes the difference; syntax (word order) is the bridge between the surface structure of language and its deep structure. But the problem with this point of view is that often it is impossible to say what a word's grammatical function is before the sentence in which it occurs is understood. Formal grammar, of the kind that is so often taught in schools, is a *descriptive* grammar. It never helped anyone to say anything or to understand what anyone else was saying. It is simply a way of talking about surface structure. Grammar, in other words, does not reveal meaning; meaning must precede grammatical analysis. Consider again the familiar words that I have been citing like *table, chair, shoe, sock, file, dog, field, take, go,* and so forth; these are all words that not only have a multiplicity of meanings but also a variety of grammatical functions. To ask anyone to identify such words when they are written in isolation is rather pointless because they can commonly be both noun and adjective, or noun and verb, or adjective and verb, or perhaps all three. How do we understand a simple statement like *open the empty bottle?* It is not by taking into account the fact that *open* is a verb and *empty* an adjective, because in the equally comprehensible sentence *Empty the open bottle*, the two words switch grammatical roles without any difference in surface structure. This complicated ambiguity of language is the reason that it is difficult to program computers to translate language or make abstracts, even when they are equipped with a "dictionary" and a "grammar." Computers lack the knowledge of the world that is required to make sense of language. Thus, a computer is befuddled by over a dozen different possible meanings of a simple expression like *time flies*. Is *time* a noun, or a verb (as in *time the racehorses*), or an adjective (like the word *fruit* in *fruit flies*)? Is *flies* a noun or a verb? A computer is said to have interpreted *out of sight, out of mind* as *invisible and insane*.

Not only is it impossible to state the grammatical function of individual words outside of a meaningful context, it can also be impossible to state the grammatical structure of entire sentences without prior understanding of their meaning. Most English teachers would parse *The onions are planted by the farmer* as a passive sentence, because it contains the three grammatical markers of the passive form—the auxiliary *are*, the participle ending -*ed*, and the preposition *by*. But the sentence *The onions are planted by the tree* is not a passive sentence, although its surface structure would appear to contain the appropriate three grammatical markers. Meaning determines the grammatical structure of these sentences, not the surface structure markers. In fact, *The onions are planted by the farmer* need not be a passive sentence, because it is just as ambiguous grammatically as *She was seated by the minister;* the grammar depends on the meaning.

In other words—and this must be the answer to the question at the beginning of this section—there is only one way in which language can be understood, that print can be comprehended, and that is by having meaning brought to it.

Comprehension Through Prediction

The assertion that language is understood by having meaning brought to it obviously cannot be taken to imply that any particular utterances or sentences can mean anything. Usually, there would be some broad general agreement about the main implications of statements, at least when they are made in real world situations. If someone in an elevator remarks "It is raining outside," few people would want to claim that it could mean that the streets are dry. And by the same argument, the meanings that listeners and readers bring to language cannot be wild guesses; the usual broad general agreement about implications makes the reckless attribution of meaning unlikely as well. If most people seem to be in agreement about the kind of meaning that can be attributed to a particular sequence of words, then some explanation must be found as to why such agreement exists.

The explanation that can be offered should not be unfamiliar. Language tends to be understood in the same way on similar occasions because listeners or readers must have a pretty good idea about the meaning that was intended in the first place. To be more precise, meaning is brought to language through prediction, which you will remember from the previous chapter means the prior elimination of unlikely alternatives. Prediction does not mean staking everything on one wild guess (which would indeed run the risk of frequent error), nor does it mean that the precise meaning is known in advance (which would of course make attention to language unnecessary in the first place). Prediction simply means that the uncertainty of the listener or reader is limited to a few probable alternatives, and provided that information can be found in the surface structure of the utterance to dispose of the remaining uncertainty—to indicate which predicted alternative is appropriate—then comprehension takes place.

Prediction is the reason that the brain is not normally overwhelmed by the possible number of alternatives in language; there are actually only very few alternatives in our minds at any time that we are comprehending what is being said. And prediction is the reason we are so rarely aware of ambiguity: We expect what the writer or speaker is likely to say and just do not contemplate alternative interpretations. We interpret *The thieves decided to head for the bank* in one way if we know they were sitting in a car and in another way if they were swimming in a river. When language is comprehended, in other words, the receiver is usually no more aware of possible ambiguity than the producer. Speakers and writers are presumed to have at least a general idea of what they intend to say and are thus unlikely to consider alternative interpretations of the language they produce. The same applies to listeners or readers. The first interpretation that comes to us is the one that makes the most sense to us at the particular time, and alternative and less likely interpretations will not be considered unless subsequent interpretations fail to be consistent or to make sense, in which case we realize our probable error and try to recapitulate. One interpretation usually satisfies us, provided it makes sense, so we do not waste time looking for a second. This is the reason that puns may be difficult to see, and also why they are mildly irritating. We do not expect to find more than one meaning for the same sequence of words.

As I indicated in the previous chapter, there is nothing very remarkable or particularly clever about this process of prediction; it goes on all the time. Prediction enables us to make sense of all the events in our daily lives. And we are no more aware of our predictions when we read than we are at any other time for the simple reason that our predictions are usually so good. We are rarely surprised because our predictions rarely let us down, even when we read a book for the first time.

What exactly do we predict when we read? The fundamental answer is meaning, although of course we look at words or letters to find the evidence that will confirm or disconfirm particular meanings. A number of detailed predictions may be made and tested simultaneously—and constantly modified—as we make our way through the actual text. Every specific prediction, however, no matter how detailed and transient, will be derived from our more general expectations about where the text as a whole might be leading.

Some Practical Implications

The preceding discussion should make it clear that it is misleading if not inaccurate to regard reading as a matter of "following the text" or to say that a listener "follows" the meaning of a speaker. Language is understood by keeping ahead of the incoming detail. By having some expectation of what the speaker or writer is likely to say, by making use of what we already know, we protect ourselves against being overwhelmed by information overload. We avoid the confusion of ambiguity and succeed in bridging the gap between the surface structure of the text and the writer's intention.

It is easy to demonstrate how we keep ahead of any words that we identify as we read. Ask a friend to turn out the light while you read aloud, so that you are suddenly deprived of visual information, and you will find that your voice is able to continue "reading" another four or five words. Your eyes were a second or more—perhaps three or four eye movements—ahead of the point your voice had reached when the lights went out. This phenomenon is known as the *eye-voice span,* a term that is rather misleading because it might suggest that we need more than a second to organize in speech the sounds of the particular word that we are looking at. But this is incorrect. We do not need a second to identify a word; the difference in time is not so much a reflection of how far thought lags behind the eye as of how far thought is ahead of the voice. We use our eyes to scout ahead so that we can make decisions about meaning, and thus about individual words, in advance. Indeed, the eye-voice span exists only when we can make sense of what we read. If we read nonsense—*dog lazy the over jumps fox quick the* rather than *The quick brown fox jumps over the lazy dog*—then eye and voice tend to converge on the same point, and the eye-voice span disappears. The span, in fact, reflects rather precisely the sense that we make of text, because it tends to extend to the end of a meaningful phrase. The four or five word span is merely an average. If the lights go out just as we are about to read . . . *and drove off into the night,* we are likely to continue aloud as far as *off* or as far as *night,* but not stop at *into* or *the*.

It is because the reader must keep ahead of the text that it is so hard for children to learn to read from material that does not make sense to them or which is so disconnected and fragmentary that prediction is impossible. Reading is similarly much more difficult for children who have been taught that they should get the words right rather than try to make sense of what is being read. Not only is "getting the words right" very much harder and slower unless meaning is brought to the text in the first place, but identifying each successive word on the line one after the other will not, in itself, give meaning. Reading is not a matter of decoding to the surface structure of speech; the sounds will not make sense of their own accord.

The difficulty of many high school "problem readers" is not that they have failed over the years to learn how to sound out words correctly, nor that they are careless about getting every word right, but rather that they read one word at a time as if meaning should be the last concern. They expect that meaning will take care of itself, although this is the reverse of the way in which sense is made of reading.

WRITTEN LANGUAGE AND SPOKEN LANGUAGE

Obviously spoken language and written language are not the same. It is not difficult to detect when a speaker reads from a text prepared for publication or when a passage that we read is the unedited transcription of a spontaneous talk. Speech and print are not different *languages*—they share a common vocabulary and the same grammatical forms—but they have different conventions for using vocabulary and grammar. It should not be considered surprising or anomalous that differences exist between spoken and written language; they are generally used for quite different purposes and addressed to quite different audiences. The grammar and vocabulary of spoken language itself are likely to vary depending on the purpose for which speech is used and the relationships between the people using it.

It is curious that the differences between written language and speech are often taken to reflect a defect in writing. Most people seem to assume—and probably rightly so—that spoken English is a reasonably efficient system. They may complain about the way various individuals *use* the language, but the language itself seems above criticism. We rarely hear suggestions that English would be a better spoken language if it had a few sounds more or less in it or if one or two grammatical structures were added or eliminated. Indeed, signs that the language is changing may be the signal for considerable outrage in the newspapers.

Written language, on the other hand, is frequently the subject of calls for improvement, ranging from spelling reform to its total abolition in beginning reading texts in favor of actual (or invented) spoken language forms. I suggest, however, that written language is different from spoken language for the good reason that spoken language has adapted itself to being heard but written language is more appropriately read. Written language is not made more comprehensible by being translated into "speech," even into the supposed speech of the reader.

The Specialization of Language

To understand why such a specialized adaptation of spoken and written language might have come about, it is necessary to examine the different demands the two language forms make on their recipients. There is, for example, the obvious fact that the spoken word dies the moment it is uttered and can only be recaptured if held in the listener's fallible memory or as the result of a good deal of mutual inconvenience as the listener asks the speaker to recapitulate. Even tape recording does little to mitigate the essential transience of speech in contrast to the facile way in which the eye can move backward and forward through written text. The reader has command over time, can attend to several words at once, select what those words will be, the order in which they will be dealt with, and the amount of time that will be spent on them. In other words, spoken language may make considerable demands on attention, which written language does not.

On the other hand, written language might seem to place a far greater burden on memory—on what we already know about language and the world—than does our everyday speech. To bring meaning to spoken language, very often all we need do is consider the circumstances in which an utterance is made. Much of our everyday spoken language is directly related to the immediate situation in which it is uttered. We may pay very little attention to the actual words the speaker is using. The relevance of the utterance is as ephemeral as the words themselves—"Pass the salt, please"—and requires putting information into long-term memory as little as it requires drawing information out from long-term memory. Written language, by contrast, generally depends on nothing but what we can and do remember. Rarely can we look around the room to make sense of what we have just read in a book.

This matter of clues to meaning must be elaborated on to consider a different kind of demand that written language places on the reader, related this time not to memory but to the far more fundamental question of how we make sense of language in the first place.

The question is how the meaning of language is verified; how can we confirm that the information we are receiving is likely to be the truth, that it makes sense, or that indeed we are understanding it correctly? What is the source of the predictions that can cut through all the ambiguity inherent in language so that we make the most reasonable and reliable interpretation? For the kind of everyday spoken language I have been talking about, the answer is simple: Look around. Even if the topic of concern is not completely clarified by what our senses can tell us of present circumstances, any uncertainty we have can probably be removed by what we know already of the speaker's nature, interests, and likely intentions. But the language of texts offers no such shortcuts. There is only one final recourse if we are not sure of what we have read, and that is to return to the text itself. For verification, for disambiguation, and to avoid error, a difficult and possibly unfamiliar kind of skill is required. That is the skill of pursuing a line of thought, looking for internal consistencies, of evaluating arguments. Both the source and the test of many of the changing predictions that are necessary for the comprehension of written language must lie in the text itself, informed by the more general expectations that readers bring from their prior knowledge. The text determines what the actual alternatives might be and whether they have been successfully predicted. For that reason alone, spoken language and written language can rarely be the same.

A Different Difference in Language

The previous section began by considering some fairly obvious differences between spoken and written language, differences which should be familiar to anyone who hopes to learn to read. But it quickly became necessary to acknowledge that the general distinctions being made were between a particular kind of speech, the "everyday spoken language directly related to the situation in which it is uttered," and a particular kind of written language, namely that of "continuous texts." To present the complete picture it must now be explained that there is another distinction that slices right across the spoken–written dimension and that is of more importance in any analysis of reading and writing.

The issue basically concerns how the words we speak or write are selected and organized in the first place. Obviously words are rarely produced at random. There is usually a necessity or reason for every word that we use, related in part to the intention we want to fulfill and to the language with which we propose to fulfill it. Both of these considerations, the reason for saying something and the linguistic vehicle we select for saying it, place considerable constraints on what we say and write. But there is a third important constraint, the one with which I am at present most concerned, and that is the environment in which the language is produced. To use language rather arbitrarily myself for the moment, I shall use the term *situation* to refer to the physical environment in which words are produced—the position in which you are standing when you say something or the location in which written words happen to be written or printed—and I shall use the word *context* to refer to the language environment in which spoken or written words occur. The context for the word *context* in the previous sentence, for example, is all the other words in that sentence and in the chapter as a whole.

A distinction must be made between *situation-dependent* and *context-depen-dent* language.

Situation-dependent speech is the spoken language with which infants first become familiar, and it is the basis upon which they begin all their learning about language. By situation-dependent I mean that the speech is directly related to the physical and social situation in which it is uttered. If someone says "Pass the salt, please," then there is likely to be some salt around, a person who would like some salt, and another person in a position to pass it. If someone says "I think it is raining again," then the streets are likely to be wet or there will be some other indication that rain has started. Given the physical situation and the speaker's intentions, it would not be possible to say anything very much different, like "I think it is raining again," if the speaker really wanted the salt passed, or vice versa.

The fact that such speech and the situation in which it is uttered (including the speaker's intentions) are closely related may seem trivial, but it is in fact crucial, because it is the basis of children's language learning. It is the way in which language is first comprehended and verified. Normally we think that such language describes the situation in which it occurs. Hear someone say "Pass the salt, please," and we can construct the probable cast of characters and the major props, even if we cannot see what is going on. But the clues also work in the other direction; the situation can make sense of the language. A child who does not yet understand what "Pass the salt, please" means can work it out from the situation in which the language is uttered. Indeed, if someone actually said "I think it is raining again," and another person passed the speaker the salt, then the child might assume that "I think it is raining again" meant "Pass the salt." This strategy of using the situation to provide clues to how unfamiliar language works is not uncommon. We all tend to use it when confronted by someone speaking a foreign language or in any other situation when we do not understand what is being said. If the waiter says something incomprehensible, we look to see if we are being offered the menu, the wine, or the bill.

Because such language is closely tied to the situation in which it occurs, it cannot be arbitrarily transferred to different situations. If "Pass the salt, please" fails to get the response we want in the restaurant, it will not do us much good to repeat it out in the street. Also, because most of the meaning and the verification of such language rests in the particular situation in which it is uttered, it tends to be elliptical and brief—"Coffee?" "Thanks"—without much evident grammar about it.

Just as there is a good deal of situation-dependent spoken language in the environment of most children, who use it to make their first sense of speech, so there is a good deal of situation-dependent *written* language in most contemporary environments, which children can again employ to make sense of reading. I am referring now to the written language of signs and labels, the ubiquitous language that we find on every product we buy, festooned around every store, on every wrapper, on every street sign, and as part of every television commercial. We do not have a convenient word in our language for such situation-dependent writing, so I refer to it as *ambient print*. It functions in exactly the same way as situation-dependent speech, because it is also closely tied to the situation in which it occurs. The situation provides learners with a clue to its meaning, and it cannot be arbitrarily changed or moved without losing its sense. The word *toothpaste* tells the reader what is in the tube and the contents of the tube tell the learner what the printed word is likely to be. Indeed, some children think the printed word *Crest* says toothpaste just as they may think that the sign *McDonald's* says hamburgers. (And the advertisers of Crest and McDonald's will tell you that these are indeed what their brand names are supposed to say.) Certainly a child who finds he is brushing his teeth with shampoo or that she has poured herself a bowl of detergent does not need an adult to point out the reading error. If you do not understand what the sign or label means, look at the situation in which it occurs. Like situation-dependent speech, ambient print is tied to where it occurs. The sign *Exit* cannot be moved to the middle of the wall because we are tired of seeing it over the door. Like situation-dependent speech, such print tends to be elliptical and independent of grammar. The situation takes the place of complexity of language.

Quite different from the situation-dependent written language of signs and labels, however, is the continuous written language of texts. This language is more complex and has to be. It does not derive or convey its meaning from the situation in which it occurs; its location offers no clues to its sense. If you do not understand something in a newspaper or novel, it will not help you to look at where the text is located in the room or into the face of the person who gave it to you. The appropriate meaning of the text remains constant, whether you look at it now in the room or an hour later in the street. It cannot be elliptical. It is grammatically complex.

Despite this independence from the specific location in which it is produced and read, however, there is just as much necessity about the written language of texts as there is about situation-dependent writing and speech. The writer is still not free to produce words arbitrarily or at random. A writer cannot decide to make the next word *rhinoceros* or *platitudinous* just because it is a long time since these words were last used. Now, however, the constraints upon the words are determined by just two things: the subject matter that the writer is talking about (what the writer wants to say) and the language the writer is employing (how the writer wants to say it). In other words, all of the constraints on what is written lie within the context of the language itself. Thus, I call such language *context dependent*. Not only does the intricate texture of a written context give every component word its meaning, but because of the redundancy in text, it is usually possible to replace a word that has been left out or to work out the meaning of an unfamiliar word.

For children learning to read in a first language and for anyone attempting to read in a second, the ability to make use of contextual clues to meaning is crucial. But the clues embedded in the immediate language environment of context-dependent writing are not the same as those in situation-dependent writing (which is one reason that children who have essential insights into reading from print may still have difficulty with continuous text). Nor are the clues of context-dependent writing those of situation-dependent speech (which is one reason why being read to is such an enormous advantage in learning to read).

The particular requirements of context-dependent writing have so impressed some theorists (Goody & Watt, 1972; Havelock, 1976; Olson, 1977) that they have argued that written language has introduced a whole new mode of thought to our basic human repertoire of intellectual skills. But context-dependent written language is not unique. Not all our spoken language is of the "everyday," situationally verifiable kind that has been discussed. Some of our spoken language can be as abstract, argumentative, and unrelated to the circumstances in which it is comprehended as an article in a scientific journal. There is also context-dependent speech. Olson (1977) claims that our ability to produce and understand such spoken language is a byproduct of our being literate. It is only because of our experience in reading that we can make sense of this kind of spoken language, which, in its form, is more like writing than everyday speech. But the contrary also applies; by hearing such speech a child becomes better equipped to read.

If prediction is the basis for the comprehension of written language, then obviously an important part of the prior knowledge of readers must be familiarity with the unique characteristics of the different forms that context-dependent language takes. The more one knows about such language, the easier it will be to read continuous text and thus to learn to read. All this is part of the reason that it must be emphasized that not only is reading learned through reading but also that learning to read begins with being read to.

THE ORGANIZATION OF TEXTS AND COMPREHENSION

Texts are not all written in the same way, even if they are written differently from the way spoken language is produced, at least not texts that are well-written and comprehensible. Instead, the content of different kinds of text is organized and presented in distinctive and characteristic ways. Each kind of text has its own conventions of layout, typography, and style—called *genre schemes*—which distinguish it from other genres or kinds of text. Novels do not have the same genre schemes as textbooks, poems, newspapers, letters, or telephone directories. Furthermore, the various kinds of text may have quite different genre schemes in different cultures. Newspapers or novels produced in France for French readers are not written and presented in the same way as those for readers elsewhere, even if they speak the same language. Often we can *see* that texts *are* different from culture to culture, even though we cannot read the language. There is nothing particularly logical or necessary about specific genre schemes—they could be different, as they usually are from one culture to another—but they have become conventional where they are employed and they serve their purposes because they are conventional.

Genre schemes help both readers and writers. Their characteristic forms help readers by giving them a basis for predicting what a text will be like, that a novel will be divided into chapters in a particular way, that a scientific article will follow a certain format, that a letter will observe typical conventions. Readers become so accustomed to the genre schemes of the texts with which they are familiar that they assume they are natural, inevitable, and universal. A text that is produced differently in a different culture may be regarded as an aberration. Indeed, we all tend to be chauvinistic about the language with which we are most intimately connected. Our own language is "natural" and the rest are "foreign." Genre schemes also help writers (if they know them), because they provide a framework for organizing what writers want to say and more importantly for anticipating and respecting what readers are likely to expect. Genre schemes facilitate communication.

Similarly, every kind of text, and every form of spoken language interaction too, has characteristic internal relationships, called *discourse structures*, which are again largely arbitrary and accidental but which serve their purposes because they are conventional. Discourse structures in conversation tell us when we may interrupt (at the end of a sentence) and when we may not; they protect speakers from interruptions while allowing others the opportunity to take a turn. In written language, readers can expect writers to observe conventional discourse structures and writers can expect readers to understand them. The structures form the basis of prediction. The manner in which chapters and paragraphs are organized and displayed in books is a matter of discourse structure, and so are the customary salutations at the beginning and end of letters.

Even stories have their conventions, whether they are spoken or written. These conventional ways of telling a story, of relating sequences of events, are known as *story grammars*. They are the framework upon which various characters, plots, motives, and resolutions are linked in related episodes and represented in ways that will be intelligible. If a story makes sense to us, if it *sounds* like a story, this is not just because the story is appropriately told but also because we know the appropriate way in which stories are told, at least in our culture. Stories must reflect the story schemes with which readers are familiar, if writers and readers are to connect.

The important function served for readers by all these conventional and characteristic structures of texts is underlined by the growing evidence that the structures are the basis for our *comprehension* of texts. If we do not know the relevant structures, then we will not understand the text, or our reading of it will be distorted. Experimental psychologists have noted that readers' comprehension of texts is very similar to the structures in the text itself. Ask people to recapitulate what they read in a story, and they will tend to do so with the same structural form as the story rather than with the same words or even "their own" words. Readers not particularly familiar with the genre scheme and discourse structure of a text, with the grammar of the story, will not only fail to comprehend aspects of the text but will recapitulate what they did understand in forms closer to their own structures. Beginning readers have even been shown to insert into their retelling of stories conventional aspects which have been omitted in the telling but which are part of their own story grammars. They put more into the story than was in it originally, because this is their way of making sense of stories.

It is also the structures in the head rather than those in the text that determine our *memory* for texts; they are the forms in which texts are remembered. Discourse structures and story grammars are part of our own cognitive structure, part of the way we organize our knowledge of the world (and therefore a reason that reading is important—it provides us with new frameworks for perceiving the world and organizing experience). The more we can anticipate and employ the formal structures that an author uses, the more we can understand and remember what we read, because the structures also form the basis of our understanding and remembering. And the more an author knows and respects the forms that the reader will predict, so the text will be more readable and memorable.

In a sense, none of this is new or surprising. The British psychologist Bartlett (1932) demonstrated experimentally over 60 years ago that the way stories are interpreted and remembered varies with the cultural backgrounds and expectations of their readers and listeners. Who would expect otherwise? But experiments and theoretical work into these matters demonstrate convincingly what in the past has perhaps been only intuitively obvious (or should have been intuitively obvious).

Two brief qualifications must be added. First, the structures of texts should be seen as the basis for comprehension but not for comprehension itself. Some researchers seem to assume that the comprehension *is* the structure of the text, that we have understood a story if we can repeat large parts of it. But comprehension is less a matter of being able to reproduce the facts in a text than of what one does or is able to do as a consequence of interacting with the structure of the text. You do not prove that you have understood anything by repeating it. And second, these structures which can be observed and ana-lyzed in the organization of texts are not structures that require our conscious attention. We need not be able to talk about a particular grammatical construction or other convention in order to understand and use it. The knowledge that enables us to make sense of the world and of language is not knowledge of which we are aware, even if we are psychologists or linguists. There is no evidence that making implicit structures explicit improves com-prehension or that by teaching them to children we help them understand. In fact without the prior understanding, such "explanations" are themselves meaningless. Children learn the structures by being helped to understand the texts in which the structures are employed, which is not the same thing as being taught the structures. Children, like all of us, are capable of compre-hending without being able to say how it is done.

THE CONVENTIONS OF LANGUAGE

There is one final characteristic of language, both spoken and written, situation-dependent and context-dependent, that I must emphasize. It is that all language is conventional. *Semiotics*—an area of study that interests a number of reading researchers—is specifically concerned with the nature of all different kinds of communicative conventions, their use, and how they develop. This is an enormous topic with multiple ramifications, but I must try to deal with it briefly, first by explaining what it means to say that all language is conventional, then why the statement is critical.

All language is conventional in the sense that every aspect of language is a matter of chance and of mutual agreement. All the various forms of language must work, they must fulfill a function, but the nature of the forms themselves is always arbitrary, a matter of historical accident; they could always be different. In fact across the 3,000 or more different languages that exist in the world, every language form is different. There is no particular logic or necessity about the specific forms of any particular language. That is what the word "conventional" means, arbitrary forms which could be different, functioning in the way they do because their form is mutually agreed on.

Thus the use of red to mean stop in traffic signs is a matter of convention. The convention works because it is mutually accepted that red should mean stop (in those cultures where red means stop). But the fact that red rather than green means stop is a matter of chance. Things could have worked out differently. Green could mean stop tomorrow provided everyone agreed on the change; there is nothing particularly compelling (or arresting) about using red. In some cultures, in certain circumstances, it is a mark of respect to remove your hat. In other cultures, the mark of respect is to keep it on. What makes removing your hat (or putting it on) a mark of respect has nothing to do with the act itself but with the mutual understanding that this is how the act is to be interpreted, the intention that it represents.

Every aspect of language is conventional, starting from the very sounds and meanings of words we use. In English, *yes* means yes, but this is only a convention. *No* could mean yes. In other languages, other words mean yes. The same applies to all the words in every language. No one has a free choice with words. No one can call anything something different from everyone else in their language community, not if they want to be understood.

Words are conventional, and so is grammar. Different languages have different grammatical forms, and there is nothing more logical or rational or efficient about one grammar than another. All languages solve the same kind of problems, but they solve them in different ways. I have already noted that story grammars, discourse structures, and genre schemes are conventions. They could be different, they are different in different languages and cultures, and they function despite their arbitrary nature because they are all matters of mutual agreement among the people who employ them.

There is an enormous range of conventions in language, many of which have not yet been mentioned. For example, there are the conventions of idiom. Language is far more than grammar and vocabulary (even though a good deal of instruction in reading, in "English" and in second languages, seems to assume that this is what language consists of). Knowledge of grammar and vocabulary gives no one a mastery of language, either in producing or in understanding it. By far the greatest part of any language, the "working" part of it, is *idiom*, the way people actually speak, and by definition idiom cannot be accounted for by vocabulary and grammar. Idiom is the way words in the vocabulary and forms in the grammar are actually used in a particular language community, and this usage is a complex and constantly changing system of conventions. Idioms cannot be translated word for word from one language to another.

There are conventions of *cohesion*. Speech does not consist of one statement after another, and paragraphs are more than a simple succession of sentences. Statements and sentences are interlocked, they cohere. I can say "I looked for John. But he had gone" but not "But he had gone. I looked for John." I would have to change the sentences to something like "John had gone. I looked for him." The pronoun and the *but* are two of a number of cohesive devices which lock sentences together in English, but they are conventions because different languages cohere in different ways. You cannot change the order of sentences in any language without having to change the sentences themselves, at least not in meaningful text. (This is a useful way of finding out whether material prepared for beginning readers is meaningful. If the order of sentences can be arbitrarily changed without anyone noticing the difference, then they do not make sense, they are not normally functioning language.)

There are tremendously subtle and intricate conventions of language, both spoken and written, concerned with *register*. This term refers to the fact that you must choose and put your words together differently depending on the subject you are talking about, the person you are talking to, and the circumstances in which you are talking. You cannot speak a language unless you employ the forms of vocabulary, grammar, idiom, and cohesion appropriate to the relevant register. Children quickly learn they must speak in one way to younger children, another way to age-mates, another way to teachers, and another way to other adults. All of the differences of register are conventional; there is no intrinsic logic about the particular form that comes to be appropriate at a particular time. Everyone who has traveled knows that you cannot carry your own conventions of language with you, not if you want to understand and be understood. Not even the nonverbal conventions of language, like how close you should stand to another person in conversation or how long you should look someone directly in the eye, are consistent from one culture to another.

Written language has its own substantial set of conventions. There are conventions of spelling, of punctuation, of the formation of letters, of the size of handwriting or type, of capitalization, of paragraphing, of page layout, of book binding. All of these could be different, and all of them are, in other languages, other cultures. Every aspect of language, in astronomical numbers of ways, is conventional.

Why should I bother to point all this out? Because it is important for readers (and writers) to know what the conventions of written language are, and it is important for teachers and researchers to understand the conventional nature of language.

Knowledge of written language conventions is essential for readers and writers because conventions are the basis of understanding and communication. Conventions make prediction possible. The forms of conventions cannot be predicted, they vary by chance or historical accident from one language community to another, and they also change with time. But knowledge of the forms makes the conventions that will be used on particular occasions predictable. To be able to read a text, we must be able to anticipate the conventions that its writer will employ. This understanding of the appropriate conventions, together with prior knowledge related to the subject matter, is the essential "nonvisual" information that readers must contribute to the act of reading. But the understanding must be mutual. To be comprehensible, the writer must anticipate and respect the conventions that the reader will predict. Conventions are the common currency of every language transaction.

Teachers and researchers should understand the conventional nature of language because it makes, or should make, a fundamental difference in the way language learning and language instruction are perceived. There is a tendency to think of language as "logical," as "rational," even as if it could be in our genes. But language is enormously complex, and all of its complexity is arbitrary and accidental. It could all be different. The implication of this is that no one ever learns language by sitting down and thinking about it, by anticipating what it will be like, or even by learning a few rules. Learning a language or learning to read involves learning a tremendous number of conventions. And these cannot be learned by rule or by rote. They must be learned, one at a time, in a sequence and context that is most meaningful for every learner.

There is one other implication of the conventional nature of language that assumes great importance when learning is considered. The conventionality of language means that language is *social* in all its aspects. Language does things for *people*, and its particular conventions—the way it does things—are matters of social contract and social identification. We talk the way people around us talk—provided we see ourselves as that kind of person. We use language in the ways that it is used by the people around us, again provided we do not see ourselves as different from them. Above and beyond all the technical aspects of reading discussed in this book and in many other books on the same topic, reading is a social activity, learned (or not learned) in a social rather than an intellectual context.

Language About Language

An interesting question about all the complexities of language that I have discussed in this chapter concerns how much they need to be consciously known by a learner. Is it necessary for beginning readers to be *instructed* in the difference between surface structure and meaning, in the fine points of grammar, or in all the other essential conventions of language, both spoken and written? Should they be able to talk about language as well as be able to use it?

There is a special word for language about language—the word is *metalanguage*. In a general sense, this entire chapter has been written in metalanguage, because it has been on the topic of language. More specifically, there are a number of *metalinguistic* terms that are frequently central to any discussion involving language—terms like *noun* and *verb*, *word* and *syllable*, *phrase* and *sentence*.

The word metalanguage may remind you of the word *metacognition*, which was introduced in chapter 1. Metacognition is thinking (or language) about thinking, just as metalanguage is language (or thinking) about language. And there is a controversy in psychology and educational research about how important ability in both metacognition and metalanguage is for learning to read and to write.

Some researchers argue that children must be aware of their own learning processes and able to talk about specific aspects of spoken and written language, if they are to learn to read. Downing (1979), for example, asserts that children who do not have metalinguistic competence are in a state of "cognitive confusion" when someone tries to teach them about reading. (Downing himself uses technical metacognitive language here. Instead of saying that children may be "in a state of cognitive confusion," he could simply describe them as "confused.") Other theorists argue that children are obviously capable of learning without being able to talk about learning—how else would babies learn to talk in the first place? We have all learned many things in our lives without being able to talk about what we were learning, or indeed, being aware at the time that we were learning. Many people can read and write phrases and paragraphs without being able to provide a linguistic definition for them or to parse a sentence.

As for being able to understand the language of language, it is also evident that many people learn to read without understanding the meaning of many metalinguistic terms. Indeed, it could be argued that terms like *word*, *sentence*, *comma*, and *period* have no meaning until we can read. They are not parts of spoken language, certainly not in any direct or conspicuous way. Like Molière's bourgeois gentilhomme, we all speak prose without knowing we are doing so until someone points it out to us (and explains the technical meaning of the word).

Why then should knowledge of metalinguistic terminology be thought to be so critical in reading instruction? The explanation seems to be that children need to understand what teachers are talking about, and if teachers find it necessary to use metalinguistic or metacognitive language, then children are in difficulty if they do not understand such language themselves. Cognitive confusion is caused by instruction that is not comprehensible. Whether it is essential for classroom teachers to employ the abstract technical language of linguistics and other specialized disciplines in teaching reading is another matter.

ISSUES

Many of the topics in this chapter are subject to endless dispute among specialists—including the nature of language, the role of grammar, and the meaning of meaning. Such issues have resisted solution or agreement for over 2000 years, and there are no reasonable grounds for believing they can ever be resolved. The issues are abstract and need have little bearing on the teaching of reading. More central is the controversy over the "relationship" of written to spoken language, which comes up frequently in this book. Some people regard written language as "parasitical" on speech. Historical, linguistic, or philosophical speculation is unlikely to settle the arguments, and the convictions of various specialists reflect faith rather than infallibility. Another matter of preference rather than evidence concerns the nature of metalinguistic discourse (is language about language any different from language about anything else?) and its necessity in classroom discourse.

SUMMARY

The sounds of language and the visual information of print are **surface structures** of language which do not represent meaning directly. Meaning resides in the **deep structure** of language, in the intentions of speakers and writers, and in the interpretations of listeners and readers. Written language and spoken language are not the same, and language also differs to the extent that it is **situation dependent** or **context dependent.** The basis of comprehension is **prediction,** made possible by the complex **conventional** nature of language.

Notes to Chapter 2 begin on page 232, covering
Surface structure and deep structure
Linguistic theories
Semiotics
Discourse analysis
Text organization and comprehension
Some technical terms
Modules and networks
Speech, writing, and "language"
More about words

3 Information and Experience

Louise Rosenblatt (1978) says there are two ways to read—for information or for experience. It is easy to tell the difference between the two. When information is what we want, we are perfectly content to get it in any way we can. No one ever says, "Don't tell me that telephone number, I want the pleasure of looking it up for myself." But when we read for experience, we are reluctant to be deprived of even a moment. We do not encourage anyone else to say "Don't bother to read the last chapter—the butler did it." Often we slow down as we near the end of a novel, as we might at the end of a good meal, to protract the experience.

The distinction between information and experience is important because the two are frequently confounded in education. Books or other texts which should be read for experience are treated only as sources of information. Rosenblatt says this is because it is easier to grade readers on the information they might be expected to acquire than on the experience they might enjoy. She satirizes such an approach in the title of an article called "What Facts Does This Poem Teach You?" (Rosenblatt, 1980).

It is often said that we live in an "information age"—but the word *information* is used very loosely. Usually it is taken to mean something like "facts" or "data." Despite its vagueness and ambiguity, the word has become ubiquitous in education, not only with reference to literacy but to learning and teaching as well. Reading and learning are both referred to as "the acquisition of information" and writing (and teaching) as its "transmission." But there is much more to education and to life than facts or data. The word *information* can be misused and misunderstood.

Information has been given a precise technical definition—which most people in education are not aware of, although it has enabled some aspects of reading to be accurately measured. I shall use the word in this strict technical sense when I examine how the visual system solves complex problems of identifying letters and words in print. On the other hand, the widespread use of the word in a more general sense in educational and psychological research—for example in the characterization of the brain as an "information-processing device"—may distort rather than facilitate efforts to understand literacy and learning. And information, when the word is used in a more general sense, cannot be measured.

First, I shall examine the technical definition of information and its relationship to another general term which can also be used technically in a very precise sense—*uncertainty*. I also look at how information can be related to comprehension and to another important concept in reading, *redundancy*. I then refer to some limitations on the way in which individuals can make use of information and also on the way in which the word itself can be used—the contrast with "experience."

INFORMATION AND UNCERTAINTY

We should not expect to be able to identify and measure information the way we measure height and weight. Information can be found in a multitude of guises—in marks on paper, in facial expressions and other bodily gestures, in the configuration of clouds, trees (and sometimes tea leaves), and in the sounds of speech. Obviously sources of information have little in common, and neither do the channels through which information passes.

Consider the mutations of information when we listen to a broadcast recording of someone talking. What we hear begins as an intention in the speaker's mind, represented in some complex and deeply mysterious way in the flux of chemical and bioelectrical activities in the structures of the brain. This intention is then translated into bursts of neural energy, dispatched from the brain at different times, rates, and directions to the musculature of the jaw, mouth, lips, tongue, vocal cords, and chest, orchestrating the expulsion of breath in such a manner that distinctive pressure waves of contrasting intensity and frequency radiate through the surrounding atmosphere. These fleeting disturbances in the molecules of the air cause the tiny diaphragm of a microphone to resonate in sympathy, triggering a flow of electrical energy along a wire quite unlike the corresponding patterns of neural energy in the nervous systems of the speaker or listener. Amplified and modulated, the electrical impulses from the microphone impress subtle combinations of magnetic forces onto a plastic tape or etch wavy lines into a plastic disk, often after being "digitized." Through further mechanical and electronic incarnations, the information may then be diffused by radio transmission (perhaps diverting through the transistors of an earth-orbiting satellite) before being reconstituted by a receiver and loud speaker into airborne pressure waves that lap against the listener's ear. And still the transformations are not done. The oscillations of the eardrum are conveyed to another resonating membrane of the inner ear across a tiny bridge of three articulating bones—the hammer, the anvil, and the stirrup. And then, perhaps most bizarrely, a pressure wave pulses back and forth through liquid in the coiling canals of the inner ear, a labyrinth carved into the skull itself, where microscopic hair cells wave like reeds with the movement of the fluid in which they are contained. The roots of these fronds are the tiny beginnings of the mighty auditory nerve, and they generate the final relays of neural impulses that travel its hundreds of thousands of separate nerve fibers, through half a dozen booster and transformer stations in various recesses of the brain, to be transformed at last into subjective experiences of meaningfulness and sound. And this meaningfulness of acoustic events can be congruent with a subjective meaningfulness and visual experience from perhaps the same words written down and reaching the brain by a completely different route through the eyes. How can all or even part of this complexity be identified and evaluated as "information"?

On Making Decisions

The answer is that information can be evaluated by looking at what it enables the "receiver"—the listener or the reader—to do. Information enables a person to make decisions, to choose among alternative possibilities or competing courses of action. Information can be assessed, not from its source or from the various forms that it can take during transmission, but from what it enables the recipient to do. Reading requires decisions, whether by a child striving to identify a single letter of the alphabet or by a scholar struggling to decipher an obscure medieval text. And anything that helps a reader to make a decision is information.

Put into other words again, *information reduces uncertainty*. The change of focus from the facilitation of decisions to the reduction of uncertainty may not seem to be much of a conceptual gain, but it permits information to be measured, or at least estimated comparatively. Information cannot be quantified directly, any more than the size or weight of a decision can be calculated directly. But it is possible to put a number to uncertainty and thus indirectly to the amount of information that eliminates or reduces that uncertainty. The trick is accomplished by defining uncertainty in terms of the number of alternatives confronting the decision-maker. If you are confronted by a lot of alternatives, you have a great deal of uncertainty; there are many different decisions you could make. If you have fewer alternatives, it may be just as hard for you to make up your mind but theoretically your uncertainty is less;

there are fewer alternative decisions you might make. The argument has nothing to do with the importance of the decision to you, only with the number of alternatives. Theoretically, your uncertainty is the same whether you must decide for or against major surgery or for having your eggs scrambled or fried. The number of alternatives is the same in each case, and so therefore is your uncertainty.

And now information can be defined more fully: *Information reduces uncertainty by the elimination of alternatives.* Information, very reasonably, is anything that moves you closer to a decision. It is beside the point whether the decision concerns the identification of particular objects or events or the selection among various choices of action. Uncertainty and information are defined in terms of the *number* of alternative decisions that could be made no matter *what* the alternatives are. However, it is easier to reach an understanding of these concepts if particular situations are taken as examples.

Suppose that the information is available in a single letter of the alphabet. Or to put the matter into plain English, suppose a child is given the task of identifying a letter written on the chalkboard. There are 26 letters of the alphabet, and the reader's uncertainty requires a decision or choice among these 26 alternatives. If the situation involves bidding in a bridge game, then the uncertainty may perhaps concern a player's strongest suit, and the number of alternatives will be four. For the simple toss of a coin, the number of alternatives is two; for the roll of a die, it is six. Sometimes the exact number of alternatives is not immediately apparent—for example, if a word rather than a letter is being read. But it may still be possible to determine when this indefinite amount of uncertainty has been reduced—for example, if the reader learns that the word begins with a particular letter or is of a particular length. Either of these pieces of information will reduce the number of alternative possibilities of what the word might be.

We can now return to the definition of information as the reduction of uncertainty. Just as the measure of uncertainty is concerned with the number of alternatives among which the decision-maker has to choose, so information is concerned with the number of alternatives that are eliminated. If the decision-maker is able to eliminate all alternatives except one and thus can make a complete decision, then the amount of information is equal to the amount of uncertainty that existed. A bridge player who receives the information that the partner's strongest suit is red has had uncertainty reduced by one half; if the information is that the strongest suit is hearts, uncertainty is reduced completely. Similarly, a child who knows the letters well enough to decide that the letter on the board is a vowel has acquired information reducing uncertainty from 26 alternatives to five. If the letter is correctly identified, then the information gained from the letter must have been equal to the original uncertainty.

Some aspects of reading involve the acquisition of information in order to make decisions, to reduce uncertainty. For the visual identification of letters and words and possibly some aspects of "reading for meaning," uncertainty can be calculated and therefore also the amount of information required to make a decision. The exact number of alternatives can be specified for letters, an approximate figure can be put to the number of words, but the number of alternatives for a meaning, if it can be estimated at all, must obviously be closely related both to the text being read and to the particular individual who is doing the reading.

COMPREHENSION AND INFORMATION

Comprehension cannot be measured in the same way that some aspects of information can. Comprehension cannot be measured at all, despite constant educational efforts to do so, because it is not a quantity of anything. Comprehension does not have dimension or weight; it is not incremental. Comprehension is not the opposite of uncertainty or even of ignorance, and therefore is not quantifiable as the accumulation of a number of facts or items of information. Rather, comprehension is more appropriately regarded as a *state*, the opposite of confusion. As I proposed in Chapter 1, comprehension is the possibility of relating whatever we are attending to in the world around us to the knowledge, intentions, and expectations we already have in our heads.

We comprehend the situation that we are in if we are not confused by it, whether we are reading a book, repairing an appliance, or trying to find our way through the traffic of an unfamiliar city. Absence of comprehension means not knowing what to do next or which way to turn—*not knowing the relevant questions to ask or not knowing how to find relevant answers*. When we cannot comprehend we cannot predict, we cannot ask questions. Absence of comprehension makes itself immediately evident to the person involved and to anyone looking on, even if it cannot be measured. I do not need a test to detect confusion in myself or in others; bewilderment does not conceal itself. If I see your brows furrow and your eyes glaze, then I know that all is not well with your comprehension. Without comprehension, there can be no reduction of uncertainty. The rote memorization of "facts" without comprehension is not uncertainty reduction. What we learn—with difficulty—under such conditions becomes informative to us only in the future, if by chance we should suddenly discover the sense it is supposed to make. Conversely, when uncertainty reduction is taking place, there must be some comprehension.

Comprehension does not entail that all uncertainty is eliminated. As readers, we comprehend when we can relate potential answers to actual questions that we are asking of the text. We usually have unanswered questions when we read a newspaper—there would not be much point in reading it if we knew everything in advance. And we do not need to have all our uncertainty reduced in order to comprehend. In fact, as we acquire information that reduces uncertainty in some ways, we usually expand our uncertainty in other ways. We find new questions to ask.

Absence of uncertainty is not a condition that we tolerate for very long; we find it boring. There is no "experience" to it. We seek uncertainty, provided we can keep it under control and clear of confusion. We comprehend when we can "make sense" of experience. Indeed, throughout the remainder of this book, I usually refer to comprehension in reading as "making sense of text," relating written language to what we know already and to what we want to know or experience.

Errors and Noise

Of course we may think we comprehend, and look as if we comprehend, but nevertheless make a mistake. Comprehension does not come with an unconditional guarantee. The way we understand something now may prove to be inappropriate later. To have a wrong idea about something is a constant possibility but again not something that can be measured. And no one else can decide for us whether we are in a state of comprehension or confusion, though they can dispute whether we are in such a state for good reason and even help us to move from one state to the other. Comprehension and confusion are the consequences of how well we cope with the particular situation that we happen to be in, with whether or not we feel we know what to do next. What may be comprehensible to you may not be comprehensible to me.

Similarly, what is information for you may not be information for me, if it does not contribute to my comprehension. And such negative information can have more than just a neutral, inconsequential effect. It can be positively disruptive.

A technical term for a signal or message that does not convey information is *noise*. The term is not restricted to acoustic events but can be applied to anything that makes communication less clear or effective, such as a difficult-to-read typeface for printed material, or poor illumination, or distraction of the reader's attention. The *static* that sometimes interferes with television reception is visual noise. Any part of a text that a reader lacks the skill or knowledge to comprehend obviously becomes noise. The present chapter offers information to readers who understand its language and general theme, but it is literally only noise for anyone else. And noise cannot easily be ignored; it is not an absence of information but rather interference that can increase uncertainty.

Because anything becomes noise if one lacks the familiarity or knowledge to understand it, reading is intrinsically more difficult for the novice than for the experienced reader. For the beginner, everything is likely to be much noisier. On the other hand, reading can be made so difficult for experienced readers that they behave no differently from beginners.

The Relativity of Information and Comprehension

What is commonly called information cannot always be measured. Facts are often called information, but the informativeness of facts depends on the prior knowledge of the person receiving them. "Paris is the capital of France" is a fact, but it is not informative to Tom who knows it already, nor to Dick who does not understand what the word "capital" means. And although the statement is informative to Harry, who was not aware of the fact before, it is not possible to say how informative it is because Harry's uncertainty cannot be calculated. We do not know how many alternative cities Harry thought might be the capital of France or how many countries he thought Paris might be the capital of. We do not even know if he cares. Quite possibly, "Paris is the capital of France" is a fact with no information value to Harry when he learns it, although it may be useful to him on a number of occasions later in his life. On the other hand, information that serves only to clutter the mind is really noise.

Information exists only when it reduces uncertainty, which is relative to the knowledge and purposes of the individual receiving it. And comprehension also depends on what an individual already knows and needs or wants to know. Comprehension does not entail assimilating or even examining all of the information in a text, but rather being able to make some sense of the text in terms of the reader's expectations and intentions. Even fluent readers must read some texts more than once in order to comprehend them or to remember a lot of detail. Reading always involves asking questions of a text (the purposeful, selective aspects of reading to which I have referred), and comprehension ensues to the extent that such questions are answered. I may not comprehend a particular text in the same way as you, but then I may not be asking the same questions. Arguments about how a novel, poem, or any other text is most appropriately or "correctly" comprehended are usually arguments about the most relevant kind of questions to ask. A child who claims to have understood a story may not have understood it in the same way as the teacher, but the child was probably not asking the same questions as the teacher. The teacher's questions may be noise to the child. A large part of comprehending literature in any conventional manner is knowing the conventional questions to ask and how to find their answers.

All the preceding discussion of information and comprehension underlines the importance in reading of what goes on behind the eyes, where prior knowledge, purposes, uncertainty, and questions reside. So also do the next two major topics that are discussed, the matter of information that is available from more than one source and the importance of having more than one source of information available.

Redundancy

Redundancy exists whenever the same information is available from more than one source, when the same alternatives can be eliminated in more than one way. And one of the basic skills of reading is the selective elimination of alternatives through the use of redundancy.

An obvious type of redundancy is repetition, when, for example, the alternative sources of information are two identical successive sentences. A different means of having the same information twice would be its concurrent presentation to the eye and to the ear—an audiovisual or multimedia situation. Repetition is an eminently popular technique in advertising, especially in television commercials, exemplifying one of the practical advantages of redundancy—that it reduces the likelihood that receivers will unwittingly make a mistake, or overlook anything, in their comprehension of the message. There are other aspects of redundancy, however, that are not always as obvious but that play a more important role in reading.

Very often the fact that the same alternatives are eliminated by two sources of information is not apparent. Consider the following pair of sentences:

1. The letter of the alphabet that I am thinking of is a vowel.
2. The letter I am thinking of is from the first half of the alphabet.

At first glance the two statements might appear to provide complementary pieces of information telling us that the letter is a vowel in the first half of the alphabet. However, if we look at the alternatives eliminated by each of the two statements, we can see that they actually contain a good deal of overlapping information. Statement 1 tells us that the letter is not *b, c, d, f, g, h, j, k, l, m, n, p, q, r, s, t, v, w, x, y, z*, and statement 2 tells us that it is not *n, o, p, q, r, s, t, u, v, w, x, y, z*. Both statements tell us that the letter is not *n, p, q, r, s, t, v, w, x, y, z*, and it is to this extent (the extent to which the excluded sets of alternatives intersect) that the statements are redundant. In fact, the only new information provided by statement 2 is that the letter is not *o* or *u*; all the other information is already provided in statement 1.

There are frequent examples of redundancy in reading. As an illustration, consider the unfinished sentence (which could perhaps be the bottom line of a right-hand page of a book):

The captain ordered the mate to drop the an-

There are four ways of reducing uncertainty about the remainder of that sentence, four alternative and therefore redundant sources of information. First, we could turn the page and see how the last word finished—this would be *visual* information. But we could also make some reasonable predictions about how the sentence will continue without turning the page. For example, we could say that the next letter is unlikely to be *b, f, j, m, p, q, r, w,* or *z* because these letters just do not occur after *an* in common words of the English language; we can therefore attribute the elimination of these alternatives to *orthographic* (or spelling) information. There are also some things that can be said about the entire word before turning the page. We know that it is most likely to be an adjective or a noun because other types of words such as articles, conjunctions, verbs, and prepositions, for example, are most unlikely to follow the word *the*; the elimination of all these additional alternatives can be attributed to *syntactic* (or grammatical) information. Finally, we can continue to eliminate alternatives even if we consider as candidates for the last word only nouns or adjectives that begin with *an* plus one of the letters not eliminated by the orthographic information already discussed. We can eliminate words like *answer* and *anagram* and *antibody* even though they are not excluded by our other criteria because our knowledge of the world tells us these are not the kinds of things that captains normally order mates to drop. The elimination of these alternatives can be attributed to *semantic* information.

Obviously, the four alternative sources of information about the incomplete word in the previous example, visual, orthographic, syntactic, and semantic, to some extent provide overlapping information. We do not need as much visual information about the next word as we would if it occurred in isolation because the other sources of information eliminate many alternatives. The four sources of information, therefore, are all to some extent redundant. And the skilled reader who can make use of the three other sources needs much less visual information than the less fluent reader. The more redundancy there is, the less visual information the skilled reader requires. In passages of continuous text, provided that the language is familiar and the content not too difficult, every other letter can be eliminated from most words, or about one word in five omitted altogether, without making the passage too difficult for a reader to comprehend.

One last point. I have talked of redundancy in reading as if it exists in the written words themselves, which of course in a sense it does. But in a more important sense, redundancy is information that is available from more than one source only when one of the alternative sources is the reader's own prior knowledge. Put another way, there is no utility in redundancy in the text if it does not reflect something the reader knows already, whether it involves the visual, orthographic, syntactic, or semantic structure of written language. The reader must know that *b* is unlikely to follow *an-* and that *anchors* are ordered dropped by captains. In making use of redundancy, the reader makes use of prior knowledge, using something that is already known to eliminate some alternatives and thus reduce the amount of visual information that is required. Redundancy represents information you do not need because you have it already.

LIMITS TO THE UTILITY OF INFORMATION

The reason for the importance of redundancy, and of prior knowledge in general, is that there are severe limits to the amount of new information we can cope with at any one time, whether through the eyes or any other sense modality. We may have questions that we want answered and potential answers to those questions may be in front of our eyes, but if our uncertainty is extensive or if we are trying to make sense of too much information, then we may not be able to handle all the information we need to reduce our uncertainty. We may fail to comprehend.

In plain language, we can try so hard to understand and to remember more of what we read that we succeed only in confusing ourselves and learning less. Limitations of the visual system and of memory are discussed in the following chapters. But there is another factor to be taken into account that may sound rather paradoxical—the more we strive to avoid error, the less likely we are to be right. We always have a choice about how wrong we will be.

Hits, Misses, and Criteria

Readers do not require a fixed amount of information in order to identify a letter or a word but can make such decisions on more or less information, depending on a number of factors. Exactly how much information a reader will seek before making a decision about a particular letter, word, or meaning depends on the difficulty of the task (which must always be defined with respect to a particular reader), on the reader's skill, and on the "cost" of making a decision.

A useful term for the amount of information that individuals require before coming to a decision is their *criterion*. If the amount of information about a particular letter, word, or meaning meets a reader's criterion for making a decision, then a choice will be made at that point, whether or not the reader has enough information to make a decision correctly. We see a letter or word when we are ready and willing to decide what it is.

An important consideration is how a person decides at what level to establish a criterion—ranging from a supercautious attitude requiring almost an absolute certainty to willingness to take a chance on minimal information, even at the risk of making a mistake. But in order to understand why a particular criterion level is established, it is necessary to understand what the effect of setting a high or low criterion might be.

The concept of criterion levels for perception developed in an area of study called *signal detection theory* and upset quite a number of venerable ideas about human perception. It is traditional to think, for example, that one either sees something or one does not and that there is no area of freedom between within which the perceiver can choose whether something is seen or not. Signal detection theory, however, shows that in many circumstances the question of whether an object is perceived depends less on the intensity of the object—on its "clarity," if you like—than on the attitude of the observer. It is also traditional to think that there is an inverse relationship between correct responses and errors, that the more correct responses there are on any particular task, the lower the number of errors must be. Signal detection theory, however, shows that the relationship is quite the reverse and that the proportion of correct responses for a given amount of information can within limits be selected by the perceiver, but that the cost of increasing the proportion of correct responses is an increase in the number of errors. In other words, the more often you want to be right, the more often you must tolerate being wrong. The paradox can be explained by discussing in a little more detail how the theory originated.

Signal detection theory was originally concerned with the ability of radar operators to distinguish between the "signals" and "noise" on their radar screens with the objective of identifying aircraft presumed to be hostile. As far as the actual situation is concerned, there are only two possibilities: a particular blip on the screen is either a signal or noise; an aircraft is present, or it is not. As far as the operator is concerned, there are also only two possibilities: a decision that the blip on the screen is an aircraft or a decision that it is not. In an ideal world, the combination of the actual situation and the operator's decision would still permit only two possibilities: either the blip is a signal, in which case the operator decides that there is an aircraft, or the blip is merely noise, in which case the decision is that there is no aircraft involved. We may call each of these two alternatives *hits* in the sense that they are both correct identifications. However, there are two other possibilities, of quite different kinds, that can be considered errors. The first type of error occurs when no aircraft is present but the operator decides that there is—this situation may be called a *false alarm*. And the other type of error occurs when there is an aircraft present but the operator decides that there is not, that the signal is actually noise—a situation that can be termed a *miss*.

The problem for the operator is that the numbers of hits, false alarms, and misses are not independent; the number of one cannot be changed without a change in the number of another. If the operator is anxious to avoid false alarms and wants to get maximum information before deciding to report an aircraft, then there will be more misses. If, on the other hand, the operator wants to maximize the number of hits, reducing the possibility of a miss by deciding in favor of an aircraft on less information, then there will also be more false alarms.

Of course, with increased skills of discrimination radar operators can improve their level of efficiency and increase the ratio of hits to false alarms, just as increased clarity of the situation will make the task easier. But in any given situation the choice is always the same between maximizing hits and minimizing false alarms. Always the perceiver has to make the choice, to decide where to set the criterion for distinguishing signal from noise, friend from foe, *a* from *b*. The higher the criterion, the fewer will be the false alarms but the fewer also will be the hits. There will be more hits if the criterion is set lower, if decisions are made on less information, but there will also be more false alarms.

Now we can approach the question of the basis upon which the criterion is established: What makes the perceiver decide to set a criterion high or low? The answer lies in the relative costs and rewards of hits, misses, and false alarms. A radar operator who is heavily penalized for false alarms will set the criterion high, risking an occasional missed identification. One who is highly rewarded for the identification of a possible enemy and excused for the occasional mistake will set the criterion low.

Readers cannot afford to set a criterion level too high before making decisions. A reader who demands too much visual information will often be unable to get it fast enough to read for sense. Readiness to take chances is critical for beginning readers who may be forced to pay too high a price for making "errors." The child who stays silent (who "misses") rather than risk a "false alarm" may please the teacher but develop a habit of setting a criterion too high for efficient reading. Poor readers often are afraid to take a chance; they may be so concerned about getting words wrong that they miss meaning altogether.

INFORMATION AND EXPERIENCE

I have gone to some length to present a technical consideration of the nature of information and its relevance in the study of reading. But my qualifications must be emphasized. *The information-processing point of view is appropriate and useful for thinking about decision-making aspects of reading, but not about reading as a whole.* Readers need to make sense of the visual information in a text in order to be able to read that text, but reading is much more than the identification of visual information. In a sense, reading is what you do with visual information; the visual information is just the raw material.

I am arguing against the view that reading is the "acquisition of information" from text or, even more specifically, that reading is a matter of receiving particular messages or facts put into a text by the writer. This is the common "communication model" (which I myself employed in earlier editions of this book), seeing text as some kind of channel along which information passes from writers to readers. Sometimes the communication metaphor becomes even more specific, with writers "encoding" messages in texts which readers in their turn must then "decode."

However, many kinds of text and considerations of reading are distorted if not fundamentally misperceived if the communication and information-processing metaphors are applied too generally. As Rosenblatt (1978) pointed out, there is reading done for the sake of experience, which is usually the case with novels and poetry and also for the stimulation and exploration of ideas. In these cases what the reader brings to the text, looks for in the text, and does as a consequence of this interaction with the text are far more important and relevant than being able to "identify" and recall the actual content of the text. Indeed, I suspect that very little reading is done for purely factual purposes, where information provided by the text is of primary importance. Such reading (outside of formal school tasks) is rarely "cover-to-cover," but rather is extremely selective and localized, limited by the specific intentions of the reader. I am referring to the occasions upon which we consult encyclopedias, dictionaries, catalogs, television guides, and telephone directories. At other times—even with newspapers and magazines—we read more for the experience generated by the reading, for the satisfaction of the act, than for the specific information that the reading provides.

The information-transmission metaphor is widespread in education, where all aspects of literacy are likely to be categorized and perceived as "communication skills." The metaphor comes, of course, from the ubiquitous electronic technology in our environment, from the radio, television, telephone, and computers. But even in these contexts the information and communication perspective is limited and narrow. For example, television is often seen as a source of either "information" or "entertainment," belittling the alternative if one does not watch programs in order to acquire facts. But not only is there another alternative, most of the so-called informational and entertainment programs in fact also present the possibility of *experience*, far more relative to each individual's knowledge and purposes than either of the other two supposed categories and probably far more important as well. Indeed, the view that education is a matter of acquiring information leads not only to misconceptions about reading (and television watching) but also about learning itself, culminating in the dubious belief that children will soon be able to do all their learning (acquire all the necessary facts) at the consoles of computers. This exclusive emphasis on information acquisition overlooks the critical importance in education, and in life in general, of experience and self-directed exploration.

The decision-making part of reading is usually only a minor part of the act as a whole, involving the identification of occasional letters, individual words, and possibly from time to time one of a limited range of meanings. Research has tended to concentrate on these restricted aspects of reading. But the information that enables you to make such identifications is not the same as the "message" that you interpret from the text, or the understanding that you bring to it, and certainly not the same as the experience that it might generate for you.

It might be best to regard the information offered by texts in a more general sense as *evidence* rather than a message, the basis for a response or understanding rather than the content of comprehension. Information may be what the brain looks for in reading, through the eyes, but it is not the end of reading. It is the basis upon which a meaning is interpreted, an experience constructed, or the exploration of an idea launched.

It is perhaps paradoxical that the concept of information is not widely understood and employed in those contexts in which it makes the most sense, namely where the reading act is limited to rather narrow identification tasks, but that it is overused and distorted as a metaphor for all of reading.

In this book, I do not use the term information in its broad and imprecise sense at all. The term is used fairly extensively in the next few chapters, but only in the strictly technical sense, in discussions of how uncertainty related to visual "input" from the eyes is resolved. Despite the time I have spent discussing information, I do not regard it as the greatest or most important aspect of reading, especially for teachers to take into account.

What is experience? It cannot be measured and is not easily defined. Perhaps it does not need definition. Experience is synonymous with *being*, with creating, exploring, and interacting with worlds—real, possible, and invented. It is engagement and participation, always involving the emotions and often including a deliberate quest for uncertainty. It is an essential condition for being human and alive.

Reading is experience. Reading about a storm is not the same thing as being in a storm, but both are experiences. We respond emotionally to both, and can learn from both. But the learning in each case is a byproduct of the experience. We do not live to acquire information, but information, like knowledge, wisdom, abilities, attitudes, and satisfactions, comes with the experience of living.

ISSUES

The chapter has been almost entirely about one of the most crucial (though often unspoken) sources of contention in education, namely whether teaching and learning should focus on the acquisition of information or the quality of experience. Almost all systematic instruction in schools (including tertiary institutions) is based on information transmission, and almost all evaluation is based on information assimilation. Whether more specific emphasis should be placed on experience, both for teachers and for students, is an issue involving values, not research.

SUMMARY

There are two fundamental reasons for reading—for **information** or for experience. Although it has a clearly defined meaning in a narrow sense, the word information is widely overused and misused. Information may be regarded as the reduction of uncertainty concerning the alternatives among which a reader must decide. How much **visual information** a reader will require is affected by the reader's willingness to risk an erroneous decision. Readers who set too high a **criterion level** for information before making decisions will find **comprehension** more difficult. Because there are limits to how much information the brain can cope with in making sense of texts, readers must make use of all forms of **redundancy** in written language—**orthographic, syntactic,** and **semantic.** Because reading is more than a matter of making decisions, the relevance of the information-processing perspective is limited.

Notes to Chapter 3 begin on page 242, covering
Measuring information and uncertainty
Measuring redundancy
Signal detection theory
Further reading
Limitations of information theory, and of "information"
Cognitive science
Computers

4 Between Eye and Brain

The eyes are given altogether too much credit for seeing. Their role in reading is frequently overemphasized. The eyes do not see at all, in a strictly literal sense. The eyes *look*, they are devices for collecting information for the brain, largely under the direction of the brain, and it is the brain that determines what we see and how we see it. Our perceptual decisions are based only partly on information from the eyes, greatly augmented by knowledge we already possess.

The present chapter is not intended to be a comprehensive physiology of the visual system, but it does outline a few characteristics of eye–brain function that make critical differences to reading. To be specific, three particular features of the visual system are considered:

1. We do not see everything that is in front of our eyes.
2. We do not see anything that is in front of our eyes immediately.
3. We do not receive information from our eyes continuously.

Together these three considerations lead to three important implications for reading, and thus also for learning to read:

1. Reading must be fast.
2. Reading must be selective.
3. Reading depends on what the reader already knows.

The remainder of this chapter considers the preceding six points in order, after elaborating on the importance of what goes on behind the eyes in reading.

TWO SIDES OF READING

Obviously, reading is not an activity that can be conducted in the dark. To read you need illumination, some print in front of you, your eyes open, and possibly your spectacles on. In other words, reading depends on some information getting through the eyes to the brain. Let us call this information that the brain receives from print *visual information*. It is easy to characterize the general nature of visual information—it is what goes away when the lights go out.

Access to visual information is a necessary part of reading, but it is not sufficient. You could have a wealth of visual information in a text before your open eyes and still not be able to read. For example, the text might be written in a language you do not understand. Knowledge of the relevant language is essential for reading, but you cannot expect to find it on the printed page. Rather it is information that you must have already, behind the eyeballs. It can be distinguished from the visual information that comes through the eyes by being called *nonvisual information* or "prior knowledge."

There are other kinds of nonvisual information apart from knowledge of language. Knowledge of subject matter is similarly important. Give many people an article on subatomic physics, the differential calculus, or the maintenance of jet engines, and they will not be able to read—not because of some inadequacy of the text, which specialists can read perfectly well, nor because there is anything wrong with their eyes, but because they lack appropriate nonvisual information. Knowledge of how to read is another kind of nonvisual information and of evident importance in making reading possible, although it has nothing to do with the lighting, the print, or the state of one's eyes. Nonvisual information is easily distinguished from visual information—it is carried around by the reader all the time; it does not go away when the lights go out.

The Trade-off Between Visual and Nonvisual Information

The distinction between visual and nonvisual information may seem obvious; nevertheless, it is so critical in reading and learning to read that I put it into diagram form (Figure 4.1).

The reason that the distinction between visual and nonvisual information is so important is simply stated—there is a reciprocal relationship between the two. Within certain limits, one can be traded off for the other. The more nonvisual information a reader has, the less visual information the reader

FIG. 4.1. Two sources of information in reading.

needs. The less nonvisual information that is available from behind the eyes, the more visual information is required. This reciprocal relationship is represented by the curved line between the two kinds of information in Figure 4.1.

Reading always involves a combination of visual and nonvisual information. It is an interaction between a reader and a text.

Informal demonstrations of the trade-off between the two sources of information in reading are not difficult to give. They are provided by the common phenomenon that popular novels and newspaper articles tend to be easy to read—they can be read relatively quickly, in poor light, despite small type and poor quality printing. They are easy to read because of what we know already; we have a minimal need for visual information. On the other hand, technical materials or difficult novels—or even the same popular novels and newspaper articles when read by someone not so familiar with the language or the conventions of the text—require more time and more effort, larger type, clearer print, and superior physical conditions. The names of familiar towns on traffic signs can be read from further away than the same size place names of unfamiliar localities. It is easier to read letters on a wall when they are arranged into meaningful words and phrases than the same size letters in the random order of an optometrist's test chart. In each case the difference has nothing to do with the quality of the visual information available in the print but with the amount of nonvisual information that the reader can bring to bear. The less nonvisual information the reader can employ, the harder it is to read.

Making Reading Difficult

Now we can see one reason why reading can be so very much harder for children, quite independently of their actual reading ability. They may have little relevant nonvisual information. Some beginning reading materials seem to be expressly designed to prevent the use of prior knowledge. At other times adults may unwittingly or even deliberately discourage its use, by prohibiting "guessing." For whatever cause, insufficiency of nonvisual information makes reading more difficult.

Insufficiency of nonvisual information can even make reading impossible,

FIG. 4.2.   The bottleneck in reading.

for the simple but inescapable reason that there is a limit to how much visual information the brain can handle at any one time. There is a bottleneck in the visual system between the eye and brain, as indicated in Figure 4.2. Because of this bottleneck a reader can temporarily become functionally blind. It is possible to look but not be able to see, no matter how good the physical conditions. A line of print which is transparently obvious to a teacher (who knows what it says in the first place) may be almost completely illegible to a child whose dependence on visual information can limit perception to just two or three letters in the middle of the line.

Being unable to discern the words for the print is not a handicap that is restricted to children. Fluent readers may find themselves in exactly the same situation for essentially the same reasons—by being given difficult material to read, by being required to pay a lot of attention to every word, or by being put into a condition of anxiety, all of which increase the demand for visual information and have the paradoxical consequence of making it harder to see the text.

Later in this chapter, I show how the relative proportions of visual and nonvisual information required in reading can be estimated and also indicate how narrow the bottleneck is, so narrow that at least three-quarters of the visual information available in text must usually be ignored. As psychologist Paul Kolers (1967) writes, "Reading is only incidentally visual." Because nonvisual information lies at the core of reading, a large part of this book is concerned with its nature, development, and use.

LIMITATIONS OF VISION

We Do Not See Everything

The fact that the eyes are open is not an indication that visual information from the world around is being received and interpreted by the brain. We do not *see* the world as its image falls upon our eyes. How could we, when that image must often be a kaleidoscopic blur as the eyes flick from place to place in their fitful investigations of the world? But the argument is more complex than the relatively simple fact that the world we see is stable although the eyes are frequently in movement. The scene we perceive has very little in common with the information the eyes receive from the surrounding world.

What goes into the open eyes is a diffuse and continual bombardment of electromagnetic radiation, minute waves of light energy that vary only in frequency, amplitude, and spatial and temporal patterning. The rays of light that impinge on the eye do not in themselves carry the color and form and texture and movement that we see; all of these familiar and meaningful aspects of perception are created within the brain. The image that presents itself to the eyes is actually lost the moment it gets there. The light-sensitive area of the eyeball, the *retina*, consists of millions of cells that transform light energy into neural impulses by a marvelously intricate process involving the bleaching and regeneration of pigment in the retinal cells. As a result of this chemical transformation, bursts of neural energy begin a complicated and relatively long and slow journey along the optic nerve—actually a bundle of many individual nerve fibers—from the back of the eyeballs to the visual areas of the brain, some 6 inches away at the back of the head. The impulses[1] that pass from the eyes to the brain undergo a number of analyses and transformations on the way. The patterned array of light that falls on the eye and the structured percept that is produced by the brain are linked by a train of nervous impulses that itself has no simple correspondence with the occurrences at either extreme of the visual system.

Not one nerve fiber runs directly from the eye to the brain; instead there are at least six interchanges where impulses along one nerve may start—or inhibit—propagation of a further pattern of impulses along the next section of the pathway. At each of these neural relay stations there are large numbers of interconnections, some of which determine that a single impulse arriving along one section may set off a complex pattern of impulses in the next, while others may relay the message only if a particular combination of signals arrives. Each interconnection point is, in fact, a place where a complex analysis and transformation takes place.

Three layers of interconnections are located in the retina of the eyes, which is, in terms of both function and embryonic development, an extension of the

---

[1]It is difficult to avoid referring to these bursts of neural energy as "messages" or "information" that the eyes send to the brain about the world. But both terms are inappropriate, with their implication that some kind of meaningful content has been put into the messages in the first place, as if the eyes know something that they are trying to communicate to the brain. It might be more apt to refer to the neural impulses that travel between eye and brain as *clues* to a world forever concealed from direct inspection. No scientist or philosopher can say what the world is "really like," because everyone's perception of the world—even when mediated by microscopes or telescopes, by photographs or x-rays—still depends on the sense the brain can make of neural impulses that have come through the dark tunnel between eye and brain. We can no more see the image of the world that falls on the retina than we can see the nerve impulses that the retina sends to the brain. The only part of vision of which we can ever be aware is the final sensation of seeing, constructed within the brain.

brain. A tremendous compression takes place within the retina itself. When the nerve fibers eventually leave the eye on their journey to the brain (the pencil-thick bundle of nerve fibers is collectively called the *optic nerve*) the impulses from about 120 million light-sensitive cells in the retina where the neural messages originate have been thinned out over a hundredfold; the optic nerve consists of barely a million neural pathways.

An interesting facet of this part of the visual system is that the retina of the eye would appear to have been constructed "the wrong way round"— probably a consequence of constructing the retina from an extension of the similarly multilayered brain surface during prenatal development, beginning as early as three weeks after conception. All of the eye's three layers of nerve cells and their interconnections, together with the vessels that provide the retina with its rich blood supply, lie *between* the light-sensitive surface of the eye and the lens. The light-sensitive cells face the world through their own cell bodies, through two other layers of nerve cells, millions upon millions of interconnecting neural networks, and the curtain of their own neural processes as they converge upon the one spot (the "blind spot") to pierce the shell of the eye at the beginning of the optic nerve.

The actual nature of the impulses that pass along this complex cable of nerves is also very different from our perception or belief of what the visual stimulus is like. Every nerve in our body is limited to conveying only one type of signal—either it fires, or it does not. The speed of the impulse may vary from nerve to nerve, but for any one nerve it is fixed; the response is "all or none." The nerve impulse is relatively slow: The fastest rate, for some of the long thick nerve fibers that travel several feet along the body, is perhaps 300 feet a second (about 200 miles an hour), but the smaller nerves, such as those in the visual system and brain, transmit at only a tenth of that speed (about 20 miles an hour, compared with the 186,000 miles a second at which light travels to the eye).

Many examples of the way in which the brain imposes stability upon the ever-changing perspective of the eyes are provided by what psychologists call the visual constancies. For example, we always see a known object as a constant size; we do not think that a person or automobile moving away from us gets smaller as the distance increases, although the actual size of the image on the retina is halved as the distance doubles. We do not think the world changes color just because the sun goes in, nor do we see a lawn as being different shades of green because parts of it are in the shade. The constancy of the visual impression belies variations in the optical information received by the eye. We "see" plates and coins as circular, although from the angle at which such objects are usually viewed the image hitting the eye is almost invariably ovoid. A cat that hides behind a chair is recognized as the same cat when it comes out again, although that information is certainly not present in the input to the eye. In fact, the distinctive forms of cats, chairs, and all other objects do not organize themselves neatly for the eye—we can distinguish them because we already know the forms we want to separate. Why else should we perceive Th as T and h and not as Π and ר or any other arrangement of parts?

One might think that at least the perception of movement is determined by whether or not the image that falls on the retina is moving, but that is not the case. If our eyes are stationary and a moving image falls across them, we do indeed normally see movement. But if a similar movement across the eyes occurs because we move our eyes voluntarily—when we look around a room, for example—we do not see the world moving. Our perception of whether or not something is moving depends as much on the knowledge we have about what our eye muscles are doing as on the visual information being received by the eye. We can easily fool our own brain by sending it false information. If we "voluntarily" move an eye up or down the page of a book by the use of our eye muscles, we do not see the book move, but if we move the eye in the same way by poking it with a finger—moving the eye without moving the eye muscles—then we do see the book in movement. The brain "thinks" that if the eye muscles have not been actively involved, then the changing image on the eye must mean external movement, and constructs our perception accordingly.

Tachistoscopes and Tunnel Vision

The preceding discussion was not intended merely to acquaint you with some of the intricacies of the visual system. The aim was to illustrate that what we think we see at any one time may be very different from what we are actually detecting visually from the world around us. It is important to know that seeing is not a simple matter of an inner eye in the brain examining snapshots or video images of complete scenes from the outside world. The brain may generate a feeling that we are able to see most of what is in front of our eyes most of the time, but that is what it is—a feeling, generated by the brain. Upon analysis we may find that in fact we see very little. The eyes are not windows, and the brain does not look through them. Not only what we see, but our conviction of seeing, is a fabrication of the brain.

For a particular example, take the case of reading. When we look at a page of print we may feel that we see entire lines at a time. In practice, we probably see very much less. And in extreme circumstances we may be almost blind. Paradoxically, the harder we try to look, the less we may actually see. To understand the research that underlies these assertions, it is necessary to acquire some familiarity with a venerable piece of psychological instrumentation and with a rather precise way of talking about very small units of time. The small unit of time is the *millisecond*, usually abbreviated to *msec*. One millisecond is a thousandth part of a second; 10 milliseconds is a hundredth of a second; 100 msec is a tenth; 250 msec, a quarter; 500 msec, a half a second; and so forth. Ten milliseconds is about the amount of time the shutter of a camera requires to be open in normal conditions to get a reasonable image on a film. It can also be sufficient time for information to be available to the eye for a single perceptual experience to result. Much more time is required for neural impulses to get from the eye to the brain or for the brain to make a perceptual decision.

The venerable piece of psychological equipment is the *tachistoscope*, a device that presents information to the eyes for very brief periods of time. In other words, a tachistoscope is a device for studying how much we can see at any one time. It does not allow the reader a second look.

In its simplest form, a tachistoscope is a slide projector that throws a picture upon a screen for a limited amount of time, usually only a fraction of a second. In experimental laboratories today, brief presentations are usually controlled with great precision by computers. One of the first discoveries made through the use of tachistoscopic devices during the 1890s was that the eye had to be exposed to visual information for very much less time than generally thought. If there is sufficient intensity, an exposure of 50 msec is more than adequate for all the information the brain can manage on any one occasion. This does not mean that 50 msec is adequate for identifying everything in a single glance; obviously it is not. You cannot inspect a page of a book for less than a second and expect to have seen every word. But 50 msec is a sufficient exposure for all the visual information that can be gained in a single fixation. It will make no difference if the source of the visual information is removed after 50 msec or left for 250 msec; nothing more will be seen. Eyes pick up usable information for only a fraction of the time that they are open.

The second significant finding from the tachistoscopic and other studies was that what could be perceived in a single brief presentation, in one glance, depended on what was presented and on the viewer's prior knowledge. If random letters of the alphabet were presented—a sequence like *KYBVOD*—then only four or five letters might be reported. But if words were presented for the same amount of time, two or three might be reported, comprising a total of perhaps 12 letters. And if the words happened to be organized into a short sentence, then four or five words, a total of perhaps 25 letters, might be perceived from the same exposure duration.

The preceding paragraph reports a most important finding and one that is central to an understanding of reading. To underline its importance, the main points are reiterated in the form of a diagram (Figure 4.3).

In the Notes section at the end of this book, it is shown that the eye and brain are *doing* the same amount of work in each of the three situations depicted in Figure 4.3. The eyes are sending the same amount of visual

K̸ B̸ O̸/D̸ J̸ W̸/G̸ (P J M S Q)̸T̸/X N̸ O̸/G̸ M̸/C̸ T̸/R S̸/O̸

Random letters: four or five

R̸EA̸D̸Y̸/(JUMP   WHEAT) P̸O̸O̸R̸ /B̸ U̸T̸

Unrelated words: about two (ten-twelve letters)

(KNIGHTS   RODE   HORSES   INTO   WAR)

A meaningful phrase: four or five words (about 25 letters)

FIG. 4.3.   What can be seen in one glance.

information to the brain and the brain is making sense of the same proportion of it. But the more sense the letters make—which means the more the brain is able to use nonvisual information—the more can be seen. The difference lies in the number of alternatives confronting the brain in making perceptual decisions. If the letters are random—or as good as random to the person trying to read them—they are basically unpredictable and demand a good deal of visual information for each identification decision. The reader consequently sees very little and is in a condition known as "tunnel vision" (Mackworth, 1965), very similar to trying to examine the world through a narrow paper tube. Everyone can have tunnel vision sometimes; it has nothing to do with the health or efficiency of the eyes. Tunnel vision is a result of trying to process too much visual information. Airline pilots can suffer from tunnel vision, especially when they have so much to attend to in trying to land a big jet. That is why it takes more than one pilot to fly such planes. All readers can be afflicted with tunnel vision when the material they are trying to read is unfamiliar, opaque, or otherwise difficult—or when through the particular demands of the task or sheer anxiety they try to handle too much visual information. Beginning readers are prime candidates for having tunnel vision much of the time, especially if the books they are supposed to read make little sense to them. Tunnel vision, in other words, is caused by information overload.

On the other hand, if the text is easily comprehended, entire lines can be seen at a time. So for a teacher who points to some words in a book and says to a child, "There, you can see that clearly enough, can't you?" the answer is probably "No." The teacher who can see the entire line probably knows what the words are in the first place. The fact that the teacher is pointing can make the situation even worse and ensure that the child sees nothing very much beyond the tip of a finger.

You cannot read if you see only a few letters at a time. Tunnel vision makes reading impossible. And the situation cannot be retrieved by trying to look at the words more often. Seeing takes time, and there is a limit to the rate at which the brain can makes its visual decisions.

Seeing Takes Time

We usually feel that we see what we are looking at immediately. But this is another illusion generated by the brain. It takes time to see anything because the brain requires time to make perceptual decisions. And the time that is required is again directly related to the number of alternatives confronting us. The more alternatives we have to consider and discard, the longer it takes the brain to make up its mind, so to speak, and for seeing to occur.

The situation is analogous to how quickly you can identify your own car in a parking lot. No matter how well you know your vehicle and no matter how close you are standing to it, the time it will take you to realize "That's mine" will vary with the number of other cars in the park. Only two cars in the park, and you will spot yours in a fraction of a second. Ten cars, and it will take considerably longer. A hundred cars, and you can be quite delayed.

For an experimental demonstration that the number of alternatives determines the speed of perception, the tachistoscope can again be used. If a single letter of the alphabet is briefly but clearly displayed, say A, the delay before the viewer succeeds in saying "A" will depend on the number of letters that could have occurred instead of A. Give the viewer no clue, so that the letter might be any one of 26 alternatives, and the delay—the "reaction time"—can be as long as 500 msec, half a second. Say in advance that the letter occurs in the first part of the alphabet or that it is a vowel, and the reaction time will be much briefer. Tell the viewer that the letter is either A or B, and reaction time may drop to as little as 200 msec. With fewer alternatives the brain of the viewer has much less work to do, and the decision comes very much faster.

In reading, it is imperative that the brain should make use of anything relevant that we already know—of nonvisual information—in order to reduce the number of alternatives. The rather slow rate at which the brain can make decisions can be extremely disruptive. If the brain has to spend too long deciding among the alternatives, the visual information that the eye makes available to the brain will be gone. That is the explanation of tunnel vision— the brain loses access to visual information before it has had time to make many decisions about it.

Visual information does not stay available to the brain for very long after being picked up by the eye. Obviously, visual information remains somewhere in the head for a short period of time, while the brain works on the information collected by the eye in the first few milliseconds of each look. Psychologists have even coined a name for the place where this information is supposed to reside between the time it has been sent back from the eye and the time the brain has made its decisions. This place is known as the *sensory store*, although it so far has remained a purely theoretical construct without any actual known location in the brain. But wherever and whatever the sensory store might be, it does not last very long. Estimates of its persistence vary from half a second to—under optimum conditions—two seconds. But it is just as well that sensory store does persist briefly because a full second is required for the brain to decide even about the limited amount that it is usually able to perceive in a single glance. The visual information that can be utilized in a single glance or tachistoscopic exposure—resulting in the identification of four or five random letters, a couple of unrelated words, or a meaningful sequence of four or five words—in fact requires a full second. The caption to Figure 4.3 could be amended to read not just "What can be seen in one glance" but also "What can be seen in one second." The basic physiological limitation on the rate at which the brain can decide among alternatives seems to put the limit on the speed at which most people can read meaningful text aloud, which is usually not much more than 250 words a minute (about 4 words a second). People who read very much faster than that rate are generally not reading aloud and not delaying to identify every word.

Information is not usually allowed to stay in sensory store for its full term of a second or so. Every time the eyes send another portion of visual information to the brain—which means every time we shift our gaze to a new focal point or at least blink to take a second look at the same place—then the arrival of new visual information erases the previous contents of sensory store. This phenomenon is referred to as *masking*. It is by the controlled use of masking in tachistoscopic experiments that psychologists have determined that the brain does indeed require a substantial amount of time to make perceptual decisions. The experiments illustrating how much can be seen in a single glance only work if a second exposure to visual information does not follow the first before the brain has had time to make sense of it. If a second exposure is presented less than half a second after the first, the viewer is unlikely to report the full four or five random letters or words that would otherwise be perceived. If the two events occur too close together—say within 50 msec of each other—then the second can completely obliterate the first. Because masking occurs before the brain has time even to decide that something has taken place, the viewer will be completely unaware of a visual event that would otherwise be seen quite clearly. Seeing is a relatively slow process.

On the other hand, because information in sensory store will not persist more than about a second under most conditions, we cannot see more simply by looking longer at one spot. The eyes must be constantly active to replenish the fading stock of visual information in sensory store. A person who stares is not seeing more, but rather is having difficulty deciding what was looked at in the first place. Because the contents of sensory store decay rapidly and cannot be replenished from an eye that remains fixed in the same position, the eyes of anyone alert to the visual environment tend to be constantly on the move, even though the brain attends to only the first few moments of every new look. Visual information is constantly subject to interruption.

Seeing Is Episodic

Our eyes are continually in movement—with our knowledge and without it. If we pause to think about it, we know that our eyes are scanning a page of text, or glancing around a room, or following a moving object. These are the eye movements we observe if we watch another person's face. These movements are rarely random—we would be quickly alarmed if our own eyes or someone else's began rolling around uncontrollably—but instead the eyes move systematically to where there is the most information or interest for us. The movements of the eye are controlled by the brain, and by examining how the brain directs the eye, we can get a basis for understanding what the brain is looking for, in general terms at least.

But first, we shall consider quite a different kind of eye movement, one not apparently under the direct control of the brain nor one that is noticeable either in ourselves or others, but that nonetheless can help to underline a point about the constructive nature of vision. Regardless of whether we are glancing around the environment, following a moving object, or maintaining a single fixation, the eyeball is in a constant state of very fast movement. This movement, or *tremor*, occurs at the rate of 50 oscillations a second. We do not notice the tremor in other people, partly because it is so fast, but also because the movement covers only a very short distance; it is more a vibration about a central position than a movement from one place to another. But although the movement is normally unnoticeable, it does have a significant role in the visual process; the tremor ensures that more than one group of retinal cells is involved in even a single glance. The tremor provides another illustration of the now familiar point that if the perceptual experience were a simple reproduction of whatever fell upon the retina, then all we should ever see would be a giddy blur.

The constant tremor of the eye is essential for vision—cancel it and our perception of the world disappears almost immediately. The cancellation has been accomplished by an ingenious experimental procedure called "stabilizing the image" on the retina (Heckenmueller, 1965; Pritchard, 1961). To stabilize the image, the information coming to the eye is made to oscillate at the same rate and over the same distance as the movement of the eye itself. The scene can be reflected through a small mirror mounted directly on the eyeball so that the image always falls on the same position on the retina, no matter what the eye is doing. The consequence of stabilizing the image on the retina is not that the viewer suddenly perceives a super-sharp picture of the world; on the contrary, perception disappears.

The image does not seem to disappear instantaneously, nor does it fade slowly like a movie scene. Instead, entire parts drop away in a very systematic fashion. If the outline of a face has been presented, meaningful parts will vanish, one by one, first perhaps the hair, then an ear, then perhaps the eyes, the nose, until the only thing remaining may be, like the Cheshire cat, the smile. Geometrical figures break up in a similarly orderly way, losing extremities first, or one side after another. The word *BEAT* might disintegrate by the loss of its initial letter, leaving *EAT*, and then by dissolution to *AT* and *A*. By itself, the letter *B* might lose one loop to become *P* and then another to leave *I*. The phenomenon should not be interpreted to mean that the cells of the retina themselves respond to—and then lose—whole words and letters or forms; rather, it shows that the brain holds on to a disappearing image in the most meaningful way possible. Presumably the overworked retinal cells, deprived of the momentary respite the tremor can give them, become fatigued and send less and less information back to the brain, while the brain continues to construct as much of a percept as it can from the diminishing material that it receives.

Other kinds of eye movement need not detain us. There is a kind of slow drift, a tendency of the eye to wander from the point of focus, which is probably not very important because the eye has picked up all the useful information it is going to get during the first few milliseconds. There are "pursuit" movements that the eye makes when it follows a moving object. The only time that the eye can move smoothly and continuously from one position to another is in the course of a pursuit movement. Looking a person up and down with a single sweep of the eyes occurs only in fiction.

The eye movement that is really of concern in reading is, in fact, a rapid, irregular, spasmodic, but surprisingly accurate jump from one position to another. It is perhaps a little inappropriate to call such an important movement a jump, so it is dignified by the far more elegant-sounding French word *saccade* (which literally translated into English, however, means "jerk").

Fixations and Regressions

A saccade is by no means a special characteristic of reading, but rather the way we normally sample our visual environment for information about the world. We are very skilled in making saccadic movements of the eye. Guided by information received in its periphery, the eye can move very rapidly and accurately from one side of the visual field to the other, from left to right, up and down, even though we may be unaware of the point or object upon which we will focus before the movement begins. Every time the eye pauses in this erratic progression, a *fixation* is said to occur.

For reading English text, fixations are generally regarded as proceeding from left to right across the page, although, of course, our eye movements must also take us from the top of the page toward the bottom and from right to left as we proceed from one line to the next. Really skilled readers often do not read "from left to right" at all—they may not make more than one fixation a line and may skip lines in reading down the page. We shall consider in a later chapter how such a method of reading can be possible. All readers, good and poor, make another kind of movement that is just another saccade but has got itself something of a bad name—a *regression*. A regression is simply a saccade that goes in the opposite direction from the line of type—from right to left along a line or from one line to an earlier one. All readers produce regressions—and for skilled readers a regression may be just as productive an eye movement as a saccade in a forward, or progressive, direction.

During the saccade, while the eye is moving from one position to another, very little is seen at all. The leaping eye is functionally blind. Information is picked up between saccades when the eye is relatively still—during fixations. The qualification "relatively" still has to be made because the eye is never absolutely stationary—there are always tremors and drifts. But neither of these types of movement seems to interrupt the important business of picking up information. The sole purpose of a saccade, in whatever direction, is to move the eye from one position to another to pick up more information. It seems possible to pick up information only once during a fixation—for the few hundredths of a second at the beginning, when information is being loaded into the sensory store. After that time, the backroom parts of the visual system are busy, perhaps for the next quarter of a second, trying to make sense of the information.

Saccades are fast as well as precise. The larger saccades are faster than the small ones, but it still takes more time to move the eye a long distance than a short one. The movement of the eyes through 100 degrees, say from the extreme left to the extreme right of the visual field, takes about 100 msec— a 10th of a second. A movement of only a 20th of that distance—about two or three words at a normal reading distance—might take 50 msec.[2] But the fact that a saccade can be made in 50 msec does not mean that we can take in new information by moving the eye 20 times a second. The limit on the rate at which we can usefully move from one fixation to another is set by the time

---

[2]There are some interesting analogies to be drawn between eye movements and hand movements. The top speed of movement for eye and hand are roughly similar, and like the eye, the hand moves faster when it moves over a greater distance. The hand performs the same kind of activity as the eye. It moves precisely and selectively to the most useful position, and it starts "picking up" only when it has arrived. But although the hands and eyes of children may move almost as fast and accurately as those of adults, they cannot always be used so efficiently. Children lack the experience of the adult and may not know so precisely what they are reaching for.

required by the brain to make sense of every new input. That is why there can be little "improvement" in the rate at which fixations are made during reading. You cannot accelerate reading by hurrying the eyes along faster.

The number of fixations varies both with the skill of the reader and the difficulty of the passage being read, but not to any remarkable extent. In fact, fixation rate settles down by about Grade 4. There is a slight tendency for skilled readers to change fixations faster than unskilled readers, but the difference is only about one extra fixation a second; adults may average four and children just starting to read change fixation about three times a second. For any reader, skilled or unskilled, reading a difficult passage may cut about one fixation a second off the fastest reading rate.

There is also not a dramatic difference between children and adults in the matter of regressions. Children tend to make more regressions than fluent readers, but not so many more, perhaps one for every four progressive fixations compared with one in six for adults. Once again, the rate of occurrence is determined as much by the difficulty of the passage as by the skill of the reader. Faced with a moderately difficult passage, skilled readers will produce as many regressions as beginning readers with a passage that they find relatively easy. Readers who do not make any regressions may be reading too slowly, too cautiously. When children make a lot of regressions, it is a signal that they are having difficulty, not a cause of difficulty. The number of regressions that readers make is an indication of the complexity to them of the passage they are trying to read.

In short, the duration of fixations and the number of regressions are not reliable guides for distinguishing between good and poor readers. What does distinguish the fluent from the less-skilled reader is the number of letters or words—or the amount of meaning—that can be identified in a single fixation. As a result, a more meaningful way to evaluate the eye movements of a poor reader and a skilled one is to count the number of fixations required to read a hundred words. Skilled readers need far fewer than the beginners because they are able to pick up more information on every fixation. A skilled reader at the "college graduate" level might pick up enough information to identify words at an average rate of over one a fixation (including regressions) or about 90 fixations per 100 words. The beginner might have to look twice for every word, or 200 fixations per 100 words. The beginner tends to have tunnel vision.

IMPLICATIONS FOR READING

I said at the beginning of this chapter that discussion of the visual system would lead to three important implications for reading and for learning to read—that reading must be fast, that it must be selective, and that it depends upon nonvisual information. By now the basic arguments underlying these implications may have become self-evident, but for emphasis they should be elaborated upon briefly.

Reading Must Be Fast

What is meant, of course, is that the brain must always move ahead quickly, to avoid becoming bogged down in the visual detail of the text to the extent that tunnel vision might result. This is not to suggest that the eyes should be speeded up. As I said earlier, reading cannot be improved by accelerating the eyeballs. There is a limit to the rate at which the brain can make sense of visual information from the eyes, and simply increasing the rate at which fixations are made would have the consequence of further overwhelming the brain rather than facilitating its decisions.

In fact, the customary reading rate of three or four fixations a second would appear to be an optimum. At a slower rate the contents of sensory store may begin to fade and the reader might be in the position of staring at nothing. At a faster rate than four fixations a second, masking can intrude so that the reader loses information before it is properly analyzed.

The "slow reading" that must be avoided is the overattention to detail that keeps the reader on the brink of tunnel vision. Trying to read text a few letters or even a whole word at a time keeps a reader functioning at the level of nonsense and precludes any hope of comprehension. The aim should be to read as much text as possible with every fixation to maintain meaningfulness. Classroom advice to slow down in case of difficulty, to be careful and examine every word closely, can easily lead to complete bewilderment.

There is no one best reading rate; that depends on the difficulty of the passage and the purpose of the reader—on whether the reader is trying to identify every word, for example, in order to read aloud, or whether the reading is "for meaning" only. The rate must be different if extensive memorization is being attempted, because rote learning cannot be accomplished quickly. Word-perfect reading aloud and extensive deliberate memorization often require that a passage should be read more than once. A reader is unlikely to comprehend while reading *slower* than 200 words a minute, because a lesser rate would imply that words were being read as isolated units rather than as meaningful sentences. As we shall see in the next chapter, limitations of memory prevent sense being built up from isolated words.

Thus, comprehension demands relatively fast reading but memorization slows the reader down. As a consequence, comprehension may be impaired and memorization become pointless in any case. If we already have a good idea of what is on the page, then slower reading is more tolerable and more time can be spared for memorization. But heavy memory burdens should be avoided when one is learning to read or unfamiliar with the language or subject matter.

Reading Must Be Selective

The brain just does not have the time to attend to all the visual information available in most texts and can be easily inundated. Nor is memory able to cope with all the information that might be available from the page. The secret of reading efficiently is not to read indiscriminately but to *sample* the text. The brain must be parsimonious, making maximum use of what is already known and analyzing the minimum of visual information required to verify or modify what can be predicted about the text. All this may sound very complicated, but in fact it is something that every experienced reader can do automatically, and almost certainly what you are doing now if you can make sense of what you read. It is no different from what you do when you look around a room or at a picture.

But like many other aspects of fluent reading, selectivity in picking up and analyzing samples of the available visual information in text comes with experience. Once again the initiative for how the eyes function rests with the brain. When the brain has got all the visual information it requires from a fixation, it directs the eyes very precisely where to move next. The saccade will be either a progressive or regressive movement, depending on whether the next information that the brain requires is further ahead or further back in the page. The brain is able to direct the eyes appropriately, in reading as in other aspects of vision, provided it "understands" what it needs to find out. The brain must always be in charge. Trying to control eye movements in reading can be like trying to steer a horse by the tail. If the eyes do not go to an appropriate place in reading, it is probably because the brain does not know where to put them, not because the reader has insufficient visual ability to switch gaze to the right place at the right time.

Reading Depends on Nonvisual Information

Everything I have said so far should underline this final point. The brain—with its purposes, expectations, and prior knowledge—has to be in control of the eyes in reading. To assert that reading should be fast does not mean recklessly so. A reader must be able to use nonvisual information to avoid being swamped by visual information from the eyes. To say that a reader should only sample the visual information does not imply that the eyes could go randomly from one part of the page to another. Rather, the reader should attend to just those parts of the text that contain the most important information for the reader's purpose, whether every word, selected words, or selected portions of words. And this again is a matter of making maximum use of what is already known.

To recapitulate, nonvisual information is knowledge we already possess that is relevant to the language and to the subject matter of what we happen to be reading, together with some additional knowledge of specific aspects of written language such as the way spelling patterns are organized. Nonvisual information is anything that can reduce the number of alternatives the brain must consider as we read. If we know that one noun is unlikely to follow another without at least a punctuation mark, then our alternatives are reduced. If we know that only a restricted range of technical terms is likely to crop up in a particular context, then again our uncertainty is reduced. Even the knowledge that certain sequences of letters are unlikely to occur in English words—for example that initial H will not be followed by another consonant—will enable a reader to eliminate many alternatives and see much more at any one time. But meaning is the most important nonvisual information of all.

The skilled reader employs no more visual information to comprehend four words in a single glance than the beginning reader who requires two fixations to identify a single word. All the additional information that skilled readers require is contributed by what they know already. When fluent readers encounter a passage that is difficult to read—because it is poorly written or crammed with new information—the number of fixations (including regressions) they make increases, and reading speed goes down. Because of the additional uncertainty in the situation, they are forced to use more visual information to try to comprehend what they read.

The relative ability to use prior knowledge has consequences in all aspects of vision. Experts—whether in reading, art, sports, or engineering—may be able to comprehend an entire situation at a single glance but the greater uncertainty of novices handicaps them with tunnel vision. When readers in a tachistoscopic experiment are presented with words in a language they do not comprehend, they are able to identify only a few letters. The fact that the words make sense to someone who knows the language is irrelevant; to the uninformed reader the letters are essentially random, and inability to see very much will result.[3] The implication for anyone involved in teaching reading should be obvious. Whenever readers cannot make sense of what they are expected to read—because the material bears no relevance to any prior

---

[3]There are similar limitations on the amount of incoming information that can be handled by all sensory systems. For example, it is possible to have a distinct hearing loss when trying to understand speech for which there is a lack of "nonacoustic information"—which to all intents and purposes is the same as nonvisual information in reading. Thus we raise our voices when attempting to converse in an unfamiliar language—and children may often be deaf in the classroom although they appear to have no hearing problems outside.

knowledge they might have—then reading will become more difficult and learning to read impossible.

ON SEEING BACKWARD

One thing the eyes and the brain cannot do is see backward. I mention this fact, which perhaps ought to be self-evident, because a belief does exist that a visual abnormality of this kind causes some children problems in learning to read. The basis of the myth is the indisputable evidence that many children at some point in their reading careers confuse reversible letters like *b* and *d*, *p* and *q*, and even words like *was* and *saw* or *much* and *chum*. But seeing backward is both a physical and a logical impossibility, and a much simpler explanation is available.

It is physically impossible to see *part* of the visual field in a different orientation from the rest—to see two dogs facing one way and one the other when they are all looking in the same direction. And it is logically impossible to see *everything* reversed because everything would still be seen in the same relationship to everything else and therefore nothing would be different; everything would still be seen the right way round. Of course, it is possible to make a mistake, to think a dog is facing east when it is facing west, especially if we are not familiar with the kind of dog, but that must be attributed to lack of adequate information or knowledge, not to a visual defect.

And indeed, the simple explanation of why so many children confuse *b* and *d* is lack of appropriate experience. The discrimination is not an easy one and can confuse adults whose information is limited, just as fluent readers of English become confused with the identification of similar letters in unfamiliar alphabets. The difference between *b* and *d* is minimal—a matter of whether the upright stroke is on the left or the right of the circle—and is not a difference that is significant or even relevant in most aspects of children's experience. A dog is a dog whichever way it faces. Those more general discriminations that do require distinctions of actual or relative direction, such as "left" and "right" or telling the time from the hands of a clock, are notoriously difficult for most children to learn.

Fluent readers do not usually mistake *b* and *d* when they read, but that is primarily because they have so many other clues and need not be concerned with individual letters. But to distinguish *b* from *d* when they occur in isolation, one at a time, is much harder, and the fact that we can normally do so with facility must be attributed to the years of experience we have had and the amount of time we are given, relatively speaking, to inspect the evidence. Being able to distinguish *b* from *d* does not make a reader, but being a reader makes the discrimination easier.

Because the difference between *b* and *d* is both unusual and difficult to perceive, it is relatively difficult for children to learn, especially if they do not understand the significance of the difference in the first place. That is why the appropriate experience for such children is not more drills on isolated letters, which are meaningless, but more meaningful reading. Children who have difficulty, perhaps confusing words like *big* and *dig*, must be reading words or sentences which are essentially meaningless (or as if they are meaningless). No one who is reading for sense could confuse words like *big* and *dig*, or *was* and *saw*, in a meaningful context. Unfortunately children with a "reversals problem" are often given concentrated exercises on distinguishing word pairs like *big* and *dig* in isolation, increasing their apprehension and bewilderment. And if they show no progress with words in isolation they may be restricted to drills with *b* and *d* alone. But letters in isolation are considerably more difficult than letters in words because an important relational clue has been removed. The difference between *b* and *d* at the beginning of a word is that the upright stroke is on the outside for *b* (as in *big*) but on the inside for *d* (as in *dig*). But "outside" and "inside" are meaningless for letters in isolation. There is only one possible way of making learning to distinguish *b* from *d* even more difficult, and that is to show them one at a time. This removes every relational clue, and puts the learner in the situation most likely to confound even experienced readers.

It is sometimes argued that children see letters backward because they *write* them that way. But writing requires quite different kinds of skill. We all recognize faces and figures that we could not possibly draw. If my drawing of a face looks like a potato, that does not mean that I see a face as a potato, it means that I am a poor artist. A child may draw a human figure as a circular head with matchstick arms and legs, but show them their own distorted efforts and an artist's representation, and they will readily show you which looks most like what they see. Children do not and cannot draw what they see, and the fact that they might write a few or many letters backward says nothing about their vision, simply that they have not yet learned the difficult task of writing letters conventionally.

A LITTLE MORE PHYSIOLOGY

Anatomically, the brain is not all of a piece. In particular it is deeply split along a center line from the back of the head to behind the nose into two roughly symmetrical hemispheres, the left and the right. These two hemispheres are relatively tenuously connected to each other, at least near the surface areas of the brain, the areas which seem to be particularly involved with the organization of cognitive and motor functions most open to conscious control. An old psychological and physiological puzzle, still not resolved, is how we piece together a coherent visual image of the scene in front of our eyes when the left half of the visual field (from both eyes) goes to one hemisphere and the right half goes to the other and there are no direct hemispheric connections between the two. Physiologically the picture is split down the middle, but subjectively the seams do not show.

It has long been known that the left hemisphere of the brain is usually largely responsible for motor and sensory control of the right side of the body and the right hemisphere for the left. Because of this general *cross-laterality*, people who suffer strokes or other forms of injury to the left side of their brain tend to lose motor control and possibly sensation in areas on the right side of their body, and damage to the right side of the brain affects the left side of the body. And it has also been known for over a century that for the majority of people, especially the right handed, areas of the left side of the brain tend to be particularly involved with language. For such people, strokes or other injuries to the right side of the brain may leave language abilities largely unimpaired, and accidents to the left side of the brain are more likely to be associated with language loss. However, this hemispheric specialization is by no means universal or necessary. About ten percent of the population has the right hemisphere primarily involved with language functions, and children who are born with or who early in life suffer damage to the left side of the brain can develop language relatively fluently with the right, although it becomes much harder to transfer language or to relearn it with the opposite hemisphere as they get older.

Many ingenious studies have been made of the general modes of functioning of the two sides of the brain, particularly with the living brains of people unfortunate enough to have had the surface connections between their two hemispheres severed by accident or unavoidable surgery. Such studies have shown that the two sides of the brain have quite different styles of operation. The left hemisphere (in most people) seems to be particularly involved in activities which are analytic and sequential (like language), for intellectual calculations and planning. In such people, the right hemisphere's characteristic responsibilities and mode of operation are more holistic and spatial; it is concerned with global, subjective, and emotional matters. The left side may be busier when we write a letter or plan an excursion, the right side when we listen to music or imagine a scene.

All this is fascinating and indeed an important step forward toward understanding the mechanisms of the brain. However, it can also be misleading and conducive to spurious and even damaging conclusions if interpreted too literally. For the great majority of people the brain functions as a whole. We draw upon the resources of both hemispheres to produce and understand language, just as we use all of our brain in the rest of our experience. It is a mistake to regard the two hemispheres as separate entities which function independently and even in opposition. Unfortunately, some educators and psychologists who know little about physiology (and some physiologists and neuroanatomists who know little about language and learning) talk as if we have two brains rather than two sides of a single brain. The hemispheres are sometimes referred to as the left and right brains, although this is literally (and only approximately) true for just a handful of people whose brains have been surgically or accidentally sectioned.

One danger of such reasoning is that it confuses a structural arrangement relevant only to the internal working of the brain with the way in which a person functions as a whole. There are no people who think only with the left or the right side of their brains, even if personalities and behavior reflect proclivities for more analytic or reflective approaches to life and learning. It is appropriate to say that a particular kind of activity or preference is dominant in a person but not that the hemisphere is dominant. It makes sense to say a person has a good spatial orientation and tends to the contemplative; this gives a way of understanding the person and perhaps adapting to idiosyncratic learning preferences. It adds nothing to say that the person is right-brain dominated, and may indeed reduce understanding by switching attention from perceptible characteristics to an assumed and probably mythical cause.

Anyone capable of learning to produce and understand the language of a familiar environment has the ability to use both sides of the brain and to do all those things the two hemispheres are supposed to specialize in. No child comes to school with only half a brain, and hemispheric specialization or "asymmetry" should not be proposed as an explanation of difficulty in learning to read, especially when there are, as we shall see, so many alternative possibilities. In particular it is wrong to work backward and to assume that because a child is slow or reluctant in learning to read there must be an imbalance or inadequacy of hemispheric function. There is no reading center in the brain. Many areas of the brain are active when we read, but none is involved in reading to the exclusion of anything else. Illness, injury, or very occasionally an inherent defect may affect the working of the brain so that ability to read is disturbed, but always some more general activity involving either language or vision will also be impaired. There is nothing physiologically or intellectually unique about reading. Reading does not make language demands on the brain that are not involved in the understanding of speech nor does reading make visual demands that the brain does not meet when we look around a room to locate an object or to distinguish faces. Advances in mapping the architecture of the brain help us mostly to understand the brain (or to further respect its complexity), not to understand language or learning.

It is important to know the possibilities and limitations of the brain, which is the reason we have already been so concerned with the mechanisms of perception and memory, but the actual manner in which the brain internally organizes its own affairs does not yet have a great relevance to education. At least, that is my view. I do not believe it would or should make the slightest difference to how reading is taught if it were discovered tomorrow that we all have a critical neural center for reading in the foot (the left foot, for most people). Instruction should always be adapted to the circumstances in which an individual learns and understands best, but this is not promoted by speculation about the brain structures of the learner.

All this is stressed because there continues to be in education what I and some other researchers believe is a readiness little short of tragic to attribute learning and teaching failures to pseudomedical or scientific causes. Failures are blamed on perceptual or cognitive handicaps with evidence no more specific than the fact that the failure occurs and a convenient medical or scientific theory happens to be around. If a plausible explanation cannot be found in terms of visual, acoustic, memory, or intellectual inadequacy, then an even vaguer "minimal learning disability" may be blamed. And the current excuse, the most popular explanation, always seems to follow the area of scientific advance which is generating the most interest and receiving the most popular attention. Failure to learn is explained in terms of fad rather than fact. The specialized insights of students of the brain are important in many respects, but they do not yet explain reading or reading problems. The relating of subtle differences in learning, behavior, attitude, and personality to presumed differences in the architecture of the brain should not become a new phrenology, as unscientific as making judgments about people's character from the bumps on their skulls.

ISSUES

The mountain of experimental data on eye movements grows with every new technological development. Basic "facts" about how the eyes move are rarely in dispute, but their interpretations are, especially when researchers feel themselves compelled to pronounce upon "the nature of reading" and "instructional implications." At issue are such matters as whether the tendency of readers (in experimental situations) to direct fixations to every word in front of their eyes means that they are actually "reading" every word, identifying one word (or letter) at a time and comprehending one word at a time, or reading the way they normally would when they, not the experimenters, control the purpose, selectivity, anticipation, and comprehension of the reading.

SUMMARY

Reading is not just a visual activity. Both **visual information** and **nonvisual information** are essential for reading, and there can be a trade-off between the two. Reading is not instantaneous; the brain cannot immediately make sense of the visual information in a page of print. The eyes move in **saccades,** pausing at **fixations** to select visual information, usually progressing in a forward direction but, when needed, in **regressions.** Slow reading interferes with comprehension. Reading is accelerated not by increasing the fixation rate but by reducing dependency on visual information, mainly through making use of meaning.

Notes to Chapter 4 begin on page 251, covering
Vision and information
Information theory and reading
The rate of visual decision-making
Eye movement in reading
On seeing backward
Hemispheric specialization

5 Bottlenecks of Memory

In Chapter 1, I talked about the diverse and massive amounts of knowledge that together comprise every individual's theory of the world. But I did not discuss how we manage to deposit and maintain all of this knowledge in the vaults of memory nor how we draw on it when we need to.

Two chapters at the end of this book are concerned with the general topic of *learning*—with the *circumstances* in which our theory of the world develops and grows. But there are some specific issues related to *how much* can get into memory at any one time that are more appropriately considered at this point. These issues are related to the bottlenecks in *perception* which I discussed in the previous chapter—for example the fact that beginning readers (or any reader confronted by an unfamiliar text) can see only a small amount at any one time, even as little as four or five letters. Now I must turn to some additional constraints that confront all readers, but especially those in difficulty. These are constraints on how quickly specific things can be taken into or out of memory.

Why should tunnel vision, the temporary inability to see what is contained in more than a small area in front of the eyes, be such a crippling handicap for readers, whatever their experience and ability? If a beginning reader can see only a few letters at a time—say the first half of a word such as *ELEP*. . .—why cannot these letters be remembered for the fraction of a second that the child requires to make a new fixation and see the rest of the word . . . *HANT*? But unfortunately, memory has its own limitations and cannot be called upon to exceed its capacity when the visual system is overworked. Fluent reading demands not only parsimony in the use of visual information but also restraint in the burdens placed on memory. In both cases there are limits on how much the brain can handle. Overloading memory does not make reading easier and can contribute to making reading impossible.

There are a number of paradoxes about the role of memory in reading. The more we try to memorize, the less we are likely to recall. The more we try to memorize, the less we are likely to comprehend, which not only makes recall more difficult—it makes recall pointless. Who wants to remember nonsense? On the other hand, the more we comprehend, the more memory will take care of itself.

An implication of these paradoxes is that the prior knowledge already in memory is far more important in reading than efforts to memorize everything in a text. To repeat a theme which by now should be familiar, the use of nonvisual information is critical.

THREE ASPECTS OF MEMORY

To begin, terms need to be clarified a little. We can use the word *memory* in a variety of ways, sometimes to refer to how well we can put something away for future use, sometimes to how long we can retain it, and sometimes to how well we can get to it. In this chapter, we consider four specific aspects or operating characteristics of memory: *input* (or how material goes in), *capacity* (how much can be held), *persistence* (how long it can be held), and *retrieval* (getting it out again). We also consider what would appear to be several kinds of memory, because memory does not always look like the same process when examined in different ways. Psychologists in fact often distinguish three kinds or aspects of memory, depending on the time that elapses between the original presentation of something to be remembered and the test to see what can be retrieved. The first aspect, termed *sensory store*, is related to information from its arrival at a receptor organ, such as the eye, until a perceptual decision is made, for example, the identification of several letters or words. The second aspect, usually called *short-term memory*, involves the brief time we can maintain attention to something immediately after its identification, for example, remembering an unfamiliar telephone number as we dial it. Finally, there is *long-term memory*, which is everything we know about the world, our total amount of nonvisual information.

These three aspects of memory are often depicted in textbook "flow diagrams" as if they are separate parts of the brain or successive stages in the process of memorization, as indicated in Figure 5.1. But such a diagram should not be taken too literally. I am not sure that it is most appropriate to refer to different "kinds" of memory, so I use the more neutral term *aspects*.

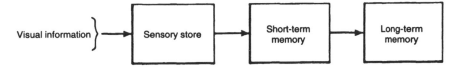

FIG. 5.1.   A typical flow diagram for memory.

There is no evidence that different memories exist in different places in the brain, nor that one memory starts functioning when the other leaves off, as the diagram might suggest. It is definitely misleading to imply that there is movement in just one direction from short-term to long-term memory, and to ignore the fact that there is always *selectivity* about how much is remembered and the manner in which remembering takes place.

However, a discussion must begin somewhere and proceed in some kind of sequence, so for convenience the three aspects of memory are dealt with in the left-to-right order. Later in the chapter an alternative representation of memory is offered.

Sensory Store

The first aspect of memory can be quickly disposed of, because it has already been encountered in the discussion of the visual system in the preceding chapter. Sensory store is a theoretical necessity rather than a known part of the brain. It is another metaphor, as is every reference to memory as a location where information is "stored." Some function or process has to be conceptualized to account for the persistence of visual information after it is received and transmitted by the eye, at the beginning of each fixation, while the brain is working on it. The operating characteristics of sensory store are quickly stated—input is very fast (the first few milliseconds of a fixation), capacity is at least large enough to hold visual information equivalent to 25 letters (although the brain may not be fast enough for us to identify anywhere near that number), persistence is very brief (about a second under optimal conditions, but normally erased before that time by another fixation), and retrieval depends on how fast sense can be made of the information.

Sensory store is of theoretical interest but has little significance for reading instruction because there is nothing that can or need be done about it. Sensory store cannot be overloaded nor can its capacity be increased by exercise. There is no evidence that children's sensory stores are less adequate than adults'. What needs to be remembered is that sense must be made of the contents of sensory store but that the contents do not persist very long. As a result, there is little point in speeding up fixations (which will simply erase sensory store faster) nor in slowing them down (which will result in blank stares). What makes the difference in reading is the effectiveness of the brain in using what is already known (nonvisual information) to make sense of incoming information (visual information) briefly held in sensory store.

Short-Term Memory

Can you repeat the sentence you are reading at this moment, without taking a second look at it? Whatever you can do to repeat what you have just read is a demonstration of the function of short-term memory. Short-term memory is—metaphorically speaking—a "working memory" or "buffer memory," where you retain in the forefront of your mind whatever you are attending to at a particular moment. As far as language is concerned, the contents of short-term memory are usually the last few words you have read or listened to or whatever thoughts you had in your mind instead. Sometimes short-term memory is occupied by what you are about to say or write, by an address you are looking for, or a telephone number you want to call. Short-term memory is whatever is holding your attention. And short-term memory is of central importance in reading. It is where you lodge the traces of what you have just read while you go on to make sense of the next few words. It is where you try to retain facts that you want to commit to rote memorization.

Short-term memory would appear to have both strengths and weaknesses in everyone, just by virtue of the way it functions. On the credit side, there does not appear to be any undue delay in getting something into short-term memory. In fact if someone asks you to call a certain telephone number, your best strategy is to get on your way to dial the number, not to stand around trying to commit the number to memory. Similarly, there does not appear to be any particular problem about retrieving items from short-term memory. If something is in short-term memory you can get it out again at once. Indeed, if you cannot immediately retrieve what you want, say the telephone number, then you might just as well go back and ask for it again. Either you have retained the number in short-term memory, in which case it is accessible without delay, or it is gone for good. Short-term memory is what we happen to be attending to at the moment, and if our attention is diverted to something else, the original content is lost.

But if short-term memory seems a reasonably efficient device as far as input and output operations are concerned, in other respects it has its limitations. Short-term memory cannot contain very much at any one time— little more than half a dozen items, in fact. A sequence of seven unrelated digits is about as much as anyone can retain. It is as if a benevolent providence had provided humanity with sufficient short-term memory capacity to make telephone calls and then had failed to prophesy area codes. For if we try to hold more than six or seven items in short-term memory, then something will be lost. If someone distracts us when we are on our way to make that telephone call, perhaps by asking us the time of day or the location of a room, then some or all of the telephone number will be forgotten and there will be absolutely no point in standing around cudgeling our brains for the number to come back. We shall just have to return and ascertain the number once again. For as much as we try to overload short-term memory, that much of its contents will be lost.

All this is the reason why short-term memory cannot be used to overcome the condition of tunnel vision. The child who has seen only *ELEP*. . . just cannot hold those letters in short-term memory, read another four or five letters, and get them all organized in a way that makes sense. As the fragments of one fixation go into short-term memory, the fragments from the previous fixation will be pushed out. This is not the same as the masking or erasure of sensory store—it is possible to hold a few items in short-term memory over a number of fixations. But holding such items in the forefront of our attention simply prevents very much more going in and has the obvious result of making reading much more difficult. Not much reading can be done if half your attention is preoccupied with earlier bits of letters and words that you are still trying to make sense of.

The second limitation of short-term memory involves its persistence. Nothing stays around very long in short-term memory. It is impossible to state an exact amount of time for the persistence of something in short-term memory, for the simple reason that its longevity depends on what you do with it. Ignore something in short-term memory for less than a second, and it will be gone. To retain it, you must keep giving it your attention. *Rehearsal* is the technical term often employed. To keep that telephone number in your head, you keep repeating it; it cannot be allowed to elude your attention. Theoretically, material can be kept in short-term memory indefinitely, but only if constantly rehearsed, a procedure that is generally impractical because it prevents you from thinking about anything else. Because we can rarely devote much attention to anything apart from what we happen to be doing at a particular moment and because life tends to be full of distraction in any case, it would therefore seem a reasonable assertion that the persistence of short-term memory is generally very brief, even if we cannot put a precise limit to it. Material in short-term memory must be dealt with as expeditiously as possible. Retaining something for longer than a fixation or two, for example, preempts attention that is required for the task on hand in reading and promotes a further loss of comprehension. The more a reader fills short-term memory with unrelated letters, bits of words, and other meaningless items, the more the letters and bits of words that the reader is currently trying to understand are likely to prove nonsense as well.

Long-Term Memory

Of course, memory is far more than whatever we happen to be thinking about at the moment. There is a vast amount that we know all the time, ranging from names and telephone numbers to all the complex interrelationships that we can perceive and predict among objects and events in the world around us, and only a small part of all of this knowledge can be the focus of our attention at any one time. Anything that persists in our minds quite independently of rehearsal or conscious knowledge is long-term memory, our continuous knowledge of the world. Long-term memory has some distinct advantages over short-term memory, especially with regard to its relative capacity. Nevertheless long-term memory cannot be used as a dump for any overflow of information from short-term memory, for long-term memory also has its limitations.

Let us begin with the positive side. Where short-term memory is restricted in its capacity to barely half a dozen items, the capacity of long-term memory would appear to be infinite. No limit has been discovered to how much can be lodged in long-term memory. Nothing has to be lost or moved aside in long-term memory to accommodate something new. We never have to forget an old friend's name to make room for the name of a new acquaintance.

Similarly, there is no apparent limit to the persistence of long-term memory. No question of rehearsal here. Memories we may not even be aware that we had, recollections of a childhood incident, for example, can quite unexpectedly revivify themselves, triggered perhaps by a few nostalgic bars of music, an old photograph, or even a certain taste or smell.

But as everyone knows, the fact that there seems to be no ultimate limit to the capacity or persistence of long-term memory does not mean that its contents are constantly accessible. It is here that some failings of long-term memory become apparent. Retrieval from long-term memory is by no means as immediate and effortless as retrieval from short-term memory.

Indeed, retention and retrieval seem quite different in long- and short-term memory. Short-term memory is like a set of half a dozen small boxes, each of which can contain one separate item, by definition immediately accessible to attention because it is attention that holds them in short-term memory in the first place. But long-term memory is more like a network of knowledge, an organized system in which each item is related in some way or another to everything else. The organization and operation of long-term memory—our theory of the world—was discussed in Chapter 1. Whether or not we can retrieve something from long-term memory depends on how it is organized. The secret of recall from long-term memory is to tap one of the interrelationships.

Sometimes the effort to get hold of something in long-term memory can be most frustrating. We know something is there but cannot find a way to get to it. An illustration is provided by the "tip-of-the-tongue" phenomenon (Brown & McNeill, 1966). We know someone's name begins with an *S* and has three syllables—and we are sure it is not Sanderson or Somerset or Sylvester. Suddenly the name appears in the set of alternatives that our mind is running through, or perhaps when someone else mentions the name, and then we recognize it at once. It was in long-term memory all the time, but not immediately accessible.

Success at retrieving something from long-term memory depends on the clues we can find to gain access to it and on how well it was organized in long-term memory in the first place. Basically, everything depends on the sense that we made of the material when we originally put it into memory. It is pointless to try to put an overflow of unrelated fragments from short-term memory into long-term memory—that is why rote learning is so often unproductive. It is not just that nonsense that goes in will be nonsense when it comes out but that it is extremely difficult to get nonsense out at all.

But there is another reason why it is not feasible to accommodate an overflow from short-term memory in long-term memory, concerned with the rate at which long-term memory can accept something new. In contrast to the practically immediate input of half a dozen items into short-term memory, committing something to long-term memory is extremely and surprisingly slow. To put one item into long-term memory takes 5 seconds—and in that 5 seconds there is little attention left over for anything else at all. The telephone number that will tax short-term memory to its capacity is at least accepted as quickly as it is read or heard, but to hold the same number in long-term memory, so that it can be dialed the next day, will require a good half minute of concentration, 5 seconds for each digit.

Committing fragments of text to long-term memory is not something that can be attempted recklessly in reading to overcome limitations of the visual system or of short-term memory. Quite the contrary, efforts to cram long-term memory will have the effect of interfering with comprehension. Beginning readers with tunnel vision, who cannot hold in short-term memory more than the few letters they see in a single fixation, are even more confounded if they try to put isolated letters or bits of words into long-term memory.

Fluent readers can find reading impossible if they overburden long-term memory, even if they are trying to read material which they would find completely comprehensible if they relaxed and were content to enjoy it. This problem can be acute for students trying to read a novel or Shakespearean play and at the same time trying to commit to memory the unfamiliar names of all the characters and every trivial detail or event. Memorization interferes with comprehension by monopolizing attention and reducing intelligibility. Most readers have encountered the perverse textbook that is incomprehensible the day before the examination—when we are trying to retain every fact—yet transparently comprehensible the day after—when all we are reading for is to discover what we missed. If you are having difficulty comprehending what you are reading right now, it may be because you are trying too hard to memorize. On the other hand—as I shall demonstrate in a number of ways—comprehension takes care of memorization. If you comprehend what you read or hear, then long-term memory will reorganize itself so efficiently and effortlessly that you will not be aware that you are learning at all.

Long-term memory is in fact extremely efficient, but only if the acquisition and organization of new material is directed by what we know already. Once again we find that it is what we know already that tips the balance, that makes reading possible. It is time to look at how prior knowledge helps to overcome the limitations of both short-term and long-term memory.

OVERCOMING MEMORY LIMITATIONS

There are some paradoxes to be resolved. The experimental evidence is that we can hold no more than half a dozen random letters in short-term memory, yet it is usually not difficult to repeat a sentence of a dozen words or more that we have just read or heard for the first time. It appears that we can put no more than one letter or digit into long-term memory every 5 seconds, yet we can commonly recall many of the larger themes and significant details that we have read in a novel or seen in a film.

To explain these discrepancies it is necessary to clarify some rather loose language that I have been using. I have been talking about retaining "material," or half a dozen "things" or "items," in short-term memory and putting just one "item" into long-term memory. What are these "things" or "items"? The answer depends on what you already know and the sense you are making of what you are reading or listening to. These "things" or "items" are units that exist in long-term memory already.

If you are looking for letters—or if you can only find letters in what you are looking at—then you can hold half a dozen letters in short-term memory. But if you are looking for words, then short-term memory will hold half a dozen words, the equivalent of four or five times as many letters.

It is a question of what you already know. Short-term memory is filled by a seven-digit telephone number, which also requires half a minute to put into long-term memory. But not if the number happens to be 123-4567 because that is a sequence that you already know. The number 1234567 will occupy just one part of short-term memory and will enter long-term memory within a few seconds because, in a sense, it is there already. Can you hold the letters *THEELEPELTJE* in short-term memory? Only if you recognize them as a word, which you will do if you can read Dutch. To put the same sequence of letters into long-term memory would require a good minute of concentration—and even then it is unlikely that you would be able to recall them all tomorrow—unless you already know the word, in which case you will commit it to memory as rapidly as the English word *teaspoon*, which is what the Dutch word happens to mean.

Psychologists refer to this process of storing the largest meaningful unit in short-term memory as *chunking*, which is a conveniently picturesque term but also a bit misleading. The term suggests that at the beginning we first attend to the small fragments (individual letters or digits) which we subsequently organize into larger units for efficiency in memory. But we are looking for the larger units all the time. When we move on to consider more specifically the processes of reading, it will be seen that written words can be identified without any reference to letters and meaning without reference to specific words. It is not that we perceive letters which we then—if we can—chunk into words but that we can perceive words or meaning in the first place and never bother the visual system or memory with letters. The "items" that we commit to memory are the largest meaningful units we can find. In other words, what we put into short-term memory is determined by the largest units that we have available in long-term memory. It is what we know and are looking for that determines the content of short-term memory, which is the reason I present an alternative diagram of memory to that of Figure 5.1. In Figure 5.2, short-term memory is shown as part of long-term memory—the part that controls what we happen to be attending to at the time. Short-term

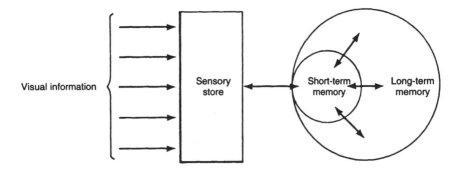

FIG. 5.2.   An alternative representation of memory.

memory is not an antechamber of long-term memory but that part of long-term memory that we use to attend to, and make sense of, a current situation.

The arrow between short-term memory and sensory store is double-ended to acknowledge that the brain is *selective* about the visual information that it attends to, and the arrows between short-term and long-term memory are double-ended to represent their continual interaction.

One final elaboration must be made. We can hold in short-term memory a few letters or a few words. But we can also put into short-term memory something far more mysterious—we can hold there large rich chunks of *meaning*. It is impossible to put a number to this—units of meaning cannot be counted the way we can count letters or words. But just as we can hold the letters contained in words in memory far more efficiently than letters that are unrelated to each other, so we can hold meaningful sequences of words in memory far more efficiently than we can hold individual unrelated words. The same applies to long-term memory; we can put an entire "meaning" away in just a few seconds—without any conscious awareness that we are doing so—even though that meaning might have been embedded in a dozen words or more. And by definition, any "meaning" that we put into long-term memory is going to be far easier to retain and retrieve because meaningfulness implies that the input is related to what we already know and makes sense to us.

We must get used to the notion that meaning does not depend on specific words. This crucial point is elaborated many times in this book. When we retain a meaningful sequence of words in memory—either short-term or long-term—we are not primarily storing the words at all but rather the meaning that we attribute to them. "Meaning" is the largest and most efficient unit of analysis that we can bring to bear from what we know already to what we are trying to read (or hear) and understand. For the moment, I offer just one illustration of the fact that not only do we look for meaning, rather than specific words, when we comprehend speech or print but also that this is the most natural thing to do.

I have said that we can hold a dozen or more words in short-term memory if they are in a meaningful sequence, but that six or seven is the limit for words that make no collective sense, like the same sequence of words in reverse. Try memorizing: *memory term short in words more or dozen a hold can we.* It is not a sequence of a dozen or so words that we can hold in short-term memory, but rather their meaning. If you ask a person to repeat a sentence, you will often get back the right meaning but not exactly the same words. The person who remembers is not so much recalling words as reconstructing a sentence from the meaning that was remembered. We do not attend to words; we attend to meanings. So a substantial "mistake" might be made in repeating exact words—the word *automobile* might be recalled as the word *car,* for example—but there is rarely the substitution of a tiny word that makes a big difference to meaning, such as *not*. We shall see, incidentally, that "errors" of this kind, that preserve meaning, are committed by fluent readers and also by children learning to read who are in the process of becoming good readers. Reading involves looking for meaning, not specific words.

Memory Without Bottlenecks

Much of what we have considered so far might be called *contrived* memory—whether by experimenters or ourselves—where remembering is in effect put under external control. In memory research, subjects are usually told what they must remember and recall. When we make a deliberate effort to commit a particular thing to memory or to get a particular thing out, we usually encounter the frustrating bottlenecks I have been describing.

But most of the time there is no particular effort involved in remembering—and memory seems to be much more efficient. I have talked about how easily something goes into long-term memory provided we can make sense of it, provided it is relevant to what we are doing at the time. These are the occasions when memory could be said to be controlled "from the inside," by the way in which the brain is naturally operating on the world or making sense of it. It is sometimes surprising to discover how much has gone into memory without our awareness. I have more to say about this in the chapter on learning, in which I stress that efficient and effortless memorizing depends on how well it is integrated with our current knowledge, ongoing purposes and predictions, the operation of the dynamic theory of the world.

I have also talked in the present chapter about how easily things can be retrieved from long-term memory, provided they are organized in relationships with relevant parts of our current theory of the world. The most relevant kind of relationship is when what we need to remember is part of what we are actually involved in at the time.

I am referring to an aspect of memory that we rely on just about every moment of the day, that is incredibly efficient and rarely lets us down. It is memory that is not contrived in any way; it functions spontaneously, without premeditation or effort. Ironically, because of their predilection for studying aspects of memory that can be brought under *control* in the laboratory, experimental psychologists have largely ignored this aspect of remembering which takes place without the conscious contrivance of the experimenters or their subjects. Because of their rather narrow viewpoint, such researchers have even persuaded themselves and many educators that remembering is normally difficult, effortful, and frequently unsuccessful.

But most of the time we remember automatically and without strain, even without awareness that we are making demands on memory. We do not usually have difficulty remembering our own name, where we live, or our telephone number. We remember our birthday and that of a few other people as well, and we remember holidays. We remember our friends' names, and how they look, and where they live, and even some of their telephone numbers. We remember everything about the world that is familiar to us. We remember that trees are called "trees" and birds "birds," even though we may not remember the names of particular kinds. We remember the meanings of just about every word we know, how these words are pronounced, and how many of them are spelled as well. We not only remember facts, we remember scenes, procedures, scenarios, scripts—all of the cognitive *schemes* discussed in Chapter 1. We remember innumerable things. We do not remember these things all the time, of course. Our heads would be continually cluttered if we did. They come to mind just when it is appropriate for us to remember them, when they help us to make sense of the world we are in at the moment.

Psychologist George Mandler (1985) has termed this everyday aspect of memory *reminding*, although he does not want to say that it is different from any other facet of memory. In fact, Mandler suggests that apparent differences in kinds of memory are really only differences in the forms of tests, in the way memory is examined. If we look at the recall of something soon after it has come to our attention, then we talk about "short-term memory." If we consider something over a longer period, then we refer to "long-term memory." And instead of looking at particular things that we (or researchers) happen quite arbitrarily to be concerned with, if we consider what we continually remember for our own purposes, then we have this phenomenon of "reminding."

And as with comprehension and with putting things into memory, the conditions that make reminding fluent and effortless are meaningfulness, relevance, and personal involvement. We remember most easily when what we need to recall is most relevant to what we are engaged in doing and when we have no anxiety about not remembering. This is all part of the continually ongoing activity of "thinking." Memory is not a special faculty of the brain that functions independently of everything else. Thinking and the "reminding" aspect of memory are inseparable.

Long-term memory is dynamic, constantly generating predictions in the form of possible or potential worlds. Reminding is an inevitable and essential aspect of that continual interaction between possible and real worlds, when our own imagination is in control of the flow of events in which we are immersed.

When we are able to read with comprehension, we are being reminded all the time. The events of the story (or the steps in the argument) carry us along as if we were experiencing them at first hand, and we rarely have to struggle to exercise our memory. We remember the meaning of particular words when we are reading those words, we recall what we have already read (and other aspects of nonvisual information) when it is appropriate to do so. And we are reminded of all manner of things that happen to be relevant to our understanding, and to our purposes in reading, at that particular time.

As a simple example, we are reminded of the appropriate meaning of the words (or we predict those meanings) in a sentence like *He wiped the tear from the child's eye*, but quite a different meaning in *He repaired the tear in the child's jacket*. Normally we would not even notice the word *tear* could have a different pronunciation and meaning than those that are appropriate for the context the word is in.

Of course, memory lets us down sometimes. We fail to remind ourselves to buy something at the store on the way home or to make a telephone call that we had planned. Often there is an explanation of why we forget—we are distracted, or confused, or possibly we may not even want to remember and we somehow suppress the recall. If we fail to recall something, it is usually not because we have suffered a permanent loss of memory. We just cannot get access for the moment (like the elusive word that stays on the wrong side of the tip of our tongue but that we recognize the moment somebody mentions it). And sometimes memory is frustratingly difficult. Remembering becomes difficult when it is conscious, when we *contrive* deliberately to remember something that has not sprung to mind at once.

Easy and *difficult* remembering differ in the way they are invoked. Easy remembering occurs involuntarily, in the normal everyday course of events. Difficult remembering is the kind we engage in deliberately, because we "want" to remember something we have not conveniently reminded ourselves of or because someone else wants us to remember something that is not part of our current frame of reference, our ongoing theory of the world. Remembering becomes difficult when we try to take charge of it "from the outside."

When we make a deliberate effort to remember something we are in a sense approaching it from the wrong end. Instead of allowing the memory to rise from the way we are currently making sense of the world, from the flow of thought, we try to dig down to it from the outside, where we have no frame of reference. Deliberate remembering is usually too contrived, too unrelated, to be successful. And the most deliberate and contrived efforts to manipulate memory occur when the control is in the hands of someone else—when we are *told* to bring something to mind. The worst conditions for memory are when someone else tells us precisely what we should remember.

Children do not need to be taught to use memory efficiently—to avoid overloading short-term memory and to refrain from forcing pointless detail into long-term memory. They naturally do these things. But reading instruction may make these natural efficiencies impossible. Anxiety while learning to read can force children into inefficient uses of memory. Reading, and therefore learning to read, depends on what you already know, on what you can make sense of. Reading teachers help to avoid overloading pupils' memories when they ensure that the material the children are expected to read makes sense to them, so that they are not required—either by the material or by the instruction—to engage in extensive and pointless memorization.

ISSUES

There is little dispute about the characteristics of memory I have outlined (though there is much technical debate about physiological aspects). Problems arise when the limitations of memory are ignored, for example, in expecting large amounts of detailed memorization to take place during reading or learning, especially when the inefficiency of memory with material that is not meaningful to the learner is overlooked.

SUMMARY

Short-term memory and **long-term memory** both have their limitations, but these are handicaps only to the readers who can make little sense of what they are doing in the first place. The differing characteristics of memory are summarized in Figure 5.3. When a reader can make sense of text and does not

	Short-term memory (working memory)	Long-term memory (permanent memory)
Capacity	limited	practically unlimited
Persistence	very brief	practically unlimited
Retrieval	immediate	depends on organization
Input	very fast	relatively slow

FIG. 5.3.   Characteristics of short-term and long-term memory.

strain to memorize, there is not even awareness of the bottlenecks of memory. Fluent readers are immediately **reminded** of what is relevant for their current situation and purposes.

Notes to Chapter 5 begin on page 256, covering
Theories of memory
Chunking
Imagery
Children's memory
Easy and difficult remembering

6 Letter Identification

The easiest route through tangled terrain may not be the most direct. Now that we are beginning an analysis of reading, an indirect approach is adopted. The point we are heading for is that fluent reading does not normally require the identification of individual letters or words, but the most convenient route to that point begins with a discussion of letter identification. Letter identification focuses on an aspect of reading where the issue can be concisely stated and specified: What is the process by which individuals who know the alphabet can discriminate and name any one of the 26 alternatives that is actually presented to them? I am talking about individual letters, not letters in sequences of any kind.

Unlike the reading of words, the question does not arise whether letters are read a bit at a time or all at once. Individual letters cannot be "sounded out" from their component parts like words; their appearance has a purely arbitrary relationship to the way they are pronounced. And there can be little question about their meaning; we "comprehend" a letter when we can say its name, and that is that.

Yet despite this simplification, letter and word identification are alike in one important aspect—they both involve the discrimination and categorization of visual information. Later we shall see that the manner in which letters are identified may be of special relevance to an understanding of the identification of words.

Before we move ahead, a digression may be in order to discuss the somewhat arbitrary use of the terms *identification* and *recognition* as labels for the process by which a letter or word (or meaning) is distinguished and named. Dictionary definitions of the two words are tortuous, but it is clear that they are not, strictly speaking, synonymous. *Identification* involves a decision that an object now confronted should be put into a particular category. There is no implication that the object being identified should have been met before. *Recognition*, on the other hand, literally means that the object now confronted has been seen before, although identification may not be involved. We recognize people when we know we have seen them before, whether or not we can put a name to them. We identify people when we put a name to them, whether or not we have met them before.

Experimental psychologists and reading specialists usually talk about letter and word recognition, but the use of the term seems doubly inappropriate. First, they would hardly consider a word to be recognized unless its name could be given; they would not consider that a child recognized a word if all the child could say about it was "That's the very same squiggle I saw yesterday." Second, skilled readers can very often attach a name to visual information that they have never met before. As a rather extreme case, do you "recognize" or "identify" the visual information *rEaDiNg* as the word *reading*? You almost certainly have never seen the word written that way before. The weight of evidence would seem to favor identification, and the term is therefore used in this book for formal purposes, such as chapter headings. But having made a point of the distinction, we need not be dogmatic about it; "identify," "recognize," "categorize," "name," and even "read" will, in general, continue to be used interchangeably; it is the process we are concerned with at the moment, not the flexible way in which language is used.

It is not strictly correct to refer to the characters that we strive to identify on particular occasions as "letters"; this implies that the perceptual decision has already been made. Whether a particular mark on the page should be characterized as a letter depends on the intention of the perceiver (whether the reader or the writer). As we have seen, IO may be identified as two letters or two numerals. Prior to an identification decision, the visual information that is IO is merely a pattern of contrasting ink marks on paper, more precisely referred to as a *visual configuration*, a *visual array*, or even a *visual stimulus*.

THEORIES OF PATTERN RECOGNITION

Letter identification is a special problem within the broader theoretical area of *pattern recognition*—the process by which any two visual configurations are "cognized" to be the same. The process of recognition is of classical philosophical concern because it has been realized for over 2,000 years that no two events are ever exactly the same; the world is always in flux, and we never see an object twice in precisely the same form, from the same angle, in the same light, or with the same eye. A topic of very general interest to psychology is what exactly determines whether two objects or events shall be considered to be equivalent. The equivalence decision clearly rests with the perceiver and not in any property of the visual array. Are *J* and *J* the same? A printer would say no. Are two automobiles of the same year, model, and color identical? Possibly to everyone except their owners. It is the perceiver, not the object, that determines equivalence. We organize our lives and our knowledge by deciding that some things should be treated as equivalent— these are the things that we put into the same category—and some as different. Those differences between objects or events that help us to place them in category systems may be called by a variety of names, such as *defining attributes* or *central attributes* or *distinctive features*; in essence, they are the differences that we choose to make *significant*. The differences that we choose to ignore, the ones that do not influence our decision, are often not noticed at all. Obviously it is more efficient to pay attention only to significant differences, particularly in view of the limited information-processing capacity of the human brain. It is, therefore, hardly surprising that we may overlook differences that we are not looking for in the first place, like the sudden absence of our friend's beard, or the pattern of his tie, or the misspelling in the newspaper headline. Human beings owe their preeminent position in the intellectual hierarchy of living organisms not so much to their ability to perceive the world in many different ways as their capacity to perceive things as the same according to criteria that they themselves establish, selectively ignoring what might be termed *differences that do not make a difference*.

The process that determines how particular letters or words are treated as equivalent has become a focus of theoretical attention because of its particular application to computer technology. There is an obvious economic as well as theoretical interest in designing computers that might be able to read. The construction of a computer with any fluent degree of reading ability has proved difficult for a number of reasons, one of which is that language can be understood only if there is an underlying understanding of the topic to which the language happens to refer, and the ability of computers to "understand" any topic is very limited indeed. Computers can copy letters, and they can compare one letter with another. But it has not proved feasible to provide a computer with rules for identifying all the printed and handwritten letters that people are able to identify, let alone words or meanings, with anything like the facility with which humans can identify them. If we consider the problems of pattern recognition from the computer point of view, we get some insights into what must be involved in the human skill.

There are two basic ways in which a computer might be constructed to recognize patterns, whether numbers, letters, words, texts, photographs, fingerprints, voiceprints, signatures, diagrams, maps, or real objects. The two ways are essentially those that appear to be open theoretically to account for the recognition of patterns by humans. The alternatives may be called *template matching* and *feature analysis*, and the best way to describe them is to imagine trying to build a computer capable of reading the 26 letters of the alphabet.

For both our models, for the template-matching and the feature-analytic devices, the ground rules have to be the same. We consider the computer to be equipped with exactly the same "input" and "output" mechanisms as a person. At the input end is an optical system or "eye" to examine visual information, and at the output end is a set of 26 alternative responses, the names of each of the letters of the alphabet. The aim, of course, is to construct a system between the input and output mechanisms to insure that when the visual array *E* is presented at the input end, the response "E" will be indicated by the output.

Template Matching

For a template-matching device, a series of internal representations must be constructed to be, in effect, a reference library for the letters that the device is required to identify. We might start with one internal representation, or *template*, for each letter of the alphabet. Each template is directly connected with an appropriate response, while between the eye and the templates we shall put a comparator or matching mechanism capable of comparing any input letter with all of the set of templates. Any letter that comes into the computer's field of view will be internalized and compared with each of the templates, at least until a match is made. Upon matching the input with a template, the computer will perform the response associated with that particular template and the identification will be complete.

There are obvious limitations to such a system. If the computer is given a template for the representation *A*, what will it do if confronted with **A** or A not to mention *A* or even A? Of course, some flexibility can be built into the system. Inputs can be normalized to iron out some of the variability; they can be scaled down to a standard size, adjusted into a particular orientation, have crooked lines straightened, small gaps filled, and minor excrescences removed; in short, a number of things can be done to increase the probability that the computer will not respond "I don't know" but will instead match an input to a template. But, unfortunately, the greater the likelihood that the computer will make a match, the greater the probability that it will make a mistake. This is the signal detection problem of Chapter 3. A computer that can normalize A to make it look like the template *A* will be likely to do the same with 4 and H. The only remedy will be to keep adding templates to try to accommodate all the different styles and types of lettering the device might meet. Even then, such a computer will be unable to make use of all the supporting knowledge that human beings have.

Critical limitations of template-matching systems, for both computer and human, lie in their relative inefficiency and costliness. A single set of templates, one for each category, is highly restricted in the number of inputs that it can match, but every increase in the number of templates adds considerably to the size, expense, and complexity of the system. The template-matching model does work, but the system copes with the diversity of input representations by cheating its way around the problem. Instead of providing the computer with templates to meet many different styles of character, it makes sure the computer eye meets only a limited set of alternatives, like the "bankers' numbers" **5 2104** that are printed on our checks.

Feature Analysis

The alternative method of pattern perception, *feature analysis*, dispenses with internal representations completely. There is no question of attempting to match the input with anything. Instead, a series of tests is made on the input. The results of each test eliminate a number of alternatives until, finally, all uncertainty is reduced and identification is achieved. The features are properties of the visual array that are subjected to tests to determine which alternative responses should be eliminated. Decisions about which alternatives each test will eliminate are made by the perceivers (or computer programmers) themselves.

To clarify the explanation, let us again imagine constructing a computer for the identification of letters, this time using feature analysis. Remember, the problem is essentially one of using rules to decide into which of a limited number of categories might a very large number of alternative events be placed. In other words this is a matter of establishing equivalences.

At the receptor end of the system, where the computer has its light-sensitive optical scanner, we establish a set of "feature analyzers." A feature analyzer is a specialized kind of detector that looks for—is sensitive to—just one kind of feature in the visual information and that passes just one kind of report back. For the sake of illustration, we might imagine that each analyzer looks for a particular distinctive feature by asking a question; one analyzer asks "Is the configuration curved?" (like *C* or *O*); another asks "Is it closed?" (like *O* or *P*); a third asks "Is it symmetrical?" (like *A* or *W*), and a fourth asks "Is there an intersection?" (as in *T* or *K*). Every analyzer is, in fact, a test, and the message it sends back is binary—either "yes" or "no," signal or no signal. Without looking too closely at the question of what constitutes a distinctive feature, we can say it is a property of visual information that can be used to differentiate some visual configurations from others—a "significant difference." By definition, a distinctive feature must be common to more than one object or event, otherwise it could not be used to put more than one into the same category. But, on the other hand, if the feature were present in all objects or events, then we could not use it to segregate them into different categories; it would not be "distinctive." In other words, a feature, if detected, permits the elimination of some of the alternative categories into which a stimulus might be allocated.

As an example, a "no" answer to the test "Is the configuration curved?" would eliminate rounded letters such as *a, b, c, d,* but not other letters such as *i, k, l, u, w, x, z.* A "yes" answer to "Is it closed?" would eliminate open letters such as *c, f, w,* but not *b, d,* or *o.* The question about symmetry would distinguish letters like *m, o, w,* and *v,* from *d, f, k, r.* Different questions eliminate different alternatives, and relatively few tests would be required to distinguish among 26 alternatives in an alphabet. In fact, if all tests eliminated about half of the alternatives, and there was no test that overlapped with any other, only five questions would be needed to identify any letter. (The logic of the previous statement is set out in the discussion of information theory in the Notes.) No one would actually suggest that as few as five tests are employed to distinguish among 26 letters, but it is reasonable to assume that there need be many fewer tests than categories—that is one of the great economic advantages of a feature-analytic system.

With an input bank of feature analyzers built into the letter-identification device, a link has to be provided to the 26 responses or output categories; "decision rules" must be devised so that the results of the individual tests are integrated and associated with the appropriate letter names. The most convenient way to set up the rules is to establish a feature list for each category, that is, for each of the 26 letters. The construction of the feature lists is the same for every category, namely a listing of the analyzers that were set up to examine the visual configuration. The feature list for every category also indicates whether each particular analyzer should send back a "yes" or "no" signal for that category. For the category *c,* for example, the feature list should specify a "yes" for the "curved?" analyzer, a "no" for the "closed?" analyzer, a "no" for the "symmetrical?" analyzer, and so forth.

The actual wiring of the letter-identification device presents no problems—every feature analyzer is connected to every category that lists a "yes" signal from it, and we arrange that a categorizing decision (an "identification") is made only when "yes" signals are received for all the analyzers listed positively on a category's feature list. In a sense, a feature list is a *specification* of what the characteristics of a particular letter should be. *Descriptions* of a letter that is being looked at—the input—are compared with specifications of what the letter might be until a match is found.

And that, in a simplified and schematic form, is a feature-analytic letter-identification device. The system is powerful, in the sense that it will do a lot of work with a minimum of effort. Unlike the template model, which to be versatile requires many templates for every decision that it might make together with complex normalizing devices, the feature-analytic device demands only a very small number of analyzers compared with the number of decisions it makes. Theoretically, such a device could decide among over a million alternatives with only 20 questions.

Functional Equivalence and Criterial Sets

A considerable advantage of the feature-analytic model over template matching is that the former has very much less trouble in adjusting to inputs that ought to be allocated to the same category but which vary in size or orientation or detail, for example, A, *A*, and *a*. The types of tests that feature analyzers apply are far better able to cope with distortion and noise than any device that requires an approximate match. But far more important, very little is added in the way of complexity or cost to provide one or more alternative feature lists for every category. With such a flexibility, the system can easily allocate not only the examples already given, but also forms as divergent as *A* to the category "A." The only adjustment that need be made to the battery of analyzers is in wiring additional connections between them and the categories to which the analyzers are relevant, so that an identification will be made on any occasion when the specifications of any of the alternative lists are satisfied.

I shall call any set of features that meet the specifications of a particular category a *criterial set*. With the type of feature-analytic device being outlined, more than one criterial set of features may exist for any one category. Obviously, the more criterial sets that exist for a given device, the more efficient that device will be in making accurate identifications.

It is also useful to give a special name to the alternative criterial sets of features that specify the same category—we shall say that they are *functionally equivalent*. *A*, *a*, and *a* are functionally equivalent for our imagined device because they are all treated as being the same as far as the category "A" is concerned. Of course, the configurations are not functionally equivalent if they are to be distinguished on a basis other than their membership of the alphabet; a printer, for example, might want them categorized into type styles. But as I pointed out earlier, it is the prerogative of the perceiver, not a characteristic of the visual configuration, to decide which differences shall be significant—which sets of features shall be criterial—in the establishment of equivalences. Functional equivalence can be determined by any systematic or arbitrary method that the pattern recognizer follows. All that is required to establish functional equivalence for quite disparate visual configurations is alternative feature lists for the same category.

Another powerful aspect of the feature-analytic model of pattern recognition is that it can work on a flexible and probabilistic basis. If a single feature list specifies the outcomes of ten analyzer tests for the categorical identification of a letter of the alphabet, a considerable amount of redundant information must be involved. Redundancy, as I noted in Chapter 3, exists when the same information is available from more than one source or when more information is available than is required to reduce the actual amount of uncertainty. Ten analyzer tests could provide enough information to select from over a thousand equally probable alternatives, and if there are only 26 alternatives, information from five of those tests could be dispensed with and there might still be enough data to make the appropriate identification. Even if analyzer information were insufficient to enable an absolutely certain selection, it might still be possible to decide which alternatives are more likely, given the particular pattern of features that is discriminated. By not demanding that *all* the specifications of a particular feature list be satisfied before a category identification is made, the system can greatly increase its repertoire of functionally equivalent criterial sets of features. Such an increase significantly enhances the efficiency of the device at a cost of little extra complexity.

The fact that different criterial sets can be established within a single feature list provides an advantage that was alluded to in the previous paragraph—a feature-analytic system can make use of redundancy. Let us say that the system already "knows" from some other source of information that the configuration it is presented with is a vowel; it has perhaps already identified the letters *THR* . . . and it has been programmed with some basic knowledge of the spelling patterns of English. The device can then exclude from consideration for the fourth letter all those feature lists that specify consonant categories, leaving considerably reduced criterial sets for selection among the remaining alternatives. (Three tests might easily distinguish among five or six vowels.)

A final powerful advantage of the feature-analytic model has also already been implied; it is a device that can easily *learn*. Every time a new feature list or criterial set is established there is an instance of learning. All that the device requires in order to learn is *feedback* from the environment. It establishes, or rejects, a new feature list for a particular category (or category for a particular feature list) by "hypothesizing" a relationship between a feature list and a category and testing whether that relationship is appropriate.

You may have noticed that the feature-analytic discussion develops easily into such topics as "learning" and "thinking." It is evident that the more efficient and sophisticated we make our imaginary letter-identifying device, the more we are likely to talk about its realization in human rather than computer terms. It is time for the computer analogy to be discarded and to direct a more specific focus on the human pattern recognizer.

The Human Letter Identifier

The analogy is discarded; I intend to use feature analysis as a model for the process by which letters are identified by readers. We learn to identify the letters of the alphabet by establishing feature lists for the required 26 categories, each of which is interrelated to a single name "A," "B," "C," and so forth. The visual system is equipped with analyzers that respond to those features in the visual environment that are distinctive for alphabetic discriminations (and many other visual discriminations as well). The results of the analyzer tests are integrated and directed to the appropriate feature lists so that letter identifications can occur. The human visual perceptual system is biologically competent to demonstrate all the most powerful aspects of the feature-analytic model outlined in the last section—to establish manifold criterial sets of features with functional equivalence, to function probabilistically, to make use of redundancy, and to learn by testing hypotheses and receiving feedback.

Two aspects of letter identification must be distinguished. The first aspect is the establishment of cognitive categories themselves and especially the allocation of category names to them, such as "A," "B," "C." This might be termed "learning to *say* the letters of the alphabet." The second aspect of letter identification is the allocation of visual configurations to various cognitive categories—the discrimination of various configurations as different, as not functionally equivalent. This might be termed "learning to *recognize* the letters of the alphabet." The greater part of perceptual learning involves finding out what exactly are the distinctive features by which various configurations should be categorized as different from each other and what are the sets of features that are criterial for particular categories. These are precisely the two aspects of object or concept learning involved in distinguishing one face from another, or cats from dogs. Categories must be established with unique names (like "cat" and "dog"), and rules must be devised for allocating particular instances to the appropriate categories.

The association of a name with a category is neither necessary nor primary in visual discrimination. It is quite possible to segregate visual configurations into different categories without having a name for them. We can see that *A* and & are different and know they should be treated differently, even though we may not have a category name, or even a specific category, for &. In fact, we cannot allocate a name to & unless first we acquire some unconscious rules for discriminating it from *A* and from every other visual configuration with which it should not be given functional equivalence. We will not learn a name for & if we cannot distinguish that particular visual configuration from *A*. The motivation for the establishment of a new category may come from either direction: either a configuration such as & cannot be related to any existing category, or a new name such as "ampersand" cannot be related to an existing category. The intermediate steps that tie the entire system together are the establishment of the first feature lists and criterial sets for the category so that the appropriate feature tests and the category name can be related.

Not only is relating a name to a category not primary; it is not difficult. The complicated part of learning to make an identification is not in remembering the name of a particular category but in discovering the criterial sets of features for that category. Children at the age when they are often learning to read are also learning thousands of new names every year—names of friends and public figures and automobiles and animals—as well as the names of letters and words. The person they learn from, the informal instructor, usually points to an object and says "That is an 'X'," in effect, leaving the child to work out what the significant differences must be. The complicated part of learning is the establishment of functional equivalences for the categories with which names are associated.

The reason that "learning names" is frequently thought to be difficult is that the intermediate steps are ignored and it is assumed that a name is applied directly to a particular visual configuration. Of course, children may find it difficult to respond with the right name for the letters *b* or *d* (or for the words *house* and *mouse*, or for an actual dog or cat) but this is not because they cannot put the name to the configuration. Their basic problem is to find out how two alternatives are significantly different. Once learners can make the discrimination, so that the appropriate functional equivalences are observed, the allocation of the correct verbal label is a relatively easy problem because the label is related directly to the category.

The Letter Identifier in Action

Is there evidence to support the feature-analytic model of the human visual system? Some of the physiological evidence has already been indicated. There is no one-to-one correspondence between the visual information impinging on the eye and anything that goes on behind the eyeball. The eye does not send "images" back to the brain; the stammering pattern of neural impulses is a representation of discrete features detected by the eye, not the transfer of a "picture." In the brain itself, there is no possibility of storing templates or even acquiring them in the first place. The brain does not deal in veridical representations; it shunts abstractions through its complex neural networks. It is true that one aspect of the brain's output, our subjective experience of the world, is generated in the form of "percepts" that might be regarded as pictures, but this experience is a *consequence* of the brain's activity, not something the brain "stores" and compares with inputs. Our visual experience is the product of the perceptual system, not part of the process.

Now we can examine evidence for the feature-analytic model from two kinds of letter-identification experiments. (Details are given in the Notes.) The basic assumption to be tested is that letters are actually conglomerates of features, of which there are perhaps a dozen different kinds. The only way in which letters can differ physically from each other is in the presence or absence of each of these features. Letters that have several features in common will be regarded as similar, and letters that are constructed of quite different feature combinations will be considered quite dissimilar in appearance. How does one assess similarity? Letters are similar—they are presumed to share many features—if they are frequently confused with each other. And letters that are rarely confused with each other are assumed to have very few features in common.

Of course, we do not very often confuse letters, and when we do the character of the error is usually influenced by nonvisual factors. We might, for example, think that the fourth letter in the sequence *REQW* . . . is a *U* not because *W* and *U* are visually similar but because we normally expect a *U* to follow *Q*. However, large numbers of visual letter confusions can be generated by experimental techniques in which the letter to be identified is so "impoverished" that viewers cannot see it clearly, although they are forced to make a guess about what the letter probably is. In other words, the experimental subjects must make letter-identification decisions on minimal visual information. The experimental assumption is that viewers who cannot see the letter clearly must lack some vital information and thus be unable to make some feature tests. And if they are unable to make certain feature tests, then the tests they are able to make will not reduce all uncertainty about the 26 alternative responses. Viewers will still be left in doubt about a few possibilities that can be differentiated only by the tests that they have been unable to perform.

The actual method of visual impairment is not important. The presentation may be a tachistoscopic brief presentation, or it may involve an image that has very little contrast with its surroundings, projected by a lamp at a very low intensity, or printed on a page under several layers of tissue paper, or hidden behind a lot of visual noise, like . As soon as viewers start making errors, one can assume that they are not getting all the information that they need to make an identification. They are deciding on something less than a criterial set of features.

There are only two possibilities if viewers are forced to identify a letter on insufficient visual information; either their guesses will be completely random, or they will respond in some systematic way. If guesses are random, there can be no prediction of what the answer will be; they will be just as likely to respond with any of the 26 letters of the alphabet, whatever the letter that is presented. If we examine the record of "confusions," the occasions when a letter is reported incorrectly, we should find that each of the other 25 letters is represented about equally often. But if responses are systematic, there are two further possibilities, both of which limit considerably the number of confusions likely to occur. One possibility, which is not very interesting, is that the viewers will always say the same thing if they cannot distinguish a letter; one might say "That's a 'k'," for example, whenever there is uncertainty. Fortunately, such a bias is easy to detect. The other and more interesting possibility is that the viewers will select only from those alternative responses that remain after the features that can be discriminated in the presentation have been taken into account. In such a circumstance, it is to be expected that the confusions will "cluster"; instead of 25 types of confusion, one for each of the possible erroneous responses, there will be only a few types.

The evidence can be summarized in a few words: Letter confusions fall into tightly packed clusters, and over two-thirds of the confusions for most letters can be accounted for by three or four confusion types. If a mistake is made in the identification of a letter, the nature of the erroneous response is highly predictable. Typical confusion clusters can be very suggestive about the kind of information the eye must be looking for in discriminating letters. Some typical confusion clusters are *(a, e, n, o, u)*, *(t, f, i)*, and *(h, m, n)* (Dunn-Rankin, 1968).

The specific conclusion to be drawn from the kind of experiment just described is that letters are indeed composed of a relatively small number of features. Letters that are easily confused, like *a* and *e* or *t* and *f*, must have a number of features in common, and those that are rarely confused, like *o* and *w* or *d* and *y*, must have few if any features in common. The general conclusion that may be drawn is that the visual system is indeed feature analytic. Letter identification is accomplished by examination of the visual environment for featural information that will eliminate all alternatives except one, thus permitting an accurate identification to be made.

There is a second line of experimental evidence supporting the view that letters are arrangements of smaller elements, and this is related to the fact that recognition is faster or easier when there are fewer alternatives for what each letter might be. The classic example of such evidence has already been described in the tunnel vision demonstration of Chapter 4, where it was shown that nonvisual information can be employed to reduce the amount of visual—or distinctive feature—information required to identify letters. There are other illustrations when the identification of words is considered in the next chapter.

WHAT IS A FEATURE?

The entire discussion of letter identification by feature analysis has been conducted without actually specifying what a feature is. The omission has been deliberate, because nobody knows what the distinctive features of letters are. Not enough is known about the structure of the human visual system to say exactly what is the featural information that the system looks for.

Of course, general statements about features can be made. There have been a number of attempts to do this, with reasoning like "The only difference between c and o is that the circle of o is 'closed'; therefore, being closed must be a distinctive feature" or "The only difference between h and n is the 'ascender' at the top of h; therefore, an ascender must be a distinctive feature." But we really do not know whether, or how, the eyes might look for "closedness" or for "ascenders." It can be argued that these hypothesized features are really properties of whole letters, and it is far from clear how a property of the whole could also be an element out of which the whole is constructed. It is obviously a reasonable assertion that the significant difference between h and n has something to do with the ascender but is an oversimplification to say that the ascender is the actual feature.

Fortunately, it is not necessary to know exactly what the features are in order to learn something about the identification process or to assist children in discriminating letters. We can trust children to locate the information required provided the appropriate informational environment is available. The appropriate informational environment is the opportunity to make comparisons and discover what the significant differences are. Remember, the primary problem of identification is to distinguish the presented configuration from all those to which it might be equivalent but is not; the configuration has to be subjected to feature analysis and put in the appropriate category. Presenting h to children 50 times and telling them it is "h" because it has an ascender will not help them to discriminate the letter. The presentation of h and other letters in pairs and groups, together with the feedback that they are *not* functionally equivalent, is the kind of information required for the visual system and brain to find out very quickly what the distinctive features really are.

ISSUES

Some of the major points of view about the physiological basis of letter recognition have been discussed in this chapter. Whether physiological evidence—for example from eye-movement or brain-function studies—

should make any difference to how reading should be taught is a contentious question. Should learners be taught "feature recognition," for example, when the status of features is hypothetical and everyone who has learned to read in the past has done so without such specialized knowledge? This is part of a general issue which comes up constantly in this book though frequently taken for granted elsewhere, whether *descriptions* of what readers do (or are hypothesized to do) should be the basis of what learners are *taught*.

SUMMARY

A feature identification model is proposed for letter identification. **Feature lists** are established to permit the allocation of visual information to specific cognitive categories, in the present case for letters. Feature lists are **specifications** of what visual information has to be like in order to be allocated to a particular category. The names of letters (and their relationships to sounds) are part of the interrelations among categories; they are not directly associated with particular visual configurations. To permit the identification of the same letter when it has different configurations, for example, A, *A*, and *a*, **functionally equivalent** feature lists are established. For each feature list there will be a number of alternative **criterial sets** to permit identification decisions on a minimum of visual information, depending on the number and nature of the alternatives.

Notes to Chapter 6 begin on page 261, covering
Recognition versus identification
Theories of pattern recognition
Making letter identification easier

7 Word Identification

The first chapter specifically concerned with reading was devoted to letter identification. In the present chapter, I shall show that word identification does not require the prior identification of letters. The chapter is restricted to considering individual or unrelated words in isolation, where there is no extrinsic clue to their identity. I am still not focusing on anything that might normally be regarded as *reading*, where a meaningful purpose and context are involved. But the chapter is another step toward a demonstration that procedures permitting the visual identification of words without the prior identification of letters also permit comprehension without the prior identification of words.

THREE THEORIES OF WORD IDENTIFICATION

There are three broad classes of theory about word identification: *whole-word identification*, *letter-by-letter identification*, and an intermediate position involving the identification of letter clusters, usually termed *spelling patterns*. In effect, these three views represent three attempts to describe the manner in which a skilled reader is able to identify words on sight. They are accounts of what a reader needs to know and do in order to be able to say what a word is. One or another of the three views is apparent in practically every approach to reading instruction.

Each of the traditional approaches to word recognition leaves more questions unanswered than it resolves. Nevertheless, each contains a kernel of truth about reading, otherwise it could not have survived to achieve a place in the folklore of the subject. In the following paragraphs, I look a little more closely at which aspects of reading each theory appears particularly competent to illuminate and which aspects it leaves in the dark.

The whole-word view is based on the premise that readers do not stop to identify individual letters (or groups of letters) in the identification of a word. The view asserts that knowledge of the alphabet and of the "sounds of letters" is irrelevant to reading. One source of support for the whole-word view has already been alluded to—the fact that a viewer can report from a single tachistoscopic presentation either four or five random letters or a similar number of words. Surely if a word can be identified as easily as a letter, then it must be just as much of a unit as a letter; a word must be recognizable as a whole, rather than as a sequence of letters. Another piece of supporting evidence is that words may be identified when none of their component letters is clearly discriminable. For example, a name may be identifiable on a distant roadside sign, or in a dim light, under conditions that would make each individual letter of that name quite illegible if presented separately. If words can be read when letters are illegible, how can word recognition depend on letter identification? Finally, there is a good deal of evidence that words can be identified as quickly as letters. It has been shown that perception is far from instantaneous and that successively presented random letters—or random words—cannot be identified faster than five or six a second (Kolers & Katzman, 1966; Newman, 1966). And if entire words can be identified as quickly as letters, how can their identification involve spelling them out letter by letter?

So much for some of the arguments in support of the whole-word point of view; now we can give equal time to the counterposition that, as a theory, it is most inadequate. One fundamental objection is that the view is not a theory at all; it has no "explanatory power" but merely rephrases the question that it pretends to answer. If words are recognized "as wholes," how are the wholes recognized? What do readers look for, and in what way is their prior knowledge of what a word looks like stored? It is no answer to say they have already learned what every word looks like, because that is the basic question: What exactly do readers know if they know what a word looks like? The qualification that words are identified "by their shapes" merely changes the name of the problem from "word identification" to "shape identification." Fluent readers are able to recognize at least 50,000 different words on sight (see Notes)—by what I shall call *immediate word identification*. Does that mean that readers have pictures of 50,000 different shapes stored in their minds and that for every word they encounter in reading they rummage through a pack of 50,000 templates in order to find a match? In what way would they sort through 50,000 alternatives? Surely not by starting at the beginning and examining each internal representation until they find a match. If we are looking for a book in a library, we do not start at the entrance and examine every volume until we come across the one with a title that matches the title we are looking for. Instead we make use of the fact that books are categorized and shelved in a predictable way; there are shortcuts for getting to the book we want. It would appear reasonable that we make use of shortcuts to make our word identification decisions quickly. We can usually find some explanation for any error that we make. We may misread *said* as *sail* or *send* (or even as *reported* in circumstances where the substitution would make sense), but never as *elephant* or *plug* or *predisposition*. In other words, we obviously do not select a word from 50,000 alternatives, but rather from a much smaller number. An unelaborated whole-word point of view cannot account for this prior elimination of alternatives.

Besides, we have already discovered that 50,000 internal representations of shapes would be far from adequate to enable us to identify 50,000 different words. Even if we could identify *HAT* by looking up an internal representation, how could the same representation enable us to identify *hat* or *hat* or any of the many other ways in which the word may be written?

The letter-by-letter theory, which the whole-word view is supposed to demolish, itself appears to have quite substantial evidence in its favor. Readers are frequently sensitive to individual letters in the identification of words. The whole-word point of view would suggest that if viewers were presented with the stimulus *fashixn* tachistoscopically, they would either identify "the whole word" without noticing the *x* or else fail to recognize the word at all because there would be no "match" with an internal representation. Instead, viewers typically identify the word but report that there is something wrong with it, not necessarily reporting that there is an *x* instead of an *o*, but offering such explanations as "There's a hair lying over the end of it"—an observation first made a century ago (Pillsbury, 1897).

Furthermore, readers are very sensitive to the *predictability* of letter sequences. Letters do not occur haphazardly in any language; in English, for example, combinations like *th, st, br,* and almost any consonant and vowel pair are more likely to occur than combinations like *tf, sr, bm, ae,* or *uo.* The knowledge that readers acquire about these differing probabilities of letter combinations is demonstrated when words containing common letter sequences are more easily identified than those with uncommon sequences. Readers can identify sequences of letters that are *not* English words just as easily as some English words, provided the sequences are "close approximations" to English—which means that they are highly probable letter combinations (Miller, Bruner, & Postman, 1954). The average reader, for example, hardly falters when presented with sequences like *vernalit* or *mossiant* or *ricaning*—yet how could these be identified "as wholes" when they have never been seen before? A letter-by-letter view might also seem to be somewhat more economical; instead of learning to recognize 50,000 words, one learns to recognize 26 letters and applies a few spelling rules, decoding every word on the spot.

A rather illogical argument is sometimes proposed to support the letter-by-letter view: Because letters in some way spell out the sound of a word,

word identification *must* be accomplished by identification of the individual letters. It would be about as compelling to suggest that we must recognize models of cars by reading the manufacturer's name on the back, simply because the name is always there to be read. Besides, the spelling of words is not a reliable guide to their sound. This question is so complex that "phonics" is given the next chapter to itself. For the moment we are not concerned with whether knowledge of letters can be used to identify words, but rather whether skilled readers normally and necessarily identify words "that they know" by a letter-by-letter analysis.

The intermediate position—that words are identified through the recognition of *clusters of letters*—has the advantage of being able to account for the relatively easy identifiability of nonwords such as *vernalit*. It argues that readers become familiar with spelling patterns, such as *ve* and *rn* and even *vern*, which are recognized and put together to form words. The larger the spelling patterns we can recognize, the easier the word identification, according to this view. The view is compatible with our normal experience that when a new word like *zygotic* or *Helsingfors* halts our reading temporarily we do not seem to break it down to the individual letters before trying to put together what its sound must be. But many of the arguments that favor the whole-word position over letter analysis also work against the letter-cluster view. It may be useful, occasionally, to work out what a word is by analysis of letters or syllables, but normal reading does not appear to proceed on this basis; in fact, it would seem impossible. There is no time to "work out" what words are by synthesizing possible sound combinations. Besides, as the letter-cluster argument is pushed to its extreme it becomes a whole-word approach because the largest and most reliable spelling patterns are words themselves.

The fact that the three traditional theories of word recognition continue to enjoy a wide acceptance obviously indicates that they rest on a fairly solid foundation of data, despite their shortcomings. No one can conclusively prove them wrong. Each approach, however, has inadequacies that are partly met by an alternative view, which would suggest that they are not mutually exclusive and that no one of them has any real claim to be the closest representation of the truth. In their place we need to find a theory of reading that will not be incompatible with any of the data but that will also offer an explanation for inadequate aspects of the three traditional views. In short, any serious attempt to understand reading must be able to explain why it might sometimes appear that words are identified as wholes and at other times through the identification of component letters or groups of letters.

A Feature-Analytic Alternative

There is another point of view that would appear to overcome the major weaknesses of the three traditional theories without being incompatible with any of the evidence in their favor. Such a theory proposes that words are indeed identified "as wholes," but that the manner of their identification involves precisely the same procedures as the identification of letters and in fact makes use of the same kind of visual information.

In the previous chapter, two models for letter identification were examined: feature analysis and template matching. The traditional whole-word theory that words are identified because of the familiarity of their "shape" is essentially a template-matching model, and arguments for its inadequacy have already been presented. The remainder of the present chapter considers the alternative, a feature-analytic model for word identification. It should be reiterated that the present chapter is concerned only with the identification of individual words in isolation, or effectively so because context is ignored. The identification of words in meaningful sequences, which is of course more representative of most reading situations, is considered in Chapter 9.

Basically, the feature-analytic model proposes that the only difference between the manner in which letters and words are identified lies in the complexity of the categories and feature lists that the perceiver employs in the analysis of visual information. The difference depends on whether the reader is looking for letters or for words; the process of looking and deciding is the same. If the reader's objective is to identify letters, then the analysis of the visual configuration is carried out with respect to the feature lists associated with the 26 letter categories, one for each letter of the alphabet. If the objective is to identify words, then there is a similar analysis of features in the visual configuration with respect to the feature lists, or specifications, of a larger number of word categories.

What are the features of words? They obviously must include the features of letters, because words are made up of letters. The arrays of marks on the printed page that can be read as words can also be distinguished as sequences of letters, so the "distinctive features" of letters that constitute a significant difference between one configuration and another must also be distinctive features of words. For example, whatever visual information permits us to distinguish between *h* and *n* must also permit us to distinguish between *hot* and *not*. And precisely the same procedures that distinguish between *h* and *n* will accomplish the discrimination between *hot* and *not*. At first glance, many more discriminations and analyses of distinctive features would appear to be required to distinguish among tens of thousands of alternative words compared with only 26 alternative letters, but we shall see that the difference is not so great. In fact, no more information—no more featural tests—may be required to identify a word in meaningful text than to identify a single letter in isolation.

If the distinctive features of the visual configurations of letters are the same as those for the visual configurations of written words, it might be expected that feature lists for letter and word categories would be similar. However, feature lists for word categories require an additional dimension to those for letters—the analysis of word configurations involves the position of features within a sequence. The number of "positions" in a word feature list reflects the number of times a particular feature could occur in the sequence of letters that constitute the word and obviously corresponds to the number of letters. A feature test that will be applied only once for the identification of a letter may be employed several times in the identification of a word, the maximum number of tests equaling the number of letters in the word. This congruence between "position" and "letter" occurs because the distinctive features of individual letters become the distributed distinctive features of words. But it does not follow that individual letters must be identified in order for words to be identified. I therefore use the term "position" rather than "letter" to avoid any implication that a word is identified from its letters, rather than by the distribution of features across its entire configuration.

There could be a few distinctive features of words that are not features of letters, for example, the total width of the word configuration and—if the word is in lower case—the relative heights of different parts. Many words in context can be identified by their contours (Haber & Haber, 1981; Haber, Haber, & Furlin, 1983). But as I have already noted, not enough is known of the visual system to assert what distinctive features actually are.

The feature-analytic view of letter identification proposes that because there is redundancy in the structure of letters—because there is more than enough featural information to distinguish among 26 alternatives—not all features need to be discriminated for a letter to be identified. Therefore, a number of alternative criterial sets of features may exist within each feature list, information about the features within any set being sufficient for an identification to be made. It would be expected that criterial sets could also exist for words to be identified, except that now they would extend over the second dimension and take into account feature combinations across the entire word. As I explained in Chapter 6 and its Notes, five or six features would be adequate to identify any letter, though there are doubtless more. That means that words, with an average length of about 5 letters, must consist of at least 25 distinctive features. The actual uncertainty of words in isolation (see Page 252) requires only half that number (and only about a quarter for words in context).

Redundancy Among Distinctive Features of Words

With experience of reading, fluent readers acquire wide knowledge about the way in which letters are grouped into words, for example that *th* and *sp* are frequent combinations and that *tf* and *sr* are not. This knowledge of the way words are spelled, or *orthographic information*, is an alternative nonvisual source of information to the *featural* or *nonvisual* information available to the eyes from the page. To the extent that both of these sources of information reduce the number of alternative ways in which a written or printed word might be constructed, there is redundancy. The duplication of information resulting from orthographic predictability is a form of *sequential redundancy*, because its source lies in the fact that the different parts of a word are not independent; the occurrence of particular alternatives in one part of the sequence of letters limits the range of alternatives that can occur anywhere else in the sequence.

The orthographic redundancy of English is enormous. If all 26 letters of the alphabet could occur without restriction in each position of a five-letter word, there could be nearly 12 million different five-letter words, compared with perhaps 10,000 that actually exist. An alphabet of seven letters would be sufficient to make 10,000 five-letter words distinguishable.

I have been referring to the sequential constraints that one letter places on the occurrence of other letters in a word. But precisely the same argument can apply to features. Obviously, if we can say that the occurrence of the letter *T* in the first position of a word restricts the possibilities for the second position to *H, R, A, E, I, O, U*, and *Y*, then we can also say that the occurrence of the features of the letter *T* restricts the possible features that can occur in the second position. In fact, we can avoid mentioning letters and specific positions altogether and say that when certain features occur in one part of a word, there are limits to the kinds of feature combinations in other parts of the word and to what the word as a whole might be. A reader implicitly knowledgeable about such limitations is able to make use of *sequential redundancy among features*, and as a result will be able to identify words with so little visual information that the identification of letters is completely bypassed. (In the same way, we are able to identify a particular make of automobile at a glance without identifying individual components, yet these "make up" the car.)

The enormous visual redundancy of written words has three consequences, all verifiable experimentally:

1. Words may be identified from as little visual information as one or two letters in isolation.
2. Words may be identified before any of their individual letters can be individually identified (and even with some letters missing).
3. Letters in words may be identified before the same letters could be discriminated in isolation.

The visual identification of words becomes very fast and efficient. Fraisse (1984) observed that experienced readers could often name written words like *house* and *tree* flashed on a screen quicker than they could name drawings of the referents of the same words, even though they had previously seen the full set of words and drawings they would be asked to identify.

To summarize, the difference between letter and word identification is simply the category system that is involved—the manner in which featural information is allocated. If the reader is examining an array of visual information in order to identify letters, the visual information will be tested and identifications made on the basis of the feature lists for the 26 categories. If the purpose is to identify words, the visual information will be tested with respect to the feature lists for words, and there will be no question of letter identification. It follows from the present argument that it should be impossible to identify a word and its component letters simultaneously, because one cannot use the same information to make two different kinds of decision.

Because letter and word identification involve the same featural information, it is not possible to identify a configuration both as a word and as a sequence of letters at the same time. We can see the configuration *cat* either as the letters *c, a, t* or as the word *cat*, but not as both simultaneously. Similarly, we can see the configuration *read* either as the word pronounced "reed" or as the word pronounced "red" but not as both at once; and *IO* can be seen either as numerals or as letters but not as both. We cannot apply the same information to two categories simultaneously, just as we cannot use the same contour as part of two figures simultaneously—we cannot see the vase and the faces of Figure 1.1 (Page 12) simultaneously.

LEARNING TO IDENTIFY WORDS

There are two aspects of learning to identify words which are analogous to the two aspects of learning to identify letters outlined at the end of the last chapter. One aspect is establishing criterial sets of functionally equivalent distinctive features for each category, the specifications for qualifying configurations, and the other is associating a name with a category. For letter identification, it was asserted that relating the name to the category was not a problem; children learn names for visual configurations all the time. In word identification, there may indeed be a problem in relating names to categories, not because children have particular difficulty in remembering the name for a category once they have found out what it is but in finding out what the name of a category is in the first place. When children are beginning to discover written language, helpful adults usually act as mediators by saying what the printed words are, leaving to the child the more complex task of discovering how to distinguish one word from another. Someone says to them "That word is 'cat'" or "This is how you write your name."

The process of finding out the name of a category may be termed *mediated word identification* and is the topic of the next chapter. Word identification must be *mediated* when a word cannot be identified on sight by allocation to a category through an existing feature list. By contrast, I refer to word identification as discussed in this chapter as *immediate word identification*. The term immediate is used not in the sense of instantaneous, which we know is not the case, but to mean not mediated, indicating that a word is identified directly from its features. The aspect of learning with which the remainder of this chapter is concerned is the establishment of appropriate visual feature lists for immediate word identification.

It will help if we consider a specific instance. A child is about to learn to recognize a particular written name, say *John*. The task confronting the child is to discover the rules for recognizing this event when it occurs again, which means finding out something about the configuration that will distinguish it from other configurations that should not be called "John." Assume that the child has already discovered that a reliable distinguishing characteristic for the configuration is not the color of the paper that it is printed on or the color of the ink, both of which may be reasonable cues for other types of identification but which will sooner or later prove to be inadequate for the allocation of visual information to word categories. Also assume that the child at this time is not confronted by *John* in a number of different type styles. The ability to name any or all of the letters of the alphabet has no direct relevance in immediate word identification, although there will be an obvious (although by no means essential) advantage for children if they have learned to distinguish even a few letters, without necessarily being able to name them, because they will have begun to acquire cues about the features that distinguish words.

That is the problem for the child, to discover cues that will distinguish *John* from other configurations. The child may decide that a good cue lies in the length of the word, or the two upright strokes, or the shape of the "fishhook" at the beginning. In selecting a cue that will be the basis for recognition of the word, a child will establish the first tentative distinctive features to be looked for in the future when testing whether to allocate a configuration to the category "John."

Exactly what the first distinctive feature will be depends on the other words from which the child tries to distinguish the configuration *John*. Until the child comes across another word that is not *John,* there is no problem; the child applies the single test and calls every configuration that passes the test *John*. But until the child comes across another word that is not *John*, there can be no learning. What brings a child to the beginning of the process of developing feature lists that will serve for reading is having to distinguish *John* from all the other configurations with which it is not functionally equivalent. The child will only really be able to identify *John* after learning not to apply that name to every other word configuration that is met. It is when the child is confronted by a configuration that should go into a different category that the soundness of the tentative discrimination is tested, and, of course, it is soon found to be wanting. If the hypothesized distinctive features were related to the length of the word, then the child would respond *John* to the configuration *Fred*. If the hypothesis involved the initial fishhook, the child would say "John" to *Jack,* or *June,* or *Jeremiah.* The more nonequivalent configurations—the more different words—children have to discriminate among, the more they will come to select as distinctive features those that will be appropriate to the eventual task of fluent reading. But until children can understand what they have to distinguish *John* from, they will never acquire an appropriate set of distinctive features for identifying that word.

The preceding statement does not mean that children must be able to *name* every other word they meet; not at all. All they have to do is see a representative sample of words that are not *John,* so that they can find out in what respects *John* is different. It does not matter if they cannot discriminate among all the other words (although in learning to identify *John* they will learn something about all other words); the beginning can be the establishment of only two categories: configurations that are *John* and configurations that are *not John.* Attempting to teach "one word at a time"—writing a word on a variety of different surfaces and occasions and insisting "This is *John;* this is *John*"—will not help children to learn the word because they will never learn how *John* may be distinguished from any other word. The notion that a child can learn to identify a word by the repetitious presentation of just that word is a template theory. But there is no way in which a child can transfer a picture of what is presented to the eyes into a storehouse in the brain. Children do not need to be told interminably what a word is; they have to be able to see what it is *not.*

Acquaintance with a wide variety of nonequivalent alternatives is everything. Through growing familiarity with the written form of language, children learn not only to discriminate distinctive features, to establish feature lists, and to recognize functional equivalences, they also learn about redundancy. And by acquiring a pool of knowledge about the redundancy of words, they learn to identify words economically, on minimal quantities of visual information; they establish large numbers of alternative criterial sets.

It is perhaps a sobering thought that just about everything that a child learns, as described in the preceding paragraph, is never explicitly taught. Among the many positive things reading teachers can do—providing relevant demonstrations, collaboration, and encouragement—they cannot include the provision of rules by which words are to be recognized. That part of learning must be left to the children themselves.

A POSTSCRIPT ABOUT WORDS

One of the inevitable consequences of examining closely a subject like reading, about which so much is taken for granted, is that it turns out to be far more complicated and less well understood than we thought it to be. An obvious first step in my discussion of word identification might have been to state clearly and precisely how many words the average fluent reader knows. This would give some useful knowledge about the dimensions of the problem. But the trouble with a simple request for a count of the words that a person knows is that the answer depends on what is meant by "word," and that in any case there is no way to compute a reliable answer.

Consider first the matter of deciding what we want to call a word. Should *cat* and *cats* or *walk* and *walked* be regarded as two different words or as two forms of the same word? Dictionaries usually provide entries only for the base or root form of words, refusing to count as different words such variations as plurals, comparatives, adjectival forms, and various verb tenses. If we want to call *cat* and *cats* or *walk* and *walked* different words (and certainly we would not regard them as functionally equivalent visually), the number of words we know on sight might turn out to be three or four times greater than the number of words the dictionary-maker would credit us with. Furthermore, common words have many meanings as in "You can *bank* on the *bank* by the river *bank*." But if the same spelling is to be regarded as (at least) three different words because *bank* has several meanings, should a preposition like *by*, which has so many different senses, be counted as 40 words or more?

The next problem is to count. Obviously, it is not good enough simply to count the number of words that a person reads or hears or produces during the course of a day, for many words will be used more than once and others will occur not at all. To count the number of *different* words a person produces, we have to examine a torrent of very familiar words. But in how big a torrent shall we look? How can we ever be certain that we have given sufficient opportunity for all the words a person knows? Without a doubt, we shall find some new words in every additional sample of a thousand that we record, but surely a law of decreasing returns would apply. After analyzing, say, 100,000 words from one person, it would seem unlikely that many new ones would be produced. But such is not the case. Very many words with which we are quite familiar occur less than once in every million, and it may take anywhere from two months to two years for a person to produce that number of words. One very extensive analysis of nearly 5 million word occurrences in popular magazines (Thorndike & Lorge, 1944) found over 3,000 words that occurred an average of less than once in every million, and almost all of these words would fall under our category of known. Here is a sample of words that occurred only once in every 5 million words: *earthiness, echelon, echidna, eclair, effluence, egad, egotistic.* One or two may be a little unusual, but by and large they are words that we can recognize.

There is something a little eerie even to think about how we might acquire and retain familiarity with the relatively infrequent words. We meet them perhaps once a year, but it is not often we have to stop and wonder "Haven't

I seen you before somewhere?" Obviously, it is not possible to count how many different words a person knows, so one has to make an estimate. And many estimates have been offered, varying from 50,000 to over 800,000, depending on the definitions used and assumptions made. This gives one good answer to the question of how many words a person might know—it is impossible to say.

When is a Word Not a Word?

Researchers who use experimental procedures in what they call reading studies frequently claim that their test materials are meaningful because they consist of lists or sequences of words that appear in dictionaries, in contrast to nonword sequences of letters like *ricaning, vernalit, msk,* or *wbc.* It may be difficult to see why strings of letters that have no relevance to readers should be regarded as meaningful, even if the letters do happen to form words. A spoken word produced without expressive or communicative intent is simply noise, and there is little reason to regard a similarly produced written word as anything different.

ISSUES

There is lively technical speculation about the neurological processes assumed to underlie the identification of written words, presumably no different from the processes underlying our remarkably efficient facility for recognizing faces, places, dogs, cats, and innumerable other objects, and no better understood. The study of word identification is often confounded by the question of whether it is necessary to say a written word to oneself—to "decode" (or "recode") it—in order to understand it. Obviously we do not need to say to ourselves that an animal that suddenly confronts us is a dog in order to understand that it is a dog; rather the wordless identification of "dogness" must precede the naming. Why then should we have to say that the written word *dog* is pronounced "dog" in order to understand it in a story? The relationship between the sounds of speech and the visual representations of written words is one of the most contentious issues in reading theory and research.

SUMMARY

Words, like letters, can be identified directly from the distinctive features that are the visual information of print. **Immediate word identification** takes place when feature analysis allocates a visual configuration to the **feature list** of a word category in cognitive structure, without the intermediate step of letter identification. **Criterial sets** of features within **functionally equivalent** feature lists permit the identification of words on minimal information, for example, when the reader can employ prior knowledge of the **orthographic redundancy** within words.

Notes to Chapter 7 begin on page 263, covering
Letter identification in words
Use of redundancy by children
Distributional redundancy among words

8 Phonics and Mediated Word Identification

The preceding chapter was concerned with *immediate* word identification, and the manner in which visual feature lists are established and used so that words can be recognized on sight, without "decoding to sound" or any other means of *mediated* word identification. In fact, the previous chapter argued that letter-by-letter identification is unnecessary and even impossible for word identification in normal reading, thus leaving no room for decoding to sound. Immediate word identification is illustrated in Figure 8.1.

But in the preceding chapter, I was talking about the identification of words where the "name" of the word—its pronunciation when read aloud—is either known to the reader or otherwise available to the learner. The learner does not need to figure out what the visual configuration "says," but only how it should be recognized on future occasions. This situation was compared with the cat-and-dog learning problem where the child is told that a particular animal is a cat and then left to discover how to recognize one another time.

Suppose, however, that the name of a word is not immediately available to the learner—that there is no one to identify an unfamiliar word, and there are

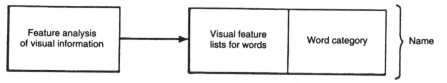

FIG. 8.1. Immediate word identification.

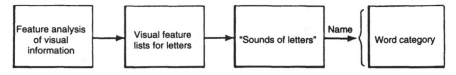

FIG. 8.2.   Mediated word identification: The phonic model.

no context cues, perhaps because the word is seen in isolation or as part of a list of unrelated words. Now the learner has a double problem, not only to discover how to recognize the word in the future but to find out what the word is in the first place. This is like trying to discover how to distinguish cats and dogs without being told whether particular animals *are* cats or dogs. In such a situation in reading, a word obviously cannot be identified *immediately*; its identification must be *mediated* by some other means of discovering what it is. The present chapter is about the use of *phonics*—a set of relationships between letters and sounds—and other methods of mediated word identification. The use of phonic rules to mediate word identification is illustrated in Figure 8.2.

In particular, this chapter examines the extent to which knowledge of the sounds associated with letters of the alphabet helps in the identification of words. For many, this process of decoding the spelling of words to their sounds is the basis of reading, a view that I do not think is tenable. It is not necessary and sometimes impossible to "say" what a written word is before we can comprehend its meaning; the naming of a word normally occurs after the identification of its meaning.

This chapter is still not the whole story of reading, even as far as words are concerned. In both the preceding and the present chapters, the assumption is made that the word a reader is trying to identify already exists in the reader's spoken language vocabulary; its meaning is known. The reader's problem is to identify the word, to discover or recognize its "name," not to learn its meaning. The next chapter deals with the situation of words that are truly new, where the meaning must be discovered as well as the name or pronunciation.

THE AIMS AND COMPLEXITY OF PHONICS

Mediated word identification is not the most critical part of reading, and phonics is not the only strategy available for mediated word identification. Nevertheless, phonics frequently plays a central role in reading instruction, and it will clear the air if we examine the nature and efficacy of phonics first of all.

Rules and Exceptions

The aim of phonics instruction is to provide readers with rules that will enable them to predict how a written word will sound from the way it is spelled. The value of teaching phonics depends on how many correspondences there are between the letters and sounds of English. A correspondence exists whenever a particular letter (or sometimes a group of letters) represents a particular sound (or absence of sound). Thus *c* is involved in at least four correspondences—with the sound /s/ as in *city*, with /k/ as in *medical*, as part of /ch/ as in *much*, and with no sound at all as in *scientist*. Alternatively, a correspondence exists whenever a particular sound is represented by a particular letter or letters, as /f/ can be represented by *f*, *ph*, and *gh*. Thus, the total number of "spelling-to-sound" correspondences must be the same as the total number of "sound-to-spelling" correspondences. But by now it is probably no surprise that any question related to language involving a simple "how many" leads to a very complicated and unsatisfactory evasion of an answer. Phonics is no exception.

The first problem concerns our expectations about rules. If we expect a rule to mean a correspondence that has no exceptions, then we will have a difficult task finding any rules in phonics at all. Here is a phonic rule that would appear to have impeccable credentials: Final *e* following a single consonant indicates that the preceding vowel should be long, as in *hat* and *hate* or *hop* and *hope*. And here are two instant exceptions: *axe* has a single consonant but a short /a/, while *ache* has a double consonant but a long /a/. We have the choice of admitting that a familiar rule is not impervious to exceptions, or else we have to make a rule for the exceptions. One explanation that might be offered is that *x* is really a double consonant, *ks*, and that *ch* is really a single consonant, *k*. But then we are in the rather peculiar position of changing the notion of what constitutes a single letter simply because we have a rule that does not fit all cases. And if we have to say that the definition of what constitutes a letter depends on the pronunciation of a word, how can we say the pronunciation of a word can be predicted from its letters? Besides, what can we say about the silent *e* at the end of *have* or *love*, which is put there only because there is a convention that English words may not end with a *v*? Or the *e* at the end of *house*, which is to indicate that the word is not a plural? Or the *o* in *money* and *women*, which is there because early printers felt that a succession of up-and-down strokes, like *mun* and *wim*, would be too difficult to decipher?

Having made the point that phonic rules will have exceptions, the next problem is to decide what constitutes an exception. Some exceptions occur so frequently and regularly that they would appear to be rules in their own right. It is quite arbitrary how anyone decides to draw the line between rules and exceptions. We have a choice of saying that the sounds of written English can be predicted by relatively few rules, although there will be quite a lot of exceptions, or by a large number of rules with relatively few exceptions. Indeed, if we care to say that some rules have only one application, for example, that *acht* is pronounced /ot/ as in "*yacht,*" then we can describe English completely in terms of rules simply because we have legislated exceptions out of existence.

If the concept of a rule seems somewhat arbitrary, the notion of what constitutes a letter is even more idiosyncratic. It is true that in one sense there can be no doubt about what a letter is—it is one of the 26 characters in the alphabet—but any attempt to construct rules of spelling-sound correspondence is doomed if we restrict our terms of reference to individual letters. To start with, there are only 26 letters compared with about 40 different sounds of speech, so many letters at least must do double duty. We find, of course, that many letters stand for more than one sound, while many sounds are represented by more than one letter. However, many sounds are not represented by single letters at all—*th, ch, ou, ue,* for example—so that we have to consider some combinations of letters as quite distinct *spelling units*—rather as if *th* were a letter in its own right (as it is in Greek, in two different forms for two different pronunciations). It has been asserted, with the help of a computer analysis of over 20,000 words (Venezky, 1967, 1970), that there are 52 "major spelling units" in English, 32 for consonants and 20 for vowels, effectively doubling the size of the alphabet.

The addition of all these extra spelling units, however, does not seem to make the structure of the English writing system very much more orderly. Some of the original letters of the alphabet are quite superfluous. There is nothing that *c* or *q* or *x* can do that could not be done by the other consonants. And many of the additional spelling units that are recognized simply duplicate the work of single letters, such as *ph* for *f* and *dg* for *j*. There are also compound vowels whose effect duplicates the silent final *e*, like *ea* in *meat* compared with *mete*. Some combinations of letters have a special value only when they occur in particular parts of a word—*gh* may be pronounced as *f* (or as nothing) at the end of a word *(rough, through)* but is pronounced just like a single *g* at the beginning *(ghost, ghastly)*. Often letters have only a relational function, sacrificing any sound of their own in order to indicate how another letter should be sounded. An obvious example is the silent *e*, another is the *u* that distinguishes the *g* in *guest* from the *g* in *gem*.

So for our basic question of phonics, what we are really asking is how many arbitrarily defined rules can account for an indeterminate number of correspondences between an indefinite set of spelling units and an uncertain number of sounds (the total and quality of which may vary from dialect to dialect).

Some aspects of spelling are simply unpredictable, certainly to a reader with a limited knowledge of word derivations, no matter how one tries to define a spelling unit. An example of a completely unpredictable spelling-to-sound correspondence is *th*, which is pronounced in one way at the beginning of words like *this, than, those, them, then, these* but in another way at the beginning of *think, thank, thatch, thong, theme,* and so on. There is only one way for a learner to tell whether *th* should be pronounced as in /this/ or as in /think/, and that is to identify the word first. On the other hand, in many dialects there is no difference between the sounds represented by *w* and *wh*, as in *witch* and *which*, so that in some cases it can be the spelling that is not predictable, not the sound. Almost all common words are exceptions—*of* requires a rule of its own for the pronunciation of *f*, and *was* for the pronunciation of *as*.

The game of finding exceptions is too easy to play. I give only one more example to illustrate the kind of difficulty one must encounter in trying to construct—or to teach—reliable rules of phonic correspondence. How are the letters *ho* pronounced, when they occur at the beginning of a word? Here are 11 possible answers; all, you will notice, quite common words: *hope, hot, hoot, hook, hour, honest, house, honey, hoist, horse, horizon.*

Of course, there are rules (or are some of them merely exceptions?) that can account for many of the pronunciations of *ho*. But there is one very significant implication in all these examples that applies to almost all English words—in order to apply phonic rules, *words must be read from right to left.* The way in which the reader pronounces *ho* depends on what comes after it, and the same applies to the *p* in *ph*, the *a* in *ate*, the *k* in *knot*, the *t* in *-tion*. The exceptions are very few, like *asp* and *ash* which are pronounced differently if preceded by a *w*, and like *f*, sometimes pronounced /v/ if preceded by *o*. The fact that sound "dependencies" in words run from right to left is an obvious difficulty for a beginning reader trying to sound out a word from left to right, or for a theorist who wants to maintain that words are identified on a left-to-right basis.

In summary, English is far from predictable as far as its spelling-sound relationships are concerned. Just how much can be done to predict the pronunciation of a relatively small number of common words with a finite number of rules we see later. But before this catalog of complications and exceptions is concluded, two points should be reiterated. The first point is that phonic rules can only be considered as probabilistic, as guides to the way words might be pronounced, and that there is rarely any indication of when a rule does or does not apply. The rule that specifies how to pronounce *ph* in *telephone* falls down in the face of *haphazard* or *shepherd*. The rule for *oe* in *doe* and *woe* will not work for *shoe*. The only way to distinguish the pronunciation of *sh* in *bishop* and *mishap*, or *th* in *father* and *fathead*, is to know the entire word in advance. The probability of being wrong if you do not know a word at all is very high. Even if individual rules were likely to be right three times out of four, there would still be only one chance in three of avoiding error in a four-letter word.

The second point is that *phonic rules look deceptively simple when you know what a word is in the first place.* I do not intend to be facetious. Teachers often feel convinced that phonic rules work because letter-sound correspondences seem obvious if a word is known in advance; the alternatives are not considered. And children may seem to apply phonic rules when they can recognize a word in any case—or because the teacher also suggests what the word is—thereby enabling them to identify or recite the phonic correspondences that happen to be appropriate.

The Efficiency of Phonics

One systematic attempt to construct a workable set of phonic rules for English was made by Berdiansky, Cronnell, and Koehler (1969). The effort had modest aims—to see how far one could go in establishing a set of correspondence rules for the 6,092 one- and two-syllable words among 9,000 different words in the comprehension vocabularies of 6- to 9-year-old children. (The remaining words, nearly one-third of the children's vocabularies, were all three or more syllables, adding too much complexity to the phonic analysis.) The words were all taken from books to which the children were normally exposed—they were the words that the children knew and ought to be able to identify if they were to be able to read the material with which they were confronted at school.

The researchers who analyzed the 6,092 words found rather more than the 52 "major spelling units" to which I have already referred—they identified 69 "grapheme units" that had to be separately distinguished in their rules. A group of letters was called a *grapheme unit*, just like a single letter, whenever its relationship to a sound could not be accounted for by any rules for single letters. Grapheme units included pairs of consonants such as *ch*, *th*; pairs of vowels such as *ea, oy*; and letters that commonly function together, such as *ck* and *qu*, as well as double consonants like *bb* and *tt*, all of which require some separate phonic explanation. The number of grapheme units should not surprise us. The previously mentioned 52 major units were not intended to represent the only spelling units that could occur but only the most frequent ones.

An arbitrary decision was made about what would constitute a rule: It would have to account for a spelling-sound correspondence occurring in at least 10 different words. Any distinctive spelling-sound correspondence and any grapheme unit that did not occur in at least 10 words was considered an "exception." Actually, the researchers made several exceptions among the exceptions. They wanted their rules to account for as many of their words as possible, and so they let several cases through the net when it seemed to them more appropriate to account for a grapheme unit with a rule rather than to stigmatize it as an exception.

The researchers discovered that their 6,000 words involved 211 distinct spelling-sound correspondences. This does not mean that 211 different sounds were represented, any more than there were 211 different grapheme units, but rather that the 69 grapheme units were related to 38 sounds in a total of 211 different ways. The results are summarized in Table 8.1.

Eighty-three of the correspondences involved consonant grapheme units, and 128 involved vowel grapheme units, including no fewer than 79 that were associated with the six "primary" single-letter vowels, *a, e, i, o, u, y.* In other words, there was a total of 79 different ways in which single vowels could be pronounced. Of the 211 correspondences, 45 were classified as exceptions, about half involving vowels and half consonants. The exclusion of 45 correspondences meant that about 10 percent of the 6,092 words had to be set aside as "exceptions."

The pronunciation of the remaining words was accounted for by a grand total of 166 rules. Sixty of these rules were concerned with the pronunciation of consonants (which are generally thought to have fairly "regular" pronunciations) and 106 with single or complex vowels.

The research that has just been outlined is important in a number of ways for understanding reading and the teaching of reading. Some conclusions that can be drawn are far-reaching in their implications. The first is very simply that phonics is complicated. Without saying anything at all about whether it is desirable to teach young children a knowledge of phonics, we now have an idea of the magnitude of the endeavor. We now know that if we really expect to give children a mastery of phonics, then we are not talking about a dozen or so rules. We are talking about 166 rules, which will still not account for hundreds of the words they might expect to meet in their early reading.

It is obvious that the most that can be expected from a knowledge of phonic rules is that they may provide a *clue* to the sound (or "name") of a configu-

TABLE 8.1.
Spelling-Sound Correspondences Among 6,092 One- and Two-Syllable Words in the Vocabularies of Nine-Year-Old Children

	Consonants	Primary Vowels	Secondary Vowels	Total
Spelling-sound correspondences	83	79	49	211
"Rules"	60	73	33	166
"Exceptions"	23	6	16	45
Grapheme units in rules	41	6	19	69

ration being examined. Phonics can provide only approximations. Even if readers do happen to know the 73 rules for the pronunciation of the six vowels, they would still have no sure way of telling which rule applies—or even that they were not dealing with an exception.

There is still one issue to be considered concerning the *effectiveness* of phonics. Is the limited degree of efficiency that might be attained worth acquiring? Other factors have to be taken into account related to the *cost* of trying to learn and use phonic rules. There is the possibility that reliance on phonics will involve readers in so much delay that short-term memory will be overloaded, and they will lose the sense of what they are reading. A tendency to rely exclusively on phonic rules may create a handicap for beginning readers whose biggest problem is to develop speed in reading. Our working memories do not have an infinite capacity, and reading is not a task that can be accomplished at too leisurely a pace. Other sources of information exist for finding out what a word in context might be, especially if the word is in the spoken vocabulary of the reader.

The Cost of "Reform"

The involved relation between the spelling of words and their sound has led to frequent suggestions for modifying the alphabet or for rationalizing the spelling system. These intentions share the same misconceptions and difficulties. A number of contemporary linguists would deny that there is anything wrong with the way most words are spelled; they argue that a good deal of information would be lost if spelling were changed. Most of the apparent inconsistencies in spelling have some historical basis; the spelling system may be complex, but it is not arbitrary—it has become what it is for quite systematic reasons. And because spelling is systematic and reflects something of the history of words, much more information is available to the reader than we normally realize. (The fact that we are not *aware* that this information is available does not mean that we do not use it; we have already seen a number of examples of the way in which we have and use a knowledge of the structure and redundancy of our language that we cannot put into words.)

Spelling reform might seem to make words easier to pronounce, but only at the cost of other information about the way words are related to each other, so that rationalizing words at the phonological level might make reading more difficult at syntactic and semantic levels. As just one example, consider the "silent *b*" in words like *bomb, bombing, bombed,* which would be an almost certain candidate for extinction if spelling reformers had their way. But the *b* is something more than a pointless appendage; it relates the previous words to others like *bombard, bombardier, bombardment* where the *b* is pronounced. And if you save yourself the trouble of a special rule about why *b* is silent in words like *bomb*, at another level there would be a new problem of explaining why *b* suddenly appears in words like *bombard*. Remove the *g* from *sign* and you must explain where it comes from in *signature*.

Another argument in favor of the present spelling system is that it is the most competent one to handle different dialects, a matter relevant also to those who would want to change the alphabet. Although there is almost universal acceptance of the idea that words should be spelled in the same way by everyone, we do not all pronounce words in the same way. If the spelling of words is to be changed so that they reflect the way they are pronounced, whose dialect will provide the standard? Is a different letter required for every different sound produced in any dialect of English we might encounter? Phonics instruction becomes even more complicated when it is realized that in many classrooms teacher and students do not speak the same dialect and that both may speak a different dialect from the authorities who suggested the particular phonic rules they are trying to follow. The teacher who tries to make children understand a phonic difference between the pronunciation of *caught* and *cot* will have a communication problem if this distinction is not one that the children observe in their own speech. The teacher may not even pronounce the two words differently, so that although the teacher thinks the message to the child is "That word is not *cot*; it is *caught*," the message coming across is "That word is not *cot*; it is *cot*."

Spelling and Meaning

The manner in which words are spelled in English is seen as a problem primarily if reading is perceived as a matter of decoding words to sound, which it is not and could not be, and if the primary function of spelling is regarded as the representation of *sounds* of words. But spelling also represents meaning, and where there is a conflict between pronunciation and meaning it is usually meaning which prevails, as if even the spelling system of written language recognized the priority of meaning. For example, the plural represented by a simple *s* in written language may be pronounced in three different ways in speech—as the /s/ sound on the end of *cats*, the /z/ sound on the end of *dogs*, and the /iz/ sound on the end of *judges*. Would writing be easier to read if the past tense of verbs were not indicated by a consistent *-ed* but rather reflected the pronunciation, so that we had such variations as *walkt* and *landid*? The reason that *medicine* and *medical* are spelled as they are is not because *c* is sometimes arbitrarily pronounced /s/ and sometimes /k/ but because the two words have the same root meaning, represented by *medic*. This commonality of meaning would be lost if the two words were spelled *medisin* and *medikal*. It should be noted, incidentally, that the consistent representation of the various pronunciations of the plural meaning by *s* or the past tense meaning by *-ed* rarely causes difficulty to readers, even beginners, provided they are reading for sense. It is not necessary for teachers to instruct children that *-ed* is often pronounced /t/ (among other things). If a child understands a word, the pronunciation will take care of itself, but the effort to produce pronunciation as a prerequisite for meaning is likely to result in neither being achieved.

Of course, spelling is a problem, both in school and out, but it is a problem of *writing*, not of reading. Knowing how to spell does not make a good reader because reading is not accomplished by the decoding of spelling. Good readers are not necessarily good spellers; we can all read words that we cannot spell. I am not saying that knowledge of spelling is unimportant, only that it has a minimal role in reading, and that undue concern with the way in which words are spelled can only interfere with a child's learning to read.

There is a frequent argument that if spelling and decoding to sound are as irrelevant to reading as the preceding analyses indicate, why should we have an alphabetic written language at all? My view is that the alphabetic system is more of a help to the writer than to the reader. For a variety of reasons, including the memory load required to reproduce every word legibly in all its featural detail, writing is a much harder skill to learn and to practice than reading, at least if the writer is to be conventionally "correct" with respect to such matters as grammar, punctuation, neatness, and so forth. Spelling may be complicated for writers (especially if they have not been taught how spelling reflects meaning as well as sound), but it still makes writing much easier than if writers had to remember and reproduce thousands and thousands of nonalphabetic ideographic forms, like writers of Chinese.

A greatly underestimated benefit of alphabetic writing is that it enables readers and writers (and teachers) to *talk about* words. Instead of asking what the word is that looks like goal posts, a circle, and a horizontal stroke with a vertical one beneath, a reader can simply say "What is the word that is spelled *h, o, t?*" Instead of having to say "Draw me (or describe to me) the shape of the word *hot*," all the writer need ask is "How do you spell *hot?*" Indeed, the fact that words can be remembered as spellings rather than as complex shapes greatly facilitates writing and learning to write. For reading it is easier to *recognize* a shape, but for writing it is easier to *recall* and *reproduce* a series of letters.

The alphabetic system may have allowed more people to learn to write, but at a cost to readers. The Chinese ideographic system can be read by people from all over China, even though they might speak languages that are mutually unintelligible. If a Cantonese speaker cannot understand what a Mandarin speaker says, they can write their conversation in the nonalphabetic writing system they both share and be mutually comprehensible. This is something English and French speakers cannot do unless they employ the small part of their own writing systems that is not alphabetic, such as arithmetic symbols like 2 + 3 = 5.

When we cannot remember or do not know how a word should be written, we have little recourse to anything but what we know about the spelling system. It does not help much in writing to look at the words before and after the one that is giving difficulty. But in reading we have some more effective alternatives before we need call upon phonics for help in identifying a word, and it is to these alternatives that we now turn.

STRATEGIES OF MEDIATED WORD IDENTIFICATION

To repeat, the problem with which we are concerned is that of a reader who encounters a word that cannot be recognized on sight, for which a visual feature list must be established, but where the reader does know what the word is to which the feature list will be assigned. The reader's problem is to identify the word by a mediated strategy.

Phonics, as we have seen, is one such strategy. But it is not the only one. An obvious alternative is simply being told what the word is. Before most children come to school, well-intentioned adults say to them "That word is *John*," "That word is *girls*" "That word is *cereal*" just as on other occasions they say, "That animal is a cat," in all cases leaving it to the child to solve the more complex problem of working out exactly how to recognize the word or animal in the future. But when the children get to school this support is frequently taken away from them, at least as far as reading is concerned. Another well-intentioned adult is likely to say to them, "Good news and bad news today, children. The bad news is that no one is ever likely to tell you what a word is again. The good news is that we are going to give you 166 rules and 45 exceptions so that you can work it out for yourselves."

Alternative Identification Strategies

Ask fluent readers what they do when they come across a word they do not recognize, and the most probable answer will be that they skip it, coming back to the word later if necessary. Passing over a word is a reasonable first strategy because it is not necessary to understand every word to understand a passage of text, and lingering to try to decipher a word may be more disruptive to comprehension than missing the word altogether. The second preferred strategy is to "guess," or predict, which again does not mean a reckless stab in the dark but making use of context to eliminate unlikely alternatives for what the unfamiliar word might be. The final strategy may be trying to work out what the word is from its spelling, but that is not so much likely to be decoding the word to sound with phonics as making use of what is already known about other words. The final strategy might be called *identification by analogy,* because all or part of the unknown word is compared with all or part of words that are known.

Examine the same question with a child who is progressing in learning to read and again you are likely to get the same sequence of strategies. The best learners tend to skip occasional unknown words (unless constrained to "read carefully" and figure out every word). The second preference, especially if there is no helpful adult around to provide assistance, is to hypothesize what a word might be based on the meaning of the text, and the final choice is to use what is known about similar-looking words. Trying to sound out words without reference to meaning is a characteristic strategy of poor readers; it is not one that leads to fluency in reading. The act of reading, on the other hand, usually helps with learning unfamiliar words, as we shall see.

What is the best method of mediated word identification? The answer depends on the situation a reader is in. Sometimes the best strategy will indeed be to ignore the unfamiliar word altogether, because sufficient meaning may be carried by the surrounding text not only to compensate for lack of understanding of the unknown word but subsequently to provide critical cues to what the unknown word might be. For a child beginning to learn to read, or confronted by text where many words are unfamiliar, the best situation is probably to have a more competent reader to turn to, if necessary by reading the entire passage to the child. But if the reader can understand enough of the passage to follow its sense, then a most effective strategy may be identification by analogy, making use of what is already known about reading.

The point is that phonics in itself is almost useless for sounding out words letter by letter, because every letter can represent too many sounds. But uncertainty about the sound of a particular letter diminishes as letters are considered not in isolation but as part of letter clusters or "spelling patterns." This has led a number of theorists to argue that the basic unit for word recognition should be regarded as the syllable rather than the individual letter, particularly syllables that rhyme with known words. And indeed it is true; the pronunciation of syllables is far less variable than the pronunciation of the individual letters that make up syllables. The trouble is that it would take a reader years to learn to read by memorizing the pronunciation of hundreds of syllables, because syllables in themselves tend to be meaning-less—there are relatively few one-syllable words—and the human brain has great difficulty in memorizing, and particularly in recalling, nonsense. What a reader can turn to for a ready-made store of syllabic information is *words* that have already been learned. It is far easier for a reader to remember the unique appearance and pronunciation of a whole word like *photograph*, for example, than to remember the alternative pronunciations of meaningless syllables or spelling units like *ph, to, gr* or *gra,* and *ph.* A single word, in other words, can provide the basis for remembering different rules of phonics, as well as the exceptions, since not only do words provide a meaningful way to organize different phonic rules in memory, they also illustrate the phonic rules at work. The 11 different ways of pronouncing *ho* cause no difficulty if one already has words like *hot, hoot, hope,* and so forth in one's sight vocabulary.

Identification by Analogy

The basis of the mediated word identification strategy of identification by analogy is looking for cues to a word's pronunciation and meaning from words that look the same. We do not learn to sound out words on the basis of individual letters or letter clusters whose sounds have been learned in isolation but rather by recognizing sequences of letters that occur in words that are already known. Such a strategy offers an additional advantage to the reader because it does more than indicate possible pronunciations for all or part of unknown words; it can offer suggestions about *meaning.* As I pointed out earlier, English spelling in general respects meaning more than sound— words that look alike tend to share the same sense. And as I have reiterated throughout this book, the basis of reading and of learning to read is meaning. The advantage of trying to identify unknown words by analogy with words that are known already is not simply that known words would provide an immediately accessible stock of pronunciations for relatively long sequences of letters but that all or part of known words can provide clues to meaning, which is always a far better clue to pronunciation than just the way an unknown word is spelled.

This is not to suggest that fluent readers cannot use their knowledge of spelling-sound correspondences to help identify unfamiliar words or that the existence of such correspondences should be concealed from children learning to read. But there are three fundamental problems with spelling-sound correspondences: the total number of rules and exceptions, the time it takes to apply them in practice, and their general unreliability. The problem of the number of rules can be solved by not trying to learn (or teach) the rules in the abstract, independently of actual words. The easiest way to learn a phonic rule is to learn a few words that exemplify it, which means—another point that will bear some reiteration—that children master phonics as a result of learning to read rather than as a prerequisite for reading. The time problem is overcome by resorting to phonics in actual reading as infrequently as possible.

The problem of the unreliability of phonic generalizations is another matter. Phonic generalizations alone will not permit a reader to decode the majority of words likely to be met in normal reading simply because there are always too many alternatives. This is the reason that producers of phonic workbooks always prefer to work with strictly controlled vocabularies—

there is not as much uncertainty of pronunciation with *The fat cat sat on the hat* as there is with *Two hungry pigeons flew behind the weary ploughman*, a sentence that makes more sense but defies phonic analysis.

Meaning Plus Phonics

But phonic generalizations can work if all they are required to do is reduce alternatives, without being expected to identify words completely or to decode them to sounds. To give an example, the use of phonics will never succeed in decoding *horse* if the word appears in isolation or is any one of thousands of alternatives. But if the reader knows that the word is either *horse, mule,* or *donkey,* then the strategy will work effectively. It is not simply that minimal phonic analysis is required to know that *mule* and *donkey* could not begin with *h*, but that not much more can be expected of phonic rules in any case. This is why I have asserted that phonics is easy—for the teacher and the child—if they know what a word is in the first place. I am not suggesting that the word has to be known absolutely. In that case neither phonics nor any other mediated word identification strategy would be required. But if the reader has a good idea of what the word might be, if there is a prediction that includes what the word actually is among the likely alternatives, then the use of phonics will probably eliminate the remaining uncertainty.

Phonic strategies cannot be expected to eliminate all uncertainty when the reader has no idea what the word might be. But if the reader can reduce alternatives in advance—by making use of nonvisual information related both to reading and to the subject matter of the text—then phonics can be made most efficient. One way to reduce uncertainty in advance is to employ the mediating technique of making use of context. Understanding of the text, in general, will reduce the number of alternatives that an unknown word might be. The other way to reduce uncertainty in advance is to employ the alternative mediating technique of identification by analogy, comparing the unknown word with known words that provide hypotheses about possible meanings and pronunciations. The reason that we can so easily read nonwords like *vernalit, mossiant,* and *ricaning* is not because we have in our heads a store of pronunciations for meaningless letter sequences like *vern, iant,* or *ric* but because these close approximations to English are made up of parts of words or even entire words that are immediately recognizable, such as *govern, vernal, lit, moss,* and so forth.

There is no simple answer to any question about the ideal method of mediated word identification. The three alternatives that have specifically been discussed—spelling-to-sound correspondences, prediction from context, and identification by analogy—are all likely to be inadequate when used alone. Although all will reduce some uncertainty, none is likely to eliminate all alternatives by itself. But used in conjunction, the strategies complement each other. A reader using phonics will rarely identify an unfamiliar word without making sense of the passage as a whole, using this understanding to eliminate unlikely alternatives in advance. To ignore alternative means of reducing uncertainty is to ignore the redundancy which is a central part of all aspects of language.

And the prior elimination of unlikely alternatives is, after all, the foundation upon which reading takes place, according to the analysis of comprehension that was offered in Chapter 3. By this analysis, phonics is neither the basis of reading nor a strategy that a reader has to depend on wholly whenever an unfamiliar word is encountered. Rather, the use of phonic rules takes a supplementary and subordinate place in normal meaningful reading, occurring so rarely and effortlessly that the reader is not usually aware of the strategies employed as unfamiliar words are tentatively identified and feature lists established. Phonic rules function almost as sentinels; they cannot decipher unknown words on their own, but they will protect the reader against making impossible hypotheses.

LEARNING MEDIATED WORD IDENTIFICATION STRATEGIES

The basis of all learning—and especially of language learning—is meaningfulness. It is pointless to expect a child to memorize lists of rules, definitions, examples, even names, if these have no apparent purpose or utility to the child. Not only will learning be difficult, but recall will be almost impossible. The mediated word identification strategies that have been discussed can fall into the category of meaningless learning if a child is expected to acquire them outside a context of meaningful reading. A child should not be expected to memorize phonic rules, or the pronunciation of isolated syllables and letter clusters, prior to learning how to read. Identification by analogy can also only be fostered after a child has begun to read.

Learning is self-directing and self-reinforcing when children are in a situation that makes sense to them, that can be related to what they know already. Rules which cannot be verbalized about many aspects of the physical world and of language are hypothesized and tested with little conscious awareness. Where children can understand a relationship they will learn the relationship, whether it is the relationship of a name to a word, of a meaning to a word, or of a spelling-sound correspondence.

What all this means is that *reading is basically a matter of increasing returns.* The more that children read, the more they will learn to read. The more they can recognize words, the easier they will be able to understand phonic correspondences, to employ context cues, and to identify new words by analogy. The more that children are able to read—or are helped to read—the more they are likely to discover and extend these strategies for themselves. There is no reason to conceal the existence of spelling-sound correspondences from children, but there is no point in impressing the rules upon an uncomprehending learner or in ignoring their limitations.

By acquiring an extensive "sight vocabulary" of immediately identifiable words, children are able to understand, remember, and utilize phonic rules and other mediated identification strategies. But such a summary statement does not imply that the way to help children read is to give them plenty of experience with flashcards and word lists. The easy way to learn words is not to work with individual words at all but with meaningful passages of text. We are considering only a limited and secondary aspect of reading when we restrict our attention to individual words. As we turn our attention to reading sequences of words that are grammatical and make sense, we find that word identification and learning are more easily explained theoretically and more easily accomplished by the child.

The time has come to complete the picture of reading by recognizing that words are rarely read or learned in meaningless isolation. Reading is easiest when it makes sense, and learning to read is also easiest when it makes sense. We are ready to view reading from a broader and more meaningful perspective.

ISSUES

The difficulty many children experience in learning phonics rules, or indeed in making sense of them, has led to the notion that such children lack "phonological awareness," that is, the ability to deconstruct the *sounds* of spoken words. It is taken for granted that the tenuous relationship between letters and sounds must be of central importance to readers of alphabetic writing systems (compared with readers of nonalphabetic systems like Chinese)—why else have an alphabet? The alternative point of view, which may be slowly gaining ground, is that the alphabet primarily serves writing and should make no substantial difference to reading.

SUMMARY

Mediated word identification is a temporary expedient for identifying unfamiliar words while establishing feature lists to permit immediate identification. Alternative strategies for mediated word identification include asking someone, using contextual cues, analogy with known words, and the use of **phonics** (spelling-sound correspondences). Attempting to decode isolated words to sound is unlikely to succeed because of the number, complexity, and unreliability of phonic generalizations. Phonic rules will help to eliminate alternative possibilities only if uncertainty can first be reduced by other means, for example, if the unfamiliar words occur in meaningful contexts. Spelling-sound correspondences are not easily or usefully learned before children acquire some familiarity with reading.

Notes to Chapter 8 begin on page 267, covering
The relevance of phonics
Phonological recoding
Phonological awareness
Word identification by analogy
The role of the alphabet

9 The Identification of Meaning

The preceding three chapters have been concerned with the identification of individual letters and individual words. They showed how the same system of feature analysis could be employed both for the identification of letters and for the direct identification of words. Word identification does not require the prior identification of letters, at least not the immediate word identification that readers accomplish when a word they are concerned with is familiar to them, a part of their "sight vocabulary." It is only when words cannot be identified immediately that the prior identification of letters may become relevant at all, and then only to a limited extent depending on the amount of contextual and other information that the reader might have available. The alternatives are summed up in Figure 9.1.

Now I want to show that comprehension, which in this chapter will be referred to as the *identification* (or apprehension) of meaning, does not require the prior identification of words. The same feature-analytic process that underlies the identification of letters and words is also available for the immediate apprehension of meaning from visual information. Although

FIG. 9.1. Immediate and mediated word identification.

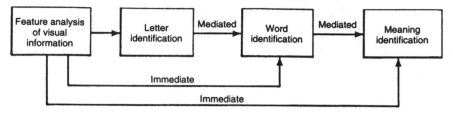

FIG. 9.2. Immediate and mediated meaning identification.

mediated meaning identification may sometimes be necessary, because for some reason meaning cannot immediately be assigned to the text, attempting to make decisions about possible meaning by the prior identification of individual words is highly inefficient and unlikely to succeed.

In other words, immediate meaning identification is as independent of the identification of individual words as immediate word identification is independent of the identification of individual letters. The alternatives are represented in Figure 9.2. The argument is presented in three steps:

1. Showing that immediate meaning identification *is* accomplished; that readers normally can and do identify meaning without or ahead of the identification of individual words.
2. Proposing how immediate meaning identification is accomplished.
3. Discussing how immediate meaning identification is learned.

In a final section, I briefly discuss the mediated identification of meaning, or what a reader does when the direct apprehension of meaning is not possible.

USING MEANING IN READING

One demonstration has already been given that readers employ meaning to assist in the identification of individual words rather than laboring to identify words in order to obtain meaning. I am referring to the experiment showing that from a single glance at a line of print—the equivalent of about one second of reading—a reader can identify four or five words if they are in a meaningful sequence but scarcely half that amount if the words are unrelated to each other. The explanation in Chapter 4 was that with meaningful text a reader could recruit nonvisual information to reduce alternatives so that the amount of visual information that the brain can handle in a second would go twice as far, to identify four or five words instead of a couple. The nonvisual information that the reader already possesses can only be meaning, or prior knowledge of the way in which words go together in language that is not only grammatical but makes sense.

A Constant Concern

It is important to understand that the reader in the situation just discussed is constantly making use of meaning; meaningfulness facilitates the identification of every word in the line. The reader does not first identify one or two words by a word identification strategy, as if they had nothing to do with the other words in the line, and then make an educated guess about the rest. Indeed, that same experiment shows that if two words had to be identified to give a clue about the others, then there would be no time left for the others to be identified. Two is the limit for words that have no meaningful relationships. Where a sequence of words does make sense, the identification of every word is facilitated, the first as well as the last, just as individual words can be identified in conditions in which none of their component letters would be individually discriminable. It is all a matter of the prior elimination of unlikely (and impossible) alternatives.

The demonstration just discussed is historic; it was first conducted and reported a century ago. But in a sense, the fact that meaning facilitates the identification of individual words is replicated every time we read, because reading would be impossible if we labored along, blindly striving to identify one word after another with no prior insights into what those words might be. The fact that eye-movement studies may show that in some circumstances the eyes briefly come to rest on all or most words is irrelevant; reading is not achieved saccadically. The eyes may "look at" words one at a time, but the brain deals with words in meaningful clusters. Slow reading is not efficient reading because it tends to create tunnel vision, overload short-term memory, and leave the reader floundering in the ambiguity of language. Yet it is impossible to read quickly language that does not make sense, as you can experience for yourself if you try to read the following passage:

> Be might words those what into insights prior no with, another after word one identify to striving blindly, along labored we if impossible be would reading because, read we time every replicated is words individual of identification the facilitates meaning that fact the, sense a in but.

The words you have just tried to read are what I hope is a meaningful English sentence—because I used it myself in the previous paragraph—written backward. Any difference between the rate and ease with which you could read the backward and forward versions of that sentence can only be attributable to whether you were able to make sense of it. If you had read the backward passage aloud, incidentally, you probably would have sounded very much like many "problem readers" at school, who struggle to identify words one at a time in a dreary monotone as if each word had nothing to do with any other. Such children seem to believe—and may well have been taught—that meaning should be their last concern; that sense will take care of itself provided they get the words right rather than that meaning facilitates the identification of words.

Professional readers, for example broadcasters, know the importance of prior understanding of what they are about to read; that is why they like to scan through a script in advance. Looking ahead also helps the silent reading of novels and technical books—we can get a general idea of what will transpire and then go back where necessary to study particular points. The general comprehension comes out of fast reading, and the slow reading that might be necessary for memorization or for reflection upon detail can only be accomplished if comprehension has already been taken care of. Conversely, meaning can interfere with some reading tasks. Proofreaders tend to overlook misprints if they attend to the sense of what they read; they see the spellings and words that should be on the page rather than those that actually are there. Sometimes proofreaders will deliberately read backward in order to give all their attention to spelling and individual words, but then of course they will overlook anomalies of meaning. Their dilemma highlights the fact that attention to individual words and to meaning are alternative and not concurrent aspects of reading.

The prior use of meaning ensures that when individual words must be identified, for example, in order to read aloud, a minimum of visual information will be used. And as a consequence, mistakes will often occur. If a reader already has a good idea of what a word might be, there is not much point in delaying to make extra certain what the word actually is. As a result it is not unusual for even highly experienced readers to make misreadings that are radically different visually—like reading *said* when the word is actually *announced* or *reported*—but that make no significant difference to the meaning. Beginning readers often show exactly the same tendency, demonstrating that children will strive for sense even as they learn to read (provided the material they are expected to learn from has some possibility of making sense in the first place). The mistakes that are made are sometimes called *miscues* rather than *errors* to avoid the connotation that they are something bad (Goodman, 1969). Such misreadings show that these beginning readers are attempting to read in the way fluent readers do, with sense taking priority over individual word identification. Of course, reading with minimal attention to individual words will sometimes result in misreadings that do make a difference to meaning, but one of the great advantages of reading for meaning in the first place is that one becomes aware of mistakes that make a difference to meaning. An important difference between children who are doing well in reading and those who are not is not that good readers make fewer mistakes, but that they go back and correct the mistakes that make a difference. Children who are not reading for sense have no chance of becoming aware of even important errors.

The Priority of Meaning

A unique illustration of the way in which the meaning takes priority over the identification of individual words was provided by Kolers (1966), who asked bilinguals fluent in English and French to read aloud from passages of text that made sense but where the actual language changed from English to French every two or three words. For example:

> His horse, followed de deux bassets, faisait la terre résonner under its even tread. Des gouttes de verglas stuck to his manteau. Une violente brise was blowing. One side de l'horizon lighted up, and dans la blancheur of the early morning light, il aperçut rabbits hopping at the bord de leur terriers.

The subjects in this experiment could read and understand such passages perfectly well, but when they had finished they often could not remember whether particular sentences or words were in English or French. Most significantly, they frequently substituted for a word in one language an appropriate word in the other. They might read *porte* when the word was *door* or *hand* when *main* was given, getting the meaning right but the language wrong. This does not mean that they were not looking at individual words at all—the passage was not completely predictable—but that they were looking at words and finding meanings, just as an English speaker might look at 2000 and understand "two thousand" while a French speaker would look at the same print and understand "deux milles."

An important and perhaps difficult point to understand from the preceding discussion is that it is possible to make meaningful decisions about words without saying exactly what the words are. In other words, we can *see* that the written word *door* means door without having to say aloud or to ourselves that the word *is* "door." Written words convey meaning directly; they are not intermediaries for spoken language. An obvious example is provided for English by words which have different spellings for the same sound, like *their* and *there*. It is easy to detect the spelling error in *The children left there books behind* because *there* represents the wrong meaning. The difference between *their* and *there*, and *read* and *reed*, and *so*, *sew*, and *sow* is evidently not that the different spellings represent different sounds, because they do not, but that the different appearances of the words indicate different meanings. The visual appearance of each word indicates meaning directly.

The fact that readers can, do, and must read directly for meaning is similarly apparent with a written language like Chinese, which does not correspond to any particular sound system. It would be pointless to argue whether the written symbol 宅 represents the Mandarin or the Cantonese word for "house" because it simply represents a *meaning*. My present assertion is that any written language is read as Chinese is read, directly for meaning. The fact that some written languages are also more or less related to the sound system of a spoken language is quite coincidental as far as the reader is concerned. As I suggested earlier, the alphabet could have originated purely for the convenience of writers. Certainly, there is no evidence that fluent readers need to identify letters in order to identify familiar words, and English spelling is, at best, an inadequate guide to the identification of words that are unfamiliar.

My final example that written language indicates meaning directly is rather poignant, because it comes from studies of brain-injured patients. People who are unable to find the exact word have been reported, for example, as reading the isolated word *ill* as "sick," *city* as "town," and *ancient* as "historic" (Marshall & Newcombe, 1966) or *injure* as "hurt," *quiet* as "listen," and *fly* as "air" (Shallice & Warrington, 1975).

COMPREHENSION AND THE REDUCTION OF UNCERTAINTY

I have tried to show that meaning can take priority over the identification of individual words in two ways, both for fluent readers and for beginners. In the first case, the meaning of a sequence of words facilitates the identification of individual words with relatively less visual information. In the second case, written words can be understood without being identified precisely. Usually both aspects of meaning identification occur simultaneously; we comprehend text using far less visual information than would be required to identify the individual words and without the necessity of identifying individual words. Both aspects of meaning identification are, in fact, reflections of the same underlying process—the use of minimal visual information to make decisions specific to implicit questions (or predictions) about meaning on the part of the reader.

I am using a rather awkward expression "meaning identification" as a synonym for comprehension in this chapter to underline the fact that the way in which a reader makes sense of text is no different from that by which individual letters or words may be identified in the same text. I could also use the rather old-fashioned psychological term *apprehension* to refer to the way meaning must be captured, but that would cloud the similarities between comprehension and letter and word identification. What is different about comprehension is that readers bring to the text implicit questions about meaning rather than about letters or words. The term *meaning identification* also helps to emphasize that comprehension is an active process. Meaning does not reside in surface structure. The meaning that readers comprehend from text is always relative to what they already know and to what they want to know. Put in another way, comprehension involves the reduction of a reader's uncertainty, asking questions and getting them answered, which is a point of view already employed in the discussion of letter and word identification. Readers must have *specifications* about meanings.

A passage of text may be perceived in at least three ways: as a sequence of letters from a certain alphabet, as a sequence of words of a particular language, or as an expression of meaning in a certain domain of knowledge or understanding. But a passage of text is none of these things, or at least it is only these things potentially. Basically, written text is a conglomeration of inkmarks on a page, variously characterized as visual information, distinctive features, or surface structure. Whatever readers perceive in text—letters, words, or meanings—depends on the prior knowledge (nonvisual information) that they happen to bring and the implicit questions they happen to be asking. The actual information that readers find (or at least seek) in the text depends on their original uncertainty.

Consider, for example, this sentence that you are reading at this moment. The visual information in the sentence can be used to make decisions about letters, for example, to say that the first letter is *c*, the second *o*, the third *n*, and so forth. Alternatively, exactly the same visual information could be used to decide that the first word is *consider*, the second word *for*, the third word *example*, and so forth. The reader employs the same visual information, selects from among the same distinctive features, but this time sees words, not letters. What readers see depends on what they are looking for, on their implicit questions or uncertainty. Finally, exactly the same visual information can be employed to make decisions about meaning in the sentence, in which case neither letters nor words would be seen individually. It is not easy to say precisely what is being identified in the case of meaning, but that is due to the conceptual difficulty of saying what meaning is—using words to describe something beyond words—not because the reader is doing anything intrinsically different. The reader is using the same source of visual information to reduce uncertainty about meaning rather than about letters or words.

As we have already seen, the amount of visual information required to make a letter or word identification depends on the extent of the reader's prior uncertainty, on the number of alternatives specified in the reader's mind (and also the degree to which the reader wants to be confident in the decisions to be made). With letters it is easy to say what the maximum number of alternatives is—26 if we are considering just one particular typeface in upper- or lowercase in the English alphabet. It is similarly easy to show that the amount of visual information required to identify each letter goes down as the number of alternatives that the letter might be (the reader's uncertainty) is reduced. The fewer the alternatives, the faster or easier a letter is identified, because fewer distinctive features need to be discriminated for a decision to be made. It is not so easy to say what the maximum number of alternatives is for words, because that depends on the range of alternatives that the reader considers in the first place, but again it is not difficult to show that the amount of visual information required to identify a word goes down as the reader's uncertainty is reduced. A word can be identified with fewer distinctive features when it comes from a couple of hundred alternatives than from many thousands. Finally, it is quite impossible to say how many alternative meanings there might be for a passage of text, because that depends entirely on what an individual reader is looking for, but it is obvious that reading is easier and faster when the reader finds the material meaningful than when comprehension is a struggle. The less uncertainty readers have about the meaning of a passage, the less visual information is required to find what they are looking for in the passage.

The Use of Nonvisual Information

In each of the preceding cases nonvisual information can be employed to reduce the reader's uncertainty in advance and to limit the amount of visual information that must be processed. The more prior knowledge a reader can bring to bear about the way letters go together in words, the less visual information is required to identify individual letters. Prediction, based on prior knowledge, eliminates unlikely alternatives in advance. Similarly, the more a reader knows about the way words go together in grammatical and meaningful phrases—because of the reader's prior knowledge of the particular language and of the topic being discussed—the less visual information is required to identify individual words. In the latter case, meaning is being used as part of nonvisual information to reduce the amount of visual information required to identify words.

Many people can follow the meaning of a novel or newspaper article at the rate of a thousand words a minute, which is four times faster than their probable speed if they were identifying every word, even with meaning to help them. There is a prevalent misconception that for this kind of fast reading the reader must be identifying only one word in every four and that this gives sufficient information at least for the gist of what is being read. But it is very easy to demonstrate that identifying one word in four will not contribute very much toward the intelligibility of a passage. Here is every fourth word from a movie review: Many———been———face———business———sour———
———If———to———. . . . The passage is even less easy to comprehend if the selected words are in groups, with correspondingly larger gaps between them. It is somewhat easier to comprehend what a passage is about if every fourth *letter* is provided rather than every fourth word, and, of course, my argument

is that reading at a thousand words a minute is possible only if the omissions occur at the *featural* level. A skilled reader may need to discriminate only a fraction of the features available in every word, but not if these features are all concentrated in a single letter.

It should not be thought that there is a special kind of distinctive feature for meaning in print, different from the distinctive features of letters and words. There is no "semantic feature," for example, that *house* and *residence* physically have in common that we should expect to find in the inkmarks on the page. What makes visual features distinctive as far as meaning is concerned is precisely what makes them distinctive for individual letters and words as well—the particular alternatives that already exist in the reader's uncertainty. The same features that can be used to distinguish the letter *m* from the letter *h* will also distinguish the word *mouse* from the word *house* and the meaning of *we went to the mill* from the meaning of *we went to the hill*. It is not possible to say what the specific features are that readers employ to distinguish meanings; this would depend upon what the reader is looking for, and, in any case, it is not possible to describe the features of letters or words either. The situation is only additionally complicated by the fact that we cannot say what a meaning is.

Capturing "Meaning"

As I pointed out in Chapter 2, in the discussion of the chasm between the surface structures and the deep structure of language, meaning lies beyond words. One cannot *say* what meaning is in general, any more than one can say what the meaning of a particular word or group of words is, except by saying other words that are themselves surface structure. The meaning itself can never be exposed. This inability to pin down meaning is not a theoretical defect or scientific oversight. We should not hope that a marvelous discovery will be made one day to enable us all to say what meanings are. Meaning, to repeat myself, cannot be captured in a net of words.

A reader does not comprehend the written word *table* by saying the spoken word *table* either aloud or silently, any more than the spoken word *table* can itself be understood simply by repeating it to oneself. (Would you understand the Spanish word *mesa* by saying it to yourself if you did not understand the language?) And neither the written nor the spoken word *table* is understood by saying silently to oneself "a four-legged flat-topped piece of furniture," or whatever other definition might come to mind, because of course the understanding of the definition would itself still have to be accounted for. There can be no understanding and no explanation unless the web of language is escaped. The actual *words*, written or spoken, are always secondary to meaning, to understanding.

We are normally unaware of *not* identifying individual words when we read because we are not thinking about words in any case. Written language (like speech) is *transparent*—we look through the actual words for the meaning beyond, and unless there are noticeable anomalies of meaning, or unless we have trouble comprehending, we are not aware of the words themselves. (When we deliberately attend to specific words, for example in the subtle matter of reading poetry, this is a consequence of asking a different kind of question in the first place. The sounds that we can give to the words do not so much contribute to a literal interpretation as establish a different— a complementary or alternative—kind of mood or meaning.)

Reading Aloud and Silently

Of course, word identification is necessary for reading aloud, but as I have tried to show, the identification of words in this way depends upon the prior identification of meaning. The voice lags behind the understanding and is always susceptible, to some extent, of diverging from the actual text. The substitution of words and even phrases with appropriate meanings is again not something that the reader will be aware of; the reader's main concern, even in reading aloud, must be with the sense of the passage. Misreadings would have to be pointed out by a listener following both the text and the reading. Misreadings of this kind are not normally made when words are not part of meaningful text, but then there is no way that meaning could be sought or utilized in words in isolation or in arbitrary lists. Besides, in such circumstances readers usually have the leisure to scrutinize sufficient visual information to identify individual words precisely (giving the words a label rather than a meaning) because nothing is lost by reading slowly.

Subvocalization (or reading silently to oneself) cannot in itself contribute to meaning or understanding any more than reading aloud can. Indeed, like reading aloud, subvocalization can only be accomplished with anything like normal speed and intonation if it is preceded by comprehension. We do not listen to ourselves mumbling parts of words or fragments of phrases and then comprehend. If anything, subvocalization slows readers down and interferes with comprehension. The habit of subvocalization can be broken without loss of comprehension (Hardyck & Petrinovich, 1970). Besides, most people do not subvocalize as much as they think. If we "listen" to ascertain whether we are subvocalizing, subvocalization is bound to occur. We can never hear ourselves not subvocalizing, but that does not mean that we subvocalize all the time. Why do we subvocalize at all? The habit may simply be a holdover from our younger days, perhaps when we were expected to read aloud. A teacher knows that children are working if their fingers are moving steadily along the lines and their lips are moving in unison. Subvocalization may also have a useful function in providing "rehearsal" to help hold in short-term memory words that cannot be immediately understood or otherwise dealt with. But in such cases subvocalization indicates lack of comprehension rather than its occurrence. There is a general tendency to subvocalize when reading becomes difficult, when we can predict less.

Prediction and Meaning

Readers do not normally attend to print with their minds blank, with no prior purpose and with no expectation of what they might find in the text. Readers normally look for meaning rather than strive to identify letters or words. The way readers look for meaning is not to consider all possibilities nor to make reckless guesses about just one, but rather to predict within the most likely range of alternatives. In this way readers can overcome the information-processing limitations of the brain and also the inherent ambiguity of language. Readers can derive meaning directly from text because they bring expectations about meaning to text. The process is normally as natural, as continuous and effortless as the way we bring meaning to every other kind of experience in our lives. We do not go through the world saying "There's a chair; there's a table; a chair is something I can sit on," struggling to make sense of every bit of information our sensory systems direct toward the brain. Instead we look out for those aspects of our environment that will make the world meaningful to us, especially with respect to our particular purposes and interests. Comprehension is not a matter of putting names to nonsense and struggling to make sense of the result, but of operating in the realm of meaningfulness all the time.

LEARNING TO IDENTIFY MEANING

There is no need for a special explanation about how children learn to apprehend meaning from print because no special process is involved. Children will naturally try to bring meaning to print. For them there is no point in language that is not meaningful, whether spoken or written. They perceive spoken language by looking for meaning, not by focusing on the sounds of words.

The Expectation of Sense

There is a classic illustration of the priority that meaning takes as children learn to talk. Even when children try to "imitate," it is meaning that they imitate, not meaningless sounds. McNeill (1967) reported an exchange between mother and child which went like this:

> *Child:* Nobody don't like me.
>
> *Mother:* No, say "Nobody likes me."

Child: Nobody don't like me.

(eight repetitions of this dialogue)

Mother: No, now listen carefully, say *"Nobody likes me."*

Child: Oh! Nobody don't likes me.

Even when children are asked to perform a language exercise, they expect that it will make sense. Like the child in the previous example, it takes them a long time to understand the task if they are required to attend to surface structure, not to meaning. Children do not need to be told the converse, to look for sense; that is their natural (and only) way of learning about language in the first place. Indeed, they will not willingly attend to any noise that does not make sense to them.

Just as children do not need to be told to look for meaning in either spoken or written language, so they also do not need to learn special procedures for finding meaning. Prediction is the basis of meaning identification, and all children who can understand the spoken language of their own environment must be experts at prediction. Besides, the very constraints of reading—the constant possibility of ambiguity, tunnel vision, and memory overload—can only serve as reminders to learners that the basis of reading must be prediction.

Certainly there is no need for a special explanation of how comprehension should be *taught*. Comprehension is not a new kind of skill that has to be learned for reading but is the basis of all learning. Rather it may happen at school that children are taught the *reverse* of comprehension, being instructed instead to take care to "decode" correctly and not to make "guesses" if they are uncertain. They may even be expected to learn to read with materials and exercises specifically designed to discourage or prevent the use of nonvisual information.

Of course, there are differences between the comprehension of written language and the comprehension of speech or of other kinds of events in the world, but these are not differences of process. The differences are simply that the reader must use the distinctive features of print to test predictions and reduce uncertainty. Children need to become familiar with these distinctive features for print and with how they are related to meaning. This familiarity and understanding cannot be taught, any more than the rules of spoken language can be taught, but formal instruction is similarly unnecessary and in fact impossible. The experience that children require to find meaning in print can only be acquired through meaningful reading, just as children develop their speech competence through using and hearing meaningful speech. And until children are able to do meaningful reading on their own account, they are clearly dependent on being read to, or at least on being assisted to read.

The Right to Ignore

A final point. It is not necessary for any readers, and especially not for beginners, to understand the meaning of *everything* that they attempt to read. Whether adults are reading novels and other lengthy texts or menus or advertisements, they always have the liberty to skip quite large passages and certainly to ignore many small details, either because they are not comprehensible or simply because they are not relevant to their interest or needs. Children, when they are learning spoken language, seem able and willing to follow adult conversations and television programs without comprehending every word. A grasp of the theme, a general interest, and the ability to make sense on the basis of a few comprehensible parts can be more than sufficient to hold a child's attention. Such partially understood material is indeed the basis for learning; no one will pay attention to any aspect of language, spoken or written, unless it contains something that is new. For children, a good deal that is not comprehensible will be tolerated for the opportunity to explore something that is new and interesting. But children are rarely given credit for their ability to ignore what they cannot understand and to attend only to that from which they will learn.

Unfortunately, the right of children to ignore what they cannot understand may be the first of their freedoms to be taken away when they enter school. Instead, attention may be focused on what each child finds incomprehensible in order to "challenge" them to further learning. Anything a child understands may be set aside as "too easy." Paradoxically, many reading materials are made intentionally meaningless. Obviously, in such cases there is no way in which children will be able to develop and profit from their ability to seek and identify meaning in text.

MEDIATED MEANING IDENTIFICATION

Reading usually involves bringing meaning *immediately* or directly to the text without awareness of individual words or their possible alternative meanings. There are occasions, however, when the meaning of the text or of particular words cannot be immediately comprehended. On these occasions, mediated meaning identification may be attempted, involving the identification of individual words before comprehension of a meaningful sequence of words as a whole. There are two cases to be considered, the first concerned with the mediated meaning identification of entire sequences of words, such as phrases and sentences, and the second concerned with the mediated identification of the meaning of occasional individual words.

I have already argued that the first is rarely possible. The meaning of a sentence as a whole is not understood by putting together the meanings of individual words (Chapter 2). Individual words have so much ambiguity—and usually alternative grammatical functions as well—that without some prior expectation about meaning there is little chance for comprehension even to begin. In addition, limitations of visual information processing and memory are difficult to overcome if the reader attempts to identify and understand every word as if it had nothing to do with its neighbors and came from many thousands of alternatives. So although some theories of reading and many methods of reading instruction would appear to be based on the assumption that comprehension of written text is achieved one word at a time, the present analysis leaves little on this topic to be discussed. To attempt to build up comprehension in such a way must be regarded as highly inefficient and unlikely to succeed.

But the second sense of mediated meaning identification—where the passage as a whole is comprehensible and perhaps just one word is unfamiliar and not understood—is a more general and useful characteristic of reading. In this case the question is not one of trying to use the meanings of individual words to construct the meaning of the whole, but rather of using the meaning of the whole to provide a possible meaning for an individual word. And not only is this possible, it is the basis of much of the language learning that we do. The bulk of the vocabulary of most literate adults must come from reading (Nagy, Herman, & Anderson, 1985). It is not necessary to understand thousands upon thousands of words to begin to learn to read—basically all that is required is a general familiarity with the words and constructions in the written material from which one is expected to learn, and then not all of those. And it seems highly unlikely that our understanding of many of the words that we have learned as a result of reading should be attributed to thousands of trips to the dictionary or to asking someone else what the word might be. We learn the meaning from the text itself.

Informal evidence that we quite coincidentally learn new words while reading comes from those words whose meaning or reference we know well but which we are not sure of pronouncing correctly, so there is no way we could have learned about them from speech. I am referring to words like *Penelope* (Penny-loap?), *misled* (mizzled? myzelled?) and *gist* (like guest or jest?), and perhaps *slough* and *orgy*, not to mention innumerable foreign words, names, and places. There is what I like to call the *facky-tious* phenomenon (*tious* to rhyme with *pious*) after the occasion when the mother of a friend commented that one did not often hear the word *facky-tious* these days. My friend confessed that he could not remember the last time he heard the word and asked what it meant. "A little sarcastic or supercilious," he was told. Something clicked. "You mean *facetious*," he said. "No," replied his mother thoughtfully, "though the two words do have a similar meaning.

Come to think of it," she added, "I don't think I've ever seen the word *facetious* in print."

The question, of course, is where she got the correct meaning of facky-tious which she had never heard in speech and had obviously never asked anyone about. And the answer must be that she learned it the way most of us learn the meaning of so many of the words that we know—by making sense of words from their context, using what is known to comprehend and learn the unfamiliar. Mediated meaning identification from context is something that fluent readers probably do frequently without awareness and is the basis not just of comprehension but of learning.

Learning new words without interference with the general comprehension of text is another example of the way in which children—and all readers—can continually learn to read by reading. The vocabulary that develops as a consequence of reading provides a permanent basis of knowledge for determining the probable meaning and pronunciation of new words. If you know both the meaning and the pronunciation of *auditor* and *visual*, you will have little difficulty in comprehending and saying a new word like *audiovisual*. The larger your capital, the faster you can add to it—whether with words or material wealth. The best way to acquire a large and useful sight vocabulary for reading is by meaningful reading. If the text makes sense, the mediation and the learning take care of themselves.

ISSUES

A persisting issue is whether in a normal reading situation individual words have to be specifically identified, one at a time, before the meaning of a phrase, sentence, or passage can be comprehended. Such issues are difficult to resolve experimentally—evidence of where the eyes are focused does not necessarily indicate what the reader is thinking about. Meaning as a concept is difficult enough to contemplate in any case. To try to pinpoint meaning by studying where the eyes fixate can be like trying to study digestion by analyzing knife and fork movements. As we shall continue to see, driving many of the controversies about the nature of reading are deep-rooted beliefs about how children should be taught.

SUMMARY

Comprehension, the basic objective of reading, also facilitates the process of reading in two ways. Immediate meaning identification makes unnecessary the prior identification of individual words, and **comprehension** of a passage as a whole facilitates the comprehension and, if necessary, the identification of individual words. **Mediated meaning identification** increases the probability of tunnel vision, memory overload, and ambiguity caused by over reliance on visual information.

10 Reading, Writing, and Thinking

So far this book has been primarily concerned with topics much broader than reading—like language, comprehension, or memory—or with small aspects of reading—like letter or word identification. In this chapter, the focus can finally be directed to reading itself, to the specific act, when something meaningful is in front of a reader's eyes, and the reader is looking at it for a purpose. What does it mean to read? What can be said to be happening? And what do readers need to know?

Reading is never an abstract, purposeless activity, although it is frequently studied in that way by researchers and theorists and regrettably still taught in that way to many learners. Readers always read *something*, they read for a *purpose*, and reading and its recollection always involve *feelings* as well as knowledge and experience.

In other words, reading can never be separated from the purposes of readers and from its consequences upon them. This chapter is mainly concerned with what reading means to readers. Reading also cannot be separated from writing or thinking, although this book is not specifically directed to either of these large topics. But their relevance cannot be ignored, so the chapter ends with brief comments on writing and thinking. The final chapter is concerned with learning to read (which also will be found inseparable from the act of reading itself).

On Definitions of Reading

Books on reading often attempt to define their terms with formal statements like "reading is extracting information from print." But such assertions do not provide any insight into reading or the way it is being discussed, and can lead to contentious debates. A definition does not justify its author using a common word differently from anyone else. Formal definitions are useful only if there is a reason for using words in a specialized, narrow, or otherwise unpredictable way, and even then they can cause more trouble than they are worth because readers prefer to interpret familiar words in familiar ways. Philosopher Karl Popper (1976) pointed out that precision can only be increased at the cost of clarity. As I have already discussed, common, easily understood words tend to have a multiplicity of meanings, and what usually gives a word an unambiguous interpretation is neither prior agreement nor fiat but the particular context in which it happens to be used. As Popper also said, it is better to *describe* how a word is used than to define it.

Take the question of whether reading necessarily involves comprehension, an issue sometimes discussed at great length. Such a question asks nothing about the nature of reading, only about the way the word is used on particular occasions. And the only possible answer is that sometimes the word reading implies comprehension, and sometimes it does not. When we suggest that someone should read a particular book, we obviously include comprehension in our recommendation—it would be redundant if not rude to say "I think you ought to read and comprehend this book." But on the other hand, our friend might reply "I've already read it, but I didn't understand it" now obviously excluding comprehension from the meaning of the word reading. Everything depends on the general sense in which words are used, even in the same conversation, in two successive sentences. If there is doubt, it is better to provide a more complete description of how the word is being used than to attempt a general definition.

Consider, for example, the differences between reading a novel, a poem, a social studies text, a mathematical formula, a telephone directory, a recipe, the formalized description of some opening moves in chess, or an advertisement in a newspaper. Novels are usually read for the *experience*, for involvement in a situation, not unlike watching a play or movie or participating in actual events, where we are caught up with the characters and motivations of individual people and with how circumstances will deal with them. To read a novel is to participate in life. A poem may evoke a much more intense experience, especially emotionally, involving a particular mental attitude and a sensitivity to the sounds as well as to the meanings of words, akin in many ways to listening to music. The social studies text may lack the direct emotional and aesthetic connection of a novel or poem, but generate more detailed analytic thought—thinking that is more "off the page" and general than the details directly presented in the print. The mathematical formula is a tool, to be lifted (with understanding) from its position in the text and used elsewhere, and the telephone directory is like a collection of keys, each of which will open the lock on a particular connection. A recipe is a description of a set of actions for the reader to follow, chess notation involves participation in a game, and a newspaper advertisement is a device for persuading readers to act in particular ways.

These descriptions are clearly inadequate for the richness that is reading. My aim in attempting a list was to illustrate the richness by demonstrating the inadequacy. And even then, I oversimplified. There is not one kind of novel or one kind of advertisement, and the same texts can be read in different ways. A novel can be read like a social studies text, and a social studies text like a novel. A newspaper advertisement may be read like a poem. Moreover, each of these different ways of reading texts is more like other forms of behavior or experience that do not involve reading than they are like other forms of reading. I equated reading a novel with watching a play, not with reading a play, and reading a recipe is obviously more like cooking a meal than like reading about any other kind of activity. There is no one activity that can be summed up as *reading*; no description that can be summarized as the "process" that is involved.

The meaning of the word reading in all these senses depends on everything that is going on—not just on what is being read, but on why a particular reader is reading. It might be said that in all of the examples I have given, answers are sought to questions that vary with the person asking them. And the only thing that makes all of these different activities reading is that the answers are being sought in print.

Because of the limitations on the amount of visual information from the text that the brain can deal with, the location and nature of the answers must to some extent be predictable. Thus the reader must have relevant expectations about the text. All questions must be couched within a prediction, a range of possible alternatives. This leads to a very broad description that I have already offered—that comprehension of text is a matter of having relevant questions to ask (that the text can answer) and of being able to find answers to at least some of those questions. To use a term I introduced earlier—reading depends on the relevance of the reader's specification of the text.

The particular questions can range from the implications of a single word to matters related to the style, symbolism, and world view of the author. I have avoided any attempt to list and characterize all these different questions because of their very specific—and sometimes specialized—nature. Instead, I have focused on three kinds of question that all fluent readers seem able to ask and answer in most reading situations, related to the identification of letters, words, and meanings. These three kinds of question are alternatives, all three cannot be asked simultaneously, and it is unnecessary for the reader to attempt to ask them in sequence. Reading is not a matter of identifying letters in order to recognize words in order to get the meaning of sentences. Meaning identification does not require the identification of individual words, just as word identification does not require the identification of letters.

Indeed, any effort on the part of a reader to identify words one at a time, without taking advantage of the sense of the whole, indicates a failure of comprehension and is unlikely to succeed. In the same way any endeavor to identify and perhaps sound out individual letters is unlikely to lead to efficient word identification.

From this perspective it does not make sense to ask whether print basically consists of letters, words, or meanings. Print is discriminable visual contrasts, inkmarks on paper, that have the potential of answering certain questions— usually implicit—that readers might ask. Print is visual information, in which readers can select distinctive features and make decisions among the alternatives in which they are interested. Readers find letters in print when they ask one kind of question and select relevant visual information; they find words in print when they ask another kind of question and use the same visual information in a different way; and they find meaning in print, in the same visual information, when they ask a different kind of question again. It should be rare for a reader to ask questions about specific letters (except when letters themselves have a particular relevance, for example, as a person's initials or as a compass direction N, S, E, or W). It should also be rare for a reader to attend specifically to words, unless again there is a particular reason to identify a word, for example, a name.

Comprehension, as I have said, is relative; it depends on getting answers to the questions being asked. A particular meaning is the answer a reader gets to a particular question. Meaning therefore also depends on the questions that are asked. A reader "gets the meaning" of a book or poem from the writer's (or a teacher's) point of view only when the reader asks questions that the writer (or teacher) implicitly expected to be asked. Disputes over the meaning of text, or the "correct" way to comprehend text, are usually disputes over the questions that should be asked. A particular skill of accomplished writers (and of accomplished teachers) is to lead readers to ask the questions that they consider appropriate. Thus, the basis of fluent reading is the ability to find answers in the visual information of written language to the particular questions that are being asked. Written language makes sense when readers can relate it to what they know already (including those occasions when learning takes place, when there is a comprehensible modification of what readers know already). And reading is interesting and relevant when it can be related to what the reader *wants* to know.

READERS AND WRITERS

Readers must bring meaning to texts; they must have a developing and constantly modifiable set of expectations about what they will find. This is their specification of the text. But obviously writers make a contribution too. They must have their own specifications. And there must be a point at which readers and writers interact. That point is the text, and this section is about the interaction, about readers, writers, and the text.

Global and Focal Predictions

So far throughout this book I have talked as if predictions are made and dealt with one at a time. But predictions are usually multiplex, varying widely in range and significance. Some predictions are overriding; they carry us across large expanses of time and space. Other predictions occurring concurrently are far more transient, arising and being disposed of relatively rapidly. Our predictions are layered and interleaved.

Consider the analogy of driving a car. We have a general expectation that we will reach a certain destination at a certain time, leading to a number of relatively long-range predictions about landmarks that will be met along the route. Call these predictions *global*, because they tend to influence large parts of the journey. No matter how much our exact path might have to be varied because of exigencies that arise on the way, swerving to avoid a pedestrian or diverting down a side street because of a traffic holdup, these overriding global predictions tend to bring us always toward our intended goal.

But while global predictions influence every decision until our intended goal is reached, we simultaneously make more detailed predictions related to specific events during the course of the journey. Call predictions of this nature *focal*, because they concern us for short periods of time only and have no lasting consequence for the journey as a whole. Focal predictions must be made, usually quite suddenly, with respect to the oncoming truck or the pedestrian or as a consequence of a minor diversion. In contrast to global predictions, we cannot usually be specific about focal predictions before the journey begins. It would be futile to try to predict before starting the specific location of incidents that are likely to occur on the way. Yet while the occasion for a focal prediction is likely to arise out of particular sets of local circumstances, the prediction itself will still be influenced by our global expectations about the journey as a whole. For example, the modified focal predictions that will result if we have to make an unexpected detour will still be influenced by our overriding expectation of eventually reaching a particular destination.

We make similar global and focal predictions when we read. While reading a novel, for example, we may be concerned with a number of quite different predictions simultaneously, some global that can persist through the entire length of the book, others more focal that can rise and be disposed of in a single fixation.

We begin a book with extremely global predictions about its content from its title and from what perhaps we have heard about it in advance. Sometimes even global predictions may fail—we discover that a book is not on the topic we anticipated. But usually global predictions about content, theme, and treatment can persist throughout the book. At a slightly more detailed level there are likely to be still quite global expectations that arise and are elaborated within every chapter. At the beginning of the book we may have such predictions about the first chapter only, but in the course of reading the first chapter expectations about the second arise, the second leads to expectations about the third, and so on to the end. Within each chapter there will be rather more focal predictions about paragraphs, each paragraph being a major source of predictions about the next. Within each paragraph there will be predictions about sentences and within each sentence predictions about words.

Lower level predictions arise more suddenly; we will rarely make focal predictions about words more than a sentence ahead of where we are reading, nor predictions about sentences more than a paragraph ahead, nor predictions about paragraphs more than a chapter ahead. The more focal the prediction, the sooner it arises (because it is based on more immediate antecedents) and the sooner it is disposed of (because it has fewer long-range consequences). In general, the more focal a prediction, the less it can be specifically formulated in advance. You would be unlikely to predict the content of the present sentence before you had read the previous sentence, although the content of the paragraph as a whole was probably predictable from the previous paragraph. On the other hand, predictions at the various levels inform each other. While focal-level predictions are largely determined by the particular situation in which they arise, they are also influenced by our more global expectations. Your focal predictions about my next sentence will depend to some extent on your comprehension of the present sentence but also on your expectations about this paragraph, this chapter, and the book as a whole. Conversely, the global predictions that we make at the book and chapter level must be constantly tested and if necessary modified by the outcomes of our predictions at more focal levels. Your comprehension of one sentence could change your view of a whole book. The entire process is at once extremely complex and highly dynamic, but in Figure 10.1, I try to illustrate the framework of it with a considerably simplified and static diagram.

In general, the expectations of Figure 10.1 should be regarded as developing from left to right; the past influences our expectations for the future. But it can occasionally help at all levels of prediction in reading to glance ahead. The sequence of reading does not have to follow the page numbering of the book. Similarly, there should perhaps be diagonal lines all over the diagram as the outcomes of local predictions have their effect on global predictions and the global expectations exert their constant influence on specific focal predictions. At any moment, the character of our existing expectations about the book, chapter, paragraph, sentence, and word is our ever-changing specification of the text.

Do not take the diagram too literally. It is not necessary to predict at every

FIG. 10.1.   Layers of prediction in reading a book.

level all of the time. We may become unsure of what a book as a whole is about and, for a while, hold our most global predictions to the chapter or even to a lower level while we try to grasp where the book might be going. Sometimes we may have so much trouble with a paragraph that we find it impossible to maintain predictions at the chapter level. At the other extreme we may find a chapter or paragraph so predictable, or so irrelevant, that we omit predictions at lower levels altogether. In plain language, we skip. It is only when we can make no predictions at all that a book will be completely incomprehensible. It should also not be thought that there are clearly defined boundaries between the different levels of prediction; the global-focal distinction does not describe alternatives but rather the extreme ends of a continuous range of possibilities.

The Writer's Point of View

I consider now the intentions of writers using the framework just employed to analyze the predictions of readers. To some extent, the patterns of predictions and intentions can be seen as reflections of each other.

Writers of books often begin with only global intentions of what the book as a whole will be about and of the way the subject will be treated. These global intentions, in due course, then determine lower level intentions for every chapter. Within each chapter will arise more focal intentions about every paragraph, and within each paragraph quite detailed focal intentions regarding sentences and words. And just as the more focal predictions of the reader (or the writer) tend to arise at shorter notice and to be dispensed with more quickly, so the more focal intentions of the writer extend over a shorter range in both directions. What I want to say in the present sentence is most specifically determined by what I wrote in the previous one and will, in turn, place a considerable constraint upon how I compose the next sentence. But these focal constraints are at the detailed level. My intention in every sentence that I write is also influenced by the more global intentions for the paragraph as a whole, and of course my intention in every paragraph reflects the topic I have selected for the chapter and more generally for the book.

The intentions of writers can be represented by exactly the same framework that I have used to represent the predictions of readers in Figure 10.1. The only difference would be that now the diagram should be captioned "Layers of intention in writing a book," with the word *intentions* replacing *expectations* at every level from global to focal. The same qualification would also apply about not taking the diagram too literally. Authors may at times be fairly sure about their global intentions at book, chapter, and even paragraph levels but be lost for focal intentions concerning particular sentences and individual words. At other times the words may flow without any clear indication of where they are going, the paragraph and other more global intentions remaining obscure.

It is from the overlapping perspectives of predictions and intentions that one can perhaps best perceive the intimate relationship between readers and writers. From the writer's point of view it might be said that a book is comprehended when the reader's predictions mirror the writer's intentions at all levels. Certainly one important aspect of writing is the intentional manipulation of the reader's predictions. A textbook writer must try to lead readers in a Socratic manner so that the answers to one set of predictive questions set up the succeeding predictions that the readers should make. In a more dramatic context an author may strive for tension by maintaining a particular degree of uncertainty in the reader's predictions at all levels throughout a book. And in a mystery story an author might quite deliberately lead readers into inappropriate predictions so that the inevitable consequence of predictive failure—surprise—becomes a part of the reading experience.

But readers should also have intentions of their own. When we read a book purely for its literary or even entertainment merit, we may willingly submit our expectations to the control of the author or poet, the willing suspension of disbelief. But with textbooks—like the present one, for example—readers should not only be pursuing certain pathways of ideas for their own particular ends, quite independently of the author, they should constantly be on guard against having their expectations entirely controlled by the author's arguments. Critical thinkers always reserve some questions of their own.

Global and Focal Conventions

The cascading diagram of Figure 10.1 can be used for a third time, to tie together much of what I have said so far about readers needing to predict what writers intend and writers needing to anticipate what readers will predict.

First I used Figure 10.1 to represent the reader's point of view, the texture of *predictions*. Then with a slight modification of labeling it was used from the writer's point of view, as a network of *intentions*. Finally it can be employed as a representation of the text itself, the meeting ground of writer intentions and reader expectations.

In what way do writers manifest their various intentions, and what is it that readers predict at the various global and focal levels? As outlined in Chapter 2, the answer is *conventions*. Conventions exist in every aspect of language; they correspond to every kind and level of intention and expectation. In considering the written language of books, Figure 10.1 needs simply to be relabeled "Layers of convention in a book," with the word *convention* replacing expectations (or intentions) at every level. There are global conventions for books as a whole—these are *genre schemes, story grammars,* and the conventions of *register*. There are conventions for the way paragraphs are arranged into chapters and chapters into books—these are the *discourse structures*. There are conventions for the way sentences are organized into paragraphs—these are the conventions of *cohesion*. There are the conventions for the organization of words in sentences, the conventions of *grammar* and of *idiom*. And there are conventions for the words themselves, the conventions of *semantics*, and for the physical representation of those words, the conventions of *spelling*.

Intentions, predictions, and conventions—all have their relatively global levels and all have their focal. The same diagram can represent all three with just the slightest change in wording. There is just one critical difference. When labeled for conventions, Figure 10.1 is, I think, one reasonably appropriate way to characterize an entire text. Texts are static, they do not change their structure from moment to moment (unless someone is working on them). But the figure offers only a way of *thinking* about readers and writers; I do not want to suggest that such a structure ever exists in its entirety or in a stable form in anyone's head. We can inquire into particular global and focal intentions or predictions in writers' and readers' minds at particular times, but we should never expect to find a complete or unchanging set of them the way the diagram might suggest, the way conventions exist in a text. Instead we would find that writers and readers, each in their own way, have in their minds a *specification* of a text, a specification of global and focal elements far less complete and detailed than Figure 10.1, but far more dynamic and changing.

The Specification of a Text

Consider the matter first from the writer's point of view. What does a writer have in mind (a) before a text is begun to direct the writing that will be done, (b) while the text is being written to ensure that it follows the writer's developing intentions, and (c) when the text is done so that the writer can say "That is what I intended to write"? My answer each time is a specification.

The specification of a text is similar in many ways to the specification of a house. Such a specification is not the house itself, nor is it the plans for a house. It is a cluster of intentions and expectations, of constraints and guidelines, which determine what the plans and ultimately the house will be like. Specifications are never complete—we would not say to the architect "This is *exactly* how we want the house" because in that case we would not need the architect. Specifications will have gaps, they may even be internally inconsistent, and during the designing of the plans we or the architect may find a need for the specifications to be changed. Indeed, specifications should be expected to change as the execution of the plans develops, so that eventually there is a match between the plans (and house) and the specifications, between the aim and its fulfilment, partly because the house was designed around the constraints of the specifications but also because the specifications were changed and developed to meet the contingencies of actually designing and building the house. A different architect might have designed a different house, but we would still say "That is what we wanted" if the design is in accordance with our final specifications.

So with the writer. The book (or any other kind of text) that the author plans will initially develop in conformity with certain specifications which do not contain all the details of the text. And as the text develops the specifications will change, partly as the demands of the text change but also as a consequence of what has already been written. Details will be developed in the specifications as focal concerns arise and are then set aside and even forgotten because they are no longer relevant. Revisions will be made to the text with reference to the specifications and the specifications will be revised in the course of writing and revising the text. And at the end, if the final text is compatible with the final specification, the author will say "That is what I wanted to write," even though the constantly changing specification at no time spelled out exactly what the book would contain at all of its global and focal levels, even though a different book might have been written to the same initial specifications on a different occasion.

So too with readers. We begin with a sketchy specification of the text ("This is a book about reading") which develops in the course of our reading, consolidating in terms of what we have read so far and elaborating when necessary for the prediction of what is to come. Focal aspects of the specification are developed to make sense of detail as we come to it but then discarded as we move on to the next detail. Apart from the occasional quotation or specific idea that might lodge in our mind, we shall in general be far more concerned with the persisting global aspects of our specification than with the transient focal ones. And at the end we will have a specification that is still not the book itself but that is our ultimate comprehension of the book (just as the specification we can put together a week or a month later is our memory of the book at that time).

Texts exist independently of writers and readers. At no time does the text in its entirety exist in either the writer's or the reader's head (unless it has been deliberately memorized after having been written, like a poem or the script of a play). But before the interaction with the text (the writing or the reading), the specification determines what the writer or reader will do. And the developing interaction with the text changes the specification and contributes to what writers and readers finish up believing they have done.

How we comprehend when we read is a matter of the richness and congruence of the specification that we bring to the text and of the extent to which we can modify the specification in the course of reading the text. What we comprehend and what we are left with in memory as a consequence of the reading depend on how our experience with the text modifies our specification. Subsequent reflection may change the specification even more, of course, which is the reason that we often cannot distinguish in memory what we read *in* a text from what we read *into* it.

Investigations into story grammars, discourse structures, and event knowledge could lead toward an understanding of how readers and writers interact with texts, not from the static point of view of the texts themselves but from the dynamic point of view of the constantly changing and developing specifications in readers' and writers' minds.

FLUENT READING AND DIFFICULT READING

This section was originally headed "Fluent Reading and Beginning Reading" to contrast the fluent manner in which experienced readers read with the stumbling, less proficient behavior of learners. But the distinction is not valid. It is usually possible to find something any beginning reader can read easily, even if it is only one word. And it is always possible to find something an experienced reader cannot read without difficulty. The advantage of a competent reader over a neophyte lies in *familiarity* with a range of different kinds of text, not in the possession of *skills* that facilitate every kind of reading.

For beginners and experienced readers alike, there is always the possibility of fluent reading and the possibility of difficult reading. There is no sudden transition from beginning reading, when nothing can be read without difficulty, to fluent reading, when all reading is easy. The more we read, the more we are able to read. Learning to read begins one word and one kind of text at a time, continues a word and a text at a time, and the learning never stops.

Every time a reader meets a new word, something new is likely to be learned about the identification and meaning of words. Every time a new text is read, something new is likely to be learned about reading different kinds of text. Learning to read is not a process of building up a repertoire of specific skills, which make all kinds of reading possible. Instead, experience increases the ability to read different kinds of text.

Even experienced readers have difficulty in reading some texts—because of the way the texts are written, or because of inadequate nonvisual information on the reader's part, and sometimes because of pressures or anxieties involved in the particular act of reading. And when otherwise "competent" readers experience difficulty in reading, they tend to read like beginners. By the same token, when beginners find easy material to read, they tend to read like experienced readers.

In other words, the critical difference is not between experienced and beginning reading, or even "good reading" and "poor reading," but between fluent reading, which even beginners can do in the right circumstances, and difficult reading, a situation in which even experienced readers can sometimes find themselves. The problem for children learning to read is that everything they might attempt to read is likely to be difficult.

Experienced readers (when they are reading fluently) can easily identify individual words if they have to. They use nonvisual information in order to comprehend and are less dependent on the identification of individual words in the text or on the surrounding words. They "take control" of the text through the four characteristics of meaningful reading—their reading is purposeful, selective, anticipatory, and based on comprehension. Inexperienced readers, on the other hand, have more trouble identifying individual words—and ironically, have more need to identify them. They depend more on the actual words in the text when they read because they can bring less prior knowledge to bear. They are less in control of their reading, more dominated by the text, lacking purpose, selectivity, appropriate anticipation, and comprehension. Experienced readers who are having difficulty reading have the characteristics of inexperienced readers.

Fluent reading involves pursuing a complex and ever changing set of objectives in order to make sense out of print in ways that are relevant to the purposes of the reader. Neither individual letter identification nor individual word identification are involved unless they are relevant to the particular requirements of the reader. Nor is every potential "meaning" on a page examined unless it has some bearing on the reader's purposes. Fluent reading is based upon a flexible specification of intentions and expectations, which change and develop as a consequence of the reader's progression through a text. Thus fluent reading demands knowledge of the conventions of the text, from vocabulary and grammar to the narrative devices employed. How much conventional knowledge is required depends on the purposes of the reader and the demands of the situation. Knowledge need not be complete, in fact provided there is sufficient comprehension to maintain the reader's attention, learning is likely to take place where specific knowledge is lacking.

The Consequences of Reading

Reading is more than just a pleasant, interesting, and informative experience. It has consequences, some of which are the typical consequences of any kind of experience we might have. Other consequences are uniquely particular to reading.

General consequences of experience are an increase in specific memories and knowledge. I have not found any studies of how much individuals normally remember from what they read (outside of artificial experimental situations looking at how much can be recalled of items determined by the researcher). But common observation would suggest that individuals remember as much about books that they find interesting and readable as they do about "real life" experiences in which they are involved. Many anecdotal reports indicate remarkable memories on the part of readers for the appearance, titles, authors, characters, settings, plots, and illustrations of books that were important to them, often extending back to childhood. With books, as with every other kind of experience, we remember what we understand and what is significant to us.

There are also specific consequences. Experience always results in learning. Experience in reading leads to more knowledge about reading itself. Not surprisingly, students who read a lot tend to read better (Anderson, Hiebert, Scott, & Wilkinson, 1985). They do not need to read better in order to read a lot, but the more they read, the more they learn about reading. The same researchers reported that students who read more also tended to have larger vocabularies, better comprehension skills, and generally did better on a range of academic subjects. In other words, reading makes people smarter.

Other things are learned through reading. I have argued at length (Smith, 1983b, 1994) that it is only through reading that anyone can learn to write. The only way to learn all the conventions of spelling, punctuation, capitalization, paragraphing, even grammar, and style, is through reading. Authors teach readers about writing.

In the next two chapters, I describe learning in metaphorical terms as the *membership of clubs*. By joining the club of readers, individuals can learn to become readers and writers. But reading also opens the doors to any club that can be the topic of a book, which probably means most of the clubs in the world and certainly many clubs that could not exist in the world as we know it. Reading is the club of clubs, the only possibility of many experiences of learning.

And finally, there are emotional concomitants and consequences of reading. Reading, like everything else, inevitably involves feelings. On the positive side, reading can provide interest and excitement, it can stimulate and alleviate curiosity, console, encourage, arouse passions, relieve loneliness, assuage tedium or anxiety, palliate sadness, and on occasion anaesthetize. On the negative side, reading can bore, confuse, and generate resentment. The emotional response to reading is treated insufficiently in most books about literacy (not excluding the present volume), although it is the primary reason most readers read, and probably the primary reason most nonreaders do not read.

Because of the range and depth of feelings involved, attitudes toward reading become habitual. Reading can become a desired activity or an undesirable one. People can become inveterate readers. They can also become inveterate nonreaders, even when they are capable of reading. One of the great tragedies of contemporary education is not so much that many students leave school unable to read and to write, but that many graduate with an antipathy to reading and writing, despite the abilities they might have. Nothing about reading or its instruction is inconsequential.

READING AND THINKING

The heading may be a trifle misleading. Reading *is* thinking, as I hope I have demonstrated throughout this chapter. And the thinking we do when we read, in order to read, is no different from the thinking we do on other occasions. Just as we cannot talk without thinking, or understand what someone is saying without thinking, or make any sense of the world without thinking, so it is impossible to read and not think. (If we sometimes say that we have spoken without thinking, we mean that we did not consider all the implications of what we said.) Reading is thinking that is partly focused on the visual information of print; it is thinking that is stimulated and directed by written language. The only time we might attempt to read without thinking is when the text we are trying to read is meaningless to us, a situation unlikely to persist in normal circumstances.

It is true that we may read a story or magazine to relax, in order not to think about particular things—but we obviously have to think enough about whatever we are reading in order to be distracted from other thoughts. If we fail to read every story with the intensity and acumen of a literary critic, it is probably not because we cannot think, but because we are not interested in reading like a literary critic.

The thought in which we engage while we are reading is like the thought we engage in while involved in any kind of experience. Fulfilling intentions, making choices, anticipating outcomes, and making sense of situations are not aspects of thinking exclusive to fluent reading. We must draw inferences, make decisions, and solve problems in order to understand what is going on in situations that involve reading and situations that do not. Reading demands no unique forms or "skills" of thought.

Thought that transpires as a consequence of reading is similarly no different from the reflection that can occur after any experience. We reconstruct an experience we have had, sometimes just for the pleasure of having it again; we wonder why events transpired the way they did, and whether they could have transpired differently. Reading can facilitate further thinking. We can join the clubs of authors, or of characters in books, who think in different ways about matters we might never otherwise contemplate and as a consequence we become more versatile and efficient thinkers ourselves. On the other hand, if we are generally not disposed to think critically in particular circumstances, or if we do not feel we have the authority to think critically about what certain "experts" are asserting, then we are unlikely to think critically when we read. The failure of children—or adults—to think in certain ways when they read may be less a matter of inadequate skill than of expectations about the manner in which they should think on any occasion (Smith, 1990).

An enormous advantage of reading over thinking in other circumstances is the *control* that it offers over events. Readers can pause in the middle of an experience for reflection. Readers can relive reading experiences, as often as they wish, and examine them from many points of view. Readers can even skip over experiences they are not interested in having or that would disrupt their flow of thought. Readers have *power*.

Reading is no different in essence from any other manifestation of thoughtful activity—but it may be the most natural and satisfying form of thinking available to us. The human brain runs on stories. Our theory of the world is largely in the form of stories. Stories are far more easily remembered and recalled than sequences of unrelated facts. The most trivial small episodes and vignettes are intrinsically more interesting than data. We cannot see random patterns or dots (or clouds or stars) without putting faces or figures to them. We cannot even observe small points of light moving randomly against a dark background without seeing them " interact" with each other in a narrative fashion (Michotte, 1946).

Thinking thrives on stories, on the construction and exploration of patterns of events and ideas, and reading often offers greater scope for engaging in stories than any other kind of activity.

ISSUES

The rift between experience and information approaches to teaching reading is less an unresolved problem than a gulf between totally antagonistic points of view, making a tremendous difference to how research is interpreted, theories developed, and teaching and learning perceived. The nature of reading itself is at issue; whether it is a process of acquiring information from print which may be turned on in any circumstances or a creative experiential interaction in an environment of print. When teachers and learners are evaluated on "performance indicators" or on the "product" or "output" of reading instruction, it is almost invariably acquisition of information rather than quality of experience that is assessed.

SUMMARY

Reading—like writing and all other forms of thinking—can never be separated from the purposes, prior knowledge, and feelings of the person engaged in the activity nor from the nature of the text being read. The **conventions** of texts permit the **expectations** of readers and the **intentions** of writers to meet. **Global** and **focal** expectations and intentions form a personal **specification** that readers and writers develop and modify as they proceed through a text. The fluency of reading depends as much on characteristics of the text and reader as on reading ability. Experienced readers who find a text difficult may read like beginners (who are likely to find most reading difficult).

Notes to Chapter 10 begin on page 279, covering
Comprehension and thinking
Reading speed
Comprehension and context
Other aspects of reading
Reading and writing

11

Learning About the World and About Language

This chapter, which introduces the topic of learning, is not specifically concerned with learning to read, a matter postponed to the next and final chapter. But this chapter is concerned with the *manner* in which children learn to read, because this is the same as the manner in which children achieve mastery of spoken language and, even earlier, begin learning about the world in general through their first elaborations of a theory of the world.

The present chapter provides an appropriate link with many of the preceding chapters, with their emphasis on comprehension in reading, because it shows that the basis of all learning, including learning how to read, is comprehension. Children learn by relating their understanding of the new to what they know already, while modifying or elaborating their prior knowledge. Learning is continuous and completely natural, and it is not necessary to propose separate "processes" of motivation and reinforcement to sustain and consolidate learning (nor should it be necessary for teachers to regard motivation and reinforcement as separate concerns that can be grafted onto reading instruction). Children may not always find it easy or even necessary to learn what we try to teach them, but they find the state of not learning anything at all intolerable.

CONSTRUCTING A THEORY OF THE WORLD

Chapter 1 discussed the complex yet precise and accurate theory of the world that we all possess. Obviously, we were not born with such a theory. The ability to construct a theory of the world and to predict from it may be innate, but the actual contents of the theory, the specific detail underlying the order and structure that we come to perceive in the world, is not part of our birthright. But equally obviously, very little of our theory can be attributed to instruction. Only a small part of what we know is actually *taught* to us. Teachers and other adults are given altogether too much credit for what we learn as children.

The Cat and Dog Problem

Consider again what it is that we know that enables us to tell the difference between cats and dogs. What were we taught that has given us this skill? It is impossible to say. Just try to write a description of cats and dogs that would enable a being from outer space—or a child who has never seen cats and dogs before—to tell the difference. Anything you might want to say about the appearance of some dogs, that they have long tails or pointed ears or furry coats, will apply to some cats and not to other dogs. The fact is that the difference between cats and dogs is *implicit*, knowledge that we cannot put into words. Nor can we communicate this knowledge by pointing to a particular part of cats and dogs and saying "That is where the difference lies."

Differences obviously exist between cats and dogs, but you cannot find and do not need language to distinguish them. Children without language can tell the difference between cats and dogs. Cats and dogs can tell the difference between cats and dogs. But if we cannot say what this difference is, how can we teach it to children? What we do, of course, is point out to children examples of the two kinds of animal. We say "That is a cat" or "There goes a dog." But pointing out examples does not teach children anything; it merely confronts them with the problem. In effect, we say "There is something I call a cat. Now you find out why." The "teacher" poses the problem and leaves the child to discover the solution.

The same argument applies to just about everything we can distinguish in the world, to all the letters of the alphabet, to numbers, chairs and tables, houses, foodstuffs, flowers, trees, utensils, and toys, to every kind of animal, bird, and fish, to every face, every car and plane and ship, thousands upon thousands of objects that we can recognize not only by sight but by other senses as well. And when did anyone tell us the rules? How often has anyone told us "Chairs can be recognized because they have four legs and a seat and possibly a back and arms"? (You can see how inadequate a description that would be.) Instead, somebody once said, "There is a chair" and left us to decide not only how to recognize chairs on other occasions but also to discover what exactly the word *chair* means, how chairs are related to everything else in the world.

With reading we do not even need someone to pose the problem in the first place. Reading at the same time presents both the problem and the possibility of its solution. Just by virtue of being a reader, every one of us has acquired a sight vocabulary of at least 50,000 words, words that we can identify on sight the way we recognize familiar faces and houses and trees. How did we acquire this enormous talent? Fifty thousand flashcards? Fifty thousand times a teacher wrote a word on a board and told us what it was? Fifty thousand times we blended together the sound of a word through phonics? We have learned to recognize words by reading.

Not only can we recognize 50,000 words on sight—and also, of course, by sound—we can usually make sense of all these words. Where have all the meanings come from? Fifty thousand trips to the dictionary? Fifty thousand vocabulary lessons? We have learned all the conventions of language through using language, by speaking it, reading it, and making sense of it. What we know about language is largely implicit, just like our knowledge of cats and dogs. So little of our knowledge of language is actually taught, we underestimate how much of language we have learned.

Most of our theory of the world, including most of our knowledge of language, whether spoken or written, is not the kind of knowledge that can be put into words; it is more like the implicit cat-and-dog kind of knowledge. Knowledge which no one can put into words is not knowledge that can be communicated by direct instruction.

How, then, do we acquire and develop the theory of the world we have in our heads? How does it become so complex and precise and efficient? There seems to be only one answer: *by testing hypotheses.*

Learning by Hypothesis Testing

Children learn by testing hypotheses. For example, a child might hypothesize that the difference between cats and dogs is that cats have pointed ears. The child can then test this hypothesis by saying "There is a cat" or "What a nice cat" or "Hi cat" when any animal with pointed ears passes by, and "There is a dog" (or "That's not a cat") for any animal without pointed ears. Any reaction tells the child whether the hypothesis is justified or not. If someone says, "Yes, there's a pretty cat" or accepts the child's statement by making no overt response, then the child has learned that the hypothesis has worked, on this occasion at least. The child's theory can be tentatively modified to include a rule that cats are animals with pointed ears. But if someone says to the child "No, that's a dog" or even "Think again, stupid," then the child knows that the hypothesis has failed. Another hypothesis must be selected and tested. Clearly more than one test will be required; it will take experience with cats and dogs before a child can be reasonably certain of having uncovered the true differences between them (whatever the differences may be). But the principle is always the same: Stay with your theory for as long as it works; modify your theory; look for another hypothesis whenever it fails.

Note that it is essential for the child to understand the problem in the first place. Children will not learn to recognize cats simply by being shown cats; they will not know what to look for. Both cats and dogs must be seen in order for the hypothesis about their relevant differences to arise. Children learn each letter of the alphabet by seeing them all; they must see what the alternatives are.

There is an intimate connection between comprehension and learning. Children's tests never go beyond their theories; they must comprehend what they are doing all the time they are learning. Anything that bewilders a child will be ignored; there is nothing to be learned there. It is not nonsense that stimulates children to learn but the possibility of making sense; that is why children grow up speaking language and not imitating the noise of the air conditioner. Children do not learn by being denied access to problems. A child learning to talk must be immersed in spoken language, and it is far better that a beginning reader having difficulties should be helped to read than be deprived of reading.

This process of hypothesis testing goes on instinctively, below the level of awareness. If we were aware of the hypotheses we test, then we could say what it is that enables us to tell the difference between cats and dogs. We are no more conscious of the hypotheses that underlie learning than we are of the predictions that underlie comprehension, or of the theory of the world itself. Indeed, there is basically no difference between comprehension and learning; hypotheses are simply tentative predictions.

LEARNING ABOUT LANGUAGE

When does all this testing take place? I think that for young children there is only one answer: They are testing hypotheses all the time. Their predictions are always tentative. This assertion is best illustrated with respect to the topic with which we are most concerned, namely language.

Bringing Meaning to Speech

Children who have just begun to talk frequently make statements that are completely obvious. A child looking out of a window with you will say something like "See big plane" although you may even have pointed the plane out in the first place. Why then should the child bother to make the statement? The answer is because the child is testing hypotheses. In fact, a child could be conducting no fewer than three different tests at the same time in that one simple situation.

The child could be testing the hypothesis that the object you can both clearly see in the sky *is* a plane, that it is not a bird or cloud or something else unidentified. When you say "Yes, I see it," you are confirming that the object is a plane. Even silence is helpful, because the child would expect you to make a correction if the hypothesis were in error. The second hypothesis that the child might be testing concerns the sounds of the language, that the name "plane" is the right name for the object, rather than "pwane," "prane," or whatever else the child might say. Once again the child can assume that if you do not take the opportunity to make a correction, then there is nothing to be corrected. A test has been successfully conducted. The third hypothesis that the child may be testing is linguistic, whether "See big plane" is a grammatically acceptable and meaningful sentence in adult language. The feedback comes when the adult says "Yes, I can see the big plane." The child learns to produce sentences in your language by using tentative sentences for which you both already know the meaning, *in a situation which you both comprehend.*

The same principle of making sense of language by understanding the situation in which it is used applies in the other direction as children learn to *comprehend* adult speech. At the beginning of language learning, infants must be able to understand what adults say before they can understand adult language. Does that statement sound paradoxical? What I mean is that children do not come to understand sentences like "Would you like a drink of juice?" or even the meaning of single words like *juice*, by figuring out the language or by having someone tell them the rules. Children learn because initially they can hypothesize the meaning of a statement from the situation in which it is uttered. An adult is usually carrying or pointing to a drink of juice when a sentence like "Would you like a drink of juice?" is spoken. This language is situation-dependent speech. From such situations a child can hypothesize what might happen the next time someone mentions *juice*. The situation provides the meaning and the utterance provides the evidence; that is all a child needs to construct hypotheses that can be tested on future occasions. Children do not learn language to make sense of words and sentences; they make sense of words and sentences in understanding how language is used (Macnamara, 1972). Adults help children to do this through "caretaker talk"—sometimes called "motherese" (and "fatherese")—engaging infants in language use, making language easy and useful. We shall see a similar phenomenon in the way adults (or other experienced readers) support children in their learning to read by reading to them and for them.

There is an interesting role for the eyes to play in these first experiences with language. Newson and Newson (1975) noted that the sharing of meaning is facilitated by a convergence of gaze. When a parent offers an infant a drink of juice, they are probably looking not at each other but at the juice that the adult is offering. When a parent says "Ah, there's a big dog" to a baby who does not understand a word of speech, the gaze of parent and baby is likely to converge on the dog. By bringing a possible meaning to the utterance the infant can hypothesize a relationship between the two, and thus test, confirm, or modify provisional rules about this relationship—a highly efficient procedure that will work only if the infant can make sense of the purpose of adult language.

I know of no research on how much spoken language children might learn simply by observation. But if a baby can hypothesize and test a potential meaning when offered juice, there is no reason why the child could not test a similar hypothesis by overhearing one adult offer another a cup of coffee, provided the entire situation can also be seen. The child could again compare probable meaning with utterance. There are obvious limits to the number of language interchanges in which infants are directly involved. It might at least seem possible that most infants overhear far more language than is actually addressed to them, though again there is no research on the issue. And by and large much of this overheard domestic language would be situationally meaningful; it would have purposes and outcomes that are both predictable and testable.

It is in fact the purposes of language, the uses to which it is put, which are the key to infant language learning. As the linguist Halliday (1973) has pointed out, children learn language and its uses simultaneously. They do not learn language, either spoken or written, which they then use for various purposes. The learning comes with the use of language and with the understanding of its uses. Language learning is incidental. Children do not learn about language as an abstraction, as an end in itself, but in the process of achieving other ends, like getting another drink of juice, learning to distinguish cats from dogs, or striving to enjoy a story from a book. The basic insight that must enable a child to make sense of speech is that its sounds are not random, they are not arbitrarily substitutable. By this I mean that the sounds of speech make a difference, they are there for a purpose. An adult cannot produce the sounds "There's a truck" when the intended meaning is "Let's go for a walk."

THREE ASPECTS OF LEARNING

Learning is the modification or elaboration of what is already known, of cognitive structure, our theory of the world. What exactly is modified or elaborated? It can be any of the three components of the theory: the category system, the rules for relating objects or events to categories (sets of distinctive features), or the complex network of interrelations among categories.

Children are constantly required to establish new categories in their cognitive structure and to discover the rules that limit the allocation of events to a new category. They have to learn that not all animals are cats and dogs but that some animals are. Children learning to sight-recognize the printed word *cat* have to establish a visual category for that word, just as they must have a category for actual cats, distinguished from other categories for dogs, and so forth. Skilled readers develop categories for every letter of the alphabet and also for every word that can be identified on sight, together, possibly, with categories for frequently occurring syllabic groups of letters, for rhymes, and for meaningful segments like plurals and tense markers. This process of learning to establish categories involves hypothesizing what are the significant differences—the only reason to establish a new category is to make a new differentiation in our experience, and the learning problem is to find the significant differences that should define the category.

Each category that we distinguish must be specified by at least one set of distinctive features. Every time children succeed in learning to recognize something new, they must have established a new set of distinctive features. But usually they go further and establish *alternative* sets of features for specifying the same categories. They learn that an *a*, *a*, or even an *A* should be categorized as the letter "a" just as many different-looking animals must be categorized as a cat. Any set of features that will serve to categorize an object is a criterial set, and alternative sets for the same category are *functionally equivalent*. As children learn, they discover more and more ways in which to make the decision that a particular object or event should be categorized in a certain way. The number of functionally equivalent criterial sets gets larger. Learning is also involved in the ability to make use of less and less featural information to comprehend text. We ran into many examples of the use of functionally equivalent criterial sets of features in our discussion of the processes of reading. Most skilled readers can identify words that have had large parts (many features) obliterated and can make sense of text that has even more features obliterated. All this is possible because we have learned to make optimal use of the information that is available, both visually and from our acquired knowledge of the language.

Finally, children constantly learn new interrelationships among categories, developing their ability to make sense of language and the world. Understanding how words go together in meaningful language makes prediction possible and, therefore, comprehension. These interrelationships are also not taught. But a child can learn them by the same process of hypothesis testing. Comprehension is the basis of a child's learning to read, but reading, in turn, contributes to a child's growing ability to comprehend by permitting elaboration of the complex structure of categories, feature lists, and interrelationships that constitute every child's theory of the world.

LEARNING ALL THE TIME

Learning is a continual and effortless process, as natural as breathing. A child does not have to be especially motivated or rewarded for learning; in fact the thrust is so natural that being deprived of the opportunity to learn is aversive.

Children will struggle to get out of situations where there is nothing to learn, just as they will struggle to escape from situations where breathing is difficult. Inability to learn is suffocating.

There is no need to worry that children who are not constantly driven and cajoled will "take the easy way out" and not learn. Young children who read the same book twenty times, even though they know the words by heart, are not avoiding more "challenging" material in order to avoid learning; they are still learning. It may not be until they know just about every word in a book that they can get on with some of the more complex aspects of reading, such as testing hypotheses about meaning and learning to use as little visual information as possible.

Underestimating Learning

It is because children learn continuously and effortlessly that adults generally fail to give them credit for the amount of learning that they do. It is a widespread adult belief that learning is a difficult and even painful activity, that it involves grappling with something which you do not understand, and therefore necessarily leaves its marks of effort and strain. But in fact, the sight of a child struggling to learn is a clear sign that learning is not taking place, that the child is confronted by something incomprehensible. When learning does occur, it is normally inconspicuous, an intrinsic but incidental part of doing something else that makes sense in its own right.

Because of this common myth that learning is effortful, many adults believe that they themselves do not learn often or without strain. They regard learning as a struggle to make sense of a textbook or set of exercises, not as something that takes place whenever they relax to read a magazine or enjoy a movie on television. But the next day they can relate a large part of what interested them in the magazine and recall a surprising amount of detail from the movie, detail which may stay with them for months or years afterward. If we can remember, we must have learned, and it is pointless to argue that this was not learning because there was no conscious effort to remember. For reasons already set out in Chapter 5, the conscious effort to memorize the magazine or movie would probably have interfered with both the comprehension and the memorization. The "making sense" and the learning go on— or are destroyed—together.

Children will not willingly stay in any situation in which there is nothing for them to learn. They are equipped with a very efficient device that prevents their wasting time in situations where there is nothing to learn. That device is called *boredom*, and boredom is something all children want to escape. A child who is bored in class is not demonstrating ill will or inability or even cussedness; boredom should convey just one very clear message for the teacher. There is nothing in the particular situation for the child to learn.

There are two reasons why there might be nothing for a child to learn in a particular situation, and hence two reasons for boredom, that arise from quite different sources. One reason why children might have nothing to learn is very simple—they know it already. Children will not attend to anything they already know. But children will also suffer and exhibit the same symptoms of boredom because they cannot make sense of what they are expected to learn. Teachers might believe that a certain exercise will improve a child's useful knowledge or skills, but unless the child can see some sense in the exercise, the instruction is a waste of time.

The Risk and Rewards of Learning

There is one other reason why children might turn their faces against learning, and that is its risk. In order to learn you must take a chance. When you test a hypothesis, there must be a possibility of being wrong. If you are certain of being right, there can be nothing to learn because you know it already. And provided there is a possibility of being wrong, you learn whether you are right or not. If you have a hypothesis about what constitutes a cat, it makes no difference whether you say "cat" and are right or say "dog" and are wrong. In fact, you often get the most useful information when you are wrong because you may be right for the wrong reason, but when you are wrong you know you have made a mistake.

Many children become reluctant to learn because they are afraid of making a mistake—consider the relative credit children are given in and out of school for being "correct" and for being "wrong."

There should be no need for special inducements to motivate a child to learn. Children are in a condition to learn whenever they are confronted by something which seems meaningful and purposeful to them, something which should be part of their own theory of the world or repertoire of skills, provided they feel there is a chance that they can learn. They learn language, basically, because it is part of the world around them; because they see other people using it, because it makes sense. Irrelevant inducements—sometimes called extrinsic reinforcement—become necessary only when a child is confronted with something that does not make sense. And forcing a child to attend to nonsense is a pointless enterprise. Bewilderment is aversive.

Nor does learning need to be extrinsically rewarded. The final exquisite virtue of learning is that it provides its own reward. Learning is satisfying, as everyone knows. It is part of the totally fulfilling and absorbing state of *flow* described by Csikszentmihalyi (1990), that we achieve only by losing ourselves in what we are doing. Deprivation of learning opportunities is boring, and failure to learn is frustrating. If a child needs reinforcement for learning, then there is only one conclusion to be drawn: that the child does not see any sense in the activity in the first place.

THE CONDITIONS OF LEARNING

I want to recapitulate and elaborate upon what I have said about learning in a rather different way. Learning is a continuous process, a natural state of the brain, and children therefore are likely to be learning all the time. There can be no other explanation for the enormous amount of unsuspected learning of the conventions of language that takes place. What then are the conditions under which these ever-learning brains succeed in learning as much about language as they do? In what kind of circumstance do children learn to read? And why is it that learning sometimes fails, as it sometimes fails for all of us, so that something which even the learner wants to master remains unlearned? Three constituents seem to determine what is learned, when it is learned, and whether indeed learning will take place at all. These may be termed *demonstrations*, which are learning conditions existing in the world around us; *engagement*, which is the interaction of the learner with a demonstration; and *sensitivity*, the learner's learning state.

Demonstrations

The first essential constituent of learning is the opportunity to see what can be done and how. Such opportunities may be termed *demonstrations* because they literally show a potential learner "This is how something is done." The world continually provides demonstrations, through people and through their products, by acts and by artifacts.

Every act is a cluster of demonstrations. A parent saying to a child "Here's your juice" is demonstrating the meaning of the word juice and the language with which juice is presented. A parent who says "There's a big dog" is demonstrating that there is a category of objects called dogs, that "dog" is the name of that category, and that the animal being referred to is a member of that category with all the appropriate distinctive features. A teacher who stands before a class demonstrates how a teacher stands before a class, how a teacher talks, how a teacher dresses, how a teacher feels about what is being taught and about the people being taught. A tired teacher demonstrates how a tired teacher behaves, a disinterested teacher demonstrates disinterest. Enthusiasm demonstrates enthusiasm. What kinds of things are demonstrated in classrooms? The fact that children are learning all the time is a time bomb in every classroom. What kind of reading do children see teachers doing? What do teachers demonstrate about their interest in reading?

Every artifact is a cluster of demonstrations. Every book demonstrates how pages are put together, how print and illustrations are organized on pages, how words are set out in sentences, and how sentences are punctuated. A book demonstrates the appearance and meaning of every word in that book. It demonstrates a particular genre scheme, discourse structure, and perhaps a story grammar too. What kinds of things do our artifacts in the classroom demonstrate? Is it possible that children, and older students, are exposed to demonstrations that books can be incomprehensible, that they can be nonsense?

An important category of demonstrations is self-generated, like those we can perform in our imagination. We can try things out in the mind—in the world inside us rather than in the world around us—and explore possible consequences without anyone actually knowing what we are doing. How much opportunity do children have for such private demonstrations?

The world is full of demonstrations, although people and the most appropriate demonstrations may not be brought together at the most appropriate times. And even when there is a relevant demonstration, learning may not take place. There has to be some kind of interaction so that "This is how something is done" becomes "This is something I can do."

Engagement

The term engagement was chosen deliberately for the productive interaction of a learner with a demonstration, because my image is of the meshing of gears. Learning occurs when the learner *engages* with a demonstration, so that it becomes, in effect, the learner's demonstration.

Most people are familiar with the experience of reading a book or magazine and stopping suddenly, not because of something they did not understand, but because their attention was engaged by a spelling they did not know. They did not start to read to have a spelling lesson, nor could they have predicted the unfamiliar spelling that they actually met, but when they encountered it—perhaps a name that they had only previously heard on radio or television—they stopped and in effect said "Ah, so that's the way that word is spelled." At such a moment we can catch ourselves in the act of learning; we have not simply responded to a spelling, we have made it a part of what we know. Sometimes it is not a spelling that stops us, but a particularly interesting fact or the answer to a question which has been puzzling us for some time.

The second example is similar. Once again we find ourselves pausing while we read, this time not because of a spelling or some other piece of information, and certainly not for lack of understanding, but simply because we have just read something that is *particularly well put*, an interesting idea appropriately expressed. This time we have engaged not with a spelling or an interesting new item of information, but with a style, a tone, a register. We are learning about language vicariously, learning how it is used from the way someone else is using it.

The two examples given were necessarily of situations in which we might actually be consciously aware of a learning moment. But such moments are rare. Perhaps we catch ourselves engaging with a new spelling or idea because it is a relatively infrequent event in our lives, because we have learned most of the things we want or expect to learn by now. New information or experiences can be surprising. But children learning the sounds, meanings, and written appearance of scores of new words every day of their lives are hardly likely to be stopped, like an adult, by the novelty of actually meeting something new. Instead, most of their learning must be like adults learning from the newspapers and the movies, an engagement so close and persistent that it does not intrude into consciousness.

Learning by engaging in the demonstrations of others is a particularly efficient and economical way for children to learn, because it limits the possibility of mistake and uncertainty. You are not likely to be in error if you let the demonstrator do your learning trials for you. This is learning by conducting experiments, where the other person (who can do it) conducts the experiment. It is hypothesis-testing where the appropriate hypothesis is easily available in the skilled performance of the demonstrator.

Children engage with particular kinds of demonstrations because "that is the kind of person they are," because they take it for granted that these are the kinds of things they should and could know. Obviously children can learn by doing things themselves. With engagement they can assimilate the demonstration of another (in an act or artifact) and make it vicariously an action—and a learning act—of their own. What I still must account for is what makes us all the kinds of person that we are; what determines whether or not engagement takes place.

Sensitivity

What makes the difference in whether we learn or do not learn from any particular demonstration? The answer cannot be motivation, a grossly overrated factor, especially in schools where it is sometimes used to cover a multitude of other possibilities. For a start, learning of the kind described in this chapter usually occurs in the absence of motivation, certainly in the sense of a deliberate, conscious intention. It makes no sense to say an infant is motivated to learn to talk or that we are motivated to remember what is in the newspaper, unless the meaning of motivation is made so general that it cannot be separated from learning.

On the other hand, motivation does not ensure learning. No matter how much they are motivated to spell, or to write fluently, or to learn a foreign language, many people still fail to learn these things. Desire and effort do not necessarily produce learning. Indeed, the only relevance of motivation to learning that I can see is that it puts us in situations where appropriate demonstrations are particularly likely to occur, and learning will certainly not take place if there is motivation *not* to learn.

Closer to the truth is that we learn when we expect to learn, when learning is taken for granted. But a *conscious* expectation is not precisely what is required. Infants may take learning to talk for granted, but not in the sense of consciously expecting it. Rather, what seems to make the difference is absence of the expectation that learning will not take place.

This is how I propose to define sensitivity, the third constituent of every learning situation: the absence of expectation that learning will not take place or that it will be difficult. Where does sensitivity come from? Every child is born with it. Children do not need to be taught that they can learn; they have this implicit expectation which they demonstrate in their earliest learning about language and about the world—they believe they are omnipotent. Experience teaches children that they have limitations, and unfortunately, experience often teaches them this unnecessarily.

Why is learning to walk usually so much easier than learning to swim? Walking must surely be the more difficult accomplishment. Infants have scarcely any motor coordination and on two tottering feet they must struggle against gravity. Little wonder walking takes several months to master. Swimming, on the other hand, can be learned in a weekend—if it is learned at all. It is learned when the learner has much better motor coordination and is in a supportive element—water. And it must be as "natural" as walking. So why the difference? Could it be that difficulty and failure are so often anticipated with swimming and not with walking?

Why is learning to talk generally so easy while learning to read is sometimes so much harder? The answer cannot be the intrinsic difficulty of reading. Infants learning to talk start with essentially nothing; they must make sense of it all for themselves. Despite the remarkable speed with which they are usually credited with learning about language, it still takes them several years to show anything approaching mastery. Reading should be learned more quickly, as it has so much language understanding to support it. And when children do learn to read, whether they learn at three years of age, or six, or ten, they learn—in the observation of many teachers—in a matter of a few weeks. The instruction may last for years, but the learning is accomplished in weeks. What is the difference? I can only think that with reading an expectation of failure is frequently communicated to the child.

The apparent "difficulty" of some learning cannot be explained away on the basis of age. Teenagers are expected to learn to drive cars—surely as complicated a matter as learning to swim, if not to read—and lo, they learn to drive cars. In fact, for anything any of us is interested in, where the learning is taken for granted, we continue to learn throughout our lives. We do not even realize we are learning, as we keep up to date with our knowledge of language, music, astronomy, automotive engineering, spelling, world affairs, the television world, or whatever—for the "kind of person" we happen to be.

Engagement takes place in the presence of appropriate demonstrations whenever we are sensitive to learning, and sensitivity is an absence of expectation that learning will not take place. Sensitivity is obviously related to two factors I mentioned earlier regarding willingness to engage in critical thinking, namely disposition and authority. Individuals who do not feel competent to think critically on particular occasions, because of the way they perceive themselves or the way others perceive them, could be said to lack sensitivity for critical thinking. If they do not feel it is appropriate or possible for them to behave in a particular way, they will also feel that it is inappropriate (and probably impossible) for them to learn to behave in those ways. Lacking the disposition and authority to learn, they will decline opportunities for the necessary engagement.

Sensitivity does not need to be accounted for; its absence does. Expectation that learning will not take place is itself learned. The ultimate irony is that our constant propensity to learn may in fact defeat learning; we can learn that particular things are not worth learning or are unlikely to be learned. Children are indiscriminate in their learning—the time bomb in the classroom—and they can learn things which they would really do much better not learning at all. Learning that something is useless, unpleasant, difficult, or improbable may be devastatingly permanent in its effect.

LEARNING—A SOCIAL EVENT

So far learning has been discussed as if it were the entire responsibility of the learner, a matter of individual effort. But this is not the case. Whether or not learning takes place usually depends more on people around learners than on the learners themselves. Personal effort does not guarantee learning, nor does conscious motivation. Learners often need do nothing in order to learn. Someone else does something, and the learner learns. Neither the learner nor the people around the learner need know that learning is taking place. Learning is usually inconspicuous.

Family and friends are generally unaware of how much even the youngest children learn of spoken language, for example. Infants do not *practice* talking, they say something—and usually they are right first time. They occasionally make mistakes, of course, and when they do, grownups regard the mistakes as cute and tell their friends. But most of the time parents find themselves saying "Where did the child learn to say that?" Learning inconspicuously and effortlessly continues into adulthood. How else would we all learn the meanings of the scores of thousands of words that we know and to talk the way we do? Where does it all come from?

The typical absence of evident error might seem to provide problems for the hypothesis testing point of view adopted earlier in this chapter. If children test hypotheses in order to learn, they must get the hypotheses right most of the time. And right or wrong, where do the hypotheses come from?

The answer to all of these questions must be—from other people. Much of what children (and adults) learn, they learn when they are not trying to learn, but when they are interested in something someone else is doing. To use a term I have already employed, children learn when they are engaged in an activity that someone else may actually be doing. They learn as if they were doing it themselves. The learning is vicarious.

Learning From Other People

George Miller (1977) recognized the importance of other people in the title of his book *Spontaneous Apprentices: Children and Language.* He argued that infants learn to talk and to understand speech by apprenticing themselves to adults or to more competent children. And they learn to talk just like the people they apprentice themselves to. Children do not even learn to talk like the people they hear talking most. (Once they get to school, children hear their teachers talking more than anyone else, but they do not grow up talking like teachers—unless they are going to become teachers themselves.)

No *modeling* is involved. It is not a matter of infants saying "I want to be like that person," and studying and practicing the other person's behavior. Instead, the child seems effortlessly to learn what the other person does. The other person is an unwitting surrogate for the child's learning. If this is trial and error learning, other people conduct the trial, and because they can already do what they are doing, there are very few errors.

A baby babbles, someone else puts the utterance into conventional language—"You want a drink of juice?"—and the child has learned something about drinks of juice, without practice, without error. One adult says to another "Pass the salt"—it could be babble as far as the infant is concerned— but their behavior allows the infant to hypothesize the meaning of the utterance. If the salt is passed, the child has learned by hypothesis testing, without error and without anyone knowing that learning has taken place.

We learn when we comprehend. (A struggle to learn is always a struggle to comprehend.) Other people help us to learn by helping us to understand. That is essentially the social nature of learning, even when we are learning from books, when it is the author's responsibility to facilitate the reader's comprehension.

Joining the Spoken Language Club

An alternative metaphor for explaining how infants learn about language (and everything else) is that they join a club (Smith, 1988). Infants join communities of people they see themselves as being like, who accept the infants as being like them, and the infants learn to be exactly like other members of the club. They learn not to be like members of the clubs they do not belong to.

A spoken language club is probably the first club most infants join, but it has exactly the same advantages as any other club they might join later in life. First, more experienced members disclose the nature of the club's activities. These are the demonstrations I have referred to in this chapter. In the spoken language club, members show the child what spoken language can be used for, how it helps to fulfil intentions in a variety of ways.

Second, when new members of the club themselves want to engage in club activities—when they want to use spoken language to fulfil their own intentions—more experienced members of the club help. They do not give newcomers *instruction* from which learning is supposed to take place, they provide *collaboration*. To be specific, other members help the infant to say what the infant is trying to say, and they help the infant to understand what the infant is trying to understand. The learner is totally involved because everything centers on the learner's intentions and interest—this is the engagement to which I referred earlier.

Children finish up talking exactly like their friends, the other members of the spoken language club they eventually affiliate with. They learn to dress and ornament themselves exactly like their friends—like the kind of person they see themselves as being. They learn the other club members' ways of perceiving the world, their attitudes, their values, their dislikes, their imperatives. They learn a *culture*—not by practice or by trial and error, but by imperceptibly yet inevitably coming to be exactly like the kind of person they see themselves as being. In other words, the clubs they join become their identity.

If we see ourselves as members of a club, and the club members do not exclude us, then we cannot help becoming like the other members because of the demonstrations and collaboration we receive. But if we are rejected by a club, or if we decide to exclude ourselves, then we not only fail to become like the club members, we often become as different from them as we can be. We lose our sensitivity—and it is usually almost impossible to get it back. It is as if we do not want to be mistaken for members of the club—except that none of the learning or failure to learn is under conscious control. Everyone fails, in one way or another, to become members of clubs of people who have mastered things like statistics, automobile engines, computer programming, algebra, identifying constellations—or reading or writing. This has nothing to do with motivation or effort—the most conspicuous things most of us have failed to learn are often things we have been most motivated to learn, and that we have spent the most "time on task" trying to learn.

The social nature of learning has been most influentially urged in recent years through the work of Lev Vygotsky. In *Mind and Society*, Vygotsky (1978) outlines his concept of a *zone of proximal development*. He demonstrates that everyone can do things with assistance that they cannot do alone, and what they can do with collaboration on one occasion they will be able to do independently on another. It is within the zone of proximal development,

Vygotsky argues, that learning takes place; it should be the area on which educational effort is focused. Successful teachers collaborate with learners in enterprises in which the learners want to be engaged, in the zone of proximal development.

ISSUES

Despite all the everyday evidence to the contrary, it is still commonly taken for granted that learning is the result of frequency and intensity of effort. Many politicians and media authorities in particular appear convinced that failure to learn indicates a lack of trying on the part of students and their teachers. Increasingly influential among specialists is the connectionist view that learning is a mindless consequence of "spreading activation" among neural networks, a new behaviorism, which may be true in a metaphorical sense but says nothing at all about the conditions of learning and teaching.

SUMMARY

Most of what individuals know about language and the world is not formally taught. Instead, children develop their theory of the world and competence in language by testing **hypotheses,** experimenting in meaningful and purposeful ways with tentative modifications of what they know already. Thus the basis of learning is **comprehension.** Children learn continuously, through **engagement** in **demonstrations** that make sense to them, whenever their natural **sensitivity** for learning is undamaged. Learning is a social activity. Children learn from what other people do and help them to do.

Notes to Chapter 11 begin on page 286, covering
Language learning
Vocabulary
Learning as a social event
Motivation

12 Learning to Use Written Language

This book is primarily about reading, therefore this chapter is primarily about learning to read. But nothing a child learns about reading—whether about letter identification, word identification, or the comprehension of print—will make any sense unless the child has an understanding of what written language does. Hence the title of this chapter. The first insight every learner must have in order to become a reader (or a writer) is that written language makes sense—an insight not always easy to achieve in educational settings.

THE IMPORTANCE OF NONVISUAL INFORMATION

There is only one way to summarize everything that a child must learn in order to become a fluent reader, and that is to say that the child must learn to use nonvisual information, or prior knowledge, efficiently when attending to written language. (And an understanding of the purposes and conventions of texts is a central part of nonvisual information.)

Learning to read does not require the memorization of letter names, or phonic rules, or a large vocabulary, all of which are in fact taken care of in the course of learning to read, and little of which will make sense to the child without some experience of reading. Nor is learning to read a matter of application to all manner of exercises and drills, which can only distract and perhaps even discourage a child from the business of learning to read. And finally, learning to read is not a matter of a child relying upon instruction, because the essential skills of reading—namely the efficient uses of nonvisual information—cannot be explicitly taught. But they can be demonstrated to children.

In a general sense, learning to read is very much like the cat-and-dog problem for children. No one can teach explicitly the relevant categories, distinctive features, and interrelationships that are involved. Yet children are perfectly capable of solving the problem for themselves provided they have the opportunities to generate and test their own hypotheses. In quite a literal sense, learning to read is like learning spoken language. No one can even begin to explain to infants what essential features and conventions of speech should be learned, let alone construct a course of study for infants to follow; yet even this complex problem is solved by children, without any apparent strain or difficulty, provided again that they have the opportunity to exercise their innate learning ability and are *helped* to use and understand speech. All that children require to master spoken language, both to produce it themselves and more fundamentally to comprehend its use by others, is to have experience of *using* language in a meaningful setting. Children easily learn about spoken language when they are involved in its use, when it has the possibility of making sense to them. And in the same way children will try to understand written language by being involved in its use, in situations where it makes sense to them and they can generate and test hypotheses.

No infallible method of instruction will ever be found to direct a child's progress in learning to read. But it was not possible to specify the precise course of a child's learning spoken language either (or learning the difference between cats and dogs for that matter). It is possible to specify the *conditions* under which children will learn to read, and these are again the general conditions that are required for learning anything—the opportunity to generate and test hypotheses in a meaningful, collaborative context. And to reiterate the constant theme, the only way a child can do all this for reading is to read. If the question arises how children can be expected to learn to read by reading before they have learned to read, the answer is very simple. At the beginning—and at any other time when it is necessary—the reading has to be done for them. Before children acquire any competence in reading, everything will have to be read to them, but as their ability expands they just need help, the opportunity to engage in reading demonstrations.

One of the beautiful things about written language that makes sense (to the child) is that it increasingly provides learning assistance to the child. Authors can take over teaching children to read. Meaningful written language, like meaningful speech, not only provides its own clues to meaning, so that children can generate appropriate learning hypotheses, but it also provides the opportunity for tests. If a beginning reader is not sure about the likely meaning of what is being attended to, the context (before *and* after) can provide clues. And the subsequent context will indicate whether the child's hypotheses were right or wrong. Reading text that makes sense is like riding a bicycle; children do not need to be told when they are falling off.

Let me list the advantages a child gains from reading meaningful written language—building vocabulary, making sense of letter-sound relationships, developing mediated meaning and word identification ability, acquiring speed, avoiding tunnel vision, preventing memory overload, relying on sense, acquiring familiarity with such relevant conventions as the appropriate discourse structure, grammar, and register—in short, increasing relevant nonvisual information and experience in using it more efficiently. And always the child will be the best guide to learning in the most efficient manner, because children will not willingly limit their vision, overload memory, or tolerate nonsense. Children also will not tolerate *not learning*, so just as there is no reason to expect that they will be satisfied with what has become simple for them, so also they should not be expected to remain in situations where no learning or comprehension is possible at all.

It is also easy to list the conditions required for children to take advantage of the learning opportunities that reading meaningful text provides. There are only four: access to meaningful and interesting reading material (ideally the child's own choice), assistance where needed (and only to the extent that it is required), a willingness to take the necessary risks (anxiety increases the proportion of visual information a reader needs), and freedom to make mistakes.

I have said little about motivation because it is not something that can be artificially promoted or maintained, certainly not by means of extrinsic "reinforcers" such as irrelevant material rewards, improved grades, or even extravagant praise. None of these is necessary for a child to learn spoken language. All the satisfaction that a child requires is in the learning itself, in the utility and understanding that result. And the impetus in the first place? Why do children set themselves the enormously time-consuming task of learning spoken language? Not, I think, in order to communicate. Children cannot understand this use of language until they have got some. And certainly not to get their material needs fulfilled or to control the behavior of others. Children are never so well looked after as before they can use language; afterwards they can be told to wait, to do without, or to do it themselves. When language fails, even adults can feel the urge to revert to earlier, nonverbal, and more assertive ways of trying to get their way. I think there can be only one reason why children apply themselves to learning spoken language—because it is *there*, a functioning part of the world around them. They learn when its sense, its utility, and its meaningfulness are demonstrated to them. And because language is meaningful, because it changes the world and is not arbitrary or capricious, not only do children succeed in learning it, but they want to learn it. Children will not stop learning anything that is meaningful to them, unless the learning becomes too difficult or too costly for them, in which case the learning itself becomes meaningless. The child's sensitivity for reading is destroyed.

Children will endeavor to understand and engage in anything they see adults doing, provided the adults demonstrate enjoyment and satisfaction in doing it. If meaningful written language exists in the child's world and is conspicuously used with satisfaction, then the child will strive to master its mystery; that is in the nature of childhood. There is no need for special explanations about why children should want to learn to read, only for why they might come to the conclusion that it is pointless or too costly.

TWO CRITICAL INSIGHTS

All this has been very general. No special theories of learning are required for how and why children learn to read. There is nothing unique about reading, whether from the point of view of the language skills involved (no different in principle from those of spoken language comprehension), the visual skills involved (no different from discriminating any aspects of the visual world), or of the situations in which learning takes place. There are, however, two special insights that children must have in order to learn to read. These insights are fundamental, in the sense that children who do not have them are bound to find reading instruction nonsensical and will not therefore succeed in learning to read. Yet not only are these insights not taught in school, much of what constitutes formal reading instruction might be seen as contrary to these insights, and thus likely to inhibit them. The insights, which I shall discuss in turn, are first, that print is meaningful, and second, that written language is not the same as speech.

Insight 1: Print Is Meaningful

There is no need to belabor why the insight that print is meaningful is an essential precondition for learning to read. Reading is a matter of making sense of print, and meaningfulness is the basis of learning. For as long as children see no sense in print, for as long as they regard it as arbitrary or nonsensical, they will find no reason to attend to print. They will not learn by trying to relate letters to sounds. Written language does not work in that way, and it is not something that can make any sense to children.

Research has offered abundant evidence that children are as much immersed in written language as they are in speech, and they respond to it with similar intelligence. I am not referring to school nor to those overrated books that are supposed to surround and somehow inspire some privileged children to literacy. I refer instead to the wealth of situation-dependent print to be found on every product in the bathroom, on every jar and package in the kitchen, in the television guide (and in television commercials), in comics, catalogs, advertising fliers, telephone directories, on street signs, store fronts, gas stations, bill-boards, at fast-food outlets, supermarkets, and department stores. All of this print is meaningful; it makes a difference. We no more predict cereal in a package labeled *detergent* than we expect *candy* in a store advertising cleaning or a concert in a television program announced as *football*.

For those not blind to it (which experienced readers are inclined to be), our visual world is an ocean of print, most of it (check your supermarket) literally right in front of our eyes. Even children who cannot yet read pay attention to it. I have told of a 3½-year-old boy who obviously could not read the words *luggage* and *footwear* on signs in a department store (because he got both of them wrong) but who nevertheless asserted that the first said "cases" and the second said "shoes" (Smith, 1976). Here was one child who could bring meaning to print long before he could read the actual print, and who therefore had acquired the insight that differences in print are meaningful.

There is only one way in which such an insight might be achieved, and that is when a child is being read to or observes print being responded to in a meaningful way. At this point, I am not referring to the reading of books or stories, but to the occasions when a child is told "That sign says 'Stop'," "That word on the door is 'Boys'," or "This is the jar for cookies." Television commercials may do the same for a child—they not only announce the product's name, desirability, and uniqueness in spoken and written language, but they even demonstrate the product at work. And just as with the spoken language of the home, there is a great deal a child might learn from this situation-dependent written language by hypothesizing a likely meaning and seeing if the hypothesis is confirmed. Children can test hypotheses about the meaning of the printed word *toys* in a store, not because anyone reads it to them, but by ascertaining whether the sign does in fact indicate the location of the toy department. There is a consistency between the print and its environment. The print that normally surrounds children is potentially meaningful, and thus provides an effective basis for learning.

There may be very little meaningful print in school, in the sense that it would not be possible to substitute one word for another. A teacher writes the words *table* or *chair* on the board but could just as well write *horse* or *cow*. The words in word lists, or the sentences in many "stories," could be changed without any child noticing anything out of place. Teachers may believe there are good reasons for a particular exercise or element of instruction, but if children cannot see the sense of the enterprise, then it can reasonably be regarded as incomprehensible. A brief list of fundamentally incomprehensible aspects of reading instruction to which children may be exposed would include:

1. The decomposition of spoken words to "sounds." The spoken word *cat*, in some contexts, can make sense, but the sounds *kuh, a, tuh* do not.
2. The decomposition of written words to letters. The printed word *cat*, in some contexts, can make sense—when it refers to a real or imaginary animal with which children can meaningfully interact. But the letters *c, a,* and *t* are arbitrary visual symbols that have nothing to do with anything else in the child's life.
3. The relating of letters to sounds. For a child who has no idea of reading to be told that some peculiar shapes called letters—which have no apparent function in the real world—are related to sounds that have no apparent independent existence in the real world must be the purest jabberwocky.
4. Meaningless drills and exercises. There are so many candidates for this category, ranging from deciding which of three ducks is facing the wrong way to underlining silent letters in words, that I shall not attempt to make a list. Children may learn to score high on repetitive and nonsensical tasks (especially if they happen to be competent readers), but such a specialized ability will not make readers of them.

The preceding kinds of activity may, through their very incomprehensibility, make learning to read more complicated, arduous, and nonsensical than it need be. It is not until children have begun reading that they have a chance of making sense of such activities at all. Children who do not have the insight that written language should make sense may never achieve it, while children who have it may be persuaded that they are wrong.

Insight 2: Written Language Is Different from Speech

The first insight was concerned primarily with written language in the form of single words (or small groups of words) like labels and signs. These kinds of print function very much like the everyday situation-dependent spoken language outside school in that cues to meaning (and constraints on interpretation) are provided largely by the physical situation in which they occur. Now I want to consider context-dependent written language, where constraints on substitutability and interpretation are placed not by the physical environment but by the syntax and semantics of the text itself. As discussed in Chapter 2, the conventions of written and spoken language are evidently not the same, and probably for very good reason, including the fact that written language has especially adapted itself for being read.

Children who expect written language to be exactly the same as speech are likely to have difficulty in predicting and comprehending its conventions and thus in learning to read. They must be familiar with how written language works. Immersion in functional language, the possibility of making sense, a plentiful experience, and the opportunity to test hypotheses would seem to be just as easily met with written language as with speech. In fact, written language might seem to have several advantages, because a number of tests can be conducted on the same piece of material, a second hypothesis tried if the first one fails. By virtue of its internal consistency the text itself can provide relevant feedback about the correctness of hypotheses.

How might children who cannot yet read acquire and develop the insight that speech and written language are not the same? Only by being read to or at least by hearing written language read aloud. When a child's predictions of written language fail because they are based on knowledge of spoken language, then the occasion exists for the insight to arise that spoken and written language are not precisely the same. And a similar process of engagement as written language is heard and comprehended will develop an understanding of the particular conventions of written language, considerably augmented, of course, as children become able to do more and more of their own reading.

The kind of reading that would most familiarize children with written language is coherent *stories*, ranging from items in newspapers and magazines to traditional fairy tales, ghost and adventure stories, history, and myth. All of these types of story are truly written *language*—produced for a purpose in a conventional medium and distinguishable from most school texts by their length, sense, and semantic and syntactic richness. There is no evidence that it is any harder for children to understand complex texts (when they are read to them or when they can explore them for themselves) than it is difficult for children to understand the complex adult speech that they hear around them and on television.

Children at school may not be provided with complex written material as part of their reading instruction for the obvious reason that they could not be expected to read it by themselves. Because most of the material in which children are likely to be interested—and from which they would be likely to learn—tends to be too difficult for them to read by themselves, less complex material is found or produced in the expectation that children will find it "simpler." And when these specially tailored-for-children texts also seem to confound beginners, the assumption may be made that the fault lies with the children or with their "language development."

And indeed, it may be the case that the language of such texts is unfamiliar to many children. But this inadequacy need not have its roots in the particular kind of spoken language with which the child is familiar nor even in the possibly limited experience of the child with print. The reason is more likely to be associated with the child's unfamiliarity with the artificial language of school books, whether of the truncated "Sam the cat sat on the mat" variety or the more florid "Down the hill, hand in hand, skipped Susie and her friend." This is also so different from any other form of language, spoken or written, that it is probably safest to put it into an exclusive category of "school language."

Of course, such material tends to be quite unpredictable for many children who consequently have enormous difficulty understanding it and learning to read from it. And ironically it may be concluded that written language is intrinsically difficult for children who would be better off learning from "spoken language written down." The text is then based on the intuition of a professional textbook writer or classroom teacher about what constitutes spoken language—or more complex still, a dialect of that language or even children's language. All of these are problems that would confound a professional linguist. The result is quite unlike written language yet has none of the advantages of speech, because it will have to be comprehended out of context. Children may learn to recite such print, but there is no evidence that it will make them readers. Any insight they might have in advance about the nature of written language is likely to be undermined, and worse, they might become persuaded that the print which they first experience in school is a model for all the written language that they will meet throughout their lives—a conviction that would be as discouraging as it is misleading.

ON INSTRUCTIONAL METHODS

I have not said anything about the best (or the worst) programs, methods, or materials for teaching children to read. This was intentional, because the conclusion to which all my analysis, research, and experience with teachers and with children in schools has led is that children do not learn to read from programs. In particular, they cannot learn from the more structured, systematic "reading skills" programs where every supposed learning step is predetermined for the child; they cannot acquire or maintain the two basic insights just discussed. Only people—and written language itself—can demonstrate how written language is *used*. Programs cannot anticipate what a child will want to do or know at a particular time. They cannot provide opportunities for engagement. And anything a program teaches that is irrelevant to a child will be learned, if it is learned at all, as something that is irrelevant.

No "method" of teaching will take care of all the contingencies. Nor should the development of a foolproof method be expected, despite the millions of dollars that have been spent in its pursuit. While some methods of teaching reading are obviously worse than others (because they are based on very weak theories of the nature of reading), the belief that one perfect method might exist to teach all children is contrary to all the evidence about the multiplicity of individual differences that every child brings to reading.

Research is of little help in the selection of appropriate methods. Research tells us that all methods of teaching reading appear to work for some children but that none works for all. Some teachers seem to succeed whatever the method they are formally believed to employ. We must conclude that the instructional method is not the critical issue. (Researchers recognize this point and have to control in their studies for the "variability" introduced first by the different abilities of children and second by the varying influences of teachers.) It might not be particularly unfair to say that many children learn to read—and many teachers succeed in helping them—despite the instructional method used.

The analysis I have made cannot be translated into a system for teaching, though it can indeed be translated into an environment for learning. In fact, the analysis explains environments in which children do learn to read, whether or not there is a program that is supposed to be teaching the child to read at the same time. These are environments in which written language makes sense, and in which an autonomous program-independent teacher has a critical role.

The Never-Ending Debate

Two basic theories of how children learn to read have been contrasted in these pages. One point of view, which this book obviously reflects, is sometimes termed "psycholinguistic," the "meaning" approach, or "whole language." The opposing point of view, which relies heavily on phonics and other exercises and drills, is generally called the "skills" approach. Between the two sides is a gulf.

Many reading theorists and researchers have taken strong positions on one side of this chasm or the other, perpetuating what Jeanne Chall (1967) called "The Great Debate" nearly thirty years ago. The debate is still unresolved. In Smith (1992) I referred to it as "never-ending," and in some lengthy Notes, beginning on page 302, I discuss why "the interminable controversy" is unlikely to end—and why it engenders such intense feelings.

For anyone who believes that there are basic skills that children must master in order to become readers and writers, and that repetitious exercises, corrections, tests, and grading are essential for learning those skills, computers constitute an ideal educational technology. With sophisticated graphics, tightly controlled instructional sequences and loops, constant testing, immediate feedback of results, and ability to remember and compare every score, computer-based literacy programs offer systematic instruction in a form that can appeal to everyone. Children enjoy them because they make "fun" out of previously tedious ritual, like the Saturday morning television cartoons. Parents like the computer programs, because the technology is contemporary and labeled "educational." Teachers may like them because they plot a path for every student and keep them on track. And administrators can find the promises and control that computer-assisted instruction offers irresistible.

Such computer programs must be questioned about what they demonstrate to learners about literacy. Yet many major publishers of reading and writing programs, from kindergarten through high school, invest in elaborate computer programs. The worksheet activities and tests contained in their print materials are now presented on the computer screen in seemingly endless profusion and variety. And the same claims of instructional efficacy are made. There is no evidence that such computer programs have succeeded in making children literate, and no convincing theories that they could succeed. Such programs could rapidly give children a totally false idea of the purposes and possibilities of literacy (Smith, 1986).

This does not mean that computers have no place in the literacy classroom. As word processors, computers have helped the youngest children to become writers, by assisting them in the physical act of writing and also in such writerly activities as drafting, editing, and preparing clean and legible copies of their texts. And when used in these and a variety of other practical ways—in simulations, games, design activities, communication links, drama, art, and music—computers seem able to stimulate children to talk more, plan more, think more, write more, and read more. The issue is not whether computers should be in classrooms, but how they should be used.

TEACHING READING

The primary role of reading teachers can be summed up in very few words— to ensure that the children have adequate demonstrations of reading being used for evident meaningful purposes and to help children to fulfill such purposes themselves. Where children see little relevance in reading, then teachers must show that reading is worthwhile. Where children find little interest in reading, then teachers must create interesting situations. No one ever taught reading to a child who was not interested in reading, and interest cannot be demanded. Teachers must themselves be conspicuous practicing users of written language.

Where children have difficulty in reading, teachers must see that they are helped to read what they would like to read. In part, this assistance can be given by developing the confidence of children to read for themselves, in their own way, taking the risk of making mistakes and being willing to ignore the completely incomprehensible. Even bizarre personal interpretations are better than none at all; children find out soon enough the mistakes that make a difference. But children will also from time to time look for help from others, either in answering specific questions or in assisting with reading generally. Such reading on behalf of the child can be provided by the teacher, an aide, by other children, or by recordings.

The Learner's Point of View

Children themselves must judge whether materials and activities are too difficult or too dull. Anything children would not listen to or understand if it were read to them is unsuitable material for them to be expected to read. A child's preference is a far better yardstick than any readability formula, and grade levels have no reality in a child's mind. Teachers need not be afraid that children will engage in reading so easy that there is nothing to learn; that would be boring. Children learn about reading as long as they read, but they can never learn to read by not reading.

There is no simple formula to ensure that reading will be comprehensible; no materials or procedures are guaranteed never to interfere with a child's progress. Instead teachers must understand the factors that make reading difficult, whether induced by the child, the teacher, or the task. For example, the concentration on visual detail that will cause tunnel vision; the overloading of short-term memory by attention to fragments of text that make little sense; logjams in long-term memory as the child strives to be ready to answer questions afterward or to write "reports"; attempts to sound out words at the expense of meaning; slow reading; anxiety not to make a mistake; lack of assistance when a child needs it for sense or even word identification; or too-insistent "correction" that may be irrelevant to the child and that may in the long run inhibit the self-correction that is an essential part of learning. All of these ways in which reading can be made harder can be characterized as limitations on the extent to which children can use nonvisual information.

And conversely, what makes reading comprehensible for children is the teacher's facilitation of the use of nonvisual information. Not only should a child come into every reading situation with relevant nonvisual information—equipped with, in plain English, an adequate prior understanding—but also the child must feel free to use it. A child's fund of knowledge and confidence should be constantly developed, but this will occur as a consequence of reading. Not only should the teacher try to avoid materials or activities that are nonsense to the child, there should be active encouragement for the child to predict, to understand, to enjoy. The worst habit for any learner is to treat text as if there were no sense to be found in it. Where there is a mismatch, where there is little likelihood that a child will comprehend the material, then the preference should be to change the material rather than to try to change the child. For older children teachers may be reluctant to change material because a certain content is expected to be learned, but they still have a choice. Students cannot learn two things at the same time; they cannot simultaneously learn to read and to master an unfamiliar subject matter like history or math. If the teacher's intention is to improve reading, then students must have material they can easily understand. If the intention is to extend subject matter knowledge—which will in turn make reading easier—then until the student can read it with some fluency the subject matter must be taught in some other way, by lecture, film, board work, or individual tuition. The two can be taught *concurrently*—the math need not wait for the reading competence any more than the reading need wait for the math skills—but they cannot be learned simultaneously.

Teaching the Hard Way

Teachers sometimes try to resolve problems the hard way, for example in expecting poor readers to improve while they are doing less reading than better readers. When children have trouble understanding text they may be given isolated word drills, while problems with word identification may provoke attention to letter identification and sound blends. But letters (and their phonic interrelations) are recognized and learned best when they are parts of words, and words are recognized and learned more easily when they are in meaningful sequences. Good readers tend to be good at letter and word identification and at phonic drills, but these more specific skills are a consequence, not a cause, of good reading (Samuels, 1971). Good readers tend also to understand the technical jargon of reading such as *letter, word, verb, sentence, paragraph,* but this again is a result of being able to read. Practice with definitions does not make readers (Downing & Oliver, 1973/1974). Knowledge of specialized words is necessary only if they are made a focal part of the instruction, if it is necessary for children to understand the words in order to be allowed to get on with the business of learning to read and write. It is not an essential prerequisite for literacy.

Children may also be confounded by instruction that is as unnecessary as it is futile, often as a consequence of a theoretical vogue among specialists. When, for example, Noam Chomsky popularized transformational linguistics as a technical method of analyzing language, many people thought children would not learn to read unless they became miniature linguists themselves and made children spend a lot of time doing transformational exercises that made no apparent difference to their language ability. After psychologists became interested in the theoretical notion of distinctive features, there were several efforts to teach children the distinctive features of letters, although no one could convincingly demonstrate what these features might be. Children who had difficulty with the alphabet or with these exercises were sometimes diagnosed as having poor feature discrimination, although they had no reported difficulty with knives and forks or dogs and cats. Phonic-based reading programs and materials have flourished whenever linguists have become particularly interested in the spelling-sound correspondences of language, and there have been moves toward teaching "prediction" as if it were something foreign to most children's experience. "Phonological awareness" is being urged as a necessity for learning to read, with the result that children may spend more time attempting to deconstruct speech than exploring written language. In all of these cases, concepts that scientists have found useful as hypothetical constructs in their attempts to understand their discipline have become something a child must learn as a prerequisite for learning to read. (How children learned to read before these concepts were devised is not explained.) There is a growing acknowledgment today of the importance of comprehension as the basis of learning, but at the same time there is a feeling that comprehension itself must be taught, that it can be broken down into a series of "comprehension skills" that presumably can be taught without comprehension.

I am not saying that it is not useful for children to know the alphabet, to build up sight vocabularies, or even to understand the relationships between the spelling of words and their sounds. But all of these are by-products of reading that make more sense as reading itself is mastered and understood. It is pointless for teacher and child to labor over activities that will not facilitate learning to read and that will become easy once reading experience develops. It is certainly not the case that teachers should never correct or make suggestions. But correction or advice may be offered too soon. A child pauses while reading aloud and half the class shouts out the next word, although the reader may be thinking about something else six words behind or ahead. Problems arise when corrections and explanations sap children's confidence or stop them in their tracks for what might be quite extraneous reasons. The teacher should always ask, "What is causing the confusion here?" Children afraid of being corrected may become afraid of speaking, reading, and writing.

The First Steps

Children begin to read with the first written word they are able to recognize. Nonvisual information is so important that reading potential is enhanced with every expansion of a child's knowledge of the world or of spoken language. (But there is no particular need for extensive prior knowledge of the world or of spoken language for a child to begin to read, just enough to make sense of the first print that will be read. Much of the knowledge and language skills of fluent readers is again a consequence of literacy rather than its cause.)

There is no "best age" for learning to read. Many children have learned to read, often spontaneously, as young as 3 years of age (Clark, 1976), and it is equally well documented that adult illiterates can learn in a few months provided their sensitivity has not been blunted by years of failure with formal reading instruction (Freire, 1972). Many of the early readers who have been studied did not have above-average intellect or any particular social or cultural privileges, they simply found reading something that was useful and straightforward to learn, usually without any particular consciousness of what they were doing. Whether a child will learn to read is not something that can be determined with reference to a calendar or the learner's "mental age."

Similarly, there is no unique mental condition of "reading readiness." Children are ready to learn to read whenever they have a purpose and intelligible opportunity for reading, not in terms of settling down to a concentrated period of systematic instruction but in an explorer's interest in signs and labels, in telephone directories and catalogs, and in stories. In educational contexts, reading readiness is often related more to the form and demands of instruction than to reading itself. Obviously, if instruction emphasizes knowledge of letter names, then a child who cannot grasp the nature of the alphabet is not ready. If instruction requires detailed attention to the sound patterns of a particular spoken language dialect, then a child who cannot do this is not ready. But none of this has anything to do with reading itself. It is difficult to see what kind of special physical, emotional, intellectual, or cultural status is required for learning to read, except the two basic insights I have already discussed.

Reading should blend smoothly into all the other visual and linguistic and intellectual enterprises of a learner's life. There is no magical day when a "pre-reader" suddenly becomes a "learner," just as there is no landmark day when learning is completed and a reader graduates. No one is a perfect reader, and we all continue to learn every time we read.

None of this is to say that all children will easily learn to read; there has always been evidence that such is unlikely to be the case. But failure need not be attributed to *dyslexia*, a disease that only strikes children who cannot read, and that is invariably cured when they can read. I have argued that there is nothing unique about reading, either visually or as far as language is concerned. There are no evident visual defects that are specific to reading, but this does not mean that there are no general visual anomalies that will interfere with learning to read. The few children who have difficulty learning to understand speech, or learning anything, may also find learning to read difficult.

But there is no convincing evidence that children who can see normally, with or without spectacles, and who have acquired a working competence in the language spoken around them, might be physically or congenitally incapable of learning to read. It cannot be denied that some children who seem "normal" and even bright in all other respects may fail to learn to read. But there can be other reasons for this failure that do not presuppose any physical dysfunction on the part of the child. Children do not learn to read who do not want to, or who see no point in doing so, or who are hostile to the teacher, or to the school, or to the social or cultural group to which they perceive the teacher and the school as belonging. Children do not learn to read who expect to fail, or who believe that learning to read will be too costly, or whose preferred image of themselves, for whatever reason, is that of a nonreader. Children do not learn to read if they have the wrong idea of the nature of reading, if they have learned—or been taught—that reading does not make sense.

TESTS AND STANDARDS

It is in the context of failure that brief reference should be made to the effects on young readers of the growing mania for constant testing and evaluation, and especially on those having difficulty in making sense of the way reading is taught.

Tests are primarily an administrative tool. They are devised and administered for a variety of bureaucratic and political reasons to categorize children and to evaluate teachers. But no reading test ever helped a child learn to read. And there is nothing in tests themselves to indicate why a child might not be succeeding in learning to read.

Problems arise in two ways. The first is that it is widely believed that the content of reading tests (or of comprehension or readiness tests) indicates what a child needs to know in order to learn to read. This is a fallacy. Tests may provide indicators of what children are able to do as a consequence of learning to read, so that children who are good readers tend to do well on tests (though not invariably) and children who are poor readers do not. But trying to teach a child to score well on individual items on a test will not teach a child how to read. Counting the number of times a child voluntarily visits the library might be a relatively sensible test indicator of reading ability, but training the child to visit the library more often would not in itself improve reading ability, though it would raise the test score. If anything, tests measure how well children have been able to make sense of formal reading instruction, to work their way through programs.

The reason for the close affinity of tests and programs is that they are both forced to treat reading in the same arbitrary and artificial way. Because someone outside the classroom must determine what is appropriate for children to do and know (and that can be measured), and because for reasons of control and standardization it is necessary to break reading down into fragmented and predetermined sequences, tests and instructional programs both tend to become concerned with the same superficial and isolated aspects that are supposed to be "components" of reading.

Thus the first problem with tests is that they give teachers and children a distorted idea of the nature of reading and of what must be done to teach a child to read (or to satisfy some outside authority that the child is being taught to read). This is perhaps not too much of a handicap for a child who is indeed learning to read, who does reasonably well on the tests, and whose exposure to meaningful reading is not limited as a consequence. But tests can be devastating for children who do not do well, partly because they may then have the opportunity to read meaningfully withdrawn from them (in favor of exercises and drills that they have already demonstrated they do not understand) and also because of the inevitable consequence for their self-esteem. The second major problem with tests is that they do nothing positive for the sensitivity of children who do badly on them.

Teachers do not need "off the shelf" tests to discover if their students are learning or if they are confused. Every teacher can tell (or should be able to tell) if a child has made progress in reading, just by talking with the child and looking at what the child is voluntarily reading. Learning to read does not inch along one item of information after another; there should be no difficulty in determining whether a child has progressed in ability and interest over a period of a few months. If the method of instruction is such that neither teacher nor child can tell whether progress is being made without recourse to a standardized test, then the instruction itself is essentially meaningless.

The best tests are "homemade," constructed on the spot to reassure the teacher that whatever a particular child is supposed to be learning at a particular time is making sense. Good teachers do this intuitively, and because such tests are a natural part of whatever activity the child is engaged in, they are both relevant and inconspicuous.

The situations that I have characterized as making reading more difficult, and thus likely to interfere with children's learning to read, are so much a fact of life in many classrooms that many teachers feel they can do little about them. Tests must be administered; instruction must be directed toward the tests; the language arts are arbitrarily and artificially fragmented; children are categorized and streamed; teachers must be accountable; certain curricula must be followed; parents and trustees must be assuaged; work must sometimes be graded; competition and anxiety are unavoidable. Much of a teacher's time is necessarily directed to classroom management, many activities are engaged in to satisfy "standards" or other demands laid down by external sources, and few teachers can find the time or the resources to provide an ideal learning environment for children all the time.

A theory of reading will not change all this (although it might provide ammunition for anyone who tries to resist). The kind of change that will make a difference in schools will not come with better theories or with better materials or even with better-informed teachers, but only with individuals taking action toward change. The problem of improving reading instruction, in the long run, is a political question. But whether teachers can change their world or not, they will still be better off to the extent that they understand about reading and about how children learn to read. Teachers who cannot relieve children of the disruptions of irrelevant demands and activities may at least protect them by pointing out that the activities have little to do with reading or with the child's learning ability. Children understand that meaningless tasks are often given to them simply to keep them occupied and quiet, but they are not helped by being led to believe that such tasks are an important part of learning to read.

THE LITERACY CLUB

There is increasing evidence that children know a great deal about literacy before they come to school (Ferreiro & Teberosky, 1982; Goelman, Oberg, & Smith, 1984). They may not have learned to read and to write, but they know how literacy is used in the community to which they belong. If their family reads books and newspapers, they know about books and newspapers. If their family consults the television guide, they know about television guides. If they leave each other messages on the refrigerator door, they know about messages on refrigerator doors. If their friends read comics or consult catalogues, they know about comics and catalogues. They know about signs, labels, lists, letters, greetings cards, telephone directories, and everything else that might be part of their personal written language environment. They also know roughly how written language works, that it consists of symbols written on lines, that it is laid out in various conventional ways. Before they can spell, they know there are rules of spelling. They have ideas of why people read, even before they can read themselves. They pretend to read and to write in their games.

There are no kits of materials or systematic exercises for teaching children how the world uses written language. They learn—usually without anyone being aware that they are learning—by participating in literate activities with people who use written language. It can all be summed up in a metaphor: Children learn about reading and writing by "joining the literacy club" (Smith, 1988). They are given demonstrations of what written language can be used for, and they receive collaboration when they become interested in using written language themselves. The assistance is usually completely casual, when someone points out that an approaching sign says "Stop" or "Burgers," the way one might say to a child "Look, there's a horse." Someone helps them to read what they are interested in reading and helps them to write what they would like to write.

Membership of the literacy club offers the same advantages as the spoken language club that I discussed in the previous chapter, and all the other clubs children might join. Children in the literacy club have opportunities to see what written language can do, they are encouraged and helped to do those things themselves, and they are not at risk of exclusion if they make mistakes or display a passing lack of interest. They learn to be like the other members of the club. (And if they learn from other demonstrations that reading and writing are boring activities or that they do not belong to the club, then they learn not to be like people who read and write.)

This does not mean that children are lost to literacy if they have not learned about reading and writing out of school. But it becomes all the more crucial for every child to have the opportunity to belong to the literacy club in school. For children who are not interested in reading and writing, it is even more important that activities in the classroom are made interesting and accessible for them. They need more demonstrations that there are worthwhile uses of literacy and more collaboration in engaging in those uses themselves. And in any case, children who have joined the club before they come to school should not then risk rejection because school definitions of literacy or perceptions of literate activities are different.

There is no need to fear that reading to learners, or writing for them, will make them passive and dependent. They will not always expect other people to do their reading and writing for them. No child has that much patience. The moment children feel they can read or write well enough to do what they want to do for themselves—often long before adults might think they are ready to do so—they reject the helping hand. It is no different when children learn to ride a bicycle. Children never want to be pushed when they can pedal away for themselves (except when the going is uphill).

Margaret Spencer (1987) describes how the authors of children's books *teach* children how to read. These are the authors of the books that children love to read, time and time again. The children already know the stories before they open the books—or the stories are so predictable that they know what is on a page before they turn it. The children know the story, according to Spencer, and the author shows them how to read it.

Jane Torrey (1969) describes how the authors of labels and television commercials might also help children to learn to read by themselves. Spontaneous self-admission into the literacy club may even explain how children succeed in learning to read when subjected to intensive classroom regimes of phonics and other worksheet activities (which then get the credit for the achievement).

Someone must do the learners' reading for them until they are able to read a few things for themselves, and they are ready to learn to read by reading. Reading to children need not take long—only until they can read enough for authors to take over. Very little actual reading ability is required for this to occur, if the right kinds of interesting and familiar materials are available (for details of such materials, ask a child). Indeed, for a child to know the stories in advance by heart may be enough to turn the child over to the authors. What matters is for the learner to be reading known or familiar texts like an experienced reader.

The role of the teacher is to support the reading and writing of all children until authors, and the children's own interest and self-perception, ensure their continued membership in the literacy club. For teachers who are themselves committed readers and writers, the opportunity to develop new club members should be a pleasure as well as a privilege.

ISSUES

Though often reduced to a "whole language versus code emphasis" disagreement, the underlying issue concerns whether the classroom practices of teachers should be guided by what they know and can see of individual student interest, comprehension, and learning or by the prescriptions of intellectual and political "authorities." Associated with the formalization of instruction is the issue of whether learning can be guaranteed or even facilitated by assessment procedures that monitor and constrain the behavior of teachers and students, with inevitable discriminatory consequences.

SUMMARY

Learning to read depends on two basic insights—that written language is meaningful and that it is different from spoken language. Learners must rely on the visual information of print as little as possible. Teachers help children learn to read by stimulating interest and facilitating written language use to a degree that formal instructional programs, with their necessarily limited objectives, cannot achieve. Teachers must ensure that all children receive the demonstrations and collaboration necessary to maintain membership of the literacy club.

Notes to Chapter 12 begin on page 291, covering
Learning to read
Reading to children
Literacy and schooling
Teachers and programs
Metalinguistic awareness
Dyslexia and learning disabilities
Evaluation, testing, and standards
The interminable controversy

Notes

NOTES TO PREFACE AND INTRODUCTION, pp. 1–6.

Psycholinguistics and Cognitive Science

The term *psycholinguistics* as used in the subtitle and other places in this book refers to an overlapping area of specialized fields of psychology and linguistics, a common ground where psychologists (who study human behavior) and linguists (who study language) meet to explore the ways in which human language is actually learned and used. In reading education, however, psycholinguistics became something of a battlecry (or term of opprobrium, depending on which side you are on). A heavily phonic approach to teaching reading has long been called "the linguistic method," and psycholinguistic became adopted in the early 1970s as the emblem of the opposing point of view (which has also been called the "meaning approach" to teaching reading).

There are two radically divergent points of view about the nature of reading. I have broadly characterized these theoretical perspectives as "inside-out" and "outside-in" (Smith, 1979), depending on where the control is presumed to originate in reading, with the reader or with the text. More generally these opposing positions have become known as "top-down" or "bottom-up" (because metaphors taken from the jargon of computer technology have a cachet of being more scientific). Top-down is roughly equivalent to my inside-out, implying that the reader determines how a text will be approached, dealt with, and interpreted. The bottom-up view is outside-in, putting the text in charge, with the letters on the page the first and final arbiters of the reader's responses. The present book, I should perhaps add, could be regarded as strongly representative of the inside-out view.

Naturally there have been attempts at compromise (or at carving out a third position), arguing for "interaction" theories which are both top-down and bottom-up at the same time. But no top-downer would want to claim that reading is not an interaction with the text in any case. Just because meaning has to be brought by the reader does not mean that *any* meaning will do (just as there may be many different

221

ways to walk through a forest, but the forest itself puts restrictions on how varied those ways might be). And as Goodman (1981) has pointed out, many interaction theories tend to be bottom-up in disguise; they sound more liberal but they still tend to give the basic power to the print.

Words can be promiscuous when used as labels for points of view, and psycholinguistic has had a particularly wayward career. Initially—in the late 1960s and early 1970s—the term primarily connoted academic studies into the nature of language and the manner in which infants learn to use it, focusing on the critical role of meaning and constructive thought. In education, the psycholinguistic perspective implied a similar focus on meaningfulness in literacy learning, opposed to fragmented prepackaged "skills-based" materials and activities. But publishers quickly produced "psycholinguistic materials" (or relabeled old materials as psycholinguistic). The principal successor to the psycholinguistic perspective in education is today known as "whole language." Once again, this was originally a term connoting a philosophy of learning, opposed to artificial decontextualized exercises and drills. But as whole language has gained influence and prominence in education, the perspective has become distorted, the theory has become a method, and publishers have begun to produce "whole language materials."

In the academic world the term psycholinguistics has also been changing its connotations—and provoking some territorial disputes. Many researchers into language learning who originally called themselves psycholinguists employed "naturalistic" methods—they *observed* how children learned or used language in natural settings, rather than experimentally manipulating learning situations. Since the mid-1970s, however, numbers of language researchers have joined forces with computer and artificial intelligence specialists in a subdiscipline called *cognitive science*. This new breed of psycholinguists frequently has a distinctly experimental and prescriptive attitude to instruction.

Nevertheless I have retained the word psycholinguistic in the title of the present edition, partly because that was the way *Understanding Reading* was titled when it first came out in 1971, but also to indicate constraints I have continued to observe in the contents of the book. The primary concern is with what readers need to know and do in order to make sense of written language. The book does not delve deeply into *sociolinguistic* issues, such as the particular social circumstances in which literacy is employed and learned (though it does not ignore the latter completely), nor into types of literate behaviors, literacy criticism, semiotics, or cultural aspects of literacy.

Research

Research into the nature of reading and reading instruction peaked in the early 1970s with the support of enormous federal grants aimed at the eradication of illiteracy. The goal was never reached, largely because (I would argue) the research and instructional efforts were frequently predicated on fragmented and decontextualized outside-in theories of reading and instruction (Smith, 1986). And with the failure, the bulk of available financial support and the focus of attention have tended to shift, first to writing and more recently to thinking, and also to the construction of standardized curricula and tests.

Despite these changes, and a universal diminution of support funds, reading research continues to be a thriving industry. The International Reading Association's *Annual Summary of Investigations Related to Reading* has abstracted well over a thousand studies annually since 1980—without claiming to catch them all. Many of these studies are byproducts of the obligatory theses or dissertations produced by graduate students, many of whom will never engage in research again. Other reports, often even more pedestrian, are generated by academics requiring publications for promotion or by the beneficiaries of research centers and other granting agencies who depend on publications to justify their existence. There is a heavy experimental emphasis in the majority of these studies, which are far removed from the realities of actual reading or classroom situations.

Barr (1986), for example, notes that only a quarter of the reports in the International Reading Association's flagship journal *Reading Research Quarterly* from 1980 to 1985 focused on instruction, and about 80 percent of those were experimental. She observed that the majority of the instructional studies involved "manipulating a single or limited number of conditions, such as teaching method and/or materials ... controlling other relevant conditions by experimental or statistical design." This approach, Barr contends, "does not consider conditions shown to be central for the instructional process, such as the number of stories actually read, the amount of time available and used, the composition of the class, and the management skills of the teacher."

For critiques of the efficacy and the morality of experimental research methodology, see Neilsen (1993) and other articles in the same volume.

I have obviously not attempted in this volume to summarize all of the research done in the name of reading. That would be impossible. Instead I have drawn primarily from what helps me to construct a coherent picture of reading and of learning to read. People with an alternative point of view could be similarly selective in order to reject my conclusions. Research in the behavioral sciences rarely resolves disputes of a fundamentally philosophical nature. Occasionally I make reference to alternative points of view, at least to set out the arguments, but this book does not attempt to be eclectic.

On Not Being Eclectic

One aspect of eclecticism is the view that science is an incremental activity—that every bit of research is valid and worthwhile, adding a nugget of truth to an always-growing accumulation of knowledge and understanding. Such a view rests on a rosy belief that researchers never start from false assumptions or finish with unreliable conclusions. All reported findings are supposed to fit together like pieces of a jigsaw puzzle, no matter how contradictory they might be. Educational textbooks are frequently pastiches of this nature, covering immense amounts of ground without the provision of navigable pathways. The alternative point of view is that scientific research is based on conceptual *paradigms*, or ways of seeing the world, which frequently conflict. They are subjectively adopted and emotionally retained. A paradigm is rarely abandoned by its adherents unless they find it totally worthless and have another to replace it with (Kuhn, 1970). The research that is done, the evidence gathered, and conclusions reached all depend on the researcher's beliefs and expectations.

Another common form of eclecticism, conspicuous in education, shuts its eyes to the possibility that conventionally-held positions might have been discredited and attempts instead to assimilate alternative points of view into established or "official" lines of thinking. Such conceptual dilution is frequently found in reviews of research produced by committees or by bureaucratic institutions. A prominent example is *Becoming a Nation of Readers: The Report of the Commission on Reading*, published by the Center for the Study of Reading at the University of Illinois (Anderson, Hiebert, Scott, & Wilkinson, 1985). This report cites—and even recommends—a variety of irreconcilable points of view about how reading is learned and should be taught, rather like arguing that vegetarianism has been shown to be good for you, but you should still eat plenty of meat.

Finally, there are eclectic approaches to teaching reading, which entail using a little bit from every prominent theorist or instructional proponent. According to such an undiscriminating view, every "authority" is probably a little bit right, and it is difficult to make decisions, so every point of view should be given its turn. Nonjudgmental approaches to instruction fail to recognize that inappropriate theories and methods can mislead the people most in need of a reliable and coherent understanding of the nature of reading, namely children trying to learn and teachers trying to teach them. It is necessary to take a position. Some current views about reading and reading instruction must be wrong.

Changes in the Fifth Edition

A principal change in this 1994 edition is the inclusion of the "Issues" sections and acknowledgment that there are deeply etched and deeply felt disputes over the nature of reading that may never be resolved, not to the extent that proponents of different points of view will be satisfied. Over the years I have come to the conclusion that the most critical need is for teachers and students to be able to make judgments and decisions rather than to trust authorities when there are conflicting points of view (the choice of authority is itself a decision, of course). To do this, one must recognize that profound differences exist. Indeed, if one wants to argue that other people are wrong, one has to admit the likelihood that one is wrong oneself (or at least that someone else might also be right) and find a reason why it is possible for two people living in the same world (if they can be said to be living in the same world) to have diametrically opposing points of view.

In Chapter 1 (and elsewhere), there are fewer references to the brain, which used to be one of my favorite words. I still regard the brain as an astonishing instrument, far more remarkable than it is often given credit for, but it makes sense much of the time to refer to the whole individual rather than to the individual's cranial contents, though it may sound less scientific. Reading, for example, is best regarded as something done by people rather than by brains. To say the brain "looks," "thinks," or "remembers" is about as appropriate as saying that the stomach enjoys a good meal. I discuss metaphor briefly in a new section in the Chapter 1 Notes.

I have deleted from Chapter 2 and its Notes almost the whole discussion and examples of Chomsky's early theories of generative transformational grammar. The theory has been much revised, is currently highly technical and tendentious, and has lost its immediate relevance for most reading research. Chomsky's great and lasting contribution to cognitive psychology, psycholinguistics, and education was that language could not be regarded as a simple matter of stimuli and responses. As George Miller (1965) wrote, Chomsky made mind more than a four-letter word. But Chomsky's theories of grammar were always provisional and technical; linguistically he has moved far beyond his position when the notions of surface structure and deep structure were first popularized (and beyond the comprehension of most nonlinguists as well). One of Chomsky's most specialized works is still widely quoted, namely his book with Halle entitled *Sound Pattern of English* (Chomsky & Halle, 1968) in which he declared that English orthography was probably an optimal system for the representation of the phonology of the language. That observation is still quoted regularly in treatises on spelling, but more as a supportive slogan than as part of a detailed analysis; a point of view with which the authors find it useful to agree. The "grammars" that reading researchers now tend to study have more to do with computer programs than with transformational linguistics. I have similarly deleted long sections of Notes on generative semantics, which did not maintain its original promise in reading research (Levin & Pinker, 1991), although like transformational grammar, it did show a way of conceptualizing a bridge between surface structure and meaning. A brief reference to an educational controversy over genre theory is added.

I have also deleted from the Notes to Chapters 2 and 11 some of the lengthier references to B. F. Skinner and behaviorism, although his austere influence survives through a number of influential figures in education, such as Bloom (taxonomy of learning), Mager (instructional objectives), and Bereiter (programs for teaching reading and writing). Skinner's name is rarely mentioned in reading research, but his antimentalistic spirit lives on in a number of hard-line cognitive science approaches, notably connectionism, which is considered in this volume.

The role of grammar has been overshadowed by the development of *modularity* and *connectionist* theories, a discussion of which I have added to the Notes in a new section on Modules and Networks, together with the brief section on Speech, Writing and "Language." As a balance, a new section on comprehension has also been added.

In Chapter 3, I have retained some of the mathematics of information theory because they underlie a supplementary argument in Chapter 4 about the uncertainty of letters, words, and meanings. I do not think they are critical in a study of reading, but they provide an illuminating line of thought for anyone who wants to pursue it. I have similarly left in the receiver operating curve of signal detection theory because of the general point that it makes. A brief section on artificial intelligence has been added.

I was not able to remove the brain from Chapter 4 ("Between Eye and Brain") because that is what the chapter is about, though I have tried to keep the discussion on as literal a level as possible. The brain reappears in later chapters but always when I am referring specifically to the organ, not to the person as a whole. My problem in trying to avoid talking about the brain as if it "learns" or "makes decisions" again emphasizes the metaphorical nature of the language we (must) use when trying to relate physiological structures to feelings or behavior.

In Chapters 6 and 7, the tables and discussions of imaginary feature lists for letters and words have been eliminated as more confusing than explanatory, together with some of the discussion on functional equivalence. Substantial sections of Chapter 7 have been rewritten for clarity, and a section on redundancy among distinctive features has been found redundant.

Some of the discussion of phonics instruction in the Notes to Chapter 8 has been deleted or transferred to Chapter 12. Chapter 8 Notes include a discussion of current claims of the importance of phonological awareness (knowledge of the sound structure of speech) and phonemic awareness (knowledge of the hypothetical boundaries of discrete sounds in speech).

A lengthy description of a redundancy experiment has been removed from Chapter 9, and also a section on Cloze that was in the Notes. In Chapter 10 Notes, a large part of "Other Aspects of Reading" has been rewritten. The Chapter 11 Notes include extensive new sections on vocabulary learning, and the Chapter 12 Notes have new sections on emergent reading and collaborative learning. The Chapter 12 Notes conclude with a rather lengthy summary of "the great debate" between "whole language" and "direct instruction," in which so many people seem compelled to participate. It would be comforting to contemplate not having to include this section in a sixth edition, but the portents are not auspicious.

A few additional terms have been added to the Glossary, and there are numerous small changes throughout the book. It would be unwise to assume that any part of the present edition of *Understanding Reading* is identical with the fourth edition.

Acknowledgment

I would never claim to have written anything "by myself," without the insights and inspiration of authors, students, teachers, and friends too numerous to be catalogued in any comprehensive way. In particular, *Understanding Reading* would not be what it is without the educational sagacity and editorial acumen of Mary-Theresa Smith.

NOTES TO CHAPTER 1, KNOWLEDGE AND COMPREHENSION, pp. 7–23.

Theories of Comprehension

Comprehension is not a topic that attracted a great deal of attention among psychologists until the 1970s, with the notable exception of Piaget. The notion that everyone commands a structure of knowledge concerning the world, into which all experience is assimilated, was a central aspect of Piaget's theorizing. Piaget's writings are voluminous and not always transparent; one might begin with *The Construction of Reality in the Child* (Piaget, 1954) or one of his collaborative efforts, such as Piaget and Inhelder (1969). Alternatively there are many useful general introductions to Piaget's thought, for example, Boden (1979), Phillips (1981), and Liben (1983).

Paradoxically, the computer has provided a great impetus to many psychologists interested in comprehension, not necessarily because the brain is conceptualized as a kind of computer (although such a notion does underlie some theorizing) but because the computer has proved a convenient tool for simulating organizations of knowledge and memory. Some experimentalists believe that theories about human cognition "lack rigor" unless they can be simulated on a computer to prove that they are at least feasible, but others find such claims constricting if not misleading. I shall talk more critically of these matters in the Notes to Chapter 3.

Karl Popper proposes that the knowledge that every individual (and every culture) has accumulated is a record of the problems they have had to solve. Popper tends to be fairly heavy going in his technical writing (e.g., Popper, 1973), but his views are expressed more concisely in an engaging autobiography (Popper, 1976) and even more clearly in a biography (Magee, 1973). Popper also points out that the brain is not the only place where knowledge can be found. Knowledge exists in books and films, in maps and diagrams, in tools and other artifacts. For someone who had never seen one, a bicycle could itself "explain" how bicycles are used. Popper thinks all of this knowledge is so substantial and so important—because it persists without necessarily being in any individual—that he gives it the name of "World 3," to distinguish it from the world of objective events and the world of subjective mental states. Computers, obviously, are part of World 3. Knowledge in World 3 is remarkably inert and sterile, however, until someone comes on the scene to "read" and comprehend it. On the other hand, we can all have knowledge—for example in the form of memorized "facts"—which is meaningless to us and might just as well be in an encyclopedia. Knowledge is useless without comprehension, wherever it is located.

Boulding (1981) argues from a behavioral scientist's point of view that human knowledge is a special system, unlike other information systems like libraries, computers, or the "real world." Human knowledge constitutes a world in itself and is not simply a combination of the "real world" and a brain. In other words—as I interpret it—we live in a world that we create, rather than in some concrete world that exists independently of us. I argue that reading can provide actual experiences in real worlds, not mere replicas of experiences in "representations" of the world. Our theory of the world is the basis of all our reality.

Yates (1985) analyzed the contents of momentary awareness—what we happen to be aware of at any particular moment—and found that though fragmentary it is always part of a complete world. Our thoughts and perceptions are never unrelated to the world as a whole. They are always capable of anticipating or simulating future events and thus provide a basis for the formulation of appropriate action. Such complex awareness, Yates argues, must reflect an underlying model of the world—a theory of the world.

Basic ideas on comprehension and learning in this and later chapters are presented at greater length in Smith (1990). Miller and Bruner are perhaps the two psychologists who have written most on a wide variety of topics relevant to comprehension. For examples of their investigations into the organization of human knowledge, see Bruner (1973, 1986) and Miller and Johnson-Laird (1975). For examples of computer-based approaches to comprehension see Just and Carpenter (1977). For schema theory, see J. Mandler (1984) and G. Mandler (1985). For thinking, see McPeck (1981), Bruner (1986), and Vygotsky (1978). Gardner (1983, 1991) presents a different point of view about thinking. Flavell (1979) is a key source on metacognition.

Prediction

Prediction as I have discussed it in this chapter is not a topic that has been widely explored, although there is an extensive psychological literature on the consequences of expectancy. Neisser (1977) explores the notion that perception is based on anticipated information from the environment and that our schemes (see below) are continually restructured through prediction and experience. Our cognitive structures are anticipations. Wildman and Kling (1978/1979) discuss "semantic, syntactic and spatial anticipation" in reading, and the effect of anticipation (or of its absence) on comprehension and recall has been investigated experimentally by Glynn and DiVesta (1979), Anderson and Pichert (1978), and Anderson, Reynolds, Schallert, and Goetz (1977). Everyone is familiar with the "double-take" reaction to unexpected semantic anomaly—like reading "he spread the warm bread with socks." Kutas and Hillyard (1980) show that encountering such a sentence actually produces a measurable surge in certain electrical potentials of the brain.

The standard reference on not having direct access to the knowledge we possess is Polanyi (1966); see also Nisbett and Wilson (1977). We do not know what we know unless we put it to use in some way, for example, by saying something or imagining saying something. We similarly do not have immediate access to thought. We can be aware of a decision that we have made, but attempts to reconstruct the "process" by which we came to that decision are inventions, even if we can hypothesize about the factors that might have weighed upon us. Normally we are only aware of thought when it has problems, when we find it difficult to make a decision, just as the only time we are normally aware of comprehension is when it is absent, when we are confused. Most of the time the brain seems able to take care of our affairs very well, without our having to become consciously involved.

Templeton (1991) has disputed that prediction plays a central role in reading, citing Fodor (1983), Perfetti (1991), Stanovich (1991), Vellutino (1991), and the "sophisticated eye-movement studies" of Rayner and Pollatsek (1989) "that show us precisely where beginning and mature readers look as they read connected text." But readers are not aware of any of this, and where they look is not necessarily a reliable indicator of what they are thinking. Prediction is a frame of mind, an adjustment to a total situation (including one's own interests and purposes), not a specific way of threading through a text. Even if alternative meanings of highly ambiguous words were "activated subliminally" in reading (whatever such a term might mean), appropriate selections must be made for comprehension to proceed. People do not normally have periods of incomprehension and uncertainty before making sense of everything they do.

Categories

There is considerable debate about the exact nature of the categorical organization of human knowledge. In particular, the hard-edged category boundaries implied by descriptions such as the one given in this chapter have been challenged. It is not always the case that something either belongs in a category or it doesn't. Some things have a greater claim to being in a category, they are more "typical," while others have only a tenuous membership, regardless of any distinctive features they might possess. Rosch (Rosch & Lloyd, 1978), for example, reports that robins are usually regarded as more typical birds than chickens, with eagles somewhere between. Penguins and emus are much closer to the boundaries between categories, which can be quite fuzzy. Rosch proposes that there are certain "natural" categories that form themselves around prototypical members, like carrots for vegetables and football for sports. The prototypical class members provide the main features of the category. Other possibilities achieve membership of the category to the extent that they share "family resemblances" with the prototypes. In a challenging and wide-ranging book taking off from Rosch's prototype theory, Lakoff (1987) rejects classical categorization theories (going back to Aristotle) and proposes instead what he calls *experiential realism*. We perceive the world in terms of holistic "basic level" categories and bodily proportions, functions and purposes, which provide metaphors for understanding the world. This is a compelling and scholarly book, technical in parts but reiterating insistently and persuasively the creative and imaginative nature of human thought.

Anderson (1991) describes how successful identification of an object enables us to predict a great deal about it, arguing that our categories therefore tell us as much about the structure of the world as about the structure of the mind. Komatsu (1992) reviews theories of conceptual or categorical structures, none of which goes anywhere near accounting for the complexity of human thought. See also Kimchi (1992) and Medin (1989) for less complicated explanations of the issues.

Schemes

It is infrequent for isolated cognitive categories to play a significant role in human thought or behavior. We usually function on the basis of much larger conceptual structures, the schemes or schemas that are constructed out of complex and often dynamic organizations of categories. The English word *schemes* is the standard term for the various kinds of abstract mental structure that enable us to make sense of the world and participate appropriately in it, but the area of study is still known as *schema theory*, perpetuating the Latin term introduced by Bartlett (1932).

One of the pioneers of schema research, Jean Mandler (1984), distinguishes three broad categories of schemes: (a) *scenes*, or spatially organized knowledge, (b) *events*, like the scripts and scenarios I have mentioned in this chapter, and (c) *stories*, which have their own "grammars" of plots, characters, settings, episodes, motives, goals, and outcomes. Some theorists—myself included—would go further to argue that stories are the primary basis of all our perception and understanding of the world. The way we perceive, comprehend, and remember events is in the form of story structures that we impose upon them, even though events may not present themselves to us in such ways.

Demonstrations that story schemes are known and employed in reading, by adults and by children, include Bower (1976), Stein and Glenn (1979), J. Mandler (1978), and J. Mandler and Johnson (1977). All basically show that comprehension requires more than just a knowledge of the world and of the language in which a text is written. Comprehension requires sharing knowledge with the author about the manner in which such a text is conventionally constructed. There is more on the structure of texts in Chapter 2 and its Notes.

Analogous to the notion that we have general conceptual frameworks that enable us to make sense of specific texts that we happen to meet (Norman & Rumelhart, 1975) is the view that we have *frames* (Minsky, 1980; Rumelhart & Ortony, 1977), *scenarios*, or *scripts* (Schank & Abelson, 1977) underlying all our routine interactions with the world. Such patterns of expectation and behavior enable us to apply general procedures for behaving appropriately in specific situations, such as finding our way around a department store or ordering a meal in a restaurant. Schemes are abstract descriptions of events or situations with "slots" for specific detail, which we try to fit in when we want to do or understand something. Comprehension, according to Rumelhart and Ortony (1977), is the confirmation of a tentative hypothesis about what schemes are relevant by finding the slots into which the details of events fit. Rumelhart (1980) sees schemes as the building blocks of cognition, comparing them with the scripts of plays that can be performed by different groups of actors in different settings. Schank (1980) provides a critical but constructive book review entitled "What's a schema anyway?"

A more general point of view is provided by Katherine Nelson (1986) and her colleagues in many research papers and in a book entitled *Event Knowledge*. They show that children are skilled at expressing ideas in "generic," abstract representations rather than as descriptions of concrete events. Asked to describe a birthday party, for example, they talk about cakes, games and gifts, about expected behavior and events, rather than about specific occurrences on a particular occasion. They speak impersonally—"you" get presents—about events with no specific location in time and place. They tell a *story*. For arguments and evidence that events are the primary focus of cognition and perception and that perception is much too fast, rich, and subtle to be constructed from the discrimination and analysis of parts, see McCabe and Balzano (1986).

The Ubiquity of Metaphors

The necessarily metaphorical nature of internal (or mental, or cognitive) processes and structures that are assumed to enable people to behave the way they do is rarely recognized. The processes and structures themselves are hypothetical. Every statement about what we do "in the mind" (or in our brains, or in our heads) should be prefaced by "as if . . ." We behave "as if we have a theory of the world," or "as if we are following a script or a scenario," or "as if our knowledge were organized into a cognitive structure."

Doubtless everything that human beings do and think is physiological, represented in the complex chemistry or neural interconnections of the brain. But no one has ever seen a thought or idea or memory in the structure of the brain; these phenomena are conceptualizations, products rather than processes. Human beings obviously think, have ideas, and remember things, but what they think or remember cannot be associated with particular parts or processes of the brain (any more than one could probe into the circuits and transistors of a television set to discover what particular program is being received). Surgeons and researchers cannot look into the brain and say "Ah, you're thinking about a tree," nor can they literally *find* a script or a scenario, a fact or a piece of knowledge, a "rule" of language or an "image" of a face. These are all metaphorical ways of talking. (Even talk about "associations" and "activitation" in the brain itself is metaphorical—there are mental connections and there are physical connections, and the relationship between the two can only be talked about in the language of analogy.) I am not condemning the fact that all talk about human thought is metaphorical—it is the only way we can talk about it. Problems arise when metaphorical usages are taken literally.

We recognize trees, but we don't have trees in the head. Nor do we literally have pictures of trees, or descriptions of them, which we compare with real trees in order to recognize them. Who or what would examine these internal pictures or descriptions? And would there be pictures or descriptions in the mind of whoever or whatever examines them? An infinite regress is unavoidable. We recognize trees "as if" we had images or descriptions of them in our mind (or brain), but such a statement should not be taken literally. The "mental images or descriptions" that we are able to generate inside our own head, in our "imagination," are themselves products of our knowledge, not the basis of it. We may try to *draw* an image or *write* a description of a tree—these physical representations may literally exist. But when we talk of images or descriptions somewhere inside us, these are metaphors. Blakemore (1990) criticizes the "homunculus fallacy" that something has been explained if an image has been constructed in the head. See also N. Goodman (1990), in the same volume.

The Narrative Basis of Thought

Continuously and inevitably, we create stories to explain and understand the world and our role in it, to remember and to anticipate events, to create worlds that might not otherwise exist. This urge to create narratives is so compelling that we impose them on otherwise meaning–less situations. We strain to find objects in blurred patterns of color and shade (Potter, 1975), we detect faces and figures in clouds and other amorphous forms, and we impose structure on random sequences of letters or numbers (Klahr, Chase, & Lovelace, 1983; Restle, 1970). When people are shown flashing points of light in a dark room, they see dramas, with objects moving to meet or to avoid each other (Michotte, 1946). When thought flows freely, in narrative form, comprehension, memory, and learning all seem to take care of themselves, as I try to show throughout this book. When the flow is broken, when comprehension, memory, and learning are manipulated from the outside, they may seem to be very difficult indeed. Often in these contrived situations, there is only boredom and bewilderment. The narrative nature of children's thought has been demonstrated by van Dongen (1987).

Rosen (1986) has argued most consistently that thought has a narrative basis. If he is correct, then reading and writing must be very fundamental human activities. In a chapter entitled "Stories of stories: Footnotes on sly gossipy practices" (Rosen, 1988), he looks at how readers creatively change stories in the retelling, in what he calls "memory as art." In a study of how children make sense of the world through the construction of stories, at home and at school, Wells (1986) refers to "the guided reinvention of knowledge." Bruner (1986) claims we all employ two modes of thought, complementary but irreconcilable—logical and intuitive (or the day view and the night view, truth seeking versus meaning making, well-formed arguments versus a good story). He proposes that the "self" develops through "autobiographical attitudes toward oneself," seen as talking to oneself about oneself, which doesn't come naturally, but requires knowledge of story conventions and genres (Bruner & Weisser, 1991). Salmon (1985) proposes three common metaphors for life—a card game (we're all dealt different hands to play as best we can), a natural cycle (birth, growth, death, regeneration), and a story (which provides everyone with an identity). Sadoski (1983) has demonstrated that reported imagery improves both comprehension and recall of stories, and Black, Freeman, and Johnson-Laird (1986) have shown that the more plausible we find a tale, the more we arc likely to understand and remember it. In other words, we understand and remember best when we can engage our imagination. Other research would no doubt show that drama, excitement, personal relevance, and familiar settings and characters are conducive to increased comprehension and recall (unless they are so familiar that they are boring). It seems unlikely to me that these are all separate avenues for coming to grips with texts or with the world; rather I would regard them as varied reflections of the more general fact that the closer an experience is to a coherent story, the more likely it is to be understood and remembered.

Thinking

An intriguing book stressing the creative and constructive nature of thought and also the brain's narrative mode of functioning is Jerome Bruner's (1986) *Actual Minds, Possible Worlds*. In *Mind in Society*, Lev Vygotsky (1978) underlines the social nature of thought, which he sees as internalized action. (Bruner would be more likely to see action as externalized thought.) Vygotsky also says profound things about the social nature of learning, which will become prominent in later chapters of this book. Some research on intelligence is really research on thinking, because it regards intelligence as just about everything that human beings do. Sternberg (1983, 1985), for example, inquires into the relationships between intelligence and the "internal world" of the individual, the external world of the individual, and the individual's experience. Sternberg's (1985) article in *Science* is a particularly concise and readable review of the variety of ways in which psychologists have thought about these relationships. Gilhooly (1982) and Gellatly (1986) are accessible and comprehensive on contemporary approaches to thinking. See also Smith (1990).

In a review article on research into metacognition, Bransford, Stein, and Vye (1982) make the typical summary observation that less successful students fail to activate knowledge that can help them to understand and remember new information. One might argue whether being unable to "activate knowledge" (which in less esoteric language means to make sense) is a cause of failure or simply a description of the condition such students find themselves in. The researchers also say that less successful students are less able to assess their own level of comprehension. But comprehension is a state rather than a process, and so is inability to comprehend. One can hardly be unaware of whether one is comprehending or confused—that is like asserting that we might be unaware of whether or not we feel hungry. Of course, we can believe we understand something when we are in error, just as we might feel hungry without needing food. But to make a mistake is not a failure of metacognition, of being out of touch with our own thought processes. It is simply a matter of being wrong.

NOTES TO CHAPTER 2, LANGUAGE: SPOKEN AND WRITTEN, pp. 25–47.

Surface Structure and Deep Structure

There is one significant exception to the statement that surface structure is the part of language which physically exists and can be measured in the world around us. That exception is the private *subvocal speech* which we "hear in our heads" when we talk to ourselves or "listen to ourselves" reading silently. It would be a mistake to believe that such an inner voice is deep structure, or indeed that it is some special but (to ourselves) observable quality of thought. Subvocal speech is just as much a *product* of thought as overt speech, the only difference being that it is uttered for our own benefit rather than anyone else's. Subvocal speech *could be* uttered aloud, just as the voice we hear in "silent" reading could be made audible to others. The inner voice is surface structure, with all the surface structure characteristics of vocabulary and grammar (albeit a little telegraphic at times). There must still be a deep structure underlying the utterances of the inner voice, a deep structure of meaning, which does not consist of sequences of words and sentences but of intangible concepts, global interrelationships, and propositions. (There is more on subvocalization in Chapter 9 and its Notes.)

Rosenberg and Simon (1977) demonstrate experimentally that there is a single underlying semantic representation, common to "information" presented in a variety of ways, in French and in English, in sentences and in pictures. McNeill (1985), reflecting on the nature and origins of language, sees parallels between speech and gesture in function, development, use, and even loss with different kinds of aphasia. In a long and rather abstruse article entitled "Against Definitions," Fodor, Garrett, Walker, and Parkes (1980) argue that sentences are not understood by recovering definitions of words. We do not understand the statement that someone is a bachelor by understanding that he is an unmarried man. "Bachelor" and "unmarried man" are not representations of each other but rather alternative representations of the same underlying meaning. Anderson and Ortony (1975) also show that the interpretation of a sentence, its "mental representation," is always much richer than the words in the text literally entail.

Gibbs (1984) argues against the notion that sentences usually have "literal meanings" in the context in which they occur (a view which he says dominates theories of language). He cites some experimental evidence that listeners do not necessarily "compute" the literal meaning of an utterance before understanding it. Golden and Guthrie (1986) show that ninth graders respond quite differently to the same short story, in the way in which they empathize with particular characters or react to events in the text, depending on their prior beliefs about what is right and natural. It is, of course, unlikely that any two people could ever experience any complex series of events, written or "real," in the same way or come away with the same understanding of what took place.

For arguments that writing is an independent language system, not derivative of speech, see Olson, Torrance, and Hildyard (1985), especially the Kolers chapter, also Vachek (1973). For arguments that written language can on occasion be spoken and spoken language written, see Tannen (1982a, 1982b).

For discussions of conventions generally, see Douglas (1968). Halliday and Hasan (1976) is the essential sourcebook for the conventions of cohesion in English, and Gregory and Carroll (1978) elucidate register. For more about the conventions of writing, see Smith (1994). Baldwin and Coady (1978) argue that punctuation rules are "empty" conventions, explaining nothing and ignored by above-average fifth grade readers.

Linguistic Theories

My very general use of the terms surface structure and deep structure should not be taken to relate explicitly to any particular linguistic theory, though the underlying distinction between physical manifestations of language and meaning is a prevailing view. Chomsky (1957), for example, in his original and revolutionary generative transformational grammar, employed the term surface structure to refer not to sound itself, and certainly not to writing, but rather as the abstract level at which "input to the phonological system" was realized. Only another transformational linguist could recognize Chomsky's surface structure if it was produced in sound or written out. Similarly, Chomsky's deep structure was never meaning, but rather "input to an underlying semantic system" which itself required transformation and interpretation. Obviously, sound (or writing) and meaning are much further apart than even the surface structures and deep structures that Chomsky talks about. Furthermore, there are a great many controversies between Chomsky and other linguists and philosophers about the connotations of these terms, and use of them has changed radically over the years (for a more recent survey, see Chomsky, 1986).

But it is not necessary to tie reading theory to a particular linguistic theory. The fact is that what for convenience I call surface structure—the physical representation—and deep structure—meaning—do not have a direct and self-evident relationship. Users of language, whether "producers" or "receivers," always have to bring sense to it.

Chomsky's thoughts on language are always significant and—when accessible to the layperson—interesting. See Chomsky (1959) for his clearest exposition, in a classic attack on the behaviorist theorizing of B. F. Skinner, and also Chomsky (1986). For a fascinating debate between Piaget and Chomsky (and even more vituperatively between their disciples), see Piattelli-Palmarini (1980).

An alternative linguistic theory, influential in the United Kingdom, is termed *systemic* (or *functional*) grammar (Butler, 1985; Halliday, 1985). The emphasis is on meaning, but from a social point of view, influenced by the anthropological theories of Firth and Malinowski. Not concerned at all with language "in the head," systemic grammar argues that every aspect of language is maintained by activity in social contexts and must be studied in those contexts. By contrast, Johnson-Laird (1982), in a system known as *procedural semantics*, proposes two-staged "mental models" in the interpretation of sentences. The first stage generates propositions at a superficial sentence level; the second stage takes into account what the listener or reader knows. The system is claimed among other things to be able to account for inferences based solely on meaning, without recourse to the constraints of logic. See also McNamara, Miller and Bransford (1991). Lakoff (1987), cited in the Notes to Chapter 1, also rejects all "objectivist grammars"—and there are many of them—which relate language to the world, in favor of a "cognitive grammar" relating language to our experiential perception of the world. From a different, evolutionary point of view, Lieberman (1984) also rejects conventional theories of language. Levin and Pinker

(1991), in the introduction to a special issue of the journal *Cognition* on "lexical and conceptual semantics," argue that attempts to show the structure in internal representations of word meanings were too complex and too *ad hoc*. The issue is technical. Lucas (1991) defends representational theories of meaning, and Shanon (1991) responds.

Many of the topics in this chapter are elaborated, from various points of view, in introductory textbooks on psycholinguistics, such as Wanner and Gleitman (1982), Taylor (1976), Glucksberg and Danks (1975), and Slobin (1979). Elementary texts on linguistics include Fromkin and Rodman (1983) and Steinberg (1982). Ortony (1979) is an edited volume on metaphor and thought. Mayor and Pugh (1987) contains excellent chapters on systems of communication and the power of literacy. Among many basic texts on semantics, see the two volumes of Lyons (1977) and also Janet Dean Fodor (1977). A classic text on the relationship between language and thought is Vygotsky (1962); see also Beveridge (1982).

For general discussions about the context of language and its uses, see Wilkinson (1971), Halliday (1973), Olson (1970), and Smith (1977a). For discussions of the consequences of writing systems and literacy, see Havelock (1976), Goody and Watt (1972), and Olson (1977).

Nystrand (1986) argues that written language is not "context-free" or "situation-independent," but that the context of texts is their "potential use." In other words, readers' understanding of the purposes for which texts were written can make the texts more predictable. Chafe and Danielwicz (1987) note that complex syntactic structures occur in "textlike" spoken language situations, like judicial proceedings and formal lectures, but for most people there is a far higher probability of experiencing such structures in print.

Semiotics

Semiotics is an abstruse and frequently opaque science that studies all manner of "signs," or communicative conventions, and their relationships to whatever it is they signify. Classic sources in semiotics are Morris (1946), Peirce (1931, 1958), and Eco (1984). None is particularly easy to read, nor is it immediately clear how their theories contribute to an understanding of why people read and write and of how they learn to do these things. Relatively clear introductions to semiotics generally are provided by Davis (1991), Suhor (1992) and Givón (1989) with earlier volumes by Culler (1981) and Deely (1982). The educator who has tried the most to make semiotics relevant to an understanding of reading and writing is Jerome Harste (see Harste, Woodward, & Burke, 1984). One aspect of semiotics to which Deely and Harste draw attention is concerned with major forms of logic and their relevance to thinking and learning generally. Two of the three forms are widely known, if not always well understood. The first is *deduction*, when known ideas or interpretive procedures are employed to develop new ideas or procedures, such as deducing what the "result" or consequence will be from a rule and an instance of that rule. Mathematics and the formal syllogisms of classical logic are examples of deductive reasoning. The second category, *induction*, relates to the inferring of causes and rules from a result, for example through the "scientific method," or hypothesis testing. Less well-known and possibly more interesting is the third category, *abduction*, when a new rule or explanation is hypothesized from a particular result or state of affairs. Such creative thinking is not normally considered part of either logic or science, but it may better characterize much of human thought, including that involved in reading or writing.

Discourse Analysis

Texts are more than simple collocations of words, arranged sequentially according to the conventions of grammar and the desire to tell a story or to explain ideas. Texts have layer upon layer of interwoven texture, and these layers are not unravelled independently of each other. One theorist, de Beaugrande (1981), proposes seven interconnected systems or "standards" in texts which both writers and readers must respect. The seven are *cohesion* (the way sentences are interlocked), *coherence* (of the parts to the whole), *intentionality*, *acceptability* (of expression and interpretation), *informativity*, *situationality* (or relevance), and *intertextuality* (relationships to texts already written or read). Readers, according to de Beaugrande, create "textual worlds" as they read, organized around over 30 different kinds of semantic relationship and over 40 types of semantic network, the four most important of which pertain to events, actions, objects, and situations. See also de Beaugrande and Dressler (1981). On the other hand, van Dijk (1980) is concerned less with all the detailed "microstructure" of texts than with "macrostructures" that involve large areas of text and reader knowledge. Kintsch and van Dijk (1975, 1978; Kintsch, 1988) have frequently collaborated to examine how texts, and readers' interpretations of texts, can be analyzed in terms of a "propositional text base," a tissue of connected assertions about states of affairs. A different point of view proposed by Meyer (1985) is that text structures involve a variety of relationships among the predicates of propositions. All of this is very complex, abstract, technical, and permeated with specialized jargon, related not just to texts but to every aspect of written and spoken language. Almost all theories of discourse analysis claim some experimental evidence that readers are sensitive to the kinds of structures the theorist believes exist in texts, but it is difficult to see how any particular theory could be disproved. Their most practical value may be in suggesting ways in which knowledge might be organized and employed on computers by experts in artificial intelligence, which is the area from which the theories originally derived. Claims that the theories are important for instruction—that students should be made aware of them—are vigorously disputed (e.g., Eisner, 1982). Most people who can read and write today learned to do so without the benefit of such specialized knowledge, which could obviously put great stress on the attentiveness and interest of beginners. What is clear is the importance of shared knowledge of the content of the text and experience of the manner in which different kinds of text are conventionally written.

For a general discussion of discourse analysis and comprehension, see Tierney and Mosenthal (1982), and more technically Flammer and Kintsch (1982), Stubbs (1982), Britton and Black (1985), and Halliday (1985). Stein (1992) is a useful but technical volume on writing and reading from a discourse analysis point of view. It contains a significant paper by Chafe (1992) noting the central role of "displaced consciousness" in reading (with the reader taking different roles and viewpoints) and also, controversially, the importance of introspection in written language research.

Halliday and his students in Australia have focused great attention on the role of genre in writing, which they believe should be explicitly taught, leading to a considerable educational controversy in that country (Cairney, 1992); there is a summary in Smith (1994). The term genre originally referred to different types of writing, such as comedy, tragedy, epic. More recently the term came to refer to different kinds of media—newspapers, periodicals, novels, nonfiction—all of which have their own conventions. Current emphasis is on complete settings, including such matters as conversations, interrogations, and classroom procedures. The core is always structure or organization—of the text alone or of the situation. Littlefair (1991) found British students' knowledge of genre after three or four years of study was directly related to the amount and breadth of the reading they did. There are some interesting discussions of genre and related topics in Cazden (1992).

Text Organization and Comprehension

Texts that are difficult to understand because of the way they are written are sometimes referred to as "inconsiderate" (Armbruster & Anderson, 1984). There is no doubt that texts can often be improved. Beck, McKeown, Omanson, and Pople (1984) revised two basal reader stories to make them more coherent without altering their plots, enhancing the comprehension of both skilled and less skilled readers. The length of the two stories was increased from 782 and 811 words to 900 and 957 words, but comprehension went up by a grade level for both second- and third-grade readers. Readability formulas based on word counts and sentence length have been generally discredited (e.g., MacGinitie, 1984). "Simplifying" reading material by fragmenting it into short sentences can greatly interfere with comprehension and recall. See also Slater (1985).

Hundreds of studies have been conducted and reported since the mid-1970s demonstrating that texts are better understood and remembered if readers (of all ages and ability) are familiar with the relevant story grammars, for example, Bower (1976), Bower, Black, and Turner (1979), Fredericksen (1975), Mandler and Johnson (1977), Reder (1980), Stein and Glenn (1979), and Walker and Meyer (1980). McGee (1982) showed that third- and fifth-grade readers were aware of text structures and used them in recall, even the poor readers (though they did so less well than better readers, who might reasonably be expected to have had greater familiarity with stories). Mandler and Goodman (1982) found that reading speed dropped when story structures were not congruent with readers' expectations and also that second sentences were read faster than the first sentences in chapters, when readers had gained an idea of what the chapter was about. Anderson and Pearson (1984) theorize about the relevance of schemes in reading comprehension. See also Grimes (1975) and Applebee (1977).

Piper (1987) has some cautions about teaching students the explicit structures of story grammar, which he sees as no different from more traditional modes of analysis which have not fared well in education. Consciousness of structure does not necessarily promote understanding, he argues, and the theories also assume that there is just one interpretation for every text. Durkin (1981) also looks critically at the significance of the "new interest" in comprehension for education. Beers (1987) argues that schema theory—and cognitive science generally—are inappropriate approaches to reading because of their underlying "machine metaphor." In a careful review, Taylor (1992) observes that concern with text structure has required students to write "hierarchical summaries" and draw diagrams and "maps" of texts—"a whole new skill to learn."

In the present book, comprehension is regarded as our cognitive state when we are able to make sense of our situation and of whatever we are trying to do. The opposite of comprehension is confusion. However, efforts to systematize education and instruction have led to a widespread view that comprehension is a process, the opposite of which is ignorance. Comprehension, like thinking, is seen as a set of skills or procedures which can and must be taught. A typical example is the analysis of Pearson, Roehler, Dole, and Duffy (1992) which breaks comprehension down into a set of seven *strategies* based on schema theory (Anderson & Pearson, 1984). These strategies—supposedly "used differentially" by "expert" and "novice" readers—include: searching for connections between what they know and new information in text; "monitoring the adequacy of their models of text meaning"; taking steps to "repair faulty comprehension" when there is failure to understand; distinguishing important from less important ideas in text; synthesizing information in and between texts; drawing inferences during and after reading for a "full, integrated understanding"; and asking conscious and unconscious questions of themselves, authors, and texts. Garner (1992) discusses "metacognition and self-monitoring strategies" as ways of getting students to ask themselves the questions that teachers would ask them.

It might be argued that comprehension is the basis rather than a consequence of the previous strategies and that they all depend on prior knowledge (including knowledge of the kinds of things that can be done with texts). There is an enormous amount of research to show the importance of prior knowledge in reading, which ought, perhaps, to be considered self-evident. No one, as far as I know, has ever proposed an opposing point of view, although some instructional methodologies pay little attention to what learners may or may not comprehend or already know—what they may find either confusing or boring.

Robinson, Faraone, Hittleman, and Unrah (1990) review comprehension research and instruction since 1783—from the expectation that comprehension occurs spontaneously or with time to the systematic teaching of strategies and self-monitoring techniques. Cairney (1990) criticizes "traditional comprehension practices" in schools as mainly directive and question based. There is a growing recognition of the role of inference in comprehension, usually discussed either in terms of skills or as internal representations, for example, Kintsch, (1988); Kintsch and van Dijk (1978) for propositional theories; Rumelhart (1980) for schema theory; and McNamara, Miller, and Bransford (1991) and Johnson-Laird, Byrne, and Schaeken (1992) for mental model theories, the latter arguing that the brain is not a logic machine but a sense-making device. There are substantial and largely nontechnical discussions of "models of the mind" from both "scientific" and "philosophical" points of view in Mohyeldin Said, Newton-Smith, Viale, and Wilkes (1990). Fodor, an erudite linguistic philosopher prolifically involved in many controversies related to language and thought, combines densely technical writing with an engaging light-heartedness, for example, a chapter entitled "Fodor's Guide to Mental Representation. The Intelligent Auntie's Vade-Mecum" in Fodor (1990).

Esoteric contemporary theories like deconstructionism and intertextuality (which tend to take all meaning out of the text and away from authors and readers) are critically discussed by Eagleton (1983) in a readably ascerbic review of literary theories from phenomenology to poststructuralism. In an extended passage on reading, Eagleton analyzes the immense amount of interpretation and prior knowledge that a reader, usually quite unconsciously, must bring to bear just to get started on a novel (he analyzes the first two sentences of an Updike novel), arguing that "the text itself is really no more than a series of 'cues' to the reader" (p. 76). For more on deconstructionism, focusing particularly on Bahktin's theory of intertextuality—the idea that the meaning of any text is determined by the complex and shifting meanings of all other texts—see Lodge (1990). Bloome and Egan-Robertson (1993) endeavor to make such theorizing relevant to classrooms.

Finally, there is a small but growing interest in *interest* as a factor in reading. Hidi, Baird, and Hildyard (1982) show that interest can interfere with comprehension because it diverts attention; children will not pay extended attention to "trivial information" in texts unless it is interesting, in which case they will remember it.

Some Technical Terms

One might think that there could not be too much complication about the fact that the basic elements of language are sounds. The word *bed*, for example, is made up of three distinctive sounds /b/, /e/, and /d/ (it is a useful convention that the sounds of language are printed between oblique // strokes). With a few perverse exceptions, each sound of the language is represented by a particular letter of the alphabet, so the number of alternative sounds in English must be about 26. Unfortunately, none of the preceding statements is correct.

English has rather more functionally different sounds than it has letters in the alphabet, about 40. These sounds have the special name *phonemes*. A variety of letters can represent a single phoneme and a variety of phonemes can be represented by a single letter or letter combination. It is necessary to be tentative in making statements about the total number of phonemes because it depends on who is talking and when. All dialects have roughly the same number of phonemes, but not always the same ones, so that words that are individually distinguishable in some dialects, such as *guard* and *god*, may not be distinguishable in others unless in a meaningful context. We often think we make distinctions between words when in fact we do not—redundancy in context is usually sufficient to indicate which alternative we intend. Many literate speakers do not have phonemes to distinguish among *Mary*, *marry*, and *merry*, or *cot*, *caught*, and *court*. Say these words one at a time and ask a listener to spell what you have just said. You may find that the listener cannot observe all the differences you think you are making. Phonemes often drop out of casual or colloquial speech.

A phoneme is not so much a single sound as a collection of sounds, all of which sound the same. If that description seems complicated, a more formal definition will not appear much better—a phoneme is a class of closely related sounds constituting the smallest unit of speech that will distinguish one utterance from another. For example, the /b/ at the beginning of the word *bed* distinguishes *bed* from words like *fed* and *led* and *red*, the /e/ in the middle distinguishes *bed* from *bad* and *bide* and *bowed*, and the /d/ distinguishes the word from such alternatives as *bet* and *beg*. So each of the three elements in *bed* will serve to distinguish the word from others, and each also is the smallest unit that can do this. Each is a *significant difference*. It does not matter if the /b/ pronounced at the beginning of *bed* is a little different from /b/ at the beginning of *bad*, or if the /b/ in *bed* is pronounced in different ways on different occasions. All the different sounds that I might make that are acceptable as the sound at the beginning of *bed* and *bad*, and that serve to distinguish them from *fed* and *fad*, and so forth qualify as being the same phoneme. A phoneme is not one sound, but a variety of sounds any of which is acceptable by listeners as making the same contrast. The actual sounds that are produced are called *phones*, and the sets of "closely related" phones that all serve as the same phoneme are called *allophones* of each other (or of the particular phoneme). Allophones are sounds that the listener learns to treat as equivalent and to hear as the same.

When electronic equipment is used to analyze sounds heard as the same, quite marked differences can be found, depending on the sound that follows them. For example, the /d/ in *dim* is basically a high-pitched rising sound, while its allophone at the beginning of *doom* is much lower pitched and falling (Liberman, Cooper, Shankweiler, & Studdert-Kennedy, 1957). A tape recorder will confirm that the two words have no /d/ sound in common. If they are recorded, it is impossible to cut the tape in order to separate the /im/ or /oom/ from the /d/. Either one is left with a distinct /di/ or /doo/ sound, or else the /d/ sound disappears altogether, leaving two quite different kinds of whistle. Other phonemes behave in equally bizarre ways. If the first part of the tape-recorded word *pit* is cut and spliced at the front of the final /at/ of a word such as *sat* or *fat*, the word that is heard is not *pat*, as we might expect, but *cat*. The /k/ from the beginning of *keep* makes *top* when joined to the /op/ from *cop* and makes *poop* when combined with the /oop/ from *coop*.

There is a simple way to demonstrate the sounds that we normally hear to be the same can be quite different. Say the word *pin* into the palm of your hand and you will feel a distinct puff of air on the /p/; however, the puff is absent when you say the word *spin*. In other words, the /p/ in *pin* is not the same as the /p/ in *spin*—and both are different from the /p/ in *limp*. If you now pay careful attention to the way you say the words, you can probably detect the difference. Usually the difference is ignored, because it is not significant. Other word pairs provide a similar demonstration—for example, *kin* and *skin* or *team* and *steam*. You may also be able to detect a difference between /k/ in *cool* and /k/ in *keen*, a difference that is allophonic in English and phonemic in Arabic, or in the /l/ at the beginning and end of *level*. Japanese often have difficulty in distinguishing between English words such as *link* and *rink* because there is no contrast at all between /l/ and /r/ in their language. In short, a phoneme is not something present in the surface level of spoken language—it is something that the listener constructs. We do not hear different sounds when we are listening to speech, but instead we hear significant differences, phonemes instead of phones. The preceding distinctions may be further illustrated by reference to writing, where a comparable situation holds. Just as the word *sound* is ambiguous in speech, because it can refer to a phone or a phoneme, so the word *letter* is ambiguous in writing. We call *a* one letter of the alphabet, as distinguished from b, c, d, and so forth, but we also talk about *a*, A, a, and so forth as being letters, although they all in a way represent the same letter. In the first case, the letter of the alphabet *a* is really a category name for a variety of written symbols such as *a*, A, a. The 26 category names for the letters in the English alphabet may be called *graphemes*, the written symbols (which are innumerable in their various forms) may be called *graphs*, and the graphs that constitute alternatives for a single grapheme are known as *allographs*.

The same defining framework can now be used for the basic elements of speech and writing. A phoneme (grapheme) is a class of closely related phones (graphs) constituting the smallest significant differences in speech (writing) that will distinguish one meaningful unit from another. The set of functionally equivalent phones (graphs) constituting a single phoneme (grapheme) are termed allophones (allographs). Allographs may not seem to have as much in common as allophones; in fact, some allographs, such as *a* and *A*, or *g* and *G*, would appear to have nothing in common at all. But they do have a *functional equivalence* in that their differences are not significant for reading, any more than the differences between allophones are significant for comprehending speech.

Linguists make several other distinctions along the same lines. A *morpheme* is the smallest meaningful part of a word. A word may consist of one or more morphemes, some "free" like *farm* or *like* because they can occur independently, and some "bound" like *-er* (meaning someone who does something) and *-s* (meaning plural) or *un-* (meaning negative), which have to be joined to a free morpheme. Thus *farmers* is three morphemes, one free and two bound, and so is *unlikely*. Different *morphs* may represent the same morpheme—thus for plurality we can have not only *-s* but *-es*, *-en*, and a lot of quite odd forms like the vowel change in *man-men* or even nothing at all, as in the singular and plural *sheep*. Morphs that constitute the same morpheme are called *allomorphs*. Meaning itself may be considered in the form of elements sometimes called *sememes*. *Bachelor* for example, comprises sememes related to maleness, age, marriage, and negation. Words in a dictionary—earlier referred to as "lexical entries"—may similarly be termed *lexemes*.

Modules and Networks

Cognitive science as a general area of theory and research related to knowledge, in both humans and computers, is a topic discussed in the Notes to Chapter 3. But within cognitive science there is a particular interest in language, including two relatively new theories that are beginning to establish a presence in educational considerations of reading which warrant brief mention at this point. One is called *modular theory* and the other *connectionism*. They are, to some extent, contradictory.

Modular theory proposes that evolution has "prewired" (or "hardwired") the human brain with special-purpose "modules" for a number of specific cognitive activities including language (meaning speech). These modules are "domain specific"—they permit certain things to be done that cannot be done in other ways or by other systems. For example, there are certain hypothetical underlying structures (like the organization of questions) that are universal to every language of the world.

No one has ever seen a module; the argument derives solely from analysis and speculation concerning the nature of language (Fodor, 1983), triggered by the rapid and relatively undirected way that the vast majority of infants learn to use spoken language, the "fast-accessing" of language, and the isolated manner in which speech ability is sometimes lost through injury or strokes. But to argue that language must be innate because of universal similarities and the fact that most people can learn to do it without difficulty might be considered a bit like arguing that car driving is innate because cars tend to be the same all over the world and most people can learn to drive them. Cars reflect human capacities and limitations, and no doubt languages do the same. For a helpful article in a useful volume on the topic of modularity (with some alternative points of view), see Maratsos (1992). Gernsbacher (1990) opposes the modularity point of view that the comprehension of language is largely syntactic with counter arguments that it is based on semantic (often narrative) components—like who is doing what to whom. Liberman and Mattingly (1989) claim that ability to distinguish an initial sound like /d/ followed by different vowel sounds from similar syllables beginning with other initial sounds is the kind of unique human capacity that supports the modular view, but Kluender, Diehl, and Killeen (1987) trained Japanese quail to do the same in 48 positive and 48 negative trials.

Rather than regard language as a specific innate capacity, Harris (1981, 1988) has the Wittgensteinian view that language is analogous to a game with complex rules, constructed socially and always changing. Quine is a prominent philosopher who also holds that language is a social art, learned on the evidence of other people's behavior through "analogic synthesis." Sentences already learned are linked to form new sentences. Gibson (1988) is a convenient summary of Quine's position. In a speculative book, Bickerton (1990) hypothesizes that language developed not from the narrow communicative systems of animals and early humans, but from representational systems, ways of forming models (or theories) of the external world based on imposed categories and relationships.

Connectionism, sometimes known as "neuroscience," "computational theory," "spreading activation," or "neural network theory," employs computers, pencil and paper, and, occasionally, actual biological materials to simulate layered networks of connections that are supposed to reflect the way neurons are organized in the cortex of the brain. The networks consist of hundreds of units, complexly connected at nodes, that have some of the properties of real neurons. Receptor units either fire or do not fire when activated by particular "inputs," they facilitate or inhibit the firing of neighboring units, and their patterns of activation at one level are organized or interpreted at intermediate levels to produce "responses" at output levels, the probability of which change with "experience." A "correct" response will be reinforced and strengthened, and "incorrect" responses weakened. Thus the networks are said to "learn" without a need for "folk psychology" concepts like "intentions," "beliefs," or "rules." This relatively simple "wetware" theory has generated enormous numbers of research projects and papers and a great deal of enthusiasm. There is a very clear discussion of it in Bereiter (1991). Much of the groundwork and many publications have come from a research group led by Rumelhart and McClelland (1987; Rumelhart, McClelland, & the "PDP Research Group," 1986), whose own particular model is termed "parallel distributed processing" (PDP for short). For a description, defense, and complex demonstration of PDP, involving the rule-less learning of the past tense of English verbs, see MacWhinney and Leinbach (1991). Crick (1989) provides a brief and comprehensible description of connectionist networks, especially PDP, and claims that they are unrealistic in important respects. They do not really work like the brain, and they use procedures not available to the brain. Crick argues that the models should be called "demonstrations" rather than simulations and that the designers have more interest in computers and engineering design than in actual brains and the way children learn.

In a stimulating volume with the unpromising title of *Artificial Intelligence in Psychology*, Boden (1989) has an elegant metaphor for the manifold "localized computations" of PDP—a classroom full of children all chatting with their neighbors about something relevant to what the class as a whole is trying to achieve, with the repeated modification of individual opinions spreading across the room from child to child until there is close to a mutually consistent opinion.

Bever (1992) argues for the necessity of both "modular and nodular" representations of knowledge. He believes that although the connectionist model (with nodes) may account for habitual behavior, a symbolic or structural system (modules) is required for new experiences; he proposes that both "structural demons" and an "habitual beast" must be interacting in the brain. The analogies are appealing, but the discussion, like everything else in the edited book on connectionism in which the chapter appears (Reilly & Sharkey, 1992) is abstruse and technical. Like many similar discussions, it is unlikely to appeal to anyone who normally talks and thinks in terms of "listening" or "understanding" rather than of "natural language processing."

"Folk psychology," with its concepts of "mental states" like desires and beliefs that are popularly supposed to underlie behavior, have come in for a good deal of criticism, notably by Stich (1983) and Fodor and Pylyshyn (1988). For a sympathetic but critical account of neuroscience by a philosopher who immersed herself in the topic, see Churchland (1986), who is in turn critically analyzed by Greenwood (1991).

Speech, Writing, and "Language"

Confusion can arise when reading is referred to as a "language process." Of course reading is a matter of language. The problem arises when the word *language* is used synonymously with the word *speech*, with reading regarded as some kind of ancillary or parasitical process rather than a language activity in its own right. When Perfetti (1985), for example, argues for the "language" basis of reading, he is asserting that reading alphabetic text depends upon "phonological awareness" of sound patterns in speech.

The priority given to speech is clearly inappropriate (though not always recognized to be so) in the case of deaf language. Deaf signing is at least as rich, flexible, and expressive as spoken language—although its development may be handicapped by efforts to anchor deaf language in speech. For powerful as well as moving discussions of the language and thought of deaf people, see Sacks (1989) and the references in that volume.

On the other hand, the word language is often used metaphorically, for example, in references to "computer language" and "body language."

More About Words

A number of my observations about the ambiguity of words are derived from the work of the linguist Fries (1945), who calculated that the 500 most common words of our language have an average of 28 distinct dictionary meanings each. The most detailed analyses of the relation between word frequencies and their different meanings are by Zipf (1960), and there are interesting and more readable summaries in Miller (1951). Miller points out that the 50 most common words of our language do the bulk of our communicative work, constituting 60 percent of talk and 40 percent of writing. A mere seven words constitute 20 percent of our language—*the, of, and, a, to, in* and *is.* The ten most common French words—*à, de, dans, sur, et, ou, que, ne, pas,* and *y*—constitute 25 percent of that language.

The eye-voice span phenomenon shows that when reading aloud we do not say the words we are looking at; the eye roves ahead over meaningful stretches of words as we organize units that make sense. There is a flurry of small studies of the eye-voice span every decade or so; a recent review is included in Gibson and Levin (1975) and earlier in Geyer (1968).

NOTES TO CHAPTER 3, INFORMATION AND EXPERIENCE, pp. 49–63.

Measuring Information and Uncertainty

Mathematics plays only a small part in this book. But a brief introduction to some elementary techniques of information theory measurement will allow some numbers to be put to the rate at which we are able to deal with visual information from the eyes (our "channel capacity"). The same techniques also permit quantification of the uncertainty or redundancy of letters and words of English (or any other language) in differing circumstances.

It is necessary to be a little circumlocutionary in putting actual figures to information and uncertainty because although both are measured with respect to alternatives, the measure is not simply the number of alternatives. Instead, information is calculated in terms of a unit called a *bit,* which always reduces by half the uncertainty on any particular occasion. Thus the card player who discovers that an opponent's strongest suit is red (either diamonds or hearts) gets one bit of information, and so does a child trying to identify a letter who is told that it comes from the second half of the alphabet. In the first case two alternatives are eliminated (the two black suits), and in the second case 13 alternatives are removed (and 13 still remain). In both cases the proportion of uncertainty reduced is a half, and therefore the amount of information received is regarded as one bit.

The uncertainty of a situation in bits is equal to the number of times a "yes or no" question would have to be asked and answered to eliminate all uncertainty if each answer reduced uncertainty by a half. Thus there are two bits of uncertainty in the card-playing example because two questions will remove all doubt, for example: *Q1. Is it a black suit? Q2. If yes, is it clubs? (If no, is it hearts?)*, or *Q1. Is it spades or diamonds? Q2. If yes, is it spades? (If no, is it hearts?)*

You can see it does not matter how the questions are posed, provided they permit a yes-no answer that will eliminate half the alternatives. The final qualification is important. Obviously, a single question such as "Is it clubs?" will eliminate all alternatives if the answer is "yes," but will still leave at least one and possibly more questions to be asked if the answer is "no." The most efficient way of reducing uncertainty when the answer can only be "yes" or "no" is by a binary split, that is, by partitioning the alternatives into two equal sets. In fact the word *bit*, which may have sounded rather colloquial, is an abbreviation of the words *binary digit*, or a number representing a choice between two alternatives.

The uncertainty of the 26 letters of the alphabet lies somewhere between four and five bits. Four bits of information will allow selection among 16 alternatives, not quite enough, the first bit reducing this number to 8, the second to 4, the third to 2, and the fourth to 1. Five bits will select among 32 alternatives, slightly too many, the first eliminating 16 and the other four removing the rest of the uncertainty. In brief, x bits of information will select among 2^x alternatives. Two bits will select among $2^2 = 4$, three bits among $2^3 = 8$, four bits among $2^4 = 16$, and so on. One question settles only $2^1 = $ two alternatives, and no questions at all requires that you have only one alternative to begin with ($2^0 = 1$). Twenty bits ("twenty questions") are theoretically sufficient to distinguish among $2^{20} = 1,048,576$ alternatives. There is a mathematical formula that shows that the theoretical uncertainty of 26 letters of the alphabet is almost precisely 4.7 bits, although, of course, it is not easy to see how one could ask just 4.7 questions. (The formula is that the uncertainty of x alternatives is $\log_2 x$, which can be looked up in a table of logarithms to the base 2. $\log_2 26 = 4.7$, since $26 = 2^{4.7}$. Can you calculate the uncertainty in a deck of 52 playing cards? Since 52 is just twice 26, the uncertainty of the cards must be one bit more than that of the alphabet, or 5.7 bits.)

Measuring Redundancy

It will be helpful to pursue the matter of redundancy a little more deeply, partly because of the importance of the concept of redundancy to reading, but also because the discussion of how *bits* of uncertainty or information are computed contained an oversimplification that can now be rectified. We shall consider two aspects of redundancy, termed *distributional* and *sequential*.

Distributional redundancy is associated with the relative probability that each of the alternatives in a particular situation can occur. Surprising as it may seem, there is less uncertainty when some alternatives are less probable than others. And because there is less uncertainty when alternatives are not equally probable, there is redundancy. The very fact that alternatives are not equally probable is an additional source of information that reduces the uncertainty of the set of alternatives as a whole. Redundancy that occurs because the probabilities of alternatives are not equally distributed is therefore called distributional redundancy.

Uncertainty is greatest when every alternative has an equal chance of occurring. Consider a coin-tossing game where there are only two alternatives, head or tail, and there are, in fact, equal chances of a head or tail turning up. The informativeness of knowing that a particular toss of the coin produced a head (or a tail) is one bit, because whatever the outcome uncertainty is reduced by a half. But now suppose that the game is not fair, and that the coin will come down head nine times out of ten. What is the uncertainty of the game now (to someone who knows the coin's bias)? The uncertainty is hardly as great as when the odds were 50–50, because then there was no reason to choose between head and tail while with the loaded coin it would be foolish knowingly to bet tail. By the same token, there is likely to be far less information on being told the outcome of a particular toss of the loaded coin. Not much uncertainty is removed if one is told that the coin has come down head because that is what was expected all the time. In fact the informativeness of a head can be computed to be about .015 bit compared with one bit if the game were fair. It is true that there is much more information in the relatively unlikely event of being told that a toss produced a tail— a total of 3.32 bits of information compared with the one bit for a tail when heads and tails are equally probable—but we can expect a tail to occur only once in every 10 tosses. The *average* amount of information available from the loaded coin will be nine-tenths of the .015 bit of information for head and one-tenth of the 3.32 bits of information for tail which when totaled is approximately .35 bit. The difference between the one bit of uncertainty (or information) for the 50–50 coin, and the .35 bit for the 90–10 loaded coin, is the distributional redundancy.

The earlier statements that every bit of information halves the number of alternatives and that the number of bits of uncertainty is the number of yes-no questions that would have to be asked and answered to eliminate all the alternatives hold only when all the alternatives are equally probable. If some alternatives are less probable than others, then an *average* amount of uncertainty or information has to be computed, taking into account both the number of alternatives and the probability of each. Because uncertainty and information are at their maximum when alternatives are equally probable, the average uncertainty of situations where this does not occur is necessarily less than the maximum, and redundancy is present.

The statement that the uncertainty of letters of the English language is 4.7 bits is perfectly true for any situation involving 26 equally probable alternatives—for example, drawing a letter from a hat containing one instance only of each of the 26 letters of the alphabet. But the letters of English do not occur in the language with equal frequency; some of them, such as *e, t, a, o, i, n, s,* occur far more often than others. In fact *e* occurs about 40 times more often than the least frequent letter, *z*. Because of this inequality, the average uncertainty of letters is somewhat less than the maximum of 4.7 bits that it would be if the letters all occurred equally often. The actual uncertainty of letters, considering their relative frequency, is 4.07 bits, the difference of about .63 bit being the distributional redundancy of English letters, a measure of the prospective informativeness that is lost because letters do not occur equally often. If letters were used equally often, we could achieve the 4.07 bits of uncertainty that the 26 letters currently have with a little over 16 letters. We could save ourselves about nine letters if we could find a way (and agree) to use the remainder equally often.

Words also have a distributional redundancy in English. One of the oldest and still least understood findings in experimental psychology concerns the "word-frequency effect," that more common words of our language can be identified on less visual information than less frequent words (Broadbent, 1967; Howes & Solomon, 1951). Computations of the distributional redundancy of letters and words in English are contained in Shannon (1951) and are discussed in Cherry (1978) and Pierce (1961).

Sequential redundancy exists when the probability of a letter or word is constrained by the presence of surrounding letters or words in the same sequence. For example, the probability that the letter *H* will follow *T* in English words is not 1 in 26 (which would be the case if all letters had an equal chance of occurring in any position) nor about 1 in 17 (taking distributional redundancy into account), but about 1 in 8 (because only eight alternatives are likely to occur following *T* in English; namely, *R, H,* or a vowel). Thus the uncertainty of any letter that follows *T* in an English word is just three bits ($2^3 = 8$). The average uncertainty of all letters in English words is about 2.5 bits (Shannon, 1951). The difference between this average uncertainty of 2.5 bits and a possible uncertainty of 4.07 bits (after allowing for distributional redundancy) is the sequential redundancy of letters in English words. An average of 2.5 bits of uncertainty means that letters in words have a probability of about 1 in 6 instead of 1 in 26. This figure, of course, is only an *average* computed over many readers, many words, and many letter positions. There is not a progressive decline in uncertainty from letter to letter, from left to right, in all words. An English word beginning with *q*, for example, has zero uncertainty about the next letter *u*, an uncertainty of about two bits for the four vowels that can follow the *u*, and then perhaps four bits of uncertainty for the next letter, which could be one of over a dozen alternatives. Other words have different uncertainty patterns, although in general the uncertainty of any letter goes down the more other letters in the word are known, irrespective of order. Because of constraints in the spelling patterns of English—due in part to the way words are pronounced—there is slightly more uncertainty at the beginning of a word than at the end, with slightly less in the middle (see Bruner & O'Dowd, 1958).

The orthographic (spelling) redundancy of print to which I have referred comprises both distributional and sequential redundancy for letters *within* words, while syntactic (grammar) and semantic (meaning) redundancy are primarily sequential redundancy *between* words. Computer software makes use of the sequential redundancy of both letters and words in order to assist writers to type (and sometimes to enable handicapped people to communicate), in combination with a "virtual keyboard" in which letters (or other symbols) appear on the screen and need only be touched or otherwise indicated in order for choices to be made. In contrast to the fixed array of keys on a "real" keyboard, the characters on a virtual keyboard can be reduced in number and kind almost instantly, from letter to letter, so that the writer is confronted only by those items most likely to be required. If a *k* has been selected, for example, only those letters likely to come next will be presented (like *l, n, r* or a vowel), reducing clutter and the time required for a decision to be made. Once one or more words have been selected, the software may be able to suggest entire words that are likely to come next, so that the writer need make only one choice, out of very few alternatives, to select an entire word. Predictive software can do more than anticipate letters and words based on their frequency in language as a whole—it can reflect probabilities of words and sequences of words in particular subject areas and even be "trained" to anticipate the probable word choices of individual writers.

Signal Detection Theory

As I said in the chapter, observers (whether radar operators or readers) always have a choice between reducing the number of their absolute errors while increasing "misses" or of achieving maximum hits while increasing the number of "false alarms." In effect, observers can place themselves at any point along a curve ranging from zero false alarms (but zero hits) to 100 percent hits (but a maximum of false alarms). This curve is called a *receiver operating characteristic*, or ROC curve, and varies with every individual and situation. At any one time an observer can choose where to be placed on the ROC curve—the criterion level selected depending on the perceived relative costs of hits, misses, and false alarms. But to shift the ROC curve as a whole—to improve the ratio of hits, misses, and false alarms—requires an improvement in the clarity of the situation (e.g., better illumination) or in the ability of the observer (e.g., more skill). Encouragement or success has the effect of moving an observer up an ROC curve, just as anxiety will move the observer down, but only a change in ability— or, for example, an increase in the availability of nonvisual information—will shift the ROC curve in its entirety.

There is an interesting example of the ability of human observers to penetrate noise and extract information-carrying signals in what Cherry (1978) calls the *cocktail party problem*. The example illustrates a point frequently made in this book that the prior knowledge of the perceiver contributes so much to comprehension. The problem is this: How can listeners in a crowd of people all talking loudly at the same time manage to follow what one person is saying and tune out everything else? The communication channel to each listener's ear is full of noise (both literally and technically), yet the individual can select from within the noise the information coming from one source only. And this "selected" voice is the only one that is heard—unless someone else happens to say something particularly relevant personally, such as the listener's name, in which case it is demonstrated that the listener has really been monitoring all the conversations all the time, "listening without hearing." It has been shown experimentally that we can follow one message even if successive words are produced by different voices, by following the sense and syntax of the message being attended to. Such a feat can be accomplished only if listeners draw upon their own knowledge of language to extract a message from all the irrelevant noise in which it is embedded.

Further Reading

Attneave (1959) discusses specifically applications of information theory to psychology. Miller (1964) reprints useful brief articles on both information theory and signal detection theory. An introductory psychology text that employs concepts from both theoretical domains is Lindsay and Norman (1977). Garner (1962, 1974) also develops psychological descriptions from an information theory point of view. A classic article on signal detection theory is Swets, Tanner, and Birdsall (1961); at a more popular level see Swets (1973) and, more technically, Pastore and Scheirer (1974).

Limitations of Information Theory and of "Information"

The first practical application of information theory was in measuring the efficiency of communication systems like telephone lines and radio links. The measure was related to the proportion of words emitted by the "transmitter" at one end of a communication channel that the "receiver" at the other end could correctly identify. Information theory had a brief but spectacular decade of influence in psychology in the 1950s and 1960s, primarily due to the erudition of George Miller (1956) in an article that referred to limits on human "capacity for processing information." For many psychologists this was a new and seductive way of talking about the brain.

Information theory became influential at a time when reading was primarily considered to be a matter of identifying letters and words. The text could be regarded as a transmitter, the reader as a receiver, and the visual system as a communication channel. The efficiency or "capacity" of this channel could be computed from the proportion of letters and words that the reader correctly identified under various conditions. The perspective and techniques were useful theoretically and enabled all kinds of interesting comparisons to be made, as I tried to indicate in the opening sections of the present Notes. They helped to demonstrate in a quantifiable way that the visual system has limitations—we cannot see everything that is in front of our eyes. The theory also offered some useful concepts, notably that of redundancy.

However, information theory itself has severe limitations, with respect to texts and to readers. It can measure "information" in its own narrow terms of reducing uncertainty among known sets of alternatives, but it can do nothing about "meaning." It cannot say how meaningful a text is, or how much understanding there might be. Outside the experimental laboratory, readers usually read for meaning rather than for information—or they get their information enveloped in meaning. And when readers do "receive information," it is usually not in the constricted sense of information theory. Statements like "More than a thousand kinds of brown algae exist" may be informative, but there is no way of saying how much uncertainty they reduce. Redundancy in spelling patterns can be calculated, but not redundancy in short stories. Information theory loses its utility once we get inside the head.

Besides, information does not seem to be what the brain is primarily concerned with (Smith, 1983a). The brain deals with understanding rather than information. Either information becomes understanding as part of our interlocked theory of the world, or it remains an isolated fact, at best potential meaning, like an item in an encyclopedia. Information can be derived from experience in the same way that vitamins can be obtained from food, but information is no more experience than vitamins are food. I now have some concern about the terms visual information and nonvisual information which I coined in the first edition of this book. The first term may be appropriate for tasks restricted to letter and word recognition, but once we get behind the eyeballs, in the "nonvisual" domain, then "knowledge" might be a better term than "information." I quietly introduced such a modification in Chapter 1 of the previous edition, although I obviously think the original distinction still has some expository usefulness.

The semantic problems are compounded by the fact that in contrast with the narrow sense in which the word information is employed in information theory, its general use these days is positively indiscriminate. Everything is information—the content of every book, journal, and television program, the entire educational curriculum, anything on a computer, even junk mail.

Rosenblatt (1978), in her distinction between reading for information and reading for experience, does not use the word information in either the narrow information theory sense or the catch-all general sense. To her, information means "facts." Perhaps because the terms information and experience have such broad general uses she actually employs quite uncommon terms for what she wants to explain. Informational reading she describes as *efferent*, meaning "carrying outward" from the text, and the alternative she terms *aesthetic*, implying involvement in the text through the senses.

In cognitive science and computer jargon, information is always "processed" rather than "understood." Almost everything now is a process in the educational research literature—and in disquisitions on teaching as well. It is rare to read of unadulterated reading, writing, comprehension, learning, or teaching, but always of the reading process, the writing process, the comprehension process, the learning process, and the teaching process. And according to my dictionary, the word *process* has broad mechanical connotations—it entails a succession of actions or operations in a specific or prescribed sequence (much like the manner in which a computer is programmed). Among cognitive scientists, reading and comprehension are now both "text processing." Writing is "word processing." Thinking is "ideas management" or "the organization of knowledge." Information processing is no longer something done by computers alone.

Perhaps to underline the growing influence of computer-based ways of thinking, the word information is being superseded by *data* (a plural word which, like *criteria* and *media*, is commonly used in the singular), and the word knowledge by *database*. Process may be losing ground to *procedures*, an artificial intelligence term, and even to *instructions*, which are what computers run on. Schemas and scenarios are seen as procedures rather than as narratives. "Procedural" knowledge is contrasted with "propositional" knowledge (Anderson, 1980). Larsen (1986) even argues that there is a need today for "procedural literacy," which is not the same thing as "computer literacy," but rather the ability to produce and understand sequences of instructions for the organization of knowledge.

Cognitive Science

I have referred several times already to cognitive scientists—the theorists and researchers who are concerned with knowledge systems in both humans and computers. Many cognitive scientists are cognitive psychologists or psycholinguists (who used to regard human thought as something unique). But now they share ideas and language with experts in advanced computer systems and artificial intelligence. They are concerned with "systems" that can organize information and make "rational" decisions. A prominent cognitive scientist, Roger Schank (1982), published a book entitled *Reading and Understanding: Teaching from the Perspective of Artificial Intelligence*. In the book he describes how he taught his daughter to read at the age of four and how he is teaching computers to read, by step-by-step procedures. (However, Schank reveals that he had been reading to his daughter on his lap since before she was a year old. He does not say how he shared this kind of experience with his computer, which was, perhaps, a laptop). The purpose of reading, Schank asserts, is to remember the information in the text, which the reader accomplishes by encoding "representations of meanings." Comprehension is important for Schank because it facilitates remembering. Two other cognitive scientists, Bransford and Stein (1984), base their "guide for improving thinking, learning, and creativity" on "insights from artificial intelligence."

A large number of studies of comprehension (or comprehension processes) from a cognitive science perspective are contained in an edited volume by Kieras and Just (1984). Olson, Duffy, and Mack (1984), for example, analyze what they term "real-time comprehension processes," in which they treat comprehension as a reader's ability to repeat what is said in the text (not what the reader might feel about the text). Reading adds to the reader's "knowledge base." Other chapters in the same volume describe computer simulations of reading, or rather of superficial characteristics of reading, such as the length of time eye fixations rest on particular words.

For more general discussions of cognitive science, see Anderson (1980), Simon (1980), and a special issue of the journal *Cognition*, edited and introduced by Norman (1993). Mandler (1985) examines cognitive science from a humanistic point of view, and Bruner (1990) fears that cognitive science has led to a "dehumanization" of cognitive psychology. The basic assumption underlying the cognitive science approach is perhaps most strongly expressed by Goldstein and Papert (1977), who declare that human beings and computers are involved in organizing and using knowledge in similar ways. They believe that artificial intelligence will "deeply transform the theory and practice of education, not just because of more intelligent machines, but by helping students understand their own thought." Boden (1989) proposes that the importance of artificial intelligence to education may be at the level of very general "powerful ideas" like the notion of "bugs" in a system. Lawler and Yazdani (1987) is an edited volume relating artificial intelligence to education, and Friedman, Klivington, and Peterson (1986) relate cognitive science and education with particular consideration to neuroscience. Spiro, Bruce, and Brewer (1980) consider the contribution of artificial intelligence to reading comprehension. More general studies of the rise of cognitive science include Gardner (1987), Baars (1986), Levin (1987), and Hirst (1988). Some notable artificial intelligence theorists believe that cognitive science is actually in a position to develop a unifying theory of mind (Newell, 1990), based on a "recursive computational information-processing brain" that achieves goals through the acquisition and use of knowledge. The unification will be achieved, Newell believes, not by critical experiments (the fundamental position is not to be challenged) but by the development of an enormous database on such topics as reaction times, learning tasks, and logical reasoning, collected by the use of computer software distributed by Newell's project to research groups dedicated to the enterprise. For a most readable and restrained overview of cognitive science issues discussed in this and the previous chapter (under "Modules and Networks"), see Blakemore and Greenfield (1987). The essence of the difference between computers and humans is of course consciousness, which most artificial intelligence theorists want to explain away as epiphenomenal if not totally illusory. Baars (1991), however, argues that consciousness is not a useless by-product of the brain but has eighteen important functions, all of which I would summarize as "making sense"—of surroundings, the self, thought, structures, analogies, and so forth. The book is technically dense in places and readable in others, making great demands on conscious functioning. For ethical dangers of the cognitive view, see McCabe (1986) in McCabe and Balzano (1986).

It can be argued that cognitive science has become an elaborate behavioristic stimulus-response system, despite the fact that it calls itself cognitive. Individuals are perceived as totally under the control of an environment, which is the source of data or information rather than of stimuli and contingencies of reinforcement. There are no intentions, feelings, or values except for what something outside the system has put into it. This is not my argument, but that of the foremost exponent of behaviorism, B. F. Skinner (1985), who claims that the only difference between cognitive science and his own theory is in the language that is used.

There are critics of cognitive science among cognitive psychologists. Neisser (1983) debates Sternberg's (1983) attempt to decompose mental states into parts, quoting J. R. R. Tolkien: "He that breaks a thing to find out what it is has left the path of wisdom." Neisser argues that the elements of Sternberg's analysis "are not separate elements in any genuine mental process; they are more like chapter headings in books on how to think." (There is a response by Sternberg in the journal in which Neisser's critique appears.) In an important article on the semantic nature of reading, Kolers and Roediger (1984) also contend that information-processing "models of mind"—full of little boxes, processes, and stages—"don't work." Information-processing models become more and more elaborate but have led to little cumulative knowledge about how information flows through supposed information systems. Kolers and Roediger recommend studying instead how the mind creates, transforms, and manipulates symbols, transferring them to new occasions. They take reading as a particular example—we remember the way we understand, and how we understand depends on what we look for. See also Beers (1987).

Computers

The discussion of cognitive science is inseparable from discussion of the relationship of computers and the brain, a complex, philosophical topic. Computers don't do anything unless told what to do and how to do it, so they are not like the human brain unless you believe that is what humans are like. Computers may do things that we can't do—like calculate thousands of prime numbers, or scrutinize complex landscapes, or generate elaborate designs—but nevertheless they are following procedures that humans give them (or which the computers develop as a consequence of earlier procedures that humans have given them). And there is no guarantee that the procedures computers follow are those used when humans make mathematical calculations, study a landscape, or paint a picture; they almost certainly are not. A computer does not have plans and intentions, except those it is given. It does not have wishes or feelings or values. These characteristics may be simulated on computers, but this does not give them human characteristics. Computers are born with nothing, not even needs. They do not have experiences. They do not understand sarcasm, or irony, or affection. They do not understand *anything*. Programming a computer is not the same thing as teaching it, and being programmed is certainly not the same thing as learning. Computers are said to have learned when they perform differently. Human beings do not necessarily behave differently as a consequence of learning and can change their behavior without learning anything.

Among many vehement arguments that computers cannot provide appropriate metaphors or models for human thought and behavior are a number by computer experts. Terry Winograd designed a renowned program (called SHRDLU) that enabled computers to make statements and answer questions about objects of different colors and shapes on a table-top. But computers don't really understand even that "carefully-constrained world," admits Winograd (1981). Their procedures are inadequate representations of reasoning. Dreyfus and Dreyfus (1986) maintain that computers can't be "intelligent" like humans because they can't replicate intuition. "Logical precision" is not enough. Computers can't even recognize patterns like human beings, say Dreyfus and Dreyfus—and they advise educators not to get involved with artificial intelligence. In a densely philosophical article entitled "Tom Swift and his procedural grandmother," Fodor (1978) sets out why computers cannot provide a theory of what it is to know the meaning of a word. Natural language cannot be reduced to computer language (or to anything else—once you say that "bachelor" means "unmarried man" there is not much more to be said). There is no way to reduce "meaning" further to "procedures" or "instructions." Boulding (1981) says that human knowledge is not like any other "system," whether in a library or a computer, because human knowledge is inseparable from the world in which we are located. See also Jones (1986) on the inability of computers to construct the social realities that determine human thought and Hausman (1985) on whether computers can create. On the other hand, Boden (1992) argues that any current inadequacy of artificial intelligence and computers to simulate aspects of human thought is due to weakness of psychological theories, not to intrinsic deficiencies of computers. Sticht, Chang, and Wood (1986) present a summary of cognitive science research in areas of reading and language (not coincidentally with a heavy emphasis on military implications, because much of the funding comes from such sources).

NOTES TO CHAPTER 4, BETWEEN EYE AND BRAIN, pp. 65–88.

Vision and Information

For a brief and interesting introduction to vision generally, see Barlow, Blakemore, and Weston-Smith (1990). Gilman and Newman (1992), Oatley (1978), and Hochberg (1978) all deal rather more technically with the constructive nature of perception. Bronowski (1978) points out picturesquely that there is no little man in the brain looking at pictures sent from the eyes (or listening to the sounds of speech transmitted from the ears). Rock (1983) insists that perception is intelligent, and based on operations similar to those which characterize thought. There are several psychology texts with a cognitive basis to their discussions of visual perception, notably Neisser (1967), Lindsay and Norman (1977), Calfee (1975), and Massaro (1975).

That there is a limit to how much print can be identified at any one time, varying according to the use a reader can make of redundancy, is not exactly a recent discovery. The illustration in this chapter of how much can be identified from a single glance at a row of random letters, random words, and meaningful sequences of words is derived directly from the researches of Cattell (1885, republished 1973) and of Erdmann and Dodge (1898). Descriptions of many similar experimental studies were included in a remarkably broad and insightful book by Huey (1908, republished in 1967) which remains the only classic in the psychology of reading. A good deal of recent research on perception in reading is basically replication of early studies with more sophisticated equipment; nothing has been demonstrated to controvert them. Yet the pioneer research was neglected by experimental psychologists for nearly half a century and is still widely unknown in education, partly because behaviorism inhibited psychologists from studying "mental phenomena" and partly because "systematic" or "operationalized" piecemeal approaches to reading instruction have concentrated on decoding and word attack—the "tunnel vision" extreme—at the expense of comprehension.

Baumann and Schneider (1979) found that a group of 24 graduate students could identify from a single 40 msec tachistoscopic exposure 3.7 random letters or 2.0 unrelated words (9.3 letters), which corresponds reasonably closely to Cattell's reported results, but a less dramatic increase to 2.4 words (11.5 letters) for words in context. However, a table showing the average results of their top, middle, and bottom eight subjects indicates that although there were only relatively slight differences among the three groups in the random letter and unrelated word conditions (my calculations show means of 5.6, 5.0, and 4.0 random letters for the top, middle, and bottom groups, respectively, with 13.7, 11.4, and 9.7 for letters in unrelated words), the top group showed a marked advantage in the words in context condition, an average of 18.2 letters (about 4 words), compared with 13.7 letters for the middle group and 11.3 letters for the bottom. Baumann and Schneider note that the better subjects in their study also made the most errors, especially in the word conditions, supporting the view that fluent reading involves risk taking, the willingness to make mistakes. Willingness to take a chance is of course a difficult variable to take into account in laboratory investigations of reading.

Other researchers using sophisticated equipment to open or narrow a "window" through which subjects can read have shown a "perceptual span" of between 21 and 31 characters (letters or spaces) in a single fixation, up to 15 on each side of the point of fixation (den Buurman, Roersema, & Gerrissen, 1981; McConkie & Rayner, 1975).

Krueger (1975) summarizes a number of studies showing that familiar letters, words, and other visual configurations are identified more rapidly and accurately than less familiar ones.

Rayner and Pollatsek (1987) demonstrated a perceptual span of up to about 18 letters under experimental conditions. The span was asymmetrical, with only 3–4 letters to the left of the fovea being reported by left-to-right readers, and imbalance in the opposite direction for readers of right-left orthographies, like Hebrew. The divergence begins to show in the earliest readers. The Rayner and Pollatsek report is a useful "tutorial" that summarizes massive amounts of eye-movement research.

Information Theory and Reading

The mathematics of information theory (Chapter 3 Notes) can be applied to show that readers identifying just four or five random letters, a couple of random words, or a meaningful sequence of four or five words are each time processing the same amount of visual information. The differences among the three conditions can be attributed to the varying amounts of nonvisual information that readers are able to contribute, derived from distributional and sequential redundancy within the print.

The random letter condition suggests that the limit for a single glance (the equivalent of a second of processing time) is about 25 bits of information. The calculation is based on a maximum of five letter identifications of about five bits of uncertainty each (5 bits = 32 alternatives). In random sequences of letters, of course, there is no distributional or sequential redundancy that a reader can utilize. That 25 bits per second is indeed a general limit on the rate of human information processing has been argued by Quastler (1956) from studies not only of letter and word identification but of the performance of piano players and "lightning calculators" as well (see also Pierce & Karlin, 1957).

How is it possible then to identify two random words, consisting on the average of 4.5 letters each, with just 25 bits of visual information? Nine or ten letters at five bits each would seem to require closer to 50 bits. But as I pointed out in the Chapter 3 Notes, because of distributional and sequential redundancy the average uncertainty of letters in English *words* is about 2.5 bits each (Shannon, 1951) making a total average uncertainty for letters in two random words of something under 25 bits. From a different perspective, random words taken from a pool of 50,000 alternatives would have an uncertainty of between 15 and 16 bits each ($2^{15} = 32,768$, $2^{16} = 65,536$), but due to distributional redundancy among words—and probably also because unusual words are unlikely to be employed in reading studies—we can probably again accept the estimate of Shannon that the average uncertainty of English words without syntactic or semantic constraints (sequential redundancy) is about 12 bits per word. So whether we look at the random word condition from the point of view of letter uncertainty in words (about 2.5 bits per letter) or of isolated word uncertainty (about 12 bits per word) the result is still that the reader is making the identification of about 9 or 10 letters or two words with roughly 25 bits of visual information. The fact that both the number of letters identified and the effective angle of vision double in the random word condition compared with the four or five letters that can be perceived in the random letter condition reflects the use that the reader can make of redundancy. In other words, the viewer in the isolated word condition contributes the equivalent of 25 bits of nonvisual information to enable twice as much to be seen in a single glance. Anyone who did not have the relevant nonvisual information would have had to rely on visual information alone and therefore have seen only half as much.

In meaningful and grammatical passages of English, there is considerable sequential redundancy among the words themselves. Speakers and authors are not free to choose any word they like whenever they please, at least not if they expect to make any sense. From statistical analyses of long passages of text and also by a "guessing game" technique in which people were actually required to guess letters and words, Shannon calculated that the average uncertainty of *words* in meaningful sequences was about seven bits (a reduction over isolated words of about a half) and that the average uncertainty of *letters* in meaningful sequences was only slightly over one bit (again reducing by half the uncertainty of letters in isolated words). On this basis, one would expect viewers in the meaningful word sequences condition to see twice as much again compared with isolated words, which is of course the experimental result. A phrase or sentence of four or five words can be seen in one glance, a total of 20 letters or more. This is four times as much as can be seen in the random letter condition, but still on the basis of the same amount of visual information: four or five random letters at about five bits each, or 20 letters in a meaningful sequence at just over one bit each. Put in another way, when reading sequences of meaningful words in text the reader can contribute at least three parts nonvisual information (in the form of prior knowledge of redundancy) to one part visual information so that four times as much can be perceived.

For a more detailed discussion of the preceding argument, see Smith and Holmes (1971). Other examinations of uncertainty and redundancy in English are included in Garner (1962, 1974) and in Miller, Bruner, and Postman (1954), the latter using carefully constructed "approximations to English." McNeill and Lindig (1973) demonstrate that what listeners perceive in spoken language also depends on how much they are looking for—individual sounds, syllables, or entire words.

The Rate of Visual Decision Making

A century after the demonstrations of a limit to how much can be seen in a single glance, other tachistoscopic studies showed that the limit cannot be attributed to any restriction on the amount of visual information that the eye can gather from the page, nor to viewers' forgetting letters or words that have already been identified before they can report them. Rather the bottleneck occurs as the brain labors to process what is transiently a considerable amount of raw visual information, organizing "seeing" after the eyes have done their work. Perceptual decision making takes time, and there is a limit to how long visual information sent back by the eyes remains available to the brain.

Subjects in the kind of tachistoscopic experiment that I have described often feel that they have potentially seen more than they are able to report. The brief presentation of visual information leaves a vaguely defined "image" that fades before subjects are fully able to attend to it. The validity of this observation was established by an experimental technique called *partial recall* (Sperling, 1960) in which subjects are required to report only four letters out of a presentation of perhaps 12 so that the required report is well within the limits of short-term memory (see Chapter 5). However, the subjects do not know *which* four letters they must report until after the visual presentation, so they must work from visual information that remains available to the brain after its source has been removed from before the eyes. At one stroke the experimental technique avoids any complication of memory by keeping the required report to a small number of items, while at the same time testing whether in fact viewers have information about all 12 items for a brief time after the eyes' work is complete.

The experimental technique involves presenting the 12 letters in three rows of four letters each. Very soon after the 50-msec presentation is ended, a tone is sounded. The subject already knows that a high tone indicates that the letters in the top row are to be reported, a low tone calls for the report of the bottom row, and an intermediate tone indicates the middle line. When this method of partial recall is employed, subjects can normally report back the four required letters, indicating that for a short while at least they have access to raw visual information about all 12 letters. The fact that subjects can report any four letters, however, does not indicate that they have identified all 12, but simply that they have time to identify four before the visual information fades. If the cue tone is delayed more than half a second after the end of the presentation the number of letters that can be reported falls off sharply. The "image" is unprocessed visual information that decays by the time about four letters have been identified.

Other evidence that visual information remains available in a sensory store for about a second and that the entire second is required if a maximum of four or five letters is to be identified has come from the masking studies described in this chapter (e.g., Averbach & Coriell, 1961; Smith & Carey, 1966). If a second visual array is presented to the eye before the brain has finished identifying the maximum number of letters that it can from the first input of visual information, then the amount reported from the first presentation declines. The second input of visual information erases information from the first presentation.

However, it can be as disruptive for reading if visual information reaches the eye too slowly as it is if too fast. Kolers and Katzman (1966), Newman (1966), and Pierce and Karlin (1957) have shown an optimum rate of about six presentations a second for receiving visual information about individual letters or words; at faster rates the brain cannot keep up and at slower speeds there tends to be a greater loss of earlier items through forgetting. These studies and the earlier calculations of Quastler (1956) all tend to support the view that the "normal reading rate" of between 200 and 300 words a minute (Tinker, 1965; S. Taylor, 1971) is an optimum; slower reading is more than inefficient, it is almost certainly disruptive to comprehension.

There is another historic strand of evidence leading to the same conclusion that perception is a judgmental process that takes time, with the amount of time required depending on the number of alternatives among which the brain must choose. I refer to the studies of *reaction times*, or of the *latency,* between the presentation of visual information to a subject and the identification response. Latency always increases with the number of alternatives within a category. For example, it took subjects an average of 410 msec to name a letter of the alphabet (out of 26 alternatives) but only 180 msec to say whether a light was flashed (a simple yes-no choice). Interestingly, short words could be identified faster (388 msec) than single letters—and no one has ever satisfactorily explained why this should be the case. I have taken these figures from a long and interesting section on vision and eye movements in Woodworth and Schlosberg's compendious *Experimental Psychology* (1954); even more basic detail about early studies of reading is included in the original Woodworth (1938) edition.

Eye Movements in Reading

Classic studies of the nature of eye movements and rate of fixation changes in reading are reported in Tinker (1951, 1958). Taylor, Frackenpohl, and Pettee (1960) report the stabilization of fixation rates by Grade 4. Llewellyn-Thomas (1962) discusses the eye movements of speed readers, who sample visual information over such a broad area that they break free of the constraint of moving their fixations along lines of type and rather move down and even up the center of pages (without, however, increasing their rate of fixations). More recent studies of eye movements in reading, involving sophisticated equipment and theorizing, are provided by Hochberg (1978), Rayner (1977, 1978), Just and Carpenter (1980), and Spragins, Lefton, and Fisher (1976). Hochberg has been influential in demonstrating that reading is a highly selective process as the brain determines in advance the best place for each fixation to fall. More generally and very technically, Treisman (1969) has argued that perception is most efficient when the viewer is in control of what the eyes will look for. Garner (1966) has also summarized a number of experiments demonstrating the selective nature of perception.

Under the laboratory conditions of most experimental studies of "reading," subjects do not have control of where they fixate their gaze or of how long fixations may last. The experimenter makes these decisions for them. In many tachistoscopic and eye-movement studies, subjects are not even free to move their heads, which are constrained by chin rests or even bite plates. Yet head movements are a conspicuous part of normal reading. To avoid head movement constraints, some reading researchers have gone to another extreme by providing helmets equipped with electronic technology for their subjects to wear while looking at a computer screen.

Many of the computer-based experiments involve bizarre reading conditions, such as words which may change during a saccade or the presence of irrelevant words or lines of x's just outside the foveal area (Rayner & Pollatsek, 1987). Important areas of the text may be removed, for example, when the letter in the center of the reader's field of vision is automatically obscured on every fixation (Rayner, 1992). The consequence that reading speed may be slowed by fifty per cent in such circumstances is cited as demonstrating that readers *need* the information in the obliterated letter, though it could be argued that it is the distraction itself that causes the disruption. For other representative eye-movement studies see Rayner and Pollatsek (1989) and Stanovich (1991).

Kimchi (1992) cites recent eye-movement studies in a critical review of efforts to determine whether wholes are perceived before parts—faces before eyes and noses, similarities rather than characteristics, and whole words rather than letters. She describes many experimental demonstrations of a "global advantage" in ambiguous situations (when for example subjects view letters constructed from smaller letters, like a large H made up of smaller Ss). Global advantage is often lost when subjects are forced to look centrally. The article summarizes difficulties encountered in experimental attempts to resolve this "enduring issue in psychology."

It might be asked why the most general and most efficient fixation rate in reading seems to be about four fixations a second when the information from a single glance persists for a second or more and at least one second is required for analyzing all the information that can be acquired from a single fixation. Why do readers appear to fixate on every word—or at least every content word (Just & Carpenter, 1980; Rayner & Pollatsek, 1987)—when they can see four or five words at a glance? There has not been a good research answer to this question, but my conjecture is that the brain is less concerned with squeezing the last bit of information from each fixation than with receiving a smooth inflow of selected visual information as it builds up a coherent understanding of the text. Successive words provide useful anchorages for the eyes as the brain does its work. Obviously, readers must already have a good idea of where to fixate if their gaze rests primarily on content words. Potter (1984) shows that limitations on the speed of eye movements may be a factor in slowing-down reading. There is a little more on eye movements and comprehension in the Notes to Chapter 9.

On Seeing Backward

Moyer and Newcomer (1977) argue and demonstrate that reversals are caused by inexperience with directionality rather than by perceptual deficits. Stanovich (1982a, 1982b) notes that normal readers may also make orientation errors ("reading or writing backward"), which are not a cause of reading difficulties.

Hemispheric Specialization

A basic article about functional differences in the cerebral hemispheres and about the occasionally bizarre consequences of their being superficially disconnected is provided by one of the earliest researchers in the area, Sperry (1968). See also Gazzaniga (1970). More recent discussions of the relationship between the hemispheres and language are included in several chapters in Caplan (1980). A readable presentation of the nature of hemispheric asymmetry, followed by some remarkable speculations about the origins of consciousness itself, can be found in Jaynes (1976, 1986). Careful research reviews leading to the conclusion that hemispheric specialization should not be considered an explanation of reading difficulties in children are reported in Naylor (1980), Young and Ellis (1981), and in the chapter by Bryden in Underwood (1978).

NOTES TO CHAPTER 5, BOTTLENECKS OF MEMORY, pp. 89–103.

Theories of Memory

One of the earliest and most coherent attempts to distinguish short-term and long-term characteristics of memory was by Norman (1969), revised and expanded into a comprehensive analysis of the processes and contents of memory (Norman, 1976). The underlying perspective also pervades the Lindsay and Norman (1977) introductory psychology text. There are useful reviews by Kintsch (1982), Baddeley (1992) and Schneider and Shiffrin (1977), who particularly emphasize the relationship between short-term memory and attention. There are of course alternative points of view. Craik and Lockhart (1972; see also Cermak & Craik, 1979) proposed an influential *levels of processing* model, arguing that the different short-term and long-term "stages" of memory are reflections of different "levels" or "depths" to which processing is done. From their point of view, additional processing is required to identify words rather than letters, or meanings rather than words. On the other hand, it is not clear that word identification *is* a deeper level of perception or memory, or that it involves more processing, than letter identification; short-term and long-term memory effects can be found with both letters and words. The argument is not really about the evidence, but about the way it is most usefully interpreted.

Lewis (1979) has also critically reviewed the short-term and long-term memory distinction, proposing that most forgetting is retrieval failure rather than storage loss and suggesting instead an active and inactive memory distinction with active memory part of the greater inactive one (similar to my Figure 5.2). A rather different view, that memory is founded on *descriptions* of varying degrees of precision and complexity, is proposed by Norman and Bobrow (1979). Vallar and Shallice (1990) examine evidence from brain-injured patients that short-term memory should not be regarded as a gateway to long-term memory, which may remain intact and fully functioning despite short-term effects.

Tulving (1985a, 1985b) proposes that there are *three* different memory systems, which he terms *episodic, semantic*, and *procedural*. He associates each with a different kind of consciousness (or absence of consciousness). Tulving's basic memory system is *procedural*; it is also the most primitive, the only one that animals have. It is also the only one of the three systems that can be completely independent of the other two. Procedural memories require overt action to become established and are not accessible to consciousness. Tulving calls this condition *anoetic* (literally, "without knowledge"). We can never be aware of what we know procedurally (except by actually doing something, possibly in the imagination). Such a memory system may be fundamental, but it is not trivial. It is probably the aspect of our memory containing the "rules" of language, which are not learned consciously (Krashen, 1985). Tulving's *semantic* memory is a subset within the procedural, and it makes possible representations of states of the world not perceptually present (i.e., which we can imagine). Semantic memory includes facts—but not in any particular order. Most people, for example, know that both John F. Kennedy and Charles de Gaulle are dead, but they cannot immediately say who died first. Semantic memory "describes" events and situations for us—it brings them to consciousness. Tulving calls this *noetic*. Finally *episodic* memory, which is nested within the semantic system, is "self-knowing," or *autonoetic*. It is our awareness of the order or sequence of events, the only conscious form of memory that includes temporal relationships. Earlier papers by Tulving and his colleagues citing research that distinguishes episodic and semantic memory include Tulving and Thomson (1973) and Tulving and Watkins (1975). See also Friendly (1977).

Tulving stresses something that few cognitive psychologists would dispute these days, that the quality of a particular memory depends on the manner and circumstances in which it was originally learned. Kolers (1975) frequently argued for a "procedural" memory, also studied experimentally by Masson and Sala (1978). See also Minsky (1980) and Anderson (1980).

A great deal of laboratory research is being done into the nature of the actual brain processes underlying memory, but much more will be needed before there is complete understanding, or indeed, an idea of what such an understanding might be like. It is clear that certain biochemical changes take place during learning, when memories are established, and that chemical interventions can apparently destroy memories, and in some circumstances possibly enhance them. But these studies fall far short of explaining how an entire statement like "July 4 is Independence Day" might be represented in the chemical composition of the brain, let alone how its meaning and comprehension might. It is not even clear how such questions should be put. For a recent comprehensive review of research into mechanisms of memory in the brain, including arguments for the possible locations of short-term and long-term memory, and procedural and propositional knowledge, see Squire (1986). From a practical educational point of view, it is difficult to see how a more refined (but still very gross) understanding of the neurological structures and chemical events underlying reading could indicate how it should be taught.

Another distinction frequently drawn is between *recognition* and *reproduction* memory. It is usually (but not always) easier to recognize a face or a place (or an object or symbol) than it is to draw it. We recognize correct spellings easier than we can produce them. At any age we can understand more of language than we can produce ourselves. This should not be taken as implying that we have two entirely different kinds of memory—that we go to one "store" for recognition and another for reproduction. It is not that we have a collection of pictures (or "images") in the brain that we can refer to for recognition. Mental images themselves have to be constructed, and we can usually recognize faces and other things easier than we can imagine them. There is probably a simple explanation—that we usually need to produce less detail for recognition than for reproduction. To recognize a face, or even a word, we may need to see only a part of it, but reproduction means that we have to generate it all, without omission or error. For factual matters, a similar distinction is frequently made between *recognition* and *recall* memory. We may be able to agree that a certain actor starred in a particular movie, yet be quite unable to think of the actor's name if asked who the star of the movie was. Once again, it is probably more complex cognitively to construct or to complete what we think is a true statement than simply to recognize the statement as true when it is produced by someone else (see Anderson, 1980). In an article entitled "Good Morning, Mr. . . . er," Burton (1992) examines how it might be that we can recognize a face without being able to recall anything else about a person and that we may remember almost everything else about someone—their occupation, nationality, where they live—but still not get their name. (Burton uses the phenomenon to support the kind of neural network theory discussed in Chapter 2; there are many frequently activated connections for categories like "actor" or "politician," but names are unique.)

The nature and role of imagery in memory is much debated. Pylyshyn (1973, 1979) vigorously rejects any suggestion that images can be stored like pictures in the brain, for inspection by "the mind's eye." Kosslyn (1980) proposes that mental images can be represented in two ways. The first possibility is indeed a form that can be viewed mentally, but this is simply transient imagination. Such images do not persist. Instead they must be constructed on the basis of the second possibility, consisting of "deeper" representations that are not pictures but more like descriptions (or specifications) from which mental images can be constructed. All this is part of a more general notion that the brain must have its own language in order to make sense of every aspect of the world. The meaning of a sentence cannot be a paraphrase of that sentence, because we would then need to explain the meaning of the paraphrase. Similarly, the meaning of a picture cannot be another picture. There must be something, inaccessible to us intellectually, which enables us to understand anything—or to feel that we understand it. The notion that the brain has its own language is argued from a linguistic point of view by Fodor (1979) and neurophysiologically by Pribram (1971).

The idea that memory is constructive, or reconstructive, rather than a simple recall of original information, also has a long history in psychology, with its own classic by Bartlett (1932). Other arguments that present perspectives influence recall of past events are offered by Cofer (1973) and J. Mandler and Johnson (1977). See Smith (1990) for an extended discussion of the role of imagination in learning, comprehension, and thinking as well as memory, and Morris (1988) for descriptions of our remarkable memory capacity for things we are interested in, like sport scores. Reber (1989) shows there are massive amounts of implicit learning, without awareness, and Bahrick and Hall (1991) demonstrate that the longer the period something is studied or experienced, the longer it is remembered. We remember names of people we know for a few years better than names we have known for a few weeks. People who do math in college can remember for half a century what they would soon forget from high school. Foreign language vocabulary fades within 3 years of one college semester, but over 60 per cent is retained 25 years later with 5 college semesters of study.

Klatzky (1980) provides a relatively nontechnical introduction to the highly technical area of memory, and there is a good summary in Calfee (1974), embedded in a discussion of reading somewhat different from the approach taken in this book. For the organization or contents of memory see an early paper by G. Mandler (1967), as well as G. Mandler (1985). For the structure or contents of memory, there are useful reviews as well as some idiosyncratic points of view in Puff (1977), Anderson and Bower (1973), and Crowder (1976). By contrast there is a very easy to comprehend paper by Jenkins (1974) relating his conversion from a traditional *associationistic* view of memory to a more meaningful cognitive approach, entitled, "Remember that Old Theory of Memory? Well, Forget It!" For a general discussion of children's memory, see Kail (1979). Because memory—at least the long-term aspect of it—and our theory of the world are alternative descriptions of the same thing, many of the general references in the Notes to Chapter 1, on knowledge and comprehension, could also be consulted.

Chunking

The two apparent bottlenecks of memory—the limited capacity of short-term memory and the slow entry into long-term memory—can both be circumvented by the strategy known as *chunking*, or organization of information into the most compact (most meaningful) unit. For example, it is easier to retain and recall the sequence of digits 1491625364964 as the first eight square numbers, or the letters JFMAMJJASOND as the initials of the months of the year, than to try to remember either sequence as a dozen or so unrelated elements. But it is a mistake to think that we normally perceive first and chunk afterward; we no more read the letters *h, o, r, s,* and *e* which we then chunk into the word *horse* than we perceive a particular nose, ears, eyes, and mouth which we then chunk into a friend's face. Chunking research and instruction both tend to get things backward, starting with arrays of ostensibly unrelated elements which the individual is supposed to group together in some meaningful way. In practice, prior knowledge and expectation of the larger grouping leads to the perception of elements in a chunked manner—if we recognize a word we do not see the individual letters. The size or character of a chunk is determined by what we are looking for in the first place (the "levels of processing" issue again). The word "chunk" became something of a minor fad term in education, with some teachers asking, "How can we teach children to chunk?" or even, "What do I do about a child who can't chunk?" But chunking is not something you learn to do, rather it is a simple consequence of what you already know; if you can recognize *horse* as a word there is no chunking problem in the first place. Chunking also has its own classic paper in the psychological literature, written with the flair suggested by its title, "The Magical Number Seven, Plus or Minus Two" (Miller, 1956). Another readable and informative paper on the same topic is by Simon (1974).

A remarkable report of how a college student increased his short-term memory span from 7 to 79 digits with 230 hours of chunking practice over 20 months is contained in Ericsson, Chase, and Falcon (1980).

Imagery

One important and common means of chunking is to employ imagery to remember; there is a substantial literature demonstrating the unsurprising fact that our recall of particularly graphic sentences that we have heard or read is more likely to be related to scenes that we imagine from descriptions provided by the words than to the words themselves (Barclay, 1973; Bransford & Franks, 1971; Bransford, Barclay, & Franks, 1972; Sachs, 1974). These papers are relevant to larger arguments that meaning lies beyond words in any case; whenever possible everyone, including children, tends to remember the meaning of words rather than the words themselves. But while we remember some sequences of words in terms of the pictures they conjure up, we also often remember scenes or pictures in terms of their descriptions. We recall a scene of birds flying over a town but not whether they were seagulls or pigeons, nor how many there were. There is nothing remarkable about any of this: We naturally try to remember in the most efficient manner possible. If a scene is easiest to remember, or most efficiently remembered, in terms of a description, because perhaps we are interested in particular things rather than in the scene as a whole, then the memorization will proceed accordingly. Not only is our recall influenced by the way we learned or perceived in the first place, but the manner of memorization will tend to reflect the most probable way in which we shall want to recall or use the information in the future. For useful discussions of the role of imagery in memory, see Paivio (1971), Tierney and Cunningham (1984), and Kintsch (1982). For a technical analysis of the relationship of words to images, see Reid (1974).

Sadoski, Goetz, and Kansinger (1988) report that readers spontaneously generate images as they read. Long, Winograd, and Bridge (1989) agree, especially when the text is interesting and facilitates image creation, which improves comprehension, memory, thinking—and enjoyment. Wilson, Rinck, McNamara, Bower, and Morrow (1993) add that readers will—when the text permits it and especially if a task requires it—construct mental models (like the floor plans of buildings) as they read about them. Jampole, Konopak, Readence, and Moser (1991) found that practice in focusing on visual, auditory, and olfactory descriptions in text enhances creative writing.

Children's Memory

There is no evidence that children have poorer or less well-developed memories than adults. Simon (1974) argues that children have the same memory capacity as adults but do not chunk as efficiently; however there is probably an adult bias behind the notion of chunking "efficiently" in the first place. We tend to chunk—or to perceive and remember in rich meaningful units—that which is most rich and meaningful to us. Recall of strings of unrelated letters and digits, which is the test by which children are usually judged to have inferior memories to those of adults, is not the most meaningful of tasks, for children especially. The number of digits a child can repeat after a single hearing increases from an average of two at the age of 2½ to six at the age of 10 (and eight for college students). But rather than suppose that children's memory capacity grows with their height and weight, one can argue that the younger children have had little experience, and see little sense, in repeating sequences of numbers, especially before they have become accustomed to using the telephone. The memory span of adults can be magically increased by teaching them little tricks or strategies, for example, to remember strings of numbers not as single digits (2, 9, 4, 3, 7, 8 . . .) but as two-digit pairs (29, 43, 78 . . .). Practice improves performance on any memory task but does not seem to improve memory beyond the particular skill into unrelated areas or activities. The best aid to memory for anyone of any age is a general understanding of the structure and purpose behind the required memorization. Skilled chess players can recall the layout of most or all of the pieces on a board after just a couple of glances while beginners can remember the positions of only a few pieces—but only if the pieces are arranged as part of an actual game. If the pieces are organized randomly then the skilled player can remember no more than the beginner, because then the skilled player's experience of hundreds of games and positions is of no relevance or utility.

Baer and Wright (1975) argue that children's memory is not inferior to adults' but that they *encode* (or organize memory) differently. Huttenlocher and Burke (1976) refer to the additional difficulty (lesser experience) of children in identifying items and especially information about order in memory tasks. Paris and Carter (1973) report that children use imagery in remembering sentences just like adults (see also G. Olson, 1973). Hudson (1986) demonstrates that "events" comprise the core of children's memory.

Easy and Difficult Remembering

As noted in the chapter, the fluent "easy" remembering that we do so efficiently most of the time has been largely neglected by experimental psychology. It is in fact due to such neglect that memory, comprehension, and learning have come to be widely regarded as difficult things to do, requiring instruction, practice, and effort. The problem is that the aspects of memory, comprehension, learning, and thinking generally that experimental psychologists have tended to study *have been* difficult, because the exigencies of experimental design demand control of all variables. The most difficult variables to control are those related to individual differences, especially in interest and prior knowledge. Not surprisingly, the more interest and knowledge we have of something, the easier it is to learn, understand, remember, and think about it. The experimental solution to such unpredictability has usually been to construct tasks that remove all possibility of interest and prior knowledge, usually achieved by the employment of nonsense materials in artificial situations. When different individuals are required to commit nonsensical matters to memory, or to recall them, they usually do badly in very predictable ways (which have become the basis of psychology's "Laws of Learning"). Unfortunately, educators looking for theories on which to base instructional techniques have tended to turn to psychology for what are essentially theories of difficult and artificial learning, comprehension, and remembering. The story is spelled out in a chapter entitled "How Education Backed the Wrong Horse" in Smith (1988).

NOTES TO CHAPTER 6, LETTER IDENTIFICATION, pp. 105–118.

Recognition versus Identification

G. Mandler (1980) makes a similar distinction to that made in this chapter between *identification* (putting a name to something) and *recognition* (deciding that something is familiar). He proposes a general theory of word recognition relevant to Chapter 9 of this book. Benton (1980) discusses the remarkable human ability to recognize patterns (in this case, faces) years after perhaps only a single partial glimpse.

Theories of Pattern Recognition

Problems and theories of pattern recognition are discussed in Lindsay and Norman (1977), Marr (1982), and Spoehr and Lehmkuhle (1982). Pinker (1984) is a basic but technical examination of contemporary theories of visual perception, including template, feature, and other more complex models and also a discussion of the nature and role of imagery. Pinker points out that there are problems with all theories—a horse, for example, would seem to consist of too many lines and curves to be easily recognized by "features" alone, yet it is inadequate to say that a horse must therefore be recognized by body parts like hooves, because the parts themselves would have to be recognized by features. The current alternative is to rely on "massively parallel" models, which search concurrently for numbers of features and for interrelationships among them. On the other hand, perhaps to show that pattern recognition should not be complicated and mystified out of proportion, Blough (1982) has shown that pigeons can easily be taught to distinguish the letters of the alphabet. When shown a particular letter on one side of a screen, they had to distinguish it from two incorrect alternatives elsewhere on the screen by pecking at the correct alternative. The pigeons, which were hungry, were rewarded with 3 seconds of eating mixed grain for every 4 successive correct answers they gave in 2700 test-trials over four days. When they made mistakes, the birds demonstrated the same confusions as humans, for example, C–G–S, M–N–W, and D–O–Q.

It is not suggested that we have visual analyzers that function solely to collect information about letters of the alphabet. Information used in letter identification is received from analyzers involved in many visual activities, of which those concerned with reading are only a small part. The same analyzers might contribute information in other circumstances to the identification of words, digits, geometric forms, faces, automobiles, or any other set of visual categories, as well as to the apprehension of meaning. The brain makes a variety of specialized uses of very general receptor systems; thus statements can be made about analyzers "looking for" alphabetic features without the implication that a benign destiny has "prewired" mankind to read the alphabet. We all have a "biological inheritance" that enables us to talk and read, to ride bicycles and play pianos, not because of some specific genetic design, but because spoken and written languages, bicycles and pianos, were progressively developed by and for human beings with precisely the biological equipment that humans are born with. For an attempt to specify possible features of English letters, see Gibson (1965).

Incidentally, it is just as appropriate to talk about distinctive features of speech as it is to refer to distinctive features of written language. In fact, the feature model for letter identification that was developed in the 1960s was inspired by a feature theory of speech perception published in the 1950s (Jakobson & Halle, 1956). In both theories a physical representation, acoustic or visual, is scanned for distinctive features which are analyzed in terms of feature lists that determine a particular categorization and perceptual experience. The number of physical features requiring to be discriminated will depend on the perceiver's uncertainty and other sources of information about the language (redundancy) that can be utilized.

Just as the basic elements of the written or printed marks on a page are regarded as distinctive features smaller than letters, so elements smaller than a single sound are conceptualized as distinctive features of speech. Distinctive features of sounds are usually regarded as components of the process by which a phoneme is articulated, such as whether or not a sound is *voiced* (whether the vocal chords vibrate as for /b/, /d/, /g/ compared with /p/, /t/, /k/), whether the sound is *nasal* (like /m/ and /n/), the sound's duration, and the position of the tongue. Each distinctive feature is a significant difference, and the discrimination of any one feature may eliminate many alternatives in the total number of possible sounds (the set of phonemes). Every feature cuts the set of alternatives in a different way, so that theoretically a total of only six distinctive features could be more than enough to distinguish among 40 alternative phonemes ($2^6 = 64$). There are many analogies between the distinctive features of print and those of speech. The total number of different features is presumed to be much smaller than the set of units that they differentiate (26 for letters, about 40 for sounds). The number of features suggested for phonemes is usually 12 or 13 (note again the redundancy). Phonemes can be confused in the same manner as letters, and the more likely two sounds are to be confused with each other, the more distinctive features they are assumed to share. Some sounds, such as /b/ and /d/, which probably differ in only one feature, are more likely to be confused than /b/ and /t/, which differ in perhaps two, and /t/ and /v/ which may differ in three features. Spoken words may also differ by only a single feature. *Ban* and *Dan*, which have only a single feature's difference, should be rather more likely to be confused than *ban* and *tan*, and much more likely than *tan* and *van*; experimental evidence suggests that assumptions of this kind are correct (Miller & Nicely, 1955).

The perception of speech is no less complex and time consuming than that of reading; what we hear is the end product of a decision-making procedure that leads to the identification (the categorization) of a sound or word or meaning prior to the perceptual experience. We rarely "hear" words and then identify them; the identification must precede the hearing, otherwise we would just hear noise. And we do not hear distinctive features of sound any more than we see distinctive features of written language; the unit that we are aware of discriminating is determined by the sense that the brain is able to make, the kind of question that it is asking. Usually we are aware only of meaning for both spoken and written language. Occasionally we may attend to particular words, but only rarely and in special circumstances will we be aware of the surface structure phonemes or letters. The features themselves evade our attention completely.

The "connectionist" theories of perception and understanding that I discussed in the Notes to Chapter 2 are essentially associative feature-analytic systems that "learn" on a probabilistic basis (without a hypothesis-testing component). Such systems are claimed to be capable of determining for themselves relevant distinctive features of such configurations as letters of the alphabet. By trial and error over enormous numbers of "epochs" (hundreds of thousands in many computer simulations), the connectionist networks mindlessly distinguish and evaluate the significant differences they should pay particular attention to (or rather, "weight")

Making Letter Identification Easier

Letter identification as I have described it in this chapter is not the easiest task for any reader. Asking someone to identify a random letter is the most difficult letter-identification task possible because there is no redundancy; the particular letter to be identified could be any one of the 26 alternatives in the alphabet, so the viewer requires a maximum of visual information and has no check if an identification is incorrectly made. Letters are much easier to identify when they come from a smaller set of alternatives or when they are not equally probable; in other words, when the viewer can make use of redundancy. And not only is it harder for viewers to identify letters without redundancy cues, it is far less familiar as an activity because the redundancy with which language is permeated is something which every language user capitalizes upon.

NOTES TO CHAPTER 7, WORD IDENTIFICATION, pp. 119–131.

For general discussions of word recognition research, see the three "cognitive psychology" texts I have already mentioned, Anderson (1980), Kieras and Just (1984), or Eysenck (1984). Goodman (1982) has some general criticism of researchers who focus on words (or letters) in their analyses of reading. See also Kimchi (1992).

In a long and technical summary of template and feature analytic theories of shape recognition, Hummel and Biederman (1992) stress the need for "structural descriptions" that include relationships among parts rather than just point by point comparisons. The authors say that enormous numbers of units and connections are required to "bind" all the parts of any figure together into possible wholes so that it can be recognized from different angles. Their connectionist solution for computer recognition of a simple figure (a cone on a rectangular block) involves a seven-layered network of mosaics of activating or inhibiting cells, the sensitivity of each varying according to experience. Biederman's research into the feature analysis of letters and words is imaginative and influential; for further technical detail see Biederman (1987). In another general examination of form recognition, Pomerantz (1983) notes that it is not understood why there is sometimes a "global preference" for what will be perceived (such as words) and sometimes a local preference (such as letters)—the difference is obviously determined by the intentions of the perceiver, not the nature of the object perceived. See also Schwab and Nussbaum (1986). Abu-Mostafa and Psaltis (1987) conclude that the only way to program a computer to be able to say that an image is a tree (as opposed to a telegraph pole) would be to program it with descriptions of all the different kinds of tree it is likely to encounter, as well as with descriptions of telegraph poles, flagstaffs, and street lights that it should not confuse trees with. Children are much better at this than computers, the authors observe.

In a useful "tutorial review," Henderson (1987) outlines the complexities and ambiguities of word recognition research, acknowledging that "surprisingly few new facts" are available to contemporary researchers than were available to Huey in 1908. Corcos and Willows (1993) summarize research showing that orthographic information (relationships among letters—or letter features—in words) facilitates word recognition and is used by readers instead of individual letter identification. Rayner and Pollatsek (1987) report that words that are predictable from prior context are recognizable after shorter fixation times.

Letter Identification in Words

There is one type of experiment which might at first sight appear to indicate that words are *not* identified more easily than letters, but which actually provides an additional demonstration that words are indeed processed on a featural basis with the reader making use of sequential redundancy. One experimental method (Smith, 1969) involves projecting letters or words at such a low intensity that there is barely any contrast with the screen on which they are shown, and then to increase the contrast slowly, gradually making more and more visual information available until observers are able to identify the word. Under this procedure the observers are not constrained by time or memory limitations and may choose to make either word or letter identifications with the information available at any moment. They typically identify letters within words before they say what an entire word is, although the entire word may still be identified before any of its letters could be identified in isolation. Although this finding is not inconsistent with the classical evidence that words can be identified before any of their component letters in isolation, it does make clear that words are, in fact, not recognized all-or-none "as wholes" but by analysis of their parts. The sequential redundancy among features that exists within the word configuration permits identification of the letters on fewer features than would be required if they were presented in isolation. Put in another way, criterial sets of features for words need not include sufficient information in any one position for the unique identification of an individual letter if all sequential redundancy were removed, but when sequential redundancy is present, it may facilitate the identification of one or more letters even before the word as a whole can be identified. The letter *h* requires fewer features to identify if presented in the sequence *hat* than if presented alone, even if the reader identifies the *h* before the *at*. The additional information that enables the earlier letter identification to be made in words is based on orthographic redundancy in the spelling of words, reducing the uncertainty of letters from over four bits (26 alternatives) to less than three (about seven alternatives), as discussed in the Notes to Chapter 3. Even if a reader has not discriminated sufficient features in the second and third positions of the configuration *hat* to identify the letters *at,* there is still some featural information available from those positions which, when combined with nonvisual information about featural redundancy within words, permits identification of the letter in the first position on minimal visual information.

There is other evidence that although words are identified "as wholes," in the sense that featural information from all parts may be taken into account in their identification, they are by no means identified on the basis of the familiarity of their shape or contour. Examples were given earlier in this chapter of the ease with which quite unfamiliar configurations like *rEaDiNg*, would be read. Entire passages printed in these peculiar configurations can be read about as fast as normal text (Smith, Lott, & Cronnell, 1969). In fact if the size of the capital letters is reduced slightly so that they do not interfere with the discriminability of the lower case letters, for example *rEADING*, then there is no difference at all in the rates at which such words and normal text are read. The result is perhaps not surprising when we reflect on the ease with which practiced readers can adapt to quite distorted forms of typography or handwriting. Indeed, the facility with which we can read passages of handwriting when individual letters and even words would be indecipherable is further evidence that reading does not depend on letter identification.

It is obviously a gross oversimplification to talk about the relative "discriminability" of individual letters of the alphabet or to assume that letters difficult to identify when standing alone must be difficult to perceive when in words. (This argument applies especially to the question of "reversals" of letter pairs like *b* and *d*, which are particularly bothersome to some children—and to adults in constrained circumstances, and now, apparently, to pigeons. Reversals were specifically considered in Chapter 4.) The criterial features of letters are not fixed and immutable. The amount of visual information required to identify a letter has relatively little to do with the physical characteristics of the actual configuration but depends much more on the reader's experience and the context in which the letter occurs. And precisely the same kind of argument applies to words. Children learning to read can often identify words in context that they cannot identify in isolation (Pearson & Studt, 1975). It is misleading to talk of children's word identification ability in terms of their "sight vocabulary" or word attack skills.

There is an extensive technical literature on the identification of letters in words, including Reicher (1969), Wheeler (1970), Meyer and Schvaneveldt (1971), Rumelhart and Siple (1974), Johnson (1975), and Cosky (1976). Silverman (1976) shows that words can be identified as integrated perceptual units, a point also made by Santa, Santa, and Smith (1977). Brand (1971) shows that distinctions can be made between letters and digits without the identification of specific letters or digits (underlining the featural aspect of identification), and in an article subtitled "Seek Not and Ye Shall Find," Johnston and McClelland (1974) describe how letters are sometimes more easily identified in words if they are not specifically looked for. Another aptly titled paper, "Forest Before Trees," by Navon (1977), shows that letters within larger visual configurations do not intrude in the recognition of the larger unit but that the larger will interfere with the perception of the smaller. Further arguments for the priority of words over letters (and of meaning over individual words) are in Kolers (1970) and Smith and Holmes (1971). For an opposing point of view, Massaro and Klitzke (1977) claim that letters always have a function in word identification (although no one argues that letter information cannot be used when the word as a whole cannot be recognized).

In a pair of complex and detailed theoretical articles, McClelland and Rumelhart (1981) and Rumelhart and McClelland (1981), two cognitive scientists, present a model for "parallel processing structures on the fly" by means of feature detectors of letters that are differentially activated or inhibited by visual information, depending on the context the letters are in, words or nonwords. This combination of neurophysiological jargon and computer methodology has produced a computer system which they claim can identify 1200 4-letter words in the same way that humans do (with word frequency effects, and letters easier in words than in nonwords). There is a summary of this work in a somewhat broader conceptual framework in McClelland (1985). See also Ellis (1984). Golden (1986), in another review, proposes a *spatial* feature analytic word recognition model sensitive to letters in specific positions, to between-letter interconnections, and also to "spatial redundancy." Words need not be recognized letter-by-letter, he concludes—and he has also constructed a computer model based on these suppositions which he claims performs like humans on letter-identification tasks in both words and nonwords.

Haber and Haber (1981) show that the outline shape of a common word is usually sufficient visual information for the unique identification of the word in a meaningful context. Haber, Haber, and Furlin (1983) showed that college students could use information about both length and shape to identify missing words in context, each kind of clue adding about 10 per cent to the probability of a correct identification, and each interacting with other contextual cues. Doggett and Richards (1975) demonstrated that longer words are more difficult to identify only if the words are unfamiliar.

Use of Redundancy by Children

There is no evidence that children need to be trained to seek or use redundancy in any way; indeed, part of the argument of this book is that all of perception depends on the use of prior knowledge and that the youngest of children demonstrate ability to limit uncertainty by eliminating unlikely alternatives in advance. Studies with young readers have found ability to use sequential redundancy very early (Lott & Smith, 1970). First-grade children who had had a limited amount of reading instruction in kindergarten were shown letters in isolation and in simple three-letter words that they could normally identify easily. The children showed themselves able to identify letters in words on less visual information than when they were presented alone. For children in fourth grade the difference between the information on which letters were identified in words and that on which the same letters were identified in isolation was equal to that of skilled adult readers, indicating that for familiar three-letter words at least, fourth-graders could make as much use of sequential featural redundancy as adults. Krueger, Keen, and Rublevich (1974) subsequently confirmed that fourth-grade children may be as good as adults in making use of redundancy among letter sequences in words and nonwords.

Distributional Redundancy Among Words

The sequential redundancy that exists among words in text—which has a critical role in making reading possible—is discussed in later chapters. But there is also a *distributional* redundancy among words, reflecting the obvious fact that some words are used far more often than others. The distributional redundancy of English words has not been formally calculated but is probably related to the maximum theoretical uncertainty of between 15 and 16 bits for a set of about 50,000 alternatives and the actual 12-bit uncertainty of isolated words computed by Shannon (1951) and discussed in the Notes to Chapter 3. Distributional redundancy among words complicates experimental studies of word identification because more frequent words are usually identified faster, more accurately, and on less visual information than less frequent words. The precise reason for this "word frequency effect" is itself the subject of a long and inconclusive debate in the technical literature (Broadbent, 1967; Broadbent & Broadbent, 1975; Howes & Solomon, 1951). See also the previous McClelland and Rumelhart references. The standard reference for relative word frequencies has long been the list of Thorndike and Lorge (1944), with a more recent compilation by Carroll, Davies, and Richman (1971).

NOTES TO CHAPTER 8, PHONICS AND MEDIATED WORD IDENTIFICATION, pp. 133–149.

The Relevance of Phonics

The analysis I have given of the relationship between the spelling of written words and the sounds of speech is mainly derived from the work of a group of researchers (Berdiansky, Cronnell, & Koehler, 1969) associated with the Southwest Regional Laboratory (SWRL), a federally sponsored research and development center in California. SWRL researchers have not only endeavored to analyze the maze of spelling-to-sound correspondences in English, based largely on the work of Venezky (1967, 1970), but also to devise instructional programs to teach these correspondences to children, both native speakers and others, in the expectation that it will make them better readers and spellers. The continuing history of this enterprise is recorded in a number of technical reports published by SWRL.

The fifty-eighth in the series of SWRL technical reports (Rhode & Cronnell, 1977) provides an analysis of a 10,000-word lexicon which they consider to be the basis of a kindergarten through sixth grade communication skills program. This time words of three or more syllables are included, a total of 27 percent of the 10,000. Ninety-nine grapheme units are distinguished, 77 related to 225 spelling-to-sound correspondence "rules" and 22 to 32 "exceptions." Eighty of the rules are associated with 48 consonant grapheme units, 111 with the six primary vowels (a/e/i/o/u/y), and 34 with 23 secondary vowel units (ai/au/etc.).

"Reading machines" that provide text-to-speech translations for the visually impaired and other computer programs that convert written to spoken language do so not by reliance on phonic rules (the last resort) but by storing the complete sounds of thousands of written words. And even then such devices have difficulty selecting the appropriate pronunciation of the 200 or more *homographs* in English, common words like *wind*, *wound*, *tear*, *read*, and *live*, which require at least syntactic and often semantic knowledge to disentangle them. Only if the electronic "reader" fails to recognize a complete word is syllabic and finally letter-sound identification attempted.

The relevance of phonics instruction is the topic of a frequently cited volume by Chall (1967) entitled *Learning to Read: The Great Debate*, although her discussion is more about how reading is taught than how it is learned, and the conclusions may not be thought to follow inevitably from the evidence presented. The debate has been renewed, though by no means concluded, by Adams (1990). The controversy, often reduced to a question of "code emphasis" (phonics exercises) versus "whole language" (meaningful texts), is discussed in Chapter 12 and its Notes.

The belief that phonics must be an indispensable part of learning to read is curiously upheld by a number of researchers despite their own demonstrations of its difficulty and limited relevance to fluent reading—for example, E. Smith and Kleiman (1979) in an article showing how words are recognized and understood without recourse to letters or sound, Weaver and Shonkoff (1978) in demonstrating the arbitrary and conflicting complexities of syllabication rules, and Liberman and Shankweiler (1979) on the difficulty children have with phoneme segmentation. (Children may have difficult recognizing, for example, that *bet* has three phonemes but *best* four, even though they can easily hear and see the difference between the words.) All of these difficulties are in fact *metalinguistic*—they do not involve language itself (as a means of expression or communication) but rather the ability to talk abstractly about language.

A small but noteworthy controversy developed out of a demonstration by Rozin, Poritsky, and Sotsky (1971) that poor readers who failed to learn through conventional phonics instruction could succeed when the Chinese characters for English meanings were substituted for the English spelling. After showing clearly that readers could extract meaning directly from written text, without the mediation of phonics, the authors rather remarkably concluded that reading would therefore best be taught by a syllabic method. Gleitman and Rozin (1973a) elaborated upon this notion of teaching reading through a syllabary, and responded vehemently (Gleitman & Rozin, 1973b) when K. Goodman (1973) commented that their proposal seemed to him to be another easy way to make learning to read difficult. The latter three articles are all contained in one lively issue of *Reading Research Quarterly*. On the relative ease with which children can learn to read in nonalphabetic written language, see also Makita (1968, 1976) for research with Japanese children. Steinberg and Yamada (1978/1979) also discuss Japanese. Park and Arbuckle (1977) compare alphabetic and ideographic aspects of Korean, while Liberman and Shankweiler (1979) observe that learners still have reading problems with the highly phonetic Serbo-Croat script. Seidenberg (1985) demonstrates that in both Chinese (logographic) and English writing systems, large numbers of high frequency words—or "familiar" words—are recognized "visually," immediately, without phonological mediation. Slower responses for less frequent words are made only by slower readers (who are presumably less experienced). Dunn-Rankin (1985) has demonstrated that readers of English are able to identify large numbers of syllables on sight. (He had noticed how familiar certain three-letter combinations had become when they caught his eye on the license plates of cars he drove behind on freeways.) Dunn-Rankin calculated that about 1500 syllables accounted for 95 percent of English words, and "appear suited to represent both the visual and phonetic aspects of speech." Obviously this is not a system to be taught, although it is required in the course of reading. Dunn-Rankin also notes that experienced readers are flexible and adaptable in the use of any clues to word identification that are available.

Phonological Recoding

The mediated identification of written words through the blending (aloud or silently) of sounds represented by their letters is frequently referred to as *phonological recoding* (or sometimes *phonological decoding*). Tremendous amounts of research into word identification and reading continue to be done based on an assumption of phonological recoding, much of it didactic and polemical in nature. It is not possible to review all of the research or even representative arguments of the major proponents—a single publisher produced six edited volumes on the topic in 1992 alone. For a typical argument that word identification has to be mediated through the identification of letters and their sounds, see Liberman and Shankweiler (1979). Mosberg (1978) critically reviews research claiming that such recoding is done "automatically." Glusko (1979) argues that even unfamiliar words or nonsense syllables (like *tave* or *heaf*) are pronounced more by analogy to known words with similar spellings (like *have* and *deaf* than by spelling-to-sound rules as such. The notion that phonics is primarily useful for discarding orthographically unlikely alternatives in meaningful situations where contextual cues eliminate most of the semantic and syntactic uncertainty in advance is supported by evidence that children who successfully attempt to use phonics look primarily at the first letters of words (Marchbanks & Levin, 1965), which happen to be the most informative (Bruner & O'Dowd, 1958), and also where the phonics (especially for consonants) is least unreliable (Broerse & Zwaan, 1966).

Walters, Komoda, and Arbuckle (1985) demonstrate that words have to be identified before they are named. Other evidence for phonological (or phonemic) recoding *after* words have been recognized is reviewed by Ellis (1984) and Besner, Davelaar, Alcott, and Parry (1984). Steinberg, Harada, Tashiro, and Harper (1980) describe teaching deaf children to read, obviously without decoding to sound. Evidence from deaf readers is also discussed by Mattingly (1985), who also argues that hearing readers can discover the pronunciation of words when ascertaining their meaning (from an internal "lexicon"), without having to decode the sounds of the letters. Baron (1979) has demonstrated experimentally that decoding to sound is not necessary for comprehension, and conversely Calfee, Arnold, and Drum (1976) have disputed the frequent but undocumented assertion that it is possible for children to decode in the absence of comprehension.

An ostensible "dual process" or "dual route" point of view asserts that readers identify some words immediately (or "directly") but other words by decoding through the letters. The difference becomes one of degree. Obviously all readers must employ alternative methods of identifying unfamiliar words. Dual process theory is considered in the Notes to Chapter 10.

Phonological Awareness

The fact that many children have difficulty learning phonics, and difficulty learning to read despite intensive instruction in phonics, has led many researchers favoring the phonological recoding view to assert that such children suffer a deficiency related to spoken language perception. (It is not uncommon for difficulties children might experience in learning to read to be attributed to "deficits" on their part, rather than to externally produced factors such as confusion, depressed interest, or learning the wrong thing). According to a widespread view, generally attributed to Isabelle Liberman and her colleagues at the Haskins Laboratories (Liberman & Liberman, 1992), the problem with such children is that they are unable to identify in spoken words the discrete sounds—or "phonological segments"—represented in writing by the letters of the alphabet. This ability to analyze hypothetical sounds has nothing to do with the understanding of speech, but is necessary for reading, according to this point of view.

Phonological awareness is occasionally termed phonemic awareness, in recognition of the fact that it involves the identification of abstract phonemes rather than actual phones in sound (see p. 239 for a discussion of the difference between phones and phonemes). As I have noted, the issue is *metalinguistic*; it does not involve the ability to use language for any expressive or communicative purpose, but only the ability to discuss language as a system.

A major problem with all these analyses of the phonemic structure of spoken words is that the "units" are completely arbitrary and hypothetical—they do not exist as distinct elements in spoken language, either in the perception or the production of speech (Liberman & Liberman, 1992). Children find it difficult to understand the statement that *bet* consists of three elements and almost impossible to understand that *best* has four (at least until they are readers). The separate sounds that letters are supposed to represent and that beginning readers are supposed to be "aware of" are fictions. Sounds are "coarticulated" in the production of speech—at any moment in saying the word *bet* the speaker might be physically producing part of the /b/, /e/ and /t/ simultaneously. It is impossible to separate the three sounds electronically—or by trying to snip independent sections out of a tape recording. The "internal structure" of speech cannot be displayed.

So although children may in some sense be aware of the fact that pairs of words rhyme, or begin with the same sound, or are "the same" or "different" in some way, to expect them to isolate the sounds in speech is a purely artificial task, based solely on the conventions of written (alphabetic) language. The code emphasis becomes not so much a matter of finding speech structures in writing, but of writing structures in speech—not something that is likely to be very easy or meaningful for children before they can read, and of limited utility afterward. Phonological awareness might be regarded as another skill, like phonics, that children may be required to learn as a separate subject from reading. It all falls apart if reading is perceived to be the decoding or recoding of written language directly into meaning, rather than through speech.

Liberman and Liberman (1992) themselves estimate that perhaps as many as 75 per cent of children will "discover the alphabetic principle . . . no matter how unhelpful the instruction" (p. 345). It might be wondered whether the remaining children are simply the victims of unhelpful instruction, especially in view of sanctions frequently imposed on confused and discouraged children who have difficulty understanding phonics (ranging from humiliation before their parents and peers to discriminatory grades and the threat of "withdrawal" into educational segregation).

Two of the foremost proponents of the phonological awareness view, Goswami and Bryant (1990), admit in a footnote in the middle of a book on *Phonological Skills and Learning to Read* coming to the "uncomfortable conclusion" that phonological awareness does not seem to be of much use to children learning to read (p. 46). An extensive review of research had demonstrated "that there is very little direct evidence that children who are learning to read do rely on letter-sound relationships to help them read words" (p. 46). On the other hand, they noted "a great deal of evidence that these young children take easily and naturally to reading words in other ways . . . they either recognize the word as a pattern or remember it as a sequence of letters" (p. 46). Goswami and Bryant's findings have not deterred others from employing the concept of phonological awareness in their theories of reading and pronouncements about instruction, often while citing the work of Goswami and Bryant but disregarding their 1990 conclusion—see Rieben and Perfetti (1991), Brady and Shankweiler (1991), and Gough, Ehri, and Treiman (1992) for numerous examples. The latter volume even includes a chapter by Goswami and Bryant (1992) themselves, citing their 1990 publication but not their uncomfortable conclusion. They still advocate teaching phonological awareness because children attempting to identify new words by analogy make extensive use of rhyme (see later discussion). Jared and Seidenberg (1991) declare that for skilled readers, phonological information contributes to the activation of word meaning only for words that occur infrequently. Even in Finnish, a language that is supposed to have almost perfect sound-symbol correspondence for its alphabetic writing system, teachers have found that a heavy emphasis on phonics instruction may confuse children about the nature of reading and cause comprehension problems later, and reading instruction in that country is moving toward a more meaning-based approach (Korkeamäki & Dreher, 1993).

Cossu, Rossini, and Marshall (1993) show that children with Down's syndrome can learn to read despite failure on tasks usually employed to assess phonological awareness. They doubt that phonological segmentation facilitates learning to read and conclude that "reading skills" should be taught, not phonological awareness skills. In an article entitled "The Relationship of Phonemic Awareness to Reading Acquisition: More Consequence Than Precondition But Still Important," Wimmer, Landerl, Linortner, and Hummer (1991) conclude from a study of Austrian children at the beginning and end of Grade 1 that phonemic awareness comes mostly with reading. It is correlated with reading and spelling achievement at end of Grade 1—but Krashen (1993) shows that children who read more tend to be better readers and spellers. Read, Yun-Fei, Hong-Yin, and Bao-Qing (1986) deduce from studies with Chinese adult readers that the ability to manipulate speech sounds depends on knowing alphabetic writing, and Scholes and Willis (1991) similarly assert that phoneme deletion—answering questions like "What is left if you remove the /k/ sound from cat?—cannot be done by nonreaders; it requires *literate* knowledge of alphabetical writing.

Word Identification by Analogy

The argument in the chapter that unfamiliar words may often be identified by analogy does not entail that phonological recoding is necessary for analogies to be made. Analogies can be made on the basis of visual characteristics—the beginning of *medication* looks like the beginning of *medical*. Goswami and Bryant (1990; see also Goswami, 1986, 1990) hold to the view that learners confronted by words they are unable to identify immediately frequently attempt to do so by piecing together the known sound of the initial consonant or consonant cluster (the "onset") with the rhyming sound of the rest of the syllable of a similarly spelled word. The unknown word *teak*, for example, is likely to rhyme with the known word *beak*, and *fight* with *night*. The view is usually referred to as "onset and rime" (presumably employing the archaic spelling to better exemplify the basic assertion that words that rhyme often share similar spelling patterns). The onset-rime unit is seen as intermediate in size between individual phones and syllables, more predictable from its spelling than a single phoneme. See also Treiman (1992) and Treiman, Goswami, and Bruck (1990) for reviews of studies of children's abilities to detect rhymes, alliteration, and other partial aspects of spoken words. Barron (1986) cites the large amounts of research showing that beginning readers, like fluent readers, use both direct and indirect (immediate and mediated) access to words—indirect when they need to.

The Role of the Alphabet

Goswami and Bryant (1990), whose uncomfortable conclusion that phonological awareness would not help children learn to read has been noted, nevertheless propose that such instruction should be continued because it will help them to spell. Unfortunately, children who spell words the way they are pronounced, as most children do naturally at the beginning (Read, 1971), spell poorly. Spelling by rule is also not an efficient strategy for spelling most common words (Brown, 1970). Although clues may be obtained from known words with similar meanings, the main requirement for good spelling is to *remember* individual spellings (Smith, 1994), a requirement that is not relevant to learning to read. Gillooly (1973) argues that there is no justification for attempts to change the current spelling of English, which he says increases reading speed and is nearly optimum for learning to read.

The complexity and unreliability of spelling-to-sound correspondences (and the reverse) may be just as misleading for writers as for readers if the primary purpose of the alphabet is seen as representing in writing the sounds of spoken language. Instead I conjecture that the main benefits of the alphabet—and they are enormous—for readers, writers, teachers, printers, and all kinds of administrators and bureaucrats is that it permits written words to be talked about and reproduced efficiently (Smith, 1994). The alphabet provides a highly economical way of *describing*, *ordering*, and *reproducing* words by their visual characteristics. If you know the names and appearance of 26 letters, you can describe uniquely many thousands of written words, asking how they should be pronounced (for readers) or how they should be visually represented (for writers). Knowledge of how to *draw* the 26 letters enables the writer to reproduce any word in our language legibly, compared with the knowledge of thousands of entire word forms required to produce ideographic text. The fact that alphabetically written words can be constructed from a relatively small number of discrete characters also has the great technological advantage of making keyboards possible, for typewriters, computers, and printing machines. And the fact that the alphabet is easily given a conventional order makes possible dictionaries and every kind of bureaucratic organization. The Chinese scholar Lin Yutang succeeded in compiling the first practical English-Chinese dictionary in the 1970s only by arbitrarily imposing an "alphabetical order" on 33 basic stroke formations in Chinese script. The alphabet is preeminently an instrument of *control*, from many points of view. Interestingly, one of the few times that public opinion in China was able to modify a national policy of Mao Tse-tung was when he tried to introduce an alphabet into Chinese writing, based on European and Russian letters (Barlow, 1981). The peasants successfully resisted this purely administrative decree on the sound linguistic ground that the new script would prevent them from reading traditional ancient Chinese writings. For a thorough discussion of cognitive and linguistic aspects of Chinese language, including reading, see Hoosain (1991). Coulmas (1992) also focuses particularly on English and Chinese in a brief overview of the different demands that various writing systems make on writers and readers. Coulmas observes that no purely logographic writing system exists. Chinese is morpho-syllabic; each character represents a morpheme (meaning) and also a syllable. There are thousands of characters, many in disuse, with probably at least 5000 in current use. Coulmas asserts that Chinese is no more difficult to read than English, and perhaps easier. For readers of classical Chinese (before post-war reforms) it is certainly easier to read a Chinese text that is hundreds of years old than an alphabetic one because alphabetic writing systems are tied to pronunciation, which changes.

Senner (1989) is an accessible collection of essays on the origin of various writing systems, showing that writing was not the invention of one particular group of people and that it appears to have had its antecedents in drawing (pictographic) rather than in spoken language. Since the development of the alphabetic system, writing has often been modified to correspond more closely with spoken language, but at the same time, spoken language has always been influenced by the structure and use of written language. Written language tends to change less rapidly than speech and therefore has tended to put a brake on spoken language change (or to drift further apart from it). Even today, many people seem to feel that written language is a particularly pure form of language, a model for what spoken language should be like. The other origin of written language, pointed out by several of the contributors to Senner's volume, is not so much conventional speech as mathematics—from keeping track of the calendar and of astronomical (and astrological) phenomena to bureaucratic and commercial record keeping.

The classic book on writing systems is Gelb (1963), although it reflects an occidental bias for crediting the Greeks with the sole discovery of an alphabet. A good case can also be made for the independent and alphabetic Sanskrit writing system devised about 3000 B.C. It all depends on whether you want to say that an alphabet must have vowel symbols that are separate from but equal to those for consonants. See also Vachek (1973). Other useful works on alphabets and writing systems include Stevenson (1983) and Sampson (1985).

NOTES TO CHAPTER 9, THE IDENTIFICATION OF MEANING, pp. 151–166.

Effects of Meaningful Context

Meaningfulness clearly has a substantial role in facilitating the identification of words in reading, reducing their uncertainty from at least 12 bits (the equivalent of 4,096 equiprobable alternatives) for words in isolation to fewer than eight bits (256 alternatives) for words in context (Chapter 4 Notes). It is really irrelevant to talk of letters at this stage—letters are not usually a concern when meaningful text is read. But as a yardstick, it is interesting to recall from the Chapter 4 discussion that the uncertainty of letters falls from 4.7 bits to scarcely one bit when context is meaningful, enabling perception of four times as much of a line of print. Not only can twice as many words be identified in a single glance when they are in a meaningful context, thus overcoming bottlenecks of information processing and memory, but problems of ambiguity and the gulf between surface structure and meaning are removed by the prior elimination from consideration of unlikely alternatives. Context has its effect not because it exists but because it can be *meaningful* and contribute information that reduces the uncertainty of individual words through sequential redundancy. Context places constraints on what each individual word might be.[1] These constraints constitute sequential redundancy, usable only if it is reflected in prior knowledge, or nonvisual information, that the reader can bring to bear. That is why I stress that the context must be *meaningful*, with all the relative connotations of that word. If a particular context is not comprehensible to a reader, or if for one reason or another the reader is reluctant to take advantage of the redundancy and reduce the amount of visual information required for any aspect of reading, then the context might just as well be nonsense, a random arrangement of marks on the page.

Meaningful context as I have been using the term exercises its constraints on word occurrence in two ways, syntactic and semantic. These are two types of restriction upon the particular words an author can select—or a reader predict—at any time. (There are other constraints on authors, such as the limited set of words a reader might be expected to understand.) Choice of words is always limited by what we want to say

---

[1]The present concern is with *language* context, the body of words in a text. But as outlined in Chapter 2, words can also be constrained by more general *situational* contexts; for example, there is a very small and highly predictable set of alternative words likely to occur on a toothpaste tube. There is also an important context in the receiver's expectations. As Olson (1970) points out, words are selected and get meaning from what the listener or reader needs to know.

(semantics) and how we want to say it (syntax). I have not tried to separate the effects of syntax and semantics in this discussion for the simple reason that I have not found a good way to do so. The theoretical analysis of Chapter 2 argued that the two are inseparable; that without meaning it is pointless to talk about grammar. Treisman (1969) attempted to unravel the two experimentally and concluded that in normal language the syntactic component is subordinate to the semantic.

There is no shortage of research demonstrating the powerful facilitatory effect of meaningful context on word identification. Indeed, there is no evidence to the contrary. But before I begin to cite this research, a fundamental point must be reiterated: *Reading does not usually involve or rely upon word identification.* Banal though it may sound, the basic point about meaningful context is that it makes reading for meaning possible and word identification unnecessary. The fact that meaningful context makes individual words easier to identify is basically as irrelevant as the fact that individual letters are easier to identify in words; the research evidence is merely a demonstration of the effect of meaningful context. Even when reading aloud is involved, so that the accurate identification of words is required, the prior apprehension of meaning is an important prerequisite. Reading aloud is difficult if prior comprehension is limited, and if word identification is given priority there will be interference with comprehension (Howe & Singer, 1975). Sharkey and Mitchell (1985) show that word recognition in meaningful contexts is frequently minimal and not very predictable, especially when the context is itself a predictable "script"—when it is a familiar narrative, in other words.

Levy (1978) reported that changing the wording but not the sense of written language did not affect a short-term memory task—meanings not specific words are retained whenever possible, even for brief periods. Sometimes context leads us astray, evidence again for the potency of meaning and prediction. Carpenter and Daneman (1981) give several examples of "garden path" texts where context misleads rather than facilitates, such as "Cinderella could not go to the ball. There were tears in her dress." Marcel (1978) even demonstrates a "subliminal" effect of what he calls "unconscious reading"—people acquiring information when they were not aware that any text had been presented (because it was flashed so briefly and then "masked"). But in a sense all reading except the most difficult and artificial is "unconscious"; we may be aware of what we read but not of the fact of reading.

For examples of how context facilitates word identification, see Morton (1969, 1982), Klein and Klein (1973), and Smith and Spoehr (1974). For a summary of the arguments of the present chapter and preceding three chapters, see Smith and Holmes (1971). In related studies demonstrating the effect of meaningfulness, Rothkopf and Coatney (1974) show that reading rate is determined by the reader's expectations of information in the text, and Rothkopf and Billington (1974) that comprehension is improved when answers to specific questions are sought and found. Smith and Kleiman (1979) summarize many experiments showing that a preceding context "somehow activates the meaning of the possible next word." Carpenter and Just (1975, 1977) examine how reading normally involves the integration of new contextual information with what is already known (again demonstrating that learning and comprehension are inseparable). Crowder and Wagner(1991) show that readers use meaning from other words to help identify specific words in text; see also Goldsmith-Phillips (1989).

Cohen (1970) and Neisser and Beller (1965) provide experimental demonstrations that meaning can be sought without the identification of words. In tasks involving a search through word lists, it took no longer to find an example of a category (such as "any flower") than to find a specific word in that category (such as *daisy*). Search tasks of this kind basically require rejecting irrelevant items on the list (much as we quickly dispose of names we are *not* looking for in a telephone directory) and show that it is not necessary to identify a word specifically to decide that it does not fall into a particular category (set of alternatives) in which we are interested. Spragins, Lefton, and Fisher (1976) have demonstrated that meaning is so prepotent that it will interfere with a search in which meaning is actually irrelevant. Neisser (1967) has an extensive discussion of such search tasks and the light they throw on visual decision-making; for a review see Martin (1979). In a study entitled "Meaning in Visual Search" that is *not* about reading, Potter (1975) reports that viewers recognize pictures as accurately and almost as fast when all they know in advance is the "meaning" (given by a name or title, such as "a boat") as when they have already seen the picture itself. McNeill and Lindig (1973) show that context effects exist with spoken language just as with written (see also Miller, Heise, & Lichten, 1951).

Context and Prediction

Some theorists have argued that *context* and *prediction* play a smaller role in reading than proposed in this book. But they tend to use the terms more narrowly than I do. For example, Stanovich (1992) concludes from eye-movement studies that "context effects" are minimal because visual information rapidly blurs outside the foveal area in the center of the field of view. Earlier, Stanovich (1986) asserted that poor readers depend more on prediction than fluent readers. But I see context in terms of a reader's *understanding* at any given point in the text of what it is about, enhanced by what has already been seen behind and sometimes ahead of where the eyes happen to fall. Such advance knowledge, primarily nonvisual rather than visual, facilitates reading by reducing the reader's uncertainty. There is a tendency to equate prediction with "guessing," a term I have never used or relied upon to describe what fluent readers do. My definition of prediction—the prior elimination of unlikely alternatives—is precisely what makes experienced readers so effective when reading texts whose language and subject matter are familiar to them. Once again, everything hinges on the purposes of the reader and on the reader's freedom to be flexible and selective.

A variety of studies have demonstrated the readiness of children to make use of context in early reading (if they are so permitted), for example, Klein, Klein, and Bertino (1974), Golinkoff (1975/1976), and Doehring (1976); see also McFarland and Rhodes (1978). Rosinski, Golinkoff, and Kukish (1975) conclude that meaning is irresistible to children; it can interfere with performance on a task because they cannot ignore it. Such studies also tend to show that use of context and reading ability increase together. This correlation is often attributed to the fact that better readers can make more use of context; less often the possibility is considered that use of context makes better readers. For the relation between ability and use of context see also Clay and Imlach (1971) and Samuels, Begy, and Chen (1975/1976). For analyses of children's errors, what Goodman calls "windows on the reading process," see Goodman (1965, 1969), Weber (1968), and Clay (1969). Studies of children's misreadings tend to highlight the important fact that many of the errors, especially those made by better readers, preserve the meaning of the context and also that errors which make a difference to meaning are often subsequently corrected by children who are reading for meaning (and therefore are not errors that need be a great cause for concern). Children who read more literally, perhaps because of an emphasis on "accuracy" during instruction, may however make nonsensical errors without being aware of them.

The paradigm example of a child learning to read by meaning alone, without any possibility of decoding to sound, must be that of Helen Keller. Henderson (1976) reports the case of a deaf child who learned to recognize 4,400 printed words in nine months at the age of six by relating them to manual signs in a meaningful context, basically in response to the child's own spontaneous inquiries. Ewoldt (1981) demonstrates that deaf children read in the same way as hearing children.

"Dual Process"

The most popular assumption about comprehension in experimentally-based research on reading is centered on the notion that there is an "internal lexicon" in the head—a kind of mental dictionary—where the meanings of words are stored. Comprehension is achieved when definitions of the words that we read are "looked up" in the internal lexicon. The concept is a metaphor, not an explanation. It fails to explain how the internal definitions are understood and does not allow for selectivity, prediction, and all the other things that readers normally do. The idea actually precludes certain explanations—for example that comprehension might on occasion be a pictorial or sensory image or a physical response, that comprehension is a state rather than a process, or that meaning is brought to language. It papers over the essential mystery of understanding. Yet the notion that such a lexicon actually exists is often taken for granted and not even debated, it is simply assumed that words are understood by being identified and "routed" to the internal lexicon. This is a great theoretical utility, it permits discussion of hypothetical "routes" between eye and understanding without any consideration of the nature of the terminus. Understanding can be dismissed simply as "lexical access." Among many discussions of the internal lexicon by linguists see Fodor (1979) and by psychologists see Morton (1969) and Rieben and Perfetti (1991). Miller and Fellbaum (1991) discuss the enormous problems of constructing an actual lexicon of English—their database of 46,000 entries includes 26 different hierarchical relationships for nouns, up to 10 levels deep with at least three different categories of distinguishing features—parts, attributes, and functions. Nevertheless such semantic decomposition is popular (see also Miller & Johnson-Laird, 1975). A notorious example is McCawley's (1968) "Kill = cause become not alive," ridiculed together with all theories of innate grammars by Robinson (1975), who disputes whether linguistics is (or should be) a science and decries what he calls "linguistic atomism." Fodor (1981) says most words are not decomposable. If people know 50,000 word meanings there must be close to 50,000 "primitive concepts," which must be innate.

Dual process theorists see two ways of getting from visual information to the internal lexicon—direct (which means an unmediated loop between word and meaning, similar to the general point of view of the present book but not necessarily in the same direction) and by phonological recoding. The idea is that the lexicon contains not only meanings but also spellings and pronunciations, information about syntactic functions, and possibly featural descriptions of various kinds. All these are alternative ways in which the lexicon can be entered, both for recognition and for production (writing and spelling).

Most researchers say both routes are possible but put different emphasis on each. Some theorists, like Gough (e.g., Gough & Walsh, 1991) argue that only a phonological route to the lexicon exists; that reading is a process of decoding (or rather deciphering) the "cipher" of English spelling. Ehri (1992) claims that access is through the spelling patterns of words, without necessarily recoding into phonological form (which nonetheless usually becomes available with recognition of meaning). Ehri calls this the *visual-phonological route*, that is used even for "direct access." She cites evidence that children "learning to read by sight" find *msk* easier to learn and remember as the word "mask" than an arbitrary spelling like *uhe*, though nonreaders do not. Some orthographic utilization in word identification is obvious, for example, in distinguishing homophones like *their* from *there*. The term orthographic structure (literally, visual structure) is usually taken to refer specifically to spelling, though it can also refer to the shape or featural detail of words as a whole and to arrangements of letters, individually or in clusters, seen as visual configurations, not as guides to pronunciation.

Van Orden, Johnson, and Hale (1988) entitle their publication unequivocally "Word Identification in Reading Proceeds From Spelling to Sound to Meaning." Barker, Torgesen, and Wagner (1992) studied 87 third graders on five tests—untimed and timed word identification, oral and silent reading of 100-word passages, and accuracy for reading nonwords—and found orthographic skills implicated in all five, from 5 percent for reading nonwords to 20 percent for oral reading of text. They also found "phonological processing skill" a more significant factor but did not note whether this was related to the instruction the children had been receiving. Seidenberg and McClelland (1989) argue that the apparent utilization of phonological information in word identification does not necessarily involve explicit use of grapheme-phoneme correspondences but is a result of statistical regularities in the covariance of the orthographic and phonological representations of words.

Perfetti (1985) does not accept the speech recoding model of Gough, which he feels is possible but not necessary. Perfetti calls his own approach a verbal efficiency theory—"verbal efficiency" meaning skill in allocating attention and memory resources to language-related aspects of reading, and language in this context meaning speech. Perfetti breaks reading down into multiplicity of separate "processes"—like word recognition, lexical access, schema access, comprehension processes and propositional encoding, and the activation of semantic and phonetic codes, with an underlying need to learn the "coding system." He relies particularly on research by Carpenter and Just (1981) that in experimental reading situations, most words are fixated upon—long words more than short, unfamiliar words more than familiar, and the last word in a sentence more than the others.

Rayner and Pollatsek (1989) argue for direct grapheme-phoneme access, not through a syllabary or whole words. Their position is rejected in a long, technical, and polemical article by Van Orden, Pennington, and Stone (1991) with a massive bibliography of the various points of view. Van Orden, Pennington, and Stone claim that flaws in dual-process theories, for example in the reading of "exception words," favor direct access models. They want to substitute a "subsymbolic psycholinguistics" alternative based on complex connectionism and "covariant learning" involving the weighting of connections. The paper is concerned solely with "initial stimulus encoding," yet among other claims its title not untypically asserts that the subject matter is "reading." Walters, Komoda, and Arbuckle (1985) offer experimental evidence that phonological recoding plays a very small part in skilled reading and that it is unnecessary unless there are detailed memory demands. For earlier, less technical reviews of dual process theories, see Henderson (1984) and Baron and Strawson (1976).

It is often assumed that decoding (or recoding) written language into speech will automatically provide meaning for written words. But spoken words must themselves be interpreted and they can be even more ambiguous than written words. Including a phonological loop in reading constitutes an additional step, not a shortcut, for understanding.

Physiological Evidence

Evidence for a direct route for understanding in reading is beginning to come in from advanced brain studies.[2] Petersen et al. (1989) used positron emission tomographic (PET) images of blood flow change to identify brain areas involved in lexical processing of spoken and written words in adults. Their results indicated a direct route from words presented visually to semantic and articulatory areas, without necessarily a phonological recoding. Raichle (1990) describes in detailed but nontechnical language procedures used to come to a similar conclusion. Subjects are asked to think about written or spoken words while the metabolic activity of their brains is recorded three-dimensionally by PET scanning of the distribution of radioactive substances.

Posner and Carr (1992) also review current brain imaging methods and their utility for studying cognitive activities like attention and reading, looking particularly at word recognition and lexical access. They report that PET imaging shows that some parts of the brain (usually the left occipital cortex) are activated when real words and "orthographically well-structured pseudowords" are read but not random letters and other complex visual patterns. Semantic judgment tasks involve the lower left prefrontal cortex. Tasks requiring phonological or articulatory processing involve a variety of temporal areas. Not surprisingly, all these studies are very complex to perform, interpret, and relate. They tend roughly to support modular theories that different properties of words are "computed" by complex sets of distinct, isolable brain systems. In reporting earlier work, Warrington and Shallice (1979) argue from neuropsychological premises that "word form" has direct access to a "semantic system," assumed to be the source of meaningfulness.

Willows, Kruk, and Corcos (1993) present a comprehensive edited review of research into visual aspects of reading and the complex neurological bases of visual perception. They complain that although reading is obviously a visual activity, very little focused attention is paid to this aspect of it compared with the emphasis on such topics as phonological awareness. This is an accurate observation, although the editors might themselves be charged with concentrating on one end of the reading process with insufficient recognition of the importance of intention, prior knowledge, and the social nature of meaning and learning. Most of the hundreds of studies cited involved tasks primarily if not exclusively focused on what the eyes do, certainly much more difficult, demanding, and possibly unnatural than reading when purpose and linguistic constraints are involved. Coltheart (1987) provides a number of useful "tutorials" in a 700-page summary of experimental approaches to reading—including word recognition, sentence comprehension, and eye movements.

---

[2] I should note here that all such studies should be interpreted very cautiously. I would not be persuaded by studies indicating that "auditory areas" of the brain, or indeed the entire brain, were invariably activated during reading, either as side effects or as part of a total response. Some profound theoretical issues about the nature of thinking and the way the brain functions need to be resolved before extrapolating from physiological to psychological phenomena. In a review of a book with a marked neurophysiological emphasis on the "psychology of reading," Underwood (1992) asks how outlines of the structure of the ganglionic structure of the eye and the function of the amygdala and hippocampus in the brain help an understanding of reading and thinks they may in fact be a distracting irrelevance because important questions are lost.

Eye Movements

The particular order and location of fixations is not a reliable guide to how readers comprehend text, especially as reading rate increases. (In the same way, the intermittent manner in which our gaze wanders around a room is not particularly suggestive of the stable perception of the room that the brain constructs.) Nevertheless, Just and Carpenter (1980) claim to present a new theory of reading based on points of fixation. For other discussions of fixations and comprehension see Kolers (1976), Kieras and Just (1984), Just and Carpenter (1984), Rayner (1983), and Groner, McConkie, and Menz (1985). Rayner and Morris (1992) claim that experiments demonstrate that "semantic preprocessing" does not control eye movements in reading. The evidence could also be taken to indicate that experiments on eye movements say nothing about reading.

Subvocalization

Edfeldt (1960) concluded that good readers engage less in "silent speech" than poor readers and that an easy text results in less subvocalization than a difficult one (which to me reflects the same underlying factor—all texts are difficult for poor readers). Kleiman (1975) in a carefully controlled study showed that recoding to speech was not necessary for the understanding of individual words (lexical access) but might be useful while "semantic integration" takes place, in other words when there might be a heavier demand on short-term memory. Baddeley, Eldridge, and Lewis (1981) argue that although memory is helped by subvocalization, inappropriate articulation requirements in experiments can disrupt short-term memory. Swanson (1984) has also shown that the need for subvocalization (which he calls phonological recoding) increases as load on memory increases, for example in the face of "comprehension questions." The need is also greater for younger readers or when reading is difficult. In any case, comprehension has to occur prior to phonological recoding; words cannot be subvocalized meaningfully in any other way. Pugh (1978) discusses both speed reading and the elimination of subvocalization and concludes that neither interferes with comprehension.

NOTES TO CHAPTER 10, READING, WRITING, AND THINKING, pp. 167–182.

Comprehension and Thinking

Reading and thinking are fundamentally inseparable, especially when reading is discussed or researched under the heading of comprehension. Vygotsky (1978) defined thinking as "internalized action," and reading might be regarded as "internalized experience." In a special "literacy" issue of *Harvard Educational Review*, Scribner and Cole (1978) argue that literacy does not change the basic way in which people reason. The contrary view is widely held, for example by Olson (1977).

In any aspect of thinking, what we know already—our "prior knowledge"—is obviously an important factor in what we can accomplish. Tierney and Cunningham (1984) discuss the importance of building up and "activating" background knowledge prior to reading. Basically this is common sense—the more we know about a topic before reading, the more we understand. But there is a decidedly mechanistic tone about theorizing which talks of the provision, utilization, and activation of any aspect of thought, which in practice can lead teachers to spend more time on preparation for reading than on reading itself, although reading is a major source of prior knowledge. Prior knowledge can on occasion be detrimental, if the text asserts something contrary to what the reader predicts (Alvermann, Smith, & Readence, 1985), especially if there are differences between the cultural perspectives of the text and the world-view of the reader (Lipson, 1983, 1984). Margolis (1987) argues that thinking is based on pattern recognition and analogy, not logic, and Johnson-Laird (1990) sees imagination as central to thinking and inference. Undergraduates given scenic photographs to look at and descriptive paragraphs to read remembered a number of pictures and paragraphs a week later—but also remembered (with a high degree of confidence) photographs they had not seen—the images they had created from paragraphs they had read (Intraub & Hoffman, 1992).

The influence of reading on children's thought and learning is not always considered beneficial. A number of writers have commented informally on the danger of children acquiring socially undesirable habits through children's literature, sometimes verging on extremes of "political correctness." A singular example is the outrage expressed by the National Rifle Association at the "reprehensible decision" of the National Council of Teachers of English to award its poetry prize to a children's author who wrote of "hateful hunters hiding behind trees" (Baker, 1993). For some considered reflections on how gender stereotypes can be reinforced through reading, see Fox (1993). For a critique of theories of children's thought, see Gardner (1991).

Kimmel and MacGinitie (1984) have shown that children may perseverate with inappropriate hypotheses while reading (and presumably in other circumstances). This is not necessarily the fault of the readers, however. Children can often cope well with paragraphs or entire texts where the "main idea" is at the beginning. But many school texts are not written in this way. Kimmel and MacGinitie show that school texts often begin with examples, analogies and even refutations, and make their point clear only at the end. Nicholson and Imlach (1981) found that prior knowledge and text could compete when children were required to answer questions about their reading. Eight-year-olds could incorrectly impose their own expectations on narrative, but on the other hand they could also "be assailed by every word in the paragraph"—a phrase first used in an important article by Thorndike (1977). Baddeley, Logie, Nimmo-Smith, and Brereton (1985) analyzed the "components" of fluent reading and found the two major factors to be vocabulary and working memory span, both of which relate to the sense which a reader can make of a text. Paradoxically, O'Brien and Myers (1985) demonstrated that comprehension difficulty could improve recall, because readers spent more time looking back. Confounding comprehension in this way is not recommended as a strategy for improving memory.

August, Flavell, and Clift (1984) showed that skilled fifth-grade readers noticed inconsistencies in stories (a missing page) more often than less skilled readers, which showed they were reading more than words. Beebe (1980) found that errors made by silent readers reduced both comprehension and recall—unless the errors were corrected or "semantically acceptable," in which case both comprehension and recall improved. Beebe's study shows clearly that reading is primarily an effort after sense. Juel and Holmes (1981) noted that poor readers spend less time on difficult words when reading silently than when reading aloud, when presumably the expectations of others control how the reading is done. In comparing oral and silent reading of sentences, the authors noted that the "same cognitive processes" were involved; reading for meaning is important in both.

Comprehension in reading does not necessarily take place immediately or all at once. Samuels (1979) and O'Shea, Sindelar, and O'Shea (1985) have shown, not surprisingly, that reading the same text more than once improves fluency, comprehension, and memory, especially for "poor readers" or for reading difficult texts. The effect is particularly pronounced if readers are cued to read for comprehension rather than for accuracy. This research underlines an important general point: It is usually more effective to read a text *quickly*, more than once, than to plod through it slowly once only. Initial "skimming," and even browsing through an entire book by glancing at occasional pages, adds to prior knowledge and facilitates subsequent efforts to make sense of the entire text.

Baldwin, Peleg-Bruckner, and McClintock (1985) wondered whether prior knowledge itself facilitated reading or whether the facilitation was attributable to the added interest that prior knowledge probably indicates. They found that for seventh- and eighth-grade children, the two factors were separate and additive. Not surprisingly, it is better to have both than to have interest without knowledge or knowledge without interest.

An ingenious eye-movement experiment by Just and Carpenter (1984) demonstrates that readers can make fast and accurate recovery from errors. When presented with sentences where mistakes of interpretation were almost certain to occur—such as with the word *sewer* in the sentence "There is also one sewer near our home who makes terrific suits"—readers made rapid and economical "regressive" eye movements directly to the misleading words. There were other references to eye-movement studies and "misleading texts" in the Notes to Chapter 9. Thompson (1981) defends the proposition that reading is generally a predictive activity but not hypothesis-testing. Prediction reduces alternatives (as argued in the present book), while hypothesis-testing focuses too much on a single possibility. For a brief consideration of Neisser's (1977) anticipatory model of cognition from a reading point of view, see Doehring and Aulls (1981).

Reading Speed

Carver (1985) criticizes studies that claim to demonstrate fast rates of reading. He asserts that "comprehension" is rarely adequately defined or measured in such studies and holds that unless readers comprehend the author's thoughts on a sentence-by-sentence basis (a procedure to which he gives the special name of *rauding*), then "skimming" rather than reading is taking place. Demonstration of rauding under laboratory conditions involves tests of recall of detail which constitute great impositions on memory. Not surprisingly, Carver's experimental subjects fail to meet such a criterion at speeds of more than 600 words a minute. But it can be argued that no one reading in normal circumstances would ever try to remember the detail of every sentence of a novel or even of a business letter. Inability to remember detail does not mean that a book was not comprehended or even that every sentence in that book was not comprehended at the appropriate time. Carver's own studies showed that "speed readers" were able to write an adequate 100-word summary of a 6000-word text after perusing it for four minutes. Carver (1992) subsequently reported that college students typically read to memorize at 138 words per minute, to study for a multiple-choice test at 299 wpm, to "comprehend complete thoughts in sentences" at 300 wpm, to skim at 450 wpm, and to scan for a target word at 600 wpm. He refers to these different reading rates as gears and says that "shifting" flexibility is needed.

Saenger (1991) discusses how silent reading facilitates rapid reading and the scanning of text, subordinating the constraints of the text to the aims and biases of the reader. The purpose of the spaces between words in alphabetic writing, Saenger argues, is to facilitate silent reading. British researchers Harding, Beech, and Sneddon (1985) found that the reason more proficient readers aged from five to nine years old appeared to "process larger units of information" was that they read faster and therefore had less of a memory handicap. Potter (1984), using a technique that delivers individual words at a controlled rate to readers (Forster, 1970), found that college students preferred a rate of 360 words a minute. At 720 words a minute, almost all the words could be read but ideas "seem to pass through the mind without being adequately retained"—on a sentence-by-sentence basis at least. At 960 to 1680 words a minute, most viewers felt they could not see most of the words or understand individual sentences, although they could be shown to have acquired some understanding. Potter, Kroll, Yachzel, and Harris (1980) corroborated that it is memory that takes time in reading. Increasing the rate of reading from 180 to 600 words a minute left comprehension unaffected but reduced memory for detail.

Comprehension and Context

There is some research showing that poor readers use context more than fluent readers (Stanovich, 1980, 1981, 1986; Stanovich, Cunningham, & Feeman, 1984; Perfetti & Roth, 1981; Perfetti, Goldman, & Hogaboam, 1979). These experimental results might appear contrary to the position argued in this book that poor readers use less nonvisual information. The resolution of this apparent paradox may be that when reading is difficult, all readers *need* context more, and as Thompson (1981) points out, "good and poor readers" reading the same text are not doing equivalent reading—one is reading easy material and the other difficult. In the experimental conditions, poor readers are forced to rely on context and every other source of available help. But there is a related factor. Experimenters, especially those with a cognitive science orientation, typically define "context" as a few words on the page on either side of a "target word" in contrived situations that emphasize word identification or memory. There is much more to nonvisual information than adjacent words on a page. Nonvisual information includes all of a reader's relevant prior knowledge, plus understanding of the text *as a whole*. In fact, adjacent words on the page should be considered *visual information*—they are not "context" so much as additional features to be analyzed if individual word identification is emphasized and difficult. And the less nonvisual information a reader can bring to bear, the more visual information, in the form of distinctive features from the text, needs to be identified. In such circumstances, readers may need supplementary features outside the boundaries of target words in order to identify those words.

Stanovich calls his view of reading *interactive-compensatory*, to indicate that readers "interact" with texts (which is indisputable) and that they compensate for local difficulties they have by attending more to surrounding detail. The point about compensation is correct, but only in situations that focus on accurate word identification rather than purposeful, meaningful reading. It could also be argued that children who cannot identify particular words on sight in contrived experimental or instructional situations are forced to use context as much as they can since phonics won't work for them.

None of the studies of "context effects" demonstrate that reading is necessarily a matter of identifying one specific word after another, although the experimental designs often suggest that this is the assumption of the researchers. Other theorists (including myself) use the term context much more broadly to include the text as a whole, the purpose of the author, and the reader's general intentions and expectations. A few theorists go even further and include the "social context" of reading as well, for example, Harste, Woodward, and Burke (1984), Heap (1980), and Iser (1978). To recapitulate the view presented in this book, features of sequences of letters are analyzed but the letters themselves need not be identified when the reader's objective is the identification of words. And features of sequences of words may be analyzed without the words themselves being identified when the purpose of reading is to find specific kinds of sense in the text. Readers can go straight to meaning in the text by means of prediction. Reading is not a matter of identifying word after word. The eyes may appear to focus on individual words during reading (Just & Carpenter, 1980), but they have to be focused somewhere. The particular focal point does not necessarily indicate that words are being identified one at a time. Freebody and Anderson (1983) dispute Stanovich's compensatory-interactive model, arguing that comprehension and prior knowledge override text factors. But they add that it is not always easy for young readers to switch away from individual word identification if that has become a habitual practice especially if there are problems related to vocabulary, text cohesion, or "schema availability" (the relevant prior knowledge).

Becker (1982) argues that skilled readers can employ two alternative "strategies": (1) identifying and trying to put together meaning from successive words (the bottom-up view) or (2) "context driven," emphasizing the sense of the passage. The latter is more of a top-down point of view—but typically still puts the text in charge. The "context" is the surrounding text, not the purposes and understanding of the reader. Aaronson and Ferres (1984) similarly identify two reading strategies. College students, both slow and fast readers, could employ (1) a "structure oriented strategy" when reading for retention or (2) a "meaning oriented strategy" when reading for comprehension. In the latter case "lexical and structural information" related primarily to individual words was lost. Fifth graders could also employ the two strategies but more often tended to use them together for both recall and comprehension, indicating less flexibility than more experienced readers.

In many of the kind of experiments that I have discussed, there is often a confusion between *decoding* (in order to identify an unfamiliar word, to say what it is) and what is termed *phonological recoding*, in order to find a meaning for the word. As I discussed in the Notes to Chapters 8 and 9, phonological recoding means putting a word into spoken language form (albeit silently) in order to "access the internal lexicon" and obtain a meaning. The phonological recoding view regards written language as parasitical on speech and says in effect that we cannot recognize the meaning of written words by the look of them, but rather have to convert them into spoken language form in order to make sense of them from their sound. Unfortunately, some theorists talk about decoding as if that automatically means getting the meaning, although phonological recoding would be a necessary additional theoretical step. Words can be identified without being understood. On the other hand, phonological recoding does not entail decoding. It is possible to name a familiar word and to find a meaning for it from the appearance of the word as a whole, without going through decoding of letters or syllables. And phonological recoding itself is by no means an essential part of reading. As argued in Chapter 9, meaning can be brought directly to the visual representation of words, without any spoken language representation, as is obviously the case for homophones like *their* and *there*, which have identical sounds but whose meaning is easily distinguished by their appearance. Once again the decoding and recoding experiments demonstrate the untoward emphasis on words in reading research that Goodman (1982) has pointed out. Reading is not normally a matter of extracting and putting together the meaning of individual words, but of bringing relevant meaning to texts.

Other Aspects of Reading

Margaret Meek Spencer (1987) emphasizes that reading always requires a text that is read for a particular purpose, a consideration which she thinks is overlooked in textbooks that treat reading in the abstract. A similar point is strongly made by Iser

(1978), who says reading requires not only a reader but a context in which the reading is taking place. Obviously the authors of textbooks cannot specify a particular situation every time they refer to "reading," but the point is well taken that the manner in which reading transpires at any particular time depends on the person reading, the text being read, and all the circumstances of the occasion. Langer (1951) and Iser (1978) both assert that a reader's involvement with a story is like involvement in actual events.

Benton (1979) identifies four characteristics of the "reading state." It is active, creative, unique (to the individual who is reading), and cooperative (between the reader and the author). For a deep understanding of how children perceive narrative, see Meek (1982) and other chapters in the same volume. For general discussions of comprehension in reading, see Flood (1984) and J. Langer (1982a). In reviewing the 1979–1980 report of the U.S. National Assessment of Reading, J. Langer (1982b) noted that the 100,000 students examined (aged 9, 13, and 17) could all comprehend reading passages and form judgments on them, though some had difficulty in elaborating or explaining their own ideas. The problem, Langer thought, was the emphasis on the "right answer," even when students were invited to give their own interpretations.

Krashen (1993) provides an excellent and concise summary of the benefits of "free voluntary reading" with regard to reading ability, comprehension, vocabulary, grammar, spelling, writing, second language learning, attitude toward school, career choice, public esteem, and self-esteem. He discusses the significance and value of every kind of reading that learners will voluntary engage in, including comic books and "romances." Elley (1989) shows that vocabulary increases with reading—or with listening to stories. Iser (1973) says that great writers make readers into better writers. In a study of geniuses, Simonton (1988) found that "omnivorous reading in childhood and adolescence correlates positively with ultimate adulthood success" (p. 111). He also noted that the geniuses he studied (like Einstein, Pasteur, and Darwin) were prolific writers throughout their lives, allowing imagery and even "play" to dominate creative aspects of their thinking. Torrance and Olson (1985) report that good readers speak in more complex utterances and use a wider range of metalinguistic words related to thinking and language. For discussions of how literacy can make a difference to an individual's knowledge of "language as an object," see Olson and Torrance (1991), particularly the chapter by Scholes and Willis (1991) arguing that learning to read promotes learning to talk and an understanding of grammar. West, Stanovich, and Mitchell (1993) examined the largely uninvestigated belief that literacy confers intellectual benefits, questioning individuals waiting alone in an airport waiting area—111 who were "reading recreationally" for ten continuous minutes and 106 others who did not read at all for ten continuous minutes (with almost equal numbers of females and males in each group). They found significant differences in vocabulary size and "cultural knowledge" in favor of the readers, who also tended to be somewhat older and to have had more educational experience. West, Stanovich, and Mitchell also discuss evidence that there are much greater opportunities for learning new words from reading than from conversation or watching television—popular magazines for example providing three times the number of opportunities—and also opportunities for learning other aspects of language and a "uniquely rich source of content knowledge."

For the richness and diversity of the roles literacy plays in individual lives (without detracting from the overriding significance of oral language and experience generally), see Heath (1986). Csikszentmihalyi (1990) has originated a concept of "flow" to denote the uniquely satisfying experience of being deeply and effortlessly involved in an activity to the extent of forgetting oneself, time, and everything else. Reading, he says, is perhaps the most often mentioned flow activity in the world. Nell (1988) describes the marked physiological effects that reading can have, both arousing and relaxing. Olson (1977) proposes that reading makes people civilized.

On the other hand, it can be also argued that literacy is often overrated (Pattanayak, 1991; Smith, 1989). Nonliterates should not be regarded as "problems" to be cured, eradicated, or declared war upon, nor should they be held responsible for social and economic crises of society. Graff (1987a, 1987b) provides compendious discussions of the history of literacy, the misunderstandings that surround it, and its social roles and functions, including a critical review of the "crisis" approach to literacy and alarms about declining standards or abilities. He asserts that the efficacy of literacy in improving an individual's life is a myth; literacy is a technology, or set of techniques, not an agent of change for individuals or societies. The "oral world" (of which writing is an extension rather than a replacement) is of continuing importance. In a more concise presentation of his views, Graff (1986) concludes that as far as the current state of the world is concerned "Literacy is neither the major problem, nor is it the main solution."

Not surprisingly, reading in a foreign language is not particularly difficult for people with a substantial vocabulary in that language. Laufer (1992) suggests there will be certain failure to read with a command of fewer than 3,000 "word families" (about 5,000 words) in the language of the text, but certain success (relative to a student's "general academic ability") if more than 5,000 word families are understood.

Looking to the not-distant future, Bolter (1991) says that readers will have to learn to read electronic texts and "hypertexts" (networks of subtexts) in different ways from linear print-reading, following routes that the writers might not even have imagined, perhaps just by touching different areas of a screen. The notion of what constitutes readers and writers will change, and also the idea of "autonomous texts" that exist independently of readers and writers, with clearly defined beginnings and ends. Bolter sees these radical changes in "writing spaces" beginning with contemporary data-bases, expert systems, computer-assisted instruction, and even a few novels.

Huey (1908) speaks such quiet common and scientific sense about reading (despite some rather dated anxieties about the "hygiene" of certain reading habits) that many theorists, including the present author, have been tempted to claim him as an intellectual predecessor. For histories of research on reading and on reading instruction see Venezky (1977), Mathews (1966), and Davies (1973). For comparative surveys of approaches to reading in different countries see Downing (1973) and Gray (1956). The Russian view, very much outside-in, is provided by Elkonin in Downing (1973), and Sakamoto (1976) discusses reading in Japan. Edited volumes covering various points of view include Singer and Ruddell (1976), Merritt (1976), and three volumes of Resnick and Weaver (1979). There are several chapters on reading in a two-volume international compendium on language edited by Lenneberg and Lenneberg (1975). For a general compendium of reading research, from a variety of points of view, see Downing and Leong (1982). Hochberg and Brooks (1976) discuss intentional aspects of reading, and Searle (1980) is an interesting but technical article on intention and language generally.

Reading and Writing

Most contemporary researchers into reading pay some attention to writing as well. They look at how readers and authors must collaborate with each other, at what reading and writing have in common, and also at what knowledge of reading and of writing contribute to each other. Nystrand (1986; also Nystrand & Wiemelt, 1991) consider reading to be a negotiation between reader and author; see also Langer and Smith-Burke (1982). Jensen (1984) reprints a number of *Language Arts* articles on "reading/writing connections." An edited volume by Mason (1989) contains chapters claiming a "revolutionary" exploration of relationships between reading and writing in the 1980s. These discussions usually focus on "teaching reading and writing together" rather than on interactions between readers and writers or on what reading and writing might contribute to each other cognitively. Shanahan (1990) explicitly entitles an edited volume *Reading and Writing Together: New Perspectives for the Classroom.* See also Tierney and Shanahan (1991) and the useful bibliography in Barnhart (1993).

In an issue of *Language Arts* devoted to the topic, Tierney and Pearson (1983) discuss reading and writing as similarly creative "composing" activities and conclude that "what drives reading and writing is . . . desire to make sense of what is happening, to make things cohere." The discussion of the implicit contract between readers and writers that enables their expectations and intentions to meet in the conventions of the text is developed more fully, and more from the writer's point of view, in Smith (1994). Tierney and LaZansky (1980) also refer to the rights and responsibilities of readers and writers as "a contractual agreement." Eckhoff (1983) shows how children's reading influences what they write. If their primers contained "stories" in which each sentence was on a separate line, children wrote their own stories in the same way. If their reading was richer and more conventional, so was their writing. Calkins (1980) found that children learned more about punctuation from their reading than from instruction and used more punctuation as a consequence. The children also adopted stylistic features of the texts they read, such as beginning sentences with "And" or ending them with "too." For a general argument that children learn to write by reading, see Smith (1994). Stotsky (1983) documents how better (more experienced) readers tend to be better writers and to produce more "syntactically mature" writing. She also found, however, that studies that used writing as an exercise to improve writing had little effect on reading. She cites several studies showing that additional reading may be as good as, or even better than, grammar study in improving writing. Jaggar, Carrara, and Weiss (1986) also examine the mutual influence of children's reading and narrative writing; see also Hansen, Newkirk, and Graves (1985).

NOTES TO CHAPTER 11, LEARNING ABOUT THE WORLD AND ABOUT LANGUAGE, pp. 183–199.

Language Learning

Important discussions of the way in which meaning is the basis of language learning include Bloom (1973), Halliday (1975), and Nelson (1973, 1974). Bloom, Rocissano, and Hood (1976) elaborate on the contribution of adult-child dialogues to language learning, and Harper (1975) considers the manner in which children actually control adult behavior to make learning possible. Bruner (1975, 1978) argues that the origin of language in children lies in their joint activities with adults; for example, from four to six months they begin to follow the direction of their parent's gaze (Scarfe & Bruner, 1975), as well as showing signs of turn-taking. See also Moerk (1977) and Moskowitz (1978). Tough (1974) also stresses that children learn language through use, not through prescription or instruction.

Many researchers have looked at how mothers help babies to learn language, for example by "scaffolding" a meaning around the use of language (Ninio & Bruner,

1978). Shatz (1978) describes how infants understand what adults mean before they understand what they say—and thereby look as if they know more than they do. Clark and Hecht (1983) review research showing how comprehension precedes the production of language. Bridges, Sinha, and Walkerdine (1981) demonstrate how infants figure out the intentions of their mothers, taking into account the circumstances in which their mothers are talking, in order to understand what they are saying. Urwin (1982) describes how convergence of gaze becomes the basis for a shared frame of reference, and Wells and Nicholls (1985) consider shared activities. Nelson (1985) proposes that children learn primarily through being involved in meaningful "events" with adults. For a semiotic perspective, see Bates (1979).

Baby talk, which is spoken by adults, not by babies, is "finely-tuned" to help children to understand and to learn language, according to Snow (1977). She demonstrates that children make as important a contribution as mothers, who can't produce baby talk unless an infant is present to cue them to do so. Book reading elicits more complex speech by both mothers and children. Cross (1977) describes the critical adjustments made by mothers in order to converse with infants who can understand but have undeveloped language skills. The Snow and Cross papers are both in Snow and Ferguson (1977), a rich collection of research papers.

Children do not learn to talk by imitation, unless imitation is defined very specifically as the deliberate use of adult utterances on appropriate occasions to achieve the same ends as adults, when the utterances are already understood. For further discussion of the active and meaningful nature of imitation by children and of its utility as a research tool, see Bloom, Hood, and Lightbown (1974) and Slobin and Welsh (1973). Certainly adults do not usually babble (in the infantile sense), yet the roots of meaningful language can be detected in infant babbling (Weir, 1962). Krashen (1976) is an important article on the *unconscious* nature of language learning (he terms it acquisition).

On "metacognition"—or knowing whether and how you know something—see especially Flavell (1979) and A. Brown (1980, 1982). Flavell (1979) argues that children cannot monitor their own or other people's mental states very well and do not have a very good understanding of goals or tasks, actions, or strategies. Flavell, Speer, Green, and August (1981) tape-recorded children working on a building-block task and reported that the children not only did not understand the task but also did not understand that they were not communicating with each other adequately. But in a commentary on this study in the same monograph, Whitehurst raises the critical question of whether the children lack independent metacognitive skills or simply experience. Brown (1980) extends her analysis to the use of study time by good and poor readers, and their relative ability in such tasks as selecting "main ideas." Once again the "skills versus experience" question should arise, but Brown believes that older students can benefit from insights into the workings of their own memories. Derry and Murphy (1986) review efforts to train learning abilities in systematic ways and conclude "executive learning skills cannot be trained easily or by direct instruction alone, but must be developed gradually and automated over an extended period of time."

An excellent introduction to Piagetian thought on children's language learning, emphasizing that it can only be understood by taking into account what a child knows already, is available in Sinclair (1970) and Sinclair-de Zwart (1973). Important studies of infant learning abilities generally, before they even turn their attention to language, are described by T. Bower (1971, 1974), Fantz (1964, 1966), Kagan (1970), and Nelson (1985). At the other extreme, the importance of meaningfulness in second language learning is discussed by McLaughlin (1977), Fillion, Smith, and Swain (1976), and Krashen (1985).

More generally, the notion that the same principles underlie both comprehension and learning has been argued by Greeno (1974) and by Haviland and Clark (1974). Donaldson and Reid (1982) demonstrate that children are natural hypothesis-testers and rule users, with a strong drive and enormous ability to make sense of the world and of what people say—especially with the help of others. See also Donaldson's (1978) excellent book on children's thinking and learning, in which she argues that children can reason perfectly well if "logical" aspects of tasks are embedded in meaningful contexts.

There are many texts on the development of language in children, including R. Brown (1973), Slobin (1979), Bloom (1970), Gleason (1989), Chukovsky (1968), Menyuk (1971), and two books with an educational emphasis, Cazden (1972) and Dale (1976). Miller (1977) is a delightful short book on the ease with which children learn language and on the difficulty adults experience in trying to study them doing so. There are also a number of edited volumes containing important original chapters, including Collins (1979), T. Moore (1973), Olson (1980), and Smith and Miller (1966). Wood (1981) examines the development of both verbal and nonverbal communication in infants, and in an edited volume, Golinkoff (1983) brings together prominent psychologists, sociologists, anthropologists, and educators for a more theoretical look at the transition from "prelinguistic" to linguistic communication. Bain (1983) is an advanced volume examining many social aspects of the development of language and behavior generally. The more general argument that comprehension and learning are inseparable is in Smith (1990), and a more complete discussion of demonstrations, engagement, and sensitivity in Smith (1981a).

Vocabulary

In an intensive study, Carey (1978) estimates that six-year-olds have mastered (to some degree) an average of 14,000 words, noting that "this massive vocabulary growth seems to occur without much help from teachers." According to Carey, there is first a "fast mapping" when a child hypothesizes a probable general meaning for a new word. A gradual process of refining and adding "partial knowledge" of meaning ensues on successive encounters, with from four to ten encounters required for word learning to be "complete." Rice (1990) describes "QUIL"—quick incidental learning—with fast mapping often occurring when the word is first encountered, followed by a long period of refinement. The initial partial comprehension of a new word includes both meaning and syntactic role; it does not need explicit assistance from adults. In one 12-minute exposure to a specially produced animated television program, five-year-olds on average "picked up" the meanings of five test words like *gramophone, nurturant, viola, makeshift, malicious,* and *artisan* that occurred seven times each. Three-year-olds picked up an average of 1.5 of these words. Mandler (1992) analyzes how babies move from preverbal perceptions of different kinds of object to conceptions that can become language. Markman (1992) examines the assumptions that 2-year-olds appear to make in learning words concerning "whole objects," taxonomic relations, and mutual exclusivity. The word *dog* is likely to mean the whole animal, not a part of it or its color—the word is likely to apply to similar objects (a cat might be a dog, but not an umbrella), and objects will not have more than one name. A similar incremental learning assumption was adopted by Nagy and Anderson (1984) and Nagy, Herman, and Anderson (1985) who used a sophisticated technique for estimating the vocabulary growth of high school students. They concluded that the students were learning an average of 3,000 new words *every year*—mostly from reading—independently of whether direct vocabulary instruction was provided by the teacher. They estimated that fifth graders could encounter more than a million words a year, between 15,000 and 55,000 of which would be unknown. From empirically derived probabilities that something would be learned of these unfamiliar words on every encounter, they calculated that a "typical middle-grade student" would learn between 1,500 and 8,250 words a year, an average of 4,875. (See also Herman, Anderson, Pearson, & Nagy, 1987.) All of these researchers see reading as the primary source of vocabulary development, and great limitations to methods of teaching based on word lists and direct instruction.

White, Graves, and Slater (1990) studied the rate of vocabulary growth of students in Grades 1 to 4 in three diverse schools. Mainly white students who spoke "standard English" at a suburban school had an average annual increase of 5,200 words; by mid Grade 4 they knew an average of about 16,000 words out of a sample of 19,050. "Economically disadvantaged" students at an inner city school had an annual growth of 3300 words with a total by mid Grade 4 of 12,000. Similarly "economically disadvantaged" students at a semirural school in Hawaii, speaking mainly a Hawaiian creole, had an annual growth of 3,500 words to a total of 12,000. The authors reported that all groups were learning "at a rapid rate to impressive size," far more than could be attributed to direct instruction. Differences were attributed to dissimilar amounts of reading and language experience and were concentrated among the less frequent words. The authors concluded that phonics had limited value and that more reading was to be encouraged.

Nagy and Herman (1987) recalibrated earlier research results and calculated that the vocabularies of Grade 3 students ranged between 4,000 and 24,000 words, with a median of 10,000 and an annual growth between Grades 3 and 12 of from 2,000 to nearly 4,000 words, and a median of 3,500. For examples of earlier studies see M. Smith (1941), Templin (1957), and a review by Anglin (1980).

Children required to learn specific new words in contrived experimental contexts—typically artificial words embedded in half a dozen unrelated sentences—usually find the task difficult. McKeown (1985), for example, required 30 fifth graders to figure out the meaning of artificial words in short sentences like "Eating lunch is a narp thing to do," and found that good readers could accomplish the task, but not poor readers (although these presumably had difficulty in reading the sentences in the first place). She concluded that "the meaning-acquisition process" is complex and difficult, even for high ability readers. But this may be a case of what might be called the Laboratory Fallacy, which asserts that children who have difficulty on an artificially contrived learning (or comprehension or memory) task, will have similar difficulty in all situations. Schatz and Baldwin (1986) showed that "context cues" are not usually reliable predictors of word meaning—not in experimental situations where texts are brief and assembled in a contrived manner. The more naturalistic approach of Nagy and Anderson and their colleagues that I have just cited suggests a different conclusion, although the technique of embedding unfamiliar words in minimal context is common in laboratories and classrooms.

McKeown (1993) shows that conventional dictionary definitions hardly facilitate learning word meanings. They are often unnecessary, focusing on words and meanings that are either too common or too uncommon to require attention, and the examples given are often misleading. McKeown suggests alternatives that focus on *describing* in familiar language the circumstances in which the word is usually ("prototypically") used. Thus instead of defining *morbid* as "not healthy or normal," she proposes "showing a great interest in horrible gruesome details, especially about death"; and for *transitory*, instead of "passing soon or quickly, lasting only a short time" (which led to student sentences like "the train was transitory"), she suggests "describes a mood or feeling that only lasts a short time." McKeown observes that such changes still do not make the traditional method of looking up a word and writing a sentence a good way of building vocabulary. Miller and Fellbaum (1991) offer a detailed discussion of complex problems of definitions and dictionaries, and Schwanenflugel (1991) is an interesting edited volume on the psychology of word meanings.

Learning as a Social Event

Vygotsky (1978) succinctly explains the social nature of learning: "Every function in the child's cultural development appears twice, on two levels. First on the social, and later on the psychological level" (p. 57). He sees an interweaving of biological "elementary" processes and sociocultural "higher" functions, imposed neither from within nor from outside but mediated always by a dialectic between individual and society. All "higher" functions like memory, attention, and perception, develop from actual relations between people which become internalized. "For the young child, to think means to recall; but for the adolescent, to recall means to think." There is a "practical intelligence" before speech, but language plays an essential role in the development of higher mental functions—it enables children to become objects of their own behavior. Cairney (1990) has called for caution in the application of Bruner's concept of "scaffolding" and Vygotsky's concept of a "zone of proximal development" in classrooms, where they may be applied in authoritarian ways—a concern shared by Bruner (1986) himself. Cairney prefers actively immersing children in literature. Brown and Ferrara (1985) examine Vygostky's theories closely, noting that children perform better and learn better with adult assistance at the *upper* level of their ability.

Walkerdine (1982) makes similar arguments in a semiotic context. She holds that language, thinking, and "context" are not separate systems but are jointly related to a basic human need to know how signs of all kinds are interpreted. In a complex and subtle discussion, Walkerdine (who has some differences with Vygotsky) also proposes the centrality of metaphor in children's thought and learning. Urwin (1982) similarly argues that learning reflects social interaction, with a semiotic emphasis on the importance of "signs." Clark and Hecht (1983) look at the relation of understanding, speech, and learning.

Brown and Palincsar (1989) demonstrate that "comprehension-learning" is social; children learn how to understand texts through discussion with other readers. Krashen (1991) argues that most language learning is natural and unconscious if there is "comprehensible input" and little or no anxiety or defensiveness. Gallistel (1990) employs a connectionist model to argue that children learn language by analogy rather than by rules, relating language they don't know to language they do know.

Fiorito and Scotto (1992) demonstrate that even the common octopus can learn by watching another octopus being rewarded with a tidbit for attacking a submerged ball of a particular color.

Motivation

The role of motivation in learning needs perhaps to be clarified, especially because failure to learn is frequently attributed to lack of motivation. However, learning continually takes place in the absence of conscious motivation, for example, the effortless growth of vocabulary. And the presence of motivation does not guarantee learning. We have all failed to learn things we have been highly motivated to learn, on which we may have expended considerable effort and "time on task." Learning normally depends not on effort but on the demonstrations, collaboration, engagement, and sensitivity that I discussed in this chapter. Interest and expectation of learning are better predictors of learning than overt motivation. At best, motivation has the beneficial effect of putting learners into situations where demonstrations and collaboration are likely to be found. And of course, anyone motivated not to learn, or anticipating failure, is likely to find the expectation fulfilled.

NOTES TO CHAPTER 12, LEARNING TO USE WRITTEN LANGUAGE, pp. 201–219.

Learning to Read

Some of the most significant pathfinding research into children's developing understanding of literacy has been done not by educators or psychologists—who tend to look at individuals in isolation, or in a personal relationship to "knowledge"—but by sociologists and anthropologists. The edited volume of Goelman, Oberg, and Smith (1984) contains summaries and reviews of research into the social basis of preschool literacy by workers in a number of disciplines and also outlines the prevailing methodologies. The primary method of research is not experimental, but observational. *Ethnographic* is the technical term for such research, also called "naturalistic research," and (by Yetta Goodman, 1978, 1980) "kid watching." Two of the main findings of this research are that children in all cultures develop insights into the forms and functions of written language before school and that these insights are based on meaning and use. The research also shows that learning about reading cannot be separated from learning about writing. As the title of this chapter indicates, learning to be literate entails learning how written language is used.

The research has also made clear that children do not need to be economically privileged or the recipients of special kinds of instructional support in order to learn about reading and writing. Ferreiro (1978, 1985), for example, who demonstrated how three- and four-year-olds gain insights about letters, words, and sentences, did much of her work in the slums of Mexico City with children whose parents were illiterate. The fact that early readers have not necessarily had advantages is also made by M. Clark (1976) in her classic book on *Young Fluent Readers*, many of whom came from large poor families and were not "good risks" for reading instruction in school. Hall and Guthrie (1982) refer to the danger of the hypothesis that minority groups and the poor use language in ways that systematically put their children at a disadvantage at school. An alternative hypothesis might be that certain approaches to instruction systematically put such children at a disadvantage. Goodman (1970) has also pointed out that children are not taught to read by having their dialect changed or by being regarded as deficient in values, speech, or attitudes, just because these are culturally different.

What children learn and think about literacy is largely determined by the practices and attitudes of people around them (Heath, 1982a). In an article that includes a useful list of references up to 1982, Teale (1982) asks how children become able to read and write without formal training, and concludes "Social interaction is the key. Natural literacy development hinges upon the experiences the child has in reading and writing activities which are mediated by literate adults, older siblings, or events in the child's everyday life."

There is an extensive documentation of the remarkable ability of children to make sense of written language without formal instruction, including Goodman (1980), Hiebert (1981), Mason (1980), and Ylisto (1977). Excellent descriptions of children learning to read independently of instruction are provided by Bissex (1980), Clark (1976), Clay (1979), and Torrey (1979). Young children's sensitivity to language generally and their often underrated ability to learn from meaningful adult demonstrations are discussed and illustrated in Gelman (1979). For what teachers can learn from children who learn to read early, see Forester (1977). See also Durkin (1966). In a review giving many examples of children's literacy learning before and during early schooling, Harste, Woodward, and Burke (1984) note that by the age of three, children assume that print is meaningful—an insight acquired from experience rather than from instruction. McCartney and Nelson (1981) show that three-year-old children use "script-based organizations of knowledge" (their own narrative constructions) to understand and recall stories. *Emergent literacy* is a new term, employed in the titles of useful books by Hall (1987) and Teale and Sulzby (1986). For more on emergent literacy in the United States, see Strickland and Morrow (1989), and in Britain, Hall (1987). Dickinson, Wolf, and Stotsky (1989) trace children's movement into literacy from early involvement in environmental print—including "emotional attachment" to books as well as to the person reading them—into the functions and conventions of written language. Stotsky (1986) proposes that written language has a different course of development from speech because it is initially built on speech competence and is used for different purposes in different circumstances.

Clay (1992/1993) reports from extensive experience that the best preparation for literacy is learning to talk and to have many opportunities for conversation. She refers specifically to bilingual schools in New Zealand concerned with the survival of the Maori language, and gives several other international examples where children read to in preschool had improved reading and speaking abilities in later years. If no books are available, competent story tellers can prepare children for literacy learning. Clay notes that children under five years of age are "amazingly good" at learning and losing languages, depending on the opportunities they have to use them. The least complicated entry into literacy learning is to begin to read and write in the language already spoken. For further discussion of language policies and literacy learning in multilingual situations, see Elley and Mangubhai (1983) for the South Pacific and Smith (1993) for South Africa.

Proficiency in oral language is not a prerequisite for learning to read. Rottenberg and Searfoss (1992) show that hearing-impaired children in a mixed preschool class learn about literacy in the same ways hearing children do—without direct instruction—and also learn about the hearing world. Hartman and Kretschmer (1992) report that hearing-impaired teenage students also learn about reading by talking and writing about what they read. For a summary of research demonstrating that children with "special needs" do not learn to read and to write differently from other learners (though they may need more time) and do not require special kinds of instruction, see Truax and Kretschmer (1993).

Reading to Children

Reading to children is frequently recommended, although it is not always made clear what exactly the practice is expected to achieve. Obviously reading to children may interest them in stories (or whatever else is read to them) and also demonstrate the interest and utility that other people find in reading. But every occasion when a child is read to can also be a reading (and writing) lesson, an opportunity to learn more about the conventions and purposes of written language. Teale (1981) reviews research into parents' reading to children. Taylor and Strickland (1986) describe many family story-reading sessions and their benefits to children. Durkin (1984) studied 23 children of "average intelligence" who had frequently transferred schools, who became "successful readers" (reading above "grade level" by Grade 5). She found that the children had supportive parents who liked stories and read to them. Dombey (1988) also discusses children's movement into the nature of stories and into reading from hearing a story read. Eldredge (1990) shows that children learn more when they are helped to read—and therefore can read material that would otherwise be too difficult for them. Ollila and Mayfield (1992) discuss the importance of early reading experiences at home, especially being read to, and Kantor, Miller, and Fernie (1992) review the evidence that children learn to read and write naturally in real-life contexts.

In a review of reading research in the 1980s, Pearson (1993) notes that even researchers who believe "the code" (phonics) should be taught explicitly are quick to add that it should be accompanied by rich experiences with language and with stories. Pearson cautiously concludes "One is hard pressed to deny the importance of reading for improving reading. One is tempted to conclude that some of the best 'practice' for enhancing reading skill occurs when students are given greater opportunity to read everyday materials." In an important section of his review, Pearson observes that the instruction of "at risk" students seems to stifle their reading development. They "tend to receive a heavy dose of phonics instruction at all grade levels and very little of the 'print awareness' focus that is characteristic of the emergent literacy tradition. While noble in purpose, the consequence of differentiated instruction for low-track students has been devastating, particularly for children of diversity. Instruction in low-track classrooms emphasizes 'the basics' as stepping stones to higher order skills." He adds that such children still tend to receive similar treatment even if they make it into "average and high-tracks."

Heath and Thomas (1984) provide a fascinating case study of a teenaged, unemployed high school dropout mother of two (co-author Charlene Thomas) herself learning to read in the course of helping her children learn to read. Heath (1985) contributes another poignant biographical study of a parent helping a child learn to read and to think in describing how she helped her own 18-year-old daughter recover from traumatic head injuries after a mountain-climbing accident. In this article, Heath emphasizes the importance of opportunities to *talk about* literate matters in order to *remain* literate. Another of her many insightful contributions is an article entitled "What No Bedtime Story Means" (Heath, 1982b). Taylor (1983) describes how children learn to read and write in their families.

More generally, Wells (1981, 1985) examines the relationship between "pre-school related activities and success in school," noting also the importance of talking about what is read and written. He also discusses the relationship between parental reading practices and children's ideas of literacy and subsequent success in school. Once again, Vygotsky (1978) becomes relevant with his conception of a "zone of proximal development" where children do things with assistance which they will soon be able to do for themselves. For more on Vygotsky and education, see Moll (1990).

Literacy and Schooling

The fact that children often learn so much before school and that cultural influences are so important does not release schools from responsibility or provide convenient justification for failures of instruction. If children have not received adequate environmental support for embarking upon literacy, then schools must provide it. The ethnographic research shows clearly the collaborative conditions under which learning to read and write takes place. If parents fail to read to children, it is all the more important that teachers read to them.

Sulzby (1985) discusses how kindergarten children, some as young as four and a half, begin to make sense of stories, from commenting on pictures to telling a story which gains more and more fidelity to the text. There was always a story behind the children's comments—and the children's versions of the story always made sense. McMahon (1983) showed that even first grade children have little difficulty—and enjoy—coordinating a text they are looking at and a tape-recorded voice reading the text. For a general, research-based review of many aspects of literacy and school, see the edited volume by Raphael (1986).

Intelligence has never been found to be an important factor in learning to read, although reading appears to contribute significantly to intelligence. Stanovich, Cunningham, and Feeman (1984) found only a low relationship between intelligence and reading ability in first-grade children. The correlation was higher by fifth grade, and the researchers attributed the increase to "reciprocal causation." They also found that children who quickly learned to read read well through life, indicating the importance of avoiding obstacles, irrelevancies, and confusions in a child's early experiences with literacy.

The influence of instruction on children's behavior has been well documented. Research on how children learn to read rarely remains uncontaminated by the influence that prior instruction has already had on them. Barr (1972, 1974) has written seminal papers on the effect of instruction on children's reading. Downing and Oliver (1973/1974), and Jenkins, Bausel, and Jenkins (1972) all report on effects of early reading instruction on children. Holdaway (1976) comments on the importance of self-correction for children learning to read and on the risk that some instructional techniques take this responsibility away from them. Eckhoff(1983) was cited in the previous chapter for demonstrating that what children read is revealed in their writing. Juel and Roper/Schneider (1985) report that what children read also shows up in how they read. In particular, texts made up of "decodable" regular words produced children whose main strategy in reading was to sound out unfamiliar words. DeFord (1981) reaches a similar conclusion.

MacGinitie and MacGinitie (1986) argue that an emphasis on "mechanics" in the primary grades teaches students not to read, and they note a deemphasis on extended writing, literature, and "content-rich reading" in high school. When students have difficulties with a text, teachers respond (or ask other students to respond) rather than bringing students back to the text. In a painstaking book-length analysis of British practices, Hull (1985) shows how the written and spoken language used in reading instruction and in content areas at all grade levels is frequently totally incomprehensible to students. He is particularly scathing when textbook or examination questions include words and phrases that students do not understand (because of their ambiguity or vacuous definitions) and complaints are then made that the students cannot read. Hull's book is published in Britain. His occasional use of Anglicisms like "lower school" (junior high) and "sixth form" (twelfth grade) will illustrate for North American teachers his point that one does not have to be ignorant or learning disabled to be confused by unfamiliar uses of common words. MacGinitie (1984), in an article entitled "Readability as a Solution Adds to the Problem," reports that attempting to "simplify" texts by making them conform to formulas restricting word and sentence length can make them more difficult to read. Pearson (1974/1975) notes that comprehensibility is not improved in early reading books by fragmenting sentences and reducing grammatical complexity, a point made in other ways by Shuy (1981) and by Gourley (1978). Furness and Graves (1980) demonstrate experimentally that emphasis on accuracy (in oral reading) can actually reduce comprehension, just as an emphasis on correct spelling will inhibit children's writing. Paradoxically, both emphases result in less learning of what is supposed to be the object of the correction. Children reluctant to make mistakes will rarely venture beyond what they know already. Hiebert (1983) takes a critical look at ability grouping.

Salmon and Claire (1984) made a two-year study of four comprehensive (secondary) schools in Britain and found that classroom collaboration, both socially and in "learning," between teachers and students and among students, resulted in better student understanding of the curriculum. Chambers, Jackson, and Rose (1993) conducted a careful analysis and evaluation of a large scale collaborative reading project in five inner-city schools that has attracted a great deal of interest in Britain—concerned with new abilities developed by teachers as well as students as a result of reflective reading, group work, and lots of talk and discussion. Significantly, although all students in the primarily 8–13-year age group gained in reading ability compared with similar students in other schools, by far the greatest gains were made by students identified as "low achievers"—an unusual and important consequence. The evaluation is discussed in more detail in Gorman, Hutchison, and Trimble (1993).

The "apprenticeship" approach to teaching reading in the United Kingdom is described by Waterland (1988). Johnston (1989) reviews British programs involving parents with their children's reading. On the other hand, Wray and Lewis (1992) report that students in British primary schools have limited experience of using books for informational material, as opposed to fiction, and when they do consult a book to "find something out," they tend to write down what they read, changing the words a little because they have been told not to copy. Goldenberg (1991) discusses the "print-drenched" atmosphere of early primary classrooms in New Zealand, with reading and writing beginning on the first day of school.

Willinsky (1990) distinguishes a view of literacy as a set of skills taught piecemeal in educational institutions from literacy as a social process, "making something of the world." He describes many attempts to "reshape the classroom" from a place of formal instruction to a place where literacy is experienced and learned through experience, which he terms the *New Literacy* and examines from historical, social, and political as well as educational perspectives. He stresses the importance of both individual voice and collaborative effort—among students and among teachers—rather than the following of timetables and agendas of others. Even where researchers have recognized the importance of active participation in literacy by the learner, he says, it is adopted as an extension of technological models of instruction. de Castell and Luke (1986) protest that "North American educators have come to see literacy as a set of context-neutral, value-free skills that can be imparted to children with near-scientific precision," and examine social and historical antecedents of this view. Courts (1991) contains a bitter attack on the skills approach to the teaching and testing of literacy (and thinking). See also Edelsky (1991) and Myers (1992) for the importance of "contexts," in school and outside, for literacy.

Mikulecky (1982) compared reading in school that was supposed to prepare students for the workplace and reading in various occupations. He found that students read less often and less competently than most workers on the job, though the students read easier material to less depth.

Books are often overrated in research and practice. Books have no unique or essential properties for literacy learning, and they are not always the easiest texts to read. Newspapers and magazines often contain material that can attract the attention of the smallest children, depending upon their interests and mood. Krashen (1987) reviews the research on comics, showing that they can be highly productive materials for developing reading interests and ability, and also that comics frequently have rich vocabularies and conceptual content.

Teachers and Programs

Atkinson (1974) exemplifies the not uncommon view that computers can teach children to read, even though the objectives are typically limited and the theory of reading underlying such programs is rarely evident or adequate. The twenty-year-old prophecy remains to be fulfilled. Jonathan Anderson (1984) surveyed commercially available computer software for language and reading in the United States, Britain, and Australia and concluded that up to 95 percent is concerned with drills and computer-managed activities. Carroll and Chall (1975) edited a report of the Committee on Reading of the U.S. National Institute of Education, discussing the research that was available or required to take advantage of modern technology and produce universal literacy. In a review of the Carroll and Chall book, Olson (1975) notes that not one of the contributing researchers queried the underlying assumption that technology could eradicate illiteracy. Eisner (1982) criticizes the idea that improved techniques and tighter evaluation will increase learning. For a general discussion of how language instruction can be fragmented into absurdity, see Shannon (1983, 1986) and Smith (1981b, 1986).

"Whole language" is the instructional philosophy that reflects most consistently the view that meaning and "natural language" are the basis of literacy learning. Kenneth and Yetta Goodman are the theorists most closely identified with the origin and development of the whole language approach. Many TAWL (Teachers Applying Whole Language) groups have been established, especially in the United States and Canada. K. Goodman (1986) sums up the whole language view:

> Many school traditions seem to have actually hindered language development. In our zeal to make it easy, we've made it hard . . . primarily by breaking whole (natural) language up into bite-size, but abstract little pieces. We took apart the language and turned it into words, syllables, and isolated sounds. Unfortunately, we also postponed its natural purpose—the communication of meaning—and turned it into a set of abstractions, unrelated to the needs and experiences of the children we sought to help. (p. 7)

Whole language's opposition to phonics and to direct instruction has aroused passionate feelings on both sides and confusion elsewhere, which I shall discuss in the final section to this chapter.

In *Report Card on Basal Readers*, Goodman, Shannon, Freeman, and Murphy (1988) criticize from a whole language point of view unnatural language and behaviors in the production and use of basal readers. Basal readers, they say, demonstrate a lack of trust in teachers, who are consequently "deskilled." Basal author Baumann (1992) responds with a defense of the books and a denial that they deskill teachers. Shannon (1993), in a polemical rejoinder, asserts that basal readers are not the direct cause of the deskilling of teachers, but part of a general capitalist *rationalization* of society over the past 150 years to limit human unpredictability and independence in favor of scientific, technological, and business principles of materials, products, processes, and control. Shannon draws upon the "critical sociological theories" of Weber, Marcuse, and Illich to characterize basals as part of a "blueprint for scientific management" under which "educational scientists, teacher educators, and school officials sought to rationalize schooling through centralized planning, analyses of teaching tasks to their elemental parts, detailed directions for teachers on how to follow those plans according to that analysis, and intricate accountability systems for instructional outcomes." See also Shannon (1989) and Smith (1986). Harste (1989) says that teachers follow basal-like instructions in classrooms even in the absence of basal readers. Amsterdam, Amman, and Simons (1990) asked first graders to repeat segments of varying lengths from controlled vocabulary basals and rewritten "more natural" forms to see which was closer to "their own" language, and thus presumably easier to read. The children did better with the latter—sometimes making segments from the basals more syntactically complex.

The whole language movement and the theory and research underlying it do not always receive their due. *Becoming a Nation of Readers*, the report of the National Academy of Education's Commission on Reading (Anderson, Hiebert, Scott, & Wilkinson, 1985) was castigated in the following manner by the editor of the International Reading Association's Annual Review of Reading Research (Weintraub, 1986):

> There's no guarantee that the big name is synonymous with quality. Even when well-funded and headed by a blue ribbon committee, a supposedly comprehensive review may be narrowly based, considerably less than comprehensive, and biased in its election of what is included and what is excluded. . . . I happen to concur that a very selective body of literature was included and some rather critical research excluded. (p. vi)

Davidson (1988) presents alternative points of view to *Becoming a Nation of Readers*, and Weaver (1988) also questions its objectivity and representativeness.

"Reading recovery" is an early intervention tutoring program devised by Clay (1985), in which children who have not "caught on" to reading after a year spend about three months getting extra help—reading entire books but also taking "temporary instructional detours" at relevant times—in "concentrated encounters" with specially trained teachers; see also Pinnell (1989) and a chapter by Clay and Cazden in Cazden (1992). Wasik and Slavin (1993) contains a useful detailed description and review of reading recovery and three other tutoring programs. Huck (1992) describes how concern with whole language has led to a growth of "literature-based" teaching, summarizing the approach and its advantages. McGee (1992) also provides a historical review of the "literature-based reading revolution" showing that younger readers are capable of quite sophisticated responses to stories. See also Morrow (1992), Meek (1988), and the discussion of a literature-based reading program which earned the International Reading Association's outstanding dissertation award for 1991–1992 (McMahon, 1992). The term "literature" in this context usually refers to books written especially for children. It has also become a buzz word used extensively by educational publishers. Tierney and Shanahan (1991) note that children who write more are more enthusiastic and competent readers, and Atwell (1987) describes an influential literature-based approach to teaching reading and writing. Alternative views on "reading and writing connections" are included in Mason (1989). There is growing recognition of the importance of self-image in learning and therefore on the relationship between teachers and students. Salmon (1988) looks at the complexities of motivation, "underachievement," and teacher-student relationships, and the impossibility of "standardization."

For social aspects of literacy and learning, see Ong (1982), Levine (1986), and several chapters in Olson, Torrance, and Hildyard (1985). Margaret Meek Spencer (Meek, 1982, 1984) is insightful on social aspects of literacy instruction. See also Meek, Armstrong, Austerfield, Graham, and Plackett (1983) regarding a not always encouraging and successful struggle to help adolescents to read. Atwell (1987) also examines teaching reading and writing to adolescents. For articles based on Yetta Goodman's concept of "kid watching" (more formally, teachers as researchers), see Jaggar and Smith-Burke (1985). An excellent compendium of research in reading and writing (termed "comprehension and composition") is Squire (1987). Hedley and Baratta (1985) contains important articles on reading, learning, and thinking generally, including ethnographic research. Tuman (1987) examines social attitudes toward reading and reading instruction.

Krashen (1985) examines the evidence and arguments that both spoken and written language are learned only by comprehension. He also examines the emotional blocks that can stand in the way of such learning. In "Learning to Read at Forty-Eight," Yatvin (1982) shares insights gained in belated efforts to learn to read Hebrew.

In addition to their interests (what they like to read about), children have their preferences—to read alone or in groups, for long or short periods, at particular times of day, with or without supervision. The best way to find out is to ask them or to observe them. A formalized characterization of "reading styles" and "learning styles" has been constructed by Carbo, Dunn, and Dunn (1987). For a discussion of this, and of other matters concerning instruction and teacher behavior from a generally whole language point of view, see Weaver (1988).

In the introductory chapter to the book *What Research Has to Say About Reading Instruction*, in a paragraph entitled "Teachers, You Have a Lot to Learn," Otto (1992) discusses dilemmas facing teachers, including the fact that there is already more reading research than a practitioner could sort out in a lifetime (with more coming faster than anyone could read it). But much of the research and argumentation is repetitious; it is not so difficult for teachers to find out what the research—and the issues—are about. The real dilemma is having to come to a decision. Kutz (1992) offers brief notes and a helpful bibliography on research by teachers, finding their own answers to questions.

Important journals related to reading research are the International Reading Association's *Reading Research Quarterly* and the National Council of Teachers of English's *Language Arts*. Significant annual volumes are the International Reading Association's *Annual Review of Reading Research* and the National Reading Conference's Yearbooks.

Metalinguistic Awareness

The notes to the previous chapter included references related to the general role of metacognition in learning—the awareness of one's own thought processes. Metalinguistic awareness is metacognition specifically related to linguistic matters, particularly (in the case of reading and writing) to the nature of written language. It is not clear that such awareness plays an important role in learning, or indeed, that such awareness can take place until after learning has occurred. It is difficult to see how terms like "letter," "word," and "sentence" can have any meaning to anyone who cannot read. Many people able to converse fluently cannot say what the difference is between nouns and verbs, or active and passive sentences, not to mention verbalizing the complexities of transformational grammars and the conventions of cohesion. Nevertheless, some theorists not only feel that metalinguistic understanding is essential for learning to read, but they define learning to read in terms of such understanding. Mason (1980) for example, in an article entitled "When do children begin to read?", associates reading with realizing that letters are discriminable patterns related to sounds. Downing (1970) found that the words *word* and *sound* were poorly understood by five-year-olds, who thought for example that "fish and chips" could be one word and that the word *sound* could be used for a variety of noises (which is of course true in normal circumstances). One implication of confusion of this kind might be that time is wasted that is spent talking about reading rather than actually helping children to read. Downing, Ollila, and Oliver (1975) discovered not surprisingly that there were cultural differences in children's "concepts" of reading and writing. They found that 72 Indian kindergarten children knew less than 92 non-Indian children about "the technical language of literacy." The difference is obviously attributable to differences (though not necessarily defects) in experience rather than instruction. The authors use typical but unfortunate evaluative language for such differences, remarking of the Indian children that "their concepts of the communicative function of reading and writing were significantly immature" and "their perception of phonemes was significantly less well developed."

In their introduction to an edited book on metalinguistics, Downing and Valtin (1985) note:

> During the 1970s there was a rapid increase in metacognition and metalinguistics ... For educators these developments presented a glittering array of new ideas that promised to throw light on children's thinking processes in learning how to read ... However, the variety of independent theoretical approaches and their accompanying terminologies has been somewhat confusing. (p. v)

In the same volume, Downing (1985) argues that reading can be broken down into subskills that require deliberate training and "task awareness," and Ehri (1985) emphasizes spelling instruction as a way to make children aware of the relation between words they hear and words they see. Metacognitive and metalinguistic theorists typically emphasize relationships of sound and spelling in reading rather than meaning. They also stress the role of cognitive *strategies*.

A. Brown (1982), for example, discusses "self-regulatory strategies" that contribute to "learning how to learn from reading," including predicting, planning, checking, and monitoring knowledge of one's own abilities. Metacognitive strategies in reading are also discussed extensively in Forrest-Pressley and Waller (1984). Brown cites extensive documentation that better readers are more efficient and effective at such tasks, though there is always the chicken-and-egg problem of whether the competence produces better readers or that experienced readers naturally gain more competence. She relates her notion of "autocritical skills" to aspects of Vygotsky's (1978) socialization theory—that collaboration provides criticism and other cognitive resources which are then internalized. Lack of such collaboration is sometimes attributed to "disadvantaged homes," for example by Feuerstein, Jensen, Hoffman, and Rand (1985), who assert that such children from such backgrounds suffer "mediational deprivation." Brown herself contrasts "disadvantaged" with middle-class children on metacognitive competences. However, she also notes that teachers treat good and poor readers differently. Shannon (1984, 1985) has reviewed a mass of research indicating that schoolchildren who are identified as poor readers, or likely to be poor readers, do less reading, less interesting reading, more difficult reading, more exercises, and receive less assistance than other children. Hiebert (1983) looked at the consequences of ability grouping and also found that more able readers get the most meaningful reading with an emphasis on meaning, while the others received a greater emphasis on accuracy (which of course makes reading more difficult). See also Stanovich (1986) on the "Matthew effect" (that the rich get richer) in reading. Stanovich acknowledges that the main reason good readers get better is the differential treatment they receive in school (but as a believer with Gough and Hillinger (1980) that reading is an "unnatural act," he favors "surgical strikes" of specific skill instruction for children with problems). Metacognitive instruction tends to become a matter of more questions in preset sequences, or more drills, before reading actually begins, according to Langer (1982a, 1982b).

Further evidence that teachers get back what they teach is provided by Mosenthal (1983), who found that teachers who concentrated on a single text and right answers got student responses showing little sign of prior knowledge or other reading. Teachers who encouraged broader thinking got more extensive and reflective responses. See also Allingston (1980) on the way in which teachers interrupt during primary-grade oral reading. Anderson, Mason, and Shirey (1984) looked closely at "reading groups" in the primary grades and concluded "There is a cornucopia of evidence that could be cited to support a stress on meaning in the reading group," compared with an emphasis on accurate oral reading. The article is a concise, readable outline of the general and educational research supporting the view that people learn and remember more when conditions require them to understand the material. The authors term this "the law of meaningful processing."

Dyslexia and Learning Disabilities

Of the allocation of blame for children's failure to learn to read there is no end. Guthrie (1973) offers one of many surveys of various systems for characterizing the disabilities of children who seem unable to capitalize on the resources available to modern reading pedagogy. Such children are frequently labeled "learning disabled," a diagnosis that is vigorously criticized by Glenn (1975) and Hart (1976). Serafica and Sigel (1970) note that some "reading disabled" children have superior visual discrimination to normal readers.

Staller (1982) reviews research on the relationship between neurological impairment and reading disability and concludes that it is not yet possible to relate dyslexic behavior to specific neurological correlates. Berninger and Colwell (1985) studied 241 children aged between ages 6 and 12 identified as having no problem, a possible problem, or a definite problem in reading—and could find no support for the use of neurodevelopmental and educational measures in the diagnosis of specific learning disabilities. Dorman (1985) criticizes research that defines or diagnoses dyslexia, because there is no agreement on what would constitute neurological evidence of neurological dysfunction in relation to reading. He concludes that "insistence upon the inclusion of [central nervous system] dysfunction in the definition and diagnosis of dyslexia seems to be putting the cart before the horse, in the sense that the neurological basis of any or all developmental reading disorders remains hypothetical." Lipson and Wixson (1986) also review reading disability research and conclude that it must "move away from the search for causative factors within the reader and toward the specification of the conditions under which different readers can and will learn." Rather than accepting deficit explanations for reading problems, Wong (1982) proposes metacognitive factors, such as inadequate self-monitoring and self-questioning (in other words, attention to the meaning of what is read). Calfee (1983) says that dyslexia ought to be viewed as a problem with the development of the mind (i.e., experience) rather than a disease of the brain. Vellutino (1987) found no evidence that dyslexia is due to a visual deficit, nor to support remediation based on exercises to improve visual perception. He adds "In any case, not enough is yet known about how the brain works to enable anyone to devise activities that would have a direct and positive effect on neurological functions responsible for such basic processes as visual perception, cross-modal transfer and serial memory." Instead he recommends lots of assisted reading.

Johnston (1985) examined three case studies of adult reading disability and found "overwhelming feelings of inadequacy and confusion," anxiety, rational and irrational use of self-defeating strategies, conflicting motives, and inappropriate attributions of cause and blame, all going back to the individual's earliest reading experiences. Clay (1979) suggests that children become reading failures by learning the wrong things. Downing (1977) argues that society creates reading disabilities, for example, by artificially establishing "critical periods" for learning and through inappropriate expectations and stereotypes. Graham (1980) shows that "learning disabled" readers may have the same word recognition skills as children who are succeeding. Individual differences always occur, of course. Some people will find it harder to learn to read than others, but not because they have special "problems." Bryant and Impey (1986) conclude that there is no essential difference between dyslexics and normal readers—dyslexics simply are at the lower end of the scale of readers. They do nothing different from normal readers except have more difficulty. For a discussion of dyslexia from a phonological coding point of view, see Rack, Snowling, and Olson (1992). In a careful examination of thirty years of research into reading failure, Hamill and McNutt (1981) could find no relationship to intelligence, perceptual or motor abilities, reasoning or even affective factors, and only a marginal correlation with spoken-language ability. Patterson (1981) reviews neuropsychological approaches to reading generally.

The consequences of reading failure are rarely adequately stressed. Reichardt (1977) talks of children "playing dead or running away" from reading situations, defensive reactions among "reading handicapped students" whose physiological responses to reading ranged from complete apathy to hypertension. More generally, Seligman (1975) discusses "learned depression" (due to lack of control over failures) and "learned laziness" (due to lack of control over rewards), both consequences of situations where the learner lacks control and understanding. Coles (1987) warns of the misuse, overuse, and dangers of the term "learning disabled." For descriptions of how "at-risk" students and their teachers can learn from each other in linguistically and culturally diverse classrooms, see Heath, Mangiola, Schachter, and Hull (1991), and Truax and Kretschmer (1993). See also Atwell (1991).

Despite all the conjectures, it should not be surprising that no one has actually succeeded in finding a specific reading center or system in the architecture of the brain. Literacy has not existed as a cultural phenomenon long enough for the brain to develop specialized reading processes. One might just as meaningfully suggest areas of the brain dedicated to cycling or sewing. It has been known for over 100 years that one side of the brain (nine times out of ten the left) is essential for the production and comprehension of language (except in infants, whose brains are much more labile). But this asymmetry does not mean that only one side of the brain is involved in language. All thinking activities involve the entire brain. Different people obviously have different preferences—some like listening to music and others would rather look at pictures—but this does not mean that they lack parts of their brains. Looking at pictures, listening to music, and reading and writing involve experience, knowledge, and feelings and cannot be restricted to one area of the brain. It is a naive interpretation of neurological, language, and learning research to imagine that reading can be learned only with the left side of the brain or with the right.

Evaluation, Testing and Standards

Testing, evaluation, and the setting of "standards" exercise great control over what teachers do in classrooms and can have lasting consequences on learners, driving the curriculum and emphasizing skills which can be taught and tested by prescription. Although many teachers express alarm over evaluation and standardization, especially when imposed upon them (and when results are publicized), a number of prominent teachers and teacher organizations have become associated with such efforts. For example, the International Reading Association and the National Council for Teachers of English joined forces with the federally funded Center for the Study of Reading in October 1992 to develop national standards (in the United States) for reading, the language arts, and English. While acknowledging diversity, it was expected that the standards would define "a common core of what is valuable in the teaching and learning of English" and reduce the "contention in the discipline," for example, over the role of phonics and the value of recommended reading lists. In announcing funding, Secretary of Education Lamar Alexander observed "If our students can't read a newspaper, write a persuasive letter, or communicate clearly with their peers, they can't succeed in today's global economy" (reported in *Reading Today*, December 1992/January 1993, *10*, 3, pp 1, 7). It was not explained how such inadequacies might be caused by an absence of standards among teachers.

Hiebert and Calfee (1992) discuss the assessment of literacy, from standardized tests to portfolios, noting the growing public demand for assessment to drive instruction and policy decisions. They refer to concern about the deprofessionalization of teachers and discouragement of students and conclude that teachers are the best judges concerning instructional decisions. D. Moore (1983) and Heath (1983) discuss naturalistic methods of assessment in reading instruction. Mayher and Brause (1986) propose that testing may often cripple language education, through pressures on children and control of teachers, while not being closely related to learning to read and write. In a book entitled *Learning Denied*, Taylor (1991) relates a dramatic example of the disruption that can occur in a child's life—in addition to the anxieties and conflicts of the teacher and the parents—as a result of testing and "early diagnosis." Giroux (1992) discusses how the testing movement ignores successful local knowledge in favor of trained "leadership," marginalized teachers, and standardization. In a concise historical review and critique of the testing movement, VanLeirsburg (1993) reports that 148 standardized reading and achievement tests have been published since 1910 and only 34 have gone out of print; the remainder are presumably still in use.

Movement away from educational research based on experimentation, tests, and numeric analyses toward more descriptive "ethnographic" studies has not proved easy for university students or staff. In an article entitled "A Crack in Time," Collins and Collins (1992) discuss the experience of a doctoral student in an institution moving with some confusion from one kind of research to the other.

The Interminable Controversy

In Smith (1992) I contend that the "never-ending debate" between advocates of whole language and those of direct instruction (or "code emphasis") will never end because it is not something that research or experimentation will resolve, or indeed that partisans are ever likely to change their minds about. The disagreement is fundamentally a dispute over whether teachers can and should be trusted to teach and learners trusted to learn. Nothing I can add at this point could adequately summarize the arguments of either side, let alone reflect the fervor involved. As I noted in the Introduction, two of the original protagonists in the dispute were still vigorously contending with each other after 25 years, in presentations transcribed in the International Reading Association newsletter *Reading Today*. Their different approaches are exemplified in their titles: Chall (1992/1993) chooses "Research Supports Direct Instruction Models" and Goodman (1992/1993) "Gurus, Professors, and the Politics of Phonics."

While acknowledging that the two approaches have a similarity of goals, Chall detects major theoretical differences: "Whole language proponents tend to view learning to read as a natural process, developing in ways similar to language [she means *spoken* language]. Therefore, like language, most whole language proponents say it is not necessary to teach reading directly. Direct instruction models, on the other hand, view reading as needing to be taught, and taught systematically." She cites the existence of many illiterate individuals as evidence that reading is not "natural" and needs to be taught, adding: "Generally, direct instruction models favor the systematic teaching and learning of the relationships of sounds and symbols. This goes under many names—phonics, decoding, phonological awareness, word analysis, word attack, phonetic analysis, sound-symbol relations, etc. Whole language, on the other hand, tends to underplay phonics. . ."

Whole language, she proposes, views reading as primarily a "language-cognitive process" (citing Goodman, 1986) while direct instruction models stress the relationship of print to spoken language. Which of the two models produces the better results? "The evidence from research is that . . . students exposed to direct instruction models achieve more at the same age and grade. The advantage is particularly strong for students 'at risk'—students from low-income families and those disposed to having reading and learning disabilities." She cites rises and falls in national assessment scores which she relates to relative emphasis placed by schools on "basic skills" at different times, and innumerable research studies, compiled and summarized in a number of sources including her classic book (Chall 1967), an article (Chall, 1989), and a book by Adams (1990). Chall concludes with a caution: "It is possible to overdo a good thing. Thus, if students get only direct instruction, they will not grow as they should because they will not read and write enough. And if whole language students do only whole language; they will miss out on learning the skills and strategies that will help them grow."

Goodman begins by asserting that whole language is "a broad, fundamental revolution in education" and that opposition to it is politically based. He says that reducing whole language "to a method of reading which is simply the opposite of an approach that stresses phonics trivializes the broad nature of this revolution." "Whole language . . . is whole, so it does not exclude phonics from reading." Because he does not regard phonics as the issue, Goodman declines to debate it and instead focuses on "why Jeanne Chall and others choose to frame the revolution in education over whether to use whole language or phonics in teaching reading." He says that "her words and her name are used by those outside the research community—including the far right—who focus on reading as a simple means of attacking public education. They quote Chall to support their claim that whole language is a conspiracy to deprive children of literacy. . . ." Goodman provides examples of attacks on whole language, in the media and in Congress, that often mistakenly conflate it with "look-say" and other "methods" of teaching reading, blaming it for illiteracy, confusion in classrooms, and even a serious public health problem, and frequently citing Chall as the authority for the condemnation of whole language and the desirability of phonics.

Goodman concludes by claiming that half a century of research about how reading and writing work, and how they are learned, supports the whole language point of view, and summarizes "a series of substantial disagreements" between himself and Chall: "We disagree on the nature of the reading and writing processes; we disagree on how kids learn to read and write; we disagree on the existence of . . . research that underlies whole language; we disagree on the ability of teachers to use their knowledge to make their own professional decisions; we even disagree on what we disagree about.

Goodman's argument that the whole language issue is a political debate is set out more fully in an article (Goodman, 1992) entitled "Why Whole Language is Today's

Agenda in Education." He cites the rapid and spontaneous growth among teachers of hundreds of local whole language support groups; capacity crowds of thousands at whole language conferences; educational change "from the ground up" as teachers employ whole language approaches in their classrooms without the permission or encouragement of school authorities; a boom in sales of children's books and concomitant decline in sales of basal readers; modification and demystifying of testing methods; and a concerted attack by the "far right" to combat the spreading influence of whole language. The name itself, and the movement attached to it, emerged from a new professionalism among North American teachers taking control of their own classrooms, rejecting "reductionist laboratory experiments . . . because they have better evidence in their own classrooms."

Language is frequently used as a blunt instrument in the debate. Advocates of whole language tend to see phonics and direct instruction as rigid, mindless, authoritarian, unfeeling, and inhuman procedures, while the whole language philosophy is seen by its opponents as unrealistic, unscientific, romantic, and anarchistic idealism, threatening to the maintenance of standards and teacher accountability. Everyone claims to have the best interests of children at heart. Goodman unwittingly provided a limitless supply of ammunition to his detractors in the title of one of his earliest publications when he characterized reading as "a psycholinguistic guessing game" (Goodman, 1967). It is frequently cited, always pejoratively. Another frequently used term—used by Goodman in his 1992/1993 title—is "guru." Proponents of direct instruction usually refer to their authorities as "researchers" or "scientists" and to the authorities of their opponents as "gurus," "radicals" or "fanatics" (with "trendy" a popular adjective among British politicians). For a critical review of the rhetoric of whole language, see Moorman, Blanton, and McLaughlin (1992), and for a critical description of the ways in which the term "whole language" is misunderstood and misused in classrooms, see Dudley-Marling and Dippo (1991).

Commissioned and funded by the U.S. Department of Education following a legislated request of Congress for an examination of the role of phonics in reading instruction, *Beginning to Read* by Adams (1990) is frequently referred to in the debate, with ardent approval by proponents of direct instruction and anathema by others. Adams cites arguments and research favoring and against teaching phonics; she acknowledges the difficulty and unnaturalness of breaking down speech into separate sounds and relating these sounds to spellings, how difficult and laborious phonics and word recognition instruction is for children before they are experienced readers, observes specifically that "spelling-sound relationships are not the basis of reading skills and knowledge" (p. 10)—and ends by "concluding" that the "symbol-sound system should be taught explicitly and early, together with phonemic awareness training." Dorothy Strickland and Bernice Cullinan, two members of a panel set up by the Center for the Study of Reading to advise the author, felt constrained to declare polite but firm disagreement in an Afterword published with the volume. They were particularly concerned by the emphasis on phonics, the references to children who have not yet begun to receive instruction as "pre-readers" rather than "emergent readers," the selection of studies, interpretation of research, and the amount of research that took place in decontextualized situations. For an interview with the author about the volume, see Robinson (1991).

Perfetti (1985) characterizes the whole language or "psycholinguistic approach" as a whole word approach, which is misleading if not incorrect because "whole word approach" typically refers to an instructional method of teaching words in isolation, in lists or on flashcards, which is far from the whole language position. Perfetti also refers to whole language as the meaning approach, adding "it is only fair to say" that such an approach is "short on specifics." He assumes that there *are* specifics that teachers need and should be given to direct their instruction. He argues that "high ability readers" are better at "decoding" than low ability readers, but high ability readers are better at everything than low ability readers, and children weak on decoding always have problems with instruction based on phonics. Another factor that particularly concerns Perfetti is *naming* something that is recognized, whether a face or a color, a letter or a word. Speed of naming rate is a distinguishing factor between high and low ability readers (Wolf, 1991)—but that does not mean that slow namers cannot read or need special treatment, only perhaps a little more patience.

Beck and Juel (1992) present typical arguments for an early need to decode—as a "tool" of reading, which they see as an alternative to "word attack" or "look-say" methods of learning by repetition. They call on substantial research support to assert that "letters correspond to the sounds in spoken language"—giving as examples *cat* and *fat*—and stress the importance of "segmentation" and "blending skills" for reading and for spelling. Schank (1982) claims he employed a similar approach in teaching his daughter and his computer to read. Ehri (1987; see also Ehri & Wilce, 1985) says that beginning readers may begin by identifying whole words on sight, but they will move from "visual cue processing" to "phonetic cue processing" in order to read larger number of words. Therefore, they argue, beginning readers should be made familiar with letters and their sounds, even perhaps before they have the opportunity to read words. It could also be argued, however, that it is the young readers' familiarity with words that enabled them to make sense of the instruction they were given about letters and sounds. The view is challenged by Stuart and Coltheart (1988). In a number of studies, Goswami (1986, 1990) has shown that children at the beginning of learning to read try to identify unfamiliar words through analogy. Ehri and Robbins (1992) argue that some "decoding skill" is required to read by analogy, for example, that *peak* may be read if *beak* is known provided the child knows a pronunciation for *p*. However, reading by analogy may also teach the pronunciation of certain letters, especially consonants in initial position. Also, despite the fact that studies of this kind are usually labeled "reading," they normally do not extend beyond the identification of words in isolation. Dreher and Zenge (1990) found that difficulty with any aspect of instruction in first grade—isolating "language segments," understanding reading as "a meaning-gathering process," and understanding terms used in instruction—was a significant predictor of reading and comprehension abilities in fifth grade.

Delpit (1988, 1991) is concerned that whole language fails to teach important conventions of written language (which she sometimes calls "skills") to empower nonmainstream students—assuming that conventions *can* be made explicit and usefully learned. Cazden (1992) cites Delpit's concern for "explicit instruction" in a discussion of teaching a "culture of power" to black children.

In a spirited attack on whole language from the phonological awareness point of view, Liberman and Liberman (1992) consistently (and not untypically) compare reading with talking, contending that the former is unnatural and difficult while the latter is natural and easy. (Gill, 1992, makes similar arguments.) But if any comparison between spoken and written language is to be made, it should be between the "receptive" or "understanding" behaviors of reading and listening or the "productive" behaviors of writing and speaking. The manner in which infants learn to understand print should be compared with the manner in which they learn to understand the spoken language that surrounds them—both are based on bringing sense to meaningful situations, and very little additional effort is required to use the eyes rather than the ears. Using the vocal apparatus is another matter, and whether it is easier to learn to reproduce the pronunciation of a word than its spelling is a moot point, but it has nothing to do with teaching reading. In another impassioned assault,

Thompson (1992) claims that whole language lacks evidence and has a philosophy of abandoning students. He objects to the enthusiasm which permeates whole language.

From the opposite point of view, Carbo (1988) criticizes many of Chall's analyses of research findings in an article entitled "Debunking the Great Phonics Myth," noting that despite a 20-year emphasis on phonics in American classrooms, at the time of writing the United States rated 49th in literacy out of 159 members of the United Nations and that New Zealand, which taught reading through a whole language approach, was ranked first. Chall (1989) is a response. There is another detailed critique of Chall's analyses of research and of the conclusions she draws in Weaver (1988), who questions the value of phonics. See also Sebasta (1981), Newman (1985), Taylor, Blum, and Logsdon (1986), and Morrow and Weinstein (1986). Goodman made several forceful counterattacks against hardline decoding critics over the years, notably Gleitman and Rozin (1973a, 1973b) in two issues of *Reading Research Quarterly* and against Mosenthal (1976/1977) in the same journal. Miller (1991) offers a friendly but pointed appraisal of the "whole language bandwagon," observing evangelism, polemics, exploitation, deification, and vagueness and noting the problem of finding a brief answer for people wondering what whole language is.

Carol Chomsky (1970), drawing extensively from her own experience and from the theorizing of Chomsky and Halle (1968), argues that spelling represents the underlying meaning structure of language rather than sound. She recommends an early introduction to writing (C. Chomsky, 1971, 1979) because it may help beginning readers make sense of phonics instruction—a view that should not be confused with the fallacious argument that children must be taught phonics to learn how to spell.

In view of the extensive and sometimes indiscriminate manner in which several of the publications included in this section are quoted, it may be relevant to note Cronbach's (1992) comment that large numbers of citations do not imply that an intended message has been widely understood and Fiske and Campbell's (1992) observation that citations do not solve problems. Vincente and Brewer (1993) remark that theoretical bias leads to misrepresentations in reading and citing original research—a bias that is increased as secondary sources are cited.

I conclude this section with two personal notes. My arguments about the limited value of phonics as a system for reading (and spelling) occasionally incite proponents of rigorous teaching methodologies to declare that I am "against phonics" or that I do not think children should learn phonics (e.g., Perfetti, 1985). But it is direct instruction, not phonics, that I reject. My only categorical proposition is that the memorization of spelling-sound correspondences as a prerequisite or alternative to reading can be a highly discouraging, disruptive, and pointless imposition on learners. But I do not suggest that the correspondences should be concealed from them. Particular correspondences and analogies might indeed be pointed out, on occasions when they happen to be helpful and relevant to the learner, when they facilitate reading rather than interrupt it. (These are the occasions when correspondences are most likely to be remembered.) All this is consistent with my conclusion that children should be *helped to read* rather than *taught about reading*.

Many of the arguments of successive editions of this book have been generally supportive of the whole language philosophy, and I am frequently identified as a proponent of whole language. Nevertheless, I have never called myself a whole language person, nor have I ever been prepared to offer a blanket testimonial for a whole language approach. I should perhaps explain my reluctance to embrace the label. (1) I dislike all labels and slogans, which I regard as open invitations for the cessation of thought. Once anything someone says or does is identified as whole language, there is no need to think further about what the person says or does; the person is pigeon-holed. I have heard teachers say they did whole language last year;

isn't there anything new? (2) I dislike all "methods" of teaching reading, and whole language, despite the best intentions of many of its adherents, has become a method. Experts talk about how to "do" whole language, whole language materials are produced, both for instruction and for assessment, and teachers look for whole language hints that they can introduce into their classrooms. Whole language becomes something that is done, not a way of thinking about children and learning. (3) Labels get stolen. People can call themselves "whole language teachers" while doing things totally alien to the underlying whole language philosophy. Worse, they can encourage or persuade other teachers to engage in certain practices without understanding what they are doing. (4) Movements become monolithic and fossilized. Whole language began as a resistance movement among individual teachers against instruction designed and dominated by people outside the classroom. Whole language was empowering. But when people argue for or against (or within) whole language on the basis of dogma rather than reason, its very *raison d'être* is subverted.

Glossary

This list does not attempt to define words as a dictionary does, but rather indicates the general way that certain terms are employed in this book. Figures in parentheses indicate the chapter in which a term was first used or primarily discussed. Terms in *italics* appear elsewhere in the glossary.

Aesthetic reading: Reading done primarily for experience; contrasted with *efferent reading* (3).

Artificial intelligence: The study of systems designed to emulate human language and thought with computer technology (preface).

Basics: See *skills learning*.

Cat and dog problem: Example of the fact that *distinctive features* cannot be explicitly taught but must be learned by the testing of *hypotheses* (11).

Category interrelationships: The various ways in which *cognitive categories* can be combined as a basis for *prediction* or action (1).

Channel capacity: Limit to the amount of *information* that can pass through any part of an information-processing system (3).

Cognition: A particular organization of knowledge in the brain, or the process of organizing such knowledge (1). See *cognitive structure*.

Cognitive categories: Prior decisions to treat some aspects of experience as the same, yet as different from other aspects of experience; the constantly developing framework of *cognitive structure* (1).

Cognitive questions: The specific information sought by the brain to make a decision among alternatives; the range of a *prediction* (1).

Cognitive science: An area of common concern in psychology, linguistics, and the design of computer systems, related to the manner in which knowledge can be acquired, stored, retrieved, and utilized (preface). See also *artificial intelligence*.

Cognitive structure: The totality of the brain's organization of knowledge; everything an individual knows (or believes) about the world. Comprises *cognitive categories, feature lists,* and *category interrelationships*. Also referred to as *long-term memory* and the *theory of the world* (1).

Comprehension: The interpretation of experience; relating new information to what is already known; asking *cognitive questions* and being able to find answers to them; a state, the absence of confusion (1).

Connectionism: A neo-associationistic theory that learning takes place when networks of "weighted" neural connections in the brain are formed or modified between "input" and "output" levels (representing stimuli and responses), and one or more interconnecting levels, without the need to hypothesize any sense, understanding, or "rules" behind the learning (2).

Constraint: The exclusion or reduced probability of certain alternatives; the mechanism of *redundancy* (3).

Context: The setting, physical or linguistic, in which words occur and that places constraints on the range of alternatives that these words might be (2).

Context-dependent language: Spoken or written language coherent within itself and not related to the concurrent physical situation in which it occurs (2).

Conventions: Arbitrary or accidental forms of behavior made meaningful by mutual understanding of and respect for their use and implications (2).

Criterial set: A set of *distinctive features* within a *feature list* that permits an *identification* to be made on minimal information from a given set of alternatives (7).

Criterion level: The amount of information an individual requires to make a particular decision, varying with the perceived uncertainty of the situation and the perceived risk and cost of making a mistake (3).

Decoding to sound: The view that reading is accomplished by transforming print into actual or subvocalized (implicit) speech through the exercise of *spelling-to-sound correspondences*. See also *phonological recoding* (8).

Declarative knowledge: See *propositional knowledge* (1).

Deep structure: The meaningful aspect of language; the interpretation of *surface structure* (2).

Demonstrations: Displays, by people or artifacts, of how something is done (11).

Direct instruction: An educational philosophy based on the belief that learning takes place most effectively when learners are told in specific detail what they should learn and are monitored closely to ensure that they do so (12). Frequently contrasted with *whole language*.

Discourse structure: Conventions concerning the organization of language, for example, turn-taking and interruption in speech, and paragraphing and repetition in texts (2).

Distinctive features: *Significant differences* among visual (or acoustic) patterns, that is, differences that make a difference. For reading, any aspect of *visual information* that permits distinctions to be made among alternative letters, words, or meanings (1, 3, 6). See also *feature lists*.

Distributional redundancy: Reduction of *uncertainty* because alternatives are not equally probable (6, 7). May exist in letters or words. See also *featural redundancy*.

Efferent reading: Reading done primarily for information; contrasted with *aesthetic reading* (3).

Engagement: The interaction of a brain with a *demonstration*; the act of learning (11).

Ethnographic research: Observation of behavior in natural contexts; nonintrusive research; also termed "naturalistic research"; contrasted with controlled experimentation (12).

Event knowledge: Hypothesized mental representations of patterns of behavior in specific events; clusters of related expectations. See *scheme* (1).

Expectations: See *prediction*.

Featural redundancy: In reading, *redundancy* among the *distinctive features* of print as a consequence of constraints upon letter or word occurrence (6, 7).

Feature analysis: A theory of pattern recognition proposing that visual configurations such as digits, letters, or words are identified by the analysis of *distinctive features* and their allocation to *feature lists*; in contrast to *template theory* (6).

Feature list: A cognitive specification or "set of rules" for particular combinations of *distinctive features* that will permit *identification* in reading (6).

Feedback: Information that permits a decision whether an *hypothesis* is right or wrong (appropriate or inappropriate) in *learning* (11).

Fixation: The pause for the selection of *visual information* as the gaze rests at one place in the text between *saccades* (4).

Functional equivalence: Specification of the same *cognitive category* by two or more *feature lists* (7).

Grammar: See *syntax*.

Grapheme: A letter of the alphabet, one of 26 alternatives (8).

Hypothesis: A tentative modification of cognitive structure (*cognitive categories, feature lists,* or *category interrelationships*) that is tested as a basis for *learning* (11).

Identification: In reading, a cognitive decision among letter, word, or meaning alternatives based on the analysis of selected *visual information* in print (6–9).

Immediate meaning identification: The *comprehension* of language without the prior identification of words (9).

Immediate word identification: The *identification* of a word on sight, without *information* from another person and without the prior *identification* of letters or letter combinations within the word (7).

Information: Any property of the physical environment that reduces *uncertainty*, eliminating or reducing the probability of alternatives among which a perceiver must decide (3).

Learning: The modification or elaboration of *cognitive structure*, specifically the establishment of new or revised *cognitive categories, category interrelationships,* or *feature lists* (11).

Letter-sound correspondence: See *spelling-to-sound correspondence*.

Lexical access: Computer-derived metaphor for making sense of words in reading or speech through reference to an internal *lexicon* (2).

Lexicon: A hypothesized mental store of knowledge about words, including their sound, spelling, and meaning. See *lexical access, logogen* (2).

Logogen: A theoretical construct for all the knowledge an individual has about a word; an entry in the internal *lexicon* (2).

Long-term memory: The totality of an individual's knowledge and beliefs, including summaries of past experience and ways of interacting with the world (5).

Mastery learning: See *skills learning*.

Meaning: A relative term; the interpretation that a reader places upon text (the answer to a *cognitive question*). Alternatively, the interpretation an author or third party expects a reader to place upon text. The consequences of *comprehension* (1).

Meaningful(ness): In reading, a text that is relevant to a reader's purpose, expectations and understanding.

Mediated meaning identification: An inferior alternative to *immediate meaning identification*, attempting to derive meaning by the prior identification of words (9).

Mediated word identification: A less efficient alternative to *immediate word identification*, requiring information from letters or letter combinations within the word (8).

Memory: See *sensory store, short-term memory,* and *long-term memory*.

Metacognition: Thought about one's own thinking, understanding, or learning (1).

Metalanguage: Language about language (2).

Metalinguistic awareness: Understanding of metalanguage, notably the way aspects of spoken and written language may be discussed in reading instruction (12).

Modular theory: Speculation that relatively independent and "hard-wired" parts of the brain are specialized for particular cognitive and perceptual functions, such as language use and face recognition (2).

Noise: A signal that conveys no information (3).

Nonvisual information: Prior knowledge "behind the eyes" that reduces *uncertainty* in advance and permits *identification* decisions with less *visual information* (4).

Orthography: Spelling; the arrangement of letters in words (8).

Perception: *Identification* decisions made by the brain; subjective awareness of these decisions (4).

Phoneme: One of about 40 discriminable classes of *significantly different* speech sounds in English (other languages have different sets of roughly the same number of phonemes) (8).

Phonetics: The scientific study of the sound structure of speech; has nothing to do with reading (8). See *phonics*.

Phonics: Reading instruction based on the assumption that reading is decoding to sound and requires learning *spelling-to-sound correspondences* (8). Sometimes mistakenly referred to as *phonetics*.

Phonological awareness: Ability to detect sounds in speech that are supposed to be represented by the letters of the alphabet (8).

Phonological recoding: Transforming written words to sound in order to understand their meaning (as opposed to understanding written words directly) (8).

Prediction: The prior elimination of unlikely alternatives; (in reading) the remaining set of alternatives among which an *identification* decision will be made from selected *visual information* in print (1).

Procedural knowledge: Knowledge of integrated sequences of behavior; see also *propositional knowledge, event knowledge* (1).

Propositional knowledge: Knowledge in the form of internalized statements, (such as facts, proverbs, formulae); also referred to as *declarative knowledge* (as opposed to *procedural knowledge*) (1).

Psycholinguistics: An area of common concern in psychology and linguistics studying how individuals learn and use language.

Redundancy: *Information* that is available from more than one source. In reading, may be present in the *visual information* of print, in the *orthography*, the *syntax*, the *meaning*, or in combinations of these sources. Redundancy may be *distributional* or *sequential*. Redundancy must always reflect *nonvisual information*; prior knowledge on the part of the reader permits redundancy to be used (3).

Regression: An eye movement (*saccade*) from right to left along a line or from bottom to top of a page (in English and similar writing systems) (4).

Saccade: Movement of the eyes as the gaze moves from one *fixation* to another in reading (4).

Scenario: A generalized mental representation of conventional patterns of behavior in specific situations. See also *scheme* (1).

Scheme: A generalized mental representation of complex patterns of behavior or events; also referred to as *schema*, plural *schemata*. See also *scenario, script, event knowledge* (1).

Script: A generalized mental representation of conventional behavior on specific occasions (1).

Semantics: The meaningful aspect of language; the study of this aspect (2).

Sensitivity: The prior learning state of the brain; readiness for *engagement;* absence of expectation that learning will not occur (11).

Sensory store: In vision, the very brief retention of *visual information* while *identification* decisions are made; also called the *visual image* (5).

Sequential redundancy: Reduction of *uncertainty* attributable to *constraints* on the number or relative probability of likely alternatives in *context* (7, 9); may exist among letters or words and as a consequence of a reader's or listener's expectations. See also *featural redundancy*.

Short-term memory: The limited and constantly changing content of what is attended to at any particular moment (5).

Significant difference: A difference in the physical properties of an event that forms the basis of an *identification* decision (6).

Situation-dependent language: Spoken or written language referring to and made meaningful by the concurrent physical situation in which it occurs (2).

Skills learning: The view that learning takes place most effectively when learners are systematically taught and rigorously tested in "the basics" of what is to be learned—in literacy, for example, the alphabet, phonics, and rules of spelling and punctuation (12). Known also as *direct instruction* and *mastery learning*.

Specification: A constantly changing outline in a reader's (or writer's) mind about the structure and content of a text; the basis of *prediction* in reading (6).

Spelling-to-sound correspondence: The co-occurrence of a particular letter or group of letters in a written word and the assumed sound of the same part of the word in speech (8).

Surface structure: The physical properties of language; for reading—*visual information* (2).

Syntax: The manner in which words are organized in meaningful language; also referred to as "grammar" (2).

Tachistoscope: A projector or other viewing device with a shutter or timer controlling the presentation of *visual information* for brief periods of time (4).

Template theory: A theory of pattern recognition that visual configurations such as digits, letters, or words can be identified by comparison with prestored representations or templates in the brain; in contrast to *featural analysis* (6).

Text: A meaningful (or potentially meaningful) instance of written language; can range from a word to an entire book.

Theory: In science, a summary of a scientist's past experience, the basis for interpreting new experience and for predicting future events (1).

Theory of the world: The brain's *theory*; also known as *cognitive structure* and *long-term memory* (1).

Transformational grammar: Part of the theory of the world of every language user; the bridge between *deep structure* and *surface structure* (2).

Uncertainty: The amount of *information* required to make an *identification* decision, determined by the number of alternative decisions that could be made, the perceived probability of each alternative, and the individual's *criterion level* for making the decision (3).

Understanding: See *comprehension*.

Visual image: See *sensory store*.

Visual information: In reading, *information* that is available to the brain through the eyes from the *surface structure* of print, for example, from the inkmarks on a page (4).

Whole language: An educational movement based on the belief that language learning takes place most effectively when learners are engaged collaboratively in meaningful and purposeful uses of language, as opposed to exercises, drills, and tests (12). Sometimes referred to as the naturalistic approach or (misleadingly) as child-centered learning, and known in Britain as real books. Frequently contrasted with *direct instruction*.

Zone of proximal development: Vygotsky's metaphor for everything a learner is able to do with assistance (though not alone). Learners quickly become able to do alone anything in the zone that they are assisted to do, and the zone then moves outward to accommodate new things that can be done with assistance (11).

References

Aaronson, Doris and Steven Ferres (1984). Reading strategies for children and adults: Some empirical evidence. *Journal of Verbal Learning and Verbal Behavior, 23*, 189–220.

Abu-Mostafa, Yaser S. and Demetri Psaltis (1987). Optical neural computers. *Scientific American, 256*(3), 88–95.

Adams, Marilyn Jagar (1990). *Beginning to Read: Learning and Thinking About Print*. Cambridge, MA: MIT Press.

Allingston, R. (1980). Teacher interruption behavior during primary-grade oral reading. *Journal of Educational Psychology, 72*(3), 371–377.

Alvermann, Donna E., Lynn C. Smith, and John E. Readence (1985). Prior knowledge activation and the comprehension of compatible and incompatible text. *Reading Research Quarterly, 20*(4), 420–436.

Amsterdam, Lisa, Paul Amman, and Herbert D. Simons (1990). Children's elicited imitations of controlled and rewritten reading texts. *Journal of Educational Research, 82*(3), 486–490.

Anderson, John R. (1980). *Cognitive Psychology and Its Implications*. San Francisco: Freeman.

Anderson, John R. (1991). The adaptive nature of human categorization. *Psychological Review, 98*(3), 409–429.

Anderson, John R. and Gordon H. Bower (1973). *Human Associative Memory*. Washington, DC: Winston.

Anderson, Jonathan (1984). The computer as tutor, tutee, tool in reading and language. *Reading, 18*(2), 67–78.

Anderson, Richard C., Elfrieda H. Hiebert, Judith A. Scott, and Ian A. G. Wilkinson (1985). *Becoming a Nation of Readers: The Report of the Commission on Reading*. Washington, DC: National Academy of Education.

Anderson, Richard C., Jana M. Mason, and Larry Shirey (1984). The reading group: An experimental investigation of a labyrinth. *Reading Research Quarterly, 20*(1), 6–38.

Anderson, Richard C. and Andrew Ortony (1975). On putting apples into bottles: A problem in polysemy. *Cognitive Psychology, 7*, 167–180.

Anderson, Richard C. and P. David Pearson (1984). A schema-theoretic view of basic processes in reading comprehension. In Pearson, P. David, Rebecca Barr, Michael L. Kamil, and Peter Mosenthal (Eds.), *Handbook of Reading Research* (Vol. 1). New York: Longman.

Anderson, Richard C. and J. W. Pichert (1978). Recall of previously unrecallable information following a shift in perspective. *Journal of Verbal Learning and Verbal Behavior, 17*, 1–12.

Anderson, Richard C., R. E. Reynolds, D. L. Schallert, and T. E. Goetz (1977). Frameworks for understanding discourse. *American Educational Research Journal, 14*, 367–381.

Anglin, Jeremy (1980). Acquiring linguistic skills: A study of sentence construction in preschool children. In Olson, David R. (Ed.), *The Social Foundations of Language.* New York: Norton.

Applebee, Arthur N. (1977). A sense of story. *Theory Into Practice, 16*, 342–347.

Armbruster, Bonnie B. and T. H. Anderson (1984). Content area textbooks. In Anderson, Richard C., Jean Osborn, and Robert J. Tierney (Eds.), *Learning to Read in American Schools: Basal Readers and Content Texts.* Hillsdale, NJ: Lawrence Erlbaum Associates.

Atkinson, Richard C. (1974). Teaching children to read using a computer. *American Psychologist, 29*, 169–178.

Attneave, Fred (1959). *Applications of Information Theory to Psychology.* New York: Holt, Rinehart and Winston.

Atwell, Nancie (1987). *In the Middle: Reading, Writing and Learning with Adolescents.* Portsmouth, NH: Heinemann.

Atwell, Nancie (1991). *Side by Side: Essays on Teaching to Learn.* Portmouth, NH: Heinemann.

August, Diane L., John H. Flavell, and Renee Clift (1984). Comparison of comprehension monitoring of skilled and less skilled readers. *Reading Research Quarterly, 20*(1), 39–53.

Averbach, E. and A. S. Coriell (1961). Short-term memory in vision. *Bell Systems Technical Journal, 40*, 309–328.

Baars, Bernard J. (1986). *The Cognitive Revolution in Psychology.* New York: Guilford.

Baars, Bernard J. (1991). *A Cognitive Theory of Consciousness.* Cambridge, UK: Cambridge University Press.

Baddeley, A. D., M. Eldridge, and V. J. Lewis (1981). The role of subvocalisation in reading. *Quarterly Journal of Experimental Psychology, 33*(A), 439–454.

Baddeley, Alan (1992). Working memory. *Science, 255*, 556–559.

Baddeley, Alan, Robert Logie, Ian Nimmo-Smith, and Neil Brereton (1985). Components of fluent reading. *Journal of Memory and Language, 24*(1), 119–131.

Baer, Donald M. and John C. Wright (1975). Developmental psychology. In Rosenzweig, Mark A. and Lyman W. Porter (Eds.), *Annual Review of Psychology, 25.*

Bahrick, Harry P. and Lynda K. Hall (1991). Lifetime maintenance of high school mathematics content. *Journal of Experimental Psychology: General, 120*(1), 20–33.

Bain, Bruce (Ed.) (1983). *The Sociogenesis of Language and Human Conduct.* New York: Plenum.

Baker, James Jay (1993). Letter to the editor. *The Council Chronical* (National Council of Teachers of English), *2*(3), 18.

Baldwin, R. Scott and James M. Coady (1978). Psycholinguistic approaches to a theory of punctuation. *Journal of Reading Behavior, 10*, 363–375.

Baldwin, R. Scott, Ziva Peleg-Bruckner, and Ann H. McClintock (1985). Effects of topic interest and prior knowledge on reading comprehension. *Reading Research Quarterly, 20*(4), 497–504.

Barclay, J. R. (1973). The role of comprehension in remembering sentences. *Cognitive Psychology, 4*, 229–252.

Barker, Theodore A., Joseph K. Torgesen, and Richard K. Wagner (1992). The role of orthographic processing skills on five different reading tasks. *Reading Research Quarterly, 27*(4), 335–345.

Barlow, Horace, Colin Blakemore, and Miranda Weston-Smith (Eds.). (1990). *Images and Understanding.* Cambridge, UK: Cambridge University Press.

Barlow, John A. (1981). Mass line leadership and thought reform in China. *American Psychologist, 36*(3), 300–309.

Barnhart, June E. (1993). The reading-writing relationship: Empirical evidence for the reconceptualization of literacy. In Johns, Jerry L. (Ed.), *Literacy: Celebration and Challenge*. Bloomington: Illinois Reading Council.

Baron, Jonathan (1979). Orthographic and word-specific mechanisms in children's reading of words. *Child Development, 50*, 60–72.

Baron, Jonathan and C. Strawson (1976). Use of orthographic and word-specific knowledge in reading words aloud. *Journal of Experimental Psychology: Human Perception and Performance, 2*, 386–393.

Barr, Rebecca C. (1972). The influence of instructional conditions on word recognition errors. *Reading Research Quarterly, 7*, 509–529.

Barr, Rebecca C. (1974). The effect of instruction on pupil reading strategies. *Reading Research Quarterly, 10*, 555–582.

Barr, Rebecca C. (1986). Commentary: Studying classroom reading instruction. *Reading Research Quarterly, 21*(3), 231–236.

Barron, Roderick W. (1986). Word recognition in early reading: A review of the direct and indirect access hypotheses. *Cognition, 24*, 93–119.

Bartlett, Frederick C. (1932). *Remembering: A Study in Experimental and Social Psychology*. London: Cambridge University Press.

Bates, Elizabeth (1979). *The Emergence of Symbols: Cognition and Communication in Infancy*. New York: Academic Press.

Baumann, James F. (1992). Basal reading programs and the deskilling of teachers: A critical examination of the argument. *Reading Research Quarterly, 27*(4), 390–398.

Baumann, James F. and Karen Wilson Schneider (1979). *Apprehension Span of Adult Fluent Readers: A Clarification of J. M. Cattell's Classic Research on Letter and Word Perception*. Madison: Wisconsin Research and Development Center for Individualized Schooling, Teaching Report #520.

Beck, Isabel L. and Connie Juel (1992). The role of decoding in learning to read. In Samuels, S. Jay and Alan E. Farstrup (Eds.), *What Research Has to Say About Reading Instruction* (2nd ed.). Newark, DE: International Reading Association.

Beck, Isabel L., Margaret G. McKeown, Richard C. Omanson, and Martha T. Pople (1984). Improving the comprehensibility of stories: The effects of revisions that improve coherence. *Reading Research Quarterly, 19*(3), 263–277.

Becker, Curtis A. (1982). The development of semantic context effects: Two processes or two strategies? *Reading Research Quarterly, 17*(4), 482–502.

Beebe, Mona J. (1980). The effect of different types of substitution miscues on reading. *Reading Research Quarterly, 15*(3), 324–336.

Beers, Terry (1987). Commentary: Schema-theoretic models of reading: Humanizing the machine. *Reading Research Quarterly, 22*(3), 369–377.

Benton, Arthur L. (1980). The neuropsychology of facial recognition. *American Psychologist, 35*(2), 176–186.

Benton, Michael (1979). Children's responses to stories. *Children's Literature in Education, 10*(2), 68–85.

Berdiansky, Betty, Bruce Cronnell, and John A. Koehler (1969). *Spelling-Sound Relations and Primary Form-Class Descriptions for Speech-Comprehension Vocabularies of 6–9 Year-Olds*. Inglewood, CA: Southwest Regional Laboratory for Educational Research and Development, Technical Report No. 15.

Bereiter, Carl (1991). Implications of connectionism for thinking about rules. *Educational Researcher, 20*(3), 10–16.

Berninger, Virginia Wise and Sarah O. Colwell (1985). Relationships between neurodevelopmental and educational findings in children aged 6 to 12 years. *Pediatrics, 75*, 697–702.

Besner, D., E. Davelaar, D. Alcott, and P. Parry (1984). Wholistic reading of alphabetic print:

Evidence from the FDM and the FBI. In Henderson, Leslie (Ed.), *Orthographies and Reading: Perspectives from Cognitive Psychology, Neuropsychology, and Linguistics*. Hillsdale, NJ: Lawrence Erlbaum Associates.

Bever, Thomas G. (1992). The demons and the beast, modular and nodular kinds of knowledge. In Reilly, Ronan G. and Noel E. Sharkey (Eds.), *Connectionist Approaches to Natural Language Processing*. Hove, UK: Lawrence Erlbaum Associates.

Beveridge, Michael (Ed.) (1982). *Children Thinking Through Language*. London: Arnold.

Bickerton, Derek (1990). *Language and Species*. Chicago: University of Chicago Press.

Biederman, Irving (1987). Recognition-by-components: A theory of human image understanding. *Psychological Review*, *94*(2), 115–147.

Bissex, Glenda L. (1980). *Gnys at Wrk: A Child Learns to Write and Read*. Cambridge, MA: Harvard University Press.

Black, Alison, Paul Freeman, and Philip N. Johnson-Laird (1986). Plausibility and the comprehension of text. *British Journal of Psychology*, *77*(1), 51–62.

Blakemore, Colin (1990). Understanding images in the brain. In Barlow, Horace, Colin Blakemore, and Miranda Weston-Smith (Eds.), *Images and Understanding*. Cambridge, UK: Cambridge University Press.

Blakemore, Colin and Susan Greenfield (Eds.) (1987). *Mindwaves: Thoughts on Intelligence, Identity and Consciousness*. Oxford, UK: Blackwell.

Bloom, Lois (1970). *Language Development: Form and Function in Emerging Grammars*. Cambridge, MA: MIT Press.

Bloom, Lois (1973). *One Word at a Time: The Use of Single Word Utterances Before Syntax*. The Hague: Mouton.

Bloom, Lois, Lois Hood, and Patsy Lightbown (1974). Imitation in language development: If, when, and why. *Cognitive Psychology*, *6*, 380–420.

Bloom, Lois, Lorraine Rocissano, and Lois Hood (1976). Adult–child discourse: Developmental interaction between information processing and linguistic knowledge. *Cognitive Psychology*, *8*, 521–552.

Bloome, David and Ann Egan-Robertson (1993). The social construction of intertextuality in classroom reading and writing lessons. *Reading Research Quarterly*, *28*(4), 304–333.

Blough, Donald S. (1982). Pigeon perception of letters of the alphabet. *Science*, *218*, 397–398.

Boden, Margaret A. (1979). *Piaget*. Brighton, Sussex: Harvester Press.

Boden, Margaret A. (1989). *Artificial Intelligence in Psychology*. Cambridge, MA: MIT Press.

Boden, Margaret A. (1992). The mind of a very special machine? *New Scientist*, *133*(1804), 34–37.

Bolter, Jay David (1991). *Writing Space: The Computer, Hypertext, and the History of Writing*. Hillsdale, NJ: Lawrence Erlbaum Associates.

Boulding, Kenneth E. (1981). Human knowledge as a special system. *Behavioral Science*, *26*, 93–102.

Bower, Gordon H. (1976). Experiments on story understanding and recall. *Quarterly Journal of Experimental Psychology*, *28*, 511–534.

Bower, Gordon H., John B. Black, and Terrence J. Turner (1979). Scripts in memory for text. *Cognitive Psychology*, *11*, 177–220.

Bower, Thomas G. R. (1971). The object in the world of the infant. *Scientific American*, *225*, 30–47.

Bower, Thomas G. R. (1974). *Development in Infancy*. San Francisco: Freeman.

Brady, Susan A. and Donald P. Shankweiler (1991). *Phonological Processes in Literacy: A Tribute to Isabelle Y. Liberman*. Hillsdale, NJ: Lawrence Erlbaum Associates.

Brand, H. (1971). Classification without identification in visual search. *Quarterly Journal of Experimental Psychology*, *23*, 178–186.

Bransford, John D., J. R. Barclay, and Jeffrey J. Franks (1972). Sentence meaning: A constructivist vs. interpretive approach. *Cognitive Psychology*, *3*, 193–209.

Bransford, John D. and Jeffrey J. Franks (1971). The abstraction of linguistic ideas. *Cognitive Psychology*, 2, 331–350.

Bransford, John D. and Barry S. Stein (1984). *The Ideal Problem Solver: A Guide for Improving Thinking, Learning and Creativity*. New York: Freeman.

Bransford, John D., Barry S. Stein, and Nancy J. Vye (1982). Helping students learn how to learn from written texts. In Singer, M. H. (Ed.), *Competent Reading, Disabled Reader: Research and Application*. Hillsdale, NJ: Lawrence Erlbaum Associates.

Bridges, Allayne, Chris Sinha, and Valerie Walkerdine (1981). The development of comprehension. In Wells, Gordon (Ed.), *Learning Through Interaction: The Study of Language Development*. Cambridge, UK: Cambridge University Press.

Britton, Bruce K. and John B. Black (Eds.) (1985). *Understanding Expository Text*. Hillsdale, NJ: Lawrence Erlbaum Associates.

Broadbent, Donald E. (1967). The word-frequency effect and response bias. *Psychological Review*, 74, 1–15.

Broadbent, Donald E. and Margaret H. P. Broadbent (1975). Some further data concerning the word frequency effect. *Journal of Experimental Psychology: General*, 104, 297–308.

Broerse, A. C. and E. J. Zwaan (1966). The information value of initial letters in the identification of words. *Journal of Verbal Learning and Verbal Behavior*, 5, 441–446.

Bronowski, Jacob (1978). *The Origins of Knowledge and Imagination*. New Haven, CT: Yale University Press.

Brown, Ann L. (1980). Metacognitive development and reading. In Spiro, Rand C., Bertram C. Bruce, and William F. Brewer (Eds.), *Theoretical Issues in Reading Comprehension: Perspectives from Cognitive Psychology, Linguistics, Artificial Intelligence, and Education*. Hillsdale, NJ: Lawrence Erlbaum Associates.

Brown, Ann L. (1982). Learning how to learn from reading. In Langer, Judith A. and M. Trika Smith-Burke (Eds.), *Reader Meets Author/Bridging the Gap*. Newark, DE: International Reading Association.

Brown, Ann L. and Roberta A. Ferrara (1985). Diagnosing zones of proximal development. In Wertsch, J. S. (Ed.), *Culture, Communication and Development*. New York: Cambridge University Press.

Brown, Ann L. and Annemarie S. Palincsar (1989). Guided, cooperative learning and individual knowledge acquisition. In Resnick, Lauren (Ed.), *Knowing, Learning, and Instruction: Essays in Honor of Robert Glaser*. Hillsdale, NJ: Lawrence Erlbaum Associates.

Brown, H. D. (1970). Categories of spelling difficulty in speakers of English as a first and second language. *Journal of Verbal Learning and Verbal Behavior*, 9, 232–236.

Brown, Roger (1973). *A First Language: The Early Stages*. Cambridge, MA: Harvard University Press.

Brown, Roger and David McNeill (1966). The "tip of the tongue" phenomenon. *Journal of Verbal Learning and Verbal Behavior*, 5(4), 325–337.

Bruner, Jerome S. (1973). *Beyond the Information Given*. New York: Norton.

Bruner, Jerome S. (1975). The ontogenesis of speech acts. *Journal of Child Language*, 2, 1–19.

Bruner, Jerome S. (1978). Acquiring the uses of language. *Canadian Journal of Psychology*, 32, 204–218.

Bruner, Jerome S. (1986). *Actual Minds, Possible Worlds*. Cambridge, MA: Harvard University Press.

Bruner, Jerome S. (1990). *Acts of Meaning*. Cambridge, MA: Harvard University Press.

Bruner, Jerome S. and D. O'Dowd (1958). A note on the informativeness of parts of words. *Language and Speech*, 1, 98–101.

Bruner, Jerome and Susan Weisser (1991). The invention of self: Autobiography and its forms. In Olson, David R. and Nancy Torrance (Eds.), *Literacy and Orality*. Cambridge, UK: Cambridge University Press.

Bryant, Peter and Lawrence Impey (1986). The similarities between normal readers and developmental and acquired dyslexics. *Cognition, 24*, 121–137.

Burton, Mike (1992). Good morning, Mr . . . er. *New Scientist, 133*(1806), 39–41.

Butler, Christopher S. (1985). *Systemic Linguistics*. London: Batsford.

Cairney, Trevor H. (1990). *Teaching Reading Comprehension: Meaning Makers at Work*. Milton Keynes: Open University.

Cairney, Trevor (1992). Mountain or mole hill: The genre debate viewed from 'down under.' *Reading, 36*, 23–29.

Calfee, Robert C. (1974). Memory and cognitive skills in reading acquisition. In Duane, Drake D. and Margaret B. Rawson (Eds.), *Reading, Perception and Language*. Baltimore: York Press.

Calfee, Robert C. (1975). *Human Experimental Psychology*. New York: Holt, Rinehart and Winston.

Calfee, Robert C. (1983). The mind of the dyslexic. In Hartwig, Elinor Linn (Ed.), *Annals of Dyslexia, Vol. 33*. Baltimore: Orton Dyslexia Society.

Calfee, Robert C., Richard Arnold, and Priscilla Drum (1976). Review of *The Psychology of Reading* (by Eleanor Gibson and Harry Levin). In *Proceedings of the National Academy of Education, 3*, 1–80.

Calkins, Lucy (1980). When children want to punctuate: Basic skills belong in context. *Language Arts, 57*, 567–573.

Caplan, David (Ed.) (1980). *Biological Studies of Mental Processes*. Cambridge, MA: MIT Press.

Carbo, Marie (1988). Debunking the great phonics myth. *Phi Delta Kappan, 70*(3), 226–240.

Carbo, Marie, Rita Dunn, and Kenneth Dunn (1987). *Teaching Students to Read Through Their Individualized Learning Styles*. Reston, VA: Prentice–Hall.

Carey, Susan (1978). The child as word learner. In Halle, M., J. Breslin, and George A. Miller (Eds.), *Linguistic Theory and Psychological Reality*. Cambridge, MA: MIT Press.

Carpenter, Patricia M. and Meredyth Daneman (1981). Lexical retrieval and error recovery in reading: A model based on eye fixations. *Journal of Verbal Learning and Verbal Behavior, 20*, 137–160.

Carpenter, Patricia A. and Marcel A. Just (1975). Sentence comprehension: A psycholinguistic processing model of verification. *Psychological Review, 82*, 45–73.

Carpenter, Patricia A. and Marcel A. Just (1977). Integrative processes in comprehension. In LaBerge, David and S. Jay Samuels (Eds.), *Basic Processes in Reading: Perception and Comprehension*. Hillsdale, NJ: Lawrence Erlbaum Associates.

Carpenter, Patricia A. and Marcel A. Just. (1981). Cognitive processes in reading: Models based on readers' eye fixations. In Lesgold, Alan M. and Charles A. Perfetti (Eds.), *Interactive Processes in Reading*. Hillsdale, NJ: Lawrence Erlbaum Associates.

Carroll, John B. and Jeanne S. Chall (Eds.) (1975). *Toward a Literate Society*. New York: McGraw–Hill.

Carroll, John B., Peter Davies, and Barry Richman (1971). *The American Heritage Word Frequency Book*. Boston: Houghton Mifflin.

Carver, Ronald P. (1985). How good are some of the world's best readers? *Reading Research Quarterly, 20*(4), 389–419.

Carver, Ronald P. (1992). Reading rate: Theory, research and practical implications. *Journal of Reading, 36*(2), 84–95.

Cattell, James McKeen (1973). Ueber die Zeit der Erkennung und Benennung von Schriftzeichen, Bildern und Farben [On the time required for recognizing and naming letters and words, pictures and colors.] *Philosophische Studien* (1885), *2*, 635–650. Translated and reprinted in Poffenberger, A. T. (Ed.), *James McKeen Cattell, Man of Science, 1860–1944* (Vol. 1). New York: Arno Press.

Cazden, Courtney B. (1972). *Child Language and Education*. New York: Holt, Rinehart and Winston.

Cazden, Courtney B. (1992). *Whole Language Plus: Essays on Literacy in the United States and New Zealand*. New York: Teachers College Press.

Cermak, Laird S. and Fergus I. M. Craik (Eds.) (1979). *Levels of Processing in Human Memory*. Hillsdale, NJ: Lawrence Erlbaum Associates.

Chafe, Wallace (1992). Immediacy and displacement in consciousness and language. In Stein, Dieter (Ed.), *Cooperating with Written Texts: The Pragmatics and Comprehension of Written Texts*. Berlin: Mouton de Gruyter, pp. 231–255.

Chafe, Wallace, and Jane Danielwicz (1987). Properties of spoken and written language. In Horowitz, Rosalind and S. Jay Samuels (Eds.), *Comprehending Oral and Written Language*. New York: Academic Press, pp. 83–113.

Chall, Jeanne S. (1967). *Learning to Read: The Great Debate*. New York: McGraw-Hill.

Chall, Jeanne S. (1989). Learning to read: The great debate 20 years later: A response to 'Debunking the great phonics myth.' *Phi Delta Kappan, 70*(7), 521–538.

Chall, Jeanne S. (1992/1993). Research supports direct instruction models. In Point/Counterpoint: Whole language versus direct instruction models. *Reading Today, 10*(3), 8–10.

Chambers, Maryl, Adrian Jackson, and Mary Rose (1993). *Children Developing as Readers: The Avon Collaborative Reading Project*. Bristol, UK: County of Avon.

Cherry, Colin (1978). *On Human Communication* (3rd ed.). Cambridge, MA: MIT Press.

Chomsky, Carol (1970). Reading, writing and phonology. *Harvard Educational Review, 40*(2), 287–309.

Chomsky, Carol (1971). Write first, read later. *Childhood Education, 47*(6), 296–299.

Chomsky, Carol (1979). Approaching spelling through invented spelling. In Resnick, Lauren B. and Phyllis A. Weaver (Eds.), *Theory and Practice of Early Reading*. Hillsdale, NJ: Lawrence Erlbaum Associates.

Chomsky, Noam (1957). *Syntactic Structures*. The Hague: Mouton.

Chomsky, Noam (1959). Review of *Verbal Learning* (by B. F. Skinner). *Language, 35*, 26–58.

Chomsky, Noam (1986). *Knowledge of Language: Its Nature, Origin and Use*. New York: Praegar.

Chomsky, Noam and Morris Halle (1968). *Sound Pattern of English*. New York: Harper and Row.

Chukovsky, Kornei (tr. Miriam Morton) (1968). *From Two to Five*. Berkeley: University of California Press.

Churchland, Patricia S. (1986). *Neurophilosophy: Toward a Unified Science of the Mind-Brain*. Cambridge, MA: MIT Press.

Clark, Eve V. and Barbara Frant Hecht (1983). Comprehension, production, and language acquisition. *Annual Review of Psychology, 34*, 325–349.

Clark, Margaret M. (1976). *Young Fluent Readers*. London: Heinemann.

Clay, Marie M. (1969). Reading errors and self-correction behavior. *British Journal of Educational Psychology, 39*(1), 49–56.

Clay, Marie M. (1979). Theoretical research and instructional change: A case study. In Resnick, Lauren B. and Phyllis A. Weaver (Eds.), *Theory and Practice of Early Reading*. Hillsdale, NJ: Lawrence Erlbaum Associates.

Clay, Marie (1985). *The Early Detection of Reading Difficulties*. Portsmouth, NH: Heinemann.

Clay, Marie (1992/1993). Language policy and literacy learning. *Reading Today, 10*(3), 3–4.

Clay, Marie M. and Robert H. Imlach (1971). Juncture, pitch and stress and reading behavior variables. *Journal of Verbal Learning and Verbal Behavior, 10*, 133–139.

Cofer, Charles N. (1973). Constructive processes in memory. *American Scientist, 61*(5), 537–543.

Cohen, Gillian (1970). Search times for combinations of visual, phonemic and semantic targets in reading prose. *Perception and Psychophysics, 8*(5B), 370–372.

Coles, Gerald (1987). *The Learning Mystique*. New York: Pantheon.

Collins, Norma Decker and James R. Collins (1992). A crack in time: A student traversing paradigms. *Journal of Reading Behavior, 24*(4), 403–411.

Collins, W. Andrew (Ed.) (1979). *Children's Language and Communication: The Minnesota Symposia on Child Psychology* (Vol. 12). Hillsdale, NJ: Lawrence Erlbaum Associates.

Coltheart, Max (Ed.) (1987). *Attention and Performance XIII: The Psychology of Reading.* Hove, UK: Lawrence Erlbaum Associates.

Corcos, Evelyne and Dale M. Willows (1993). The processing of orthographic information. In Willows, Dale M., Richard S. Kruk, and Evelyne Corcos (Eds.), *Visual Processes in Reading and Reading Disabilities*. Hillsdale, NJ: Lawrence Erlbaum Associates.

Cosky, Michael J. (1976). The role of letter recognition in word recognition. *Memory and Cognition, 4*(2), 207–214.

Cossu, G., F. Rossini, and John C. Marshall (1993). When reading is acquired but phonemic awareness is not: A study of literacy in Down's syndrome. *Cognition, 46*, 129–138.

Coulmas, Florian (1992). On the relationship between writing system, written language, and text processing. In Stein, Dieter (Ed.), *Cooperating with Written Texts: The Pragmatics and Comprehension of Written Texts*. Berlin: Mouton de Gruyter.

Courts, Patrick L. (1991). *Literacy and Empowerment: The Meaning Makers*. New York: Bergin and Garvey.

Craik, Fergus I. M. and Robert S. Lockhart (1972). Levels of processing: A framework for memory research. *Journal of Verbal Learning and Verbal Behavior, 11*, 671–684.

Crick, Francis (1989). The recent excitement about neural networks. *Nature, 337*, 129–132.

Cronbach, Lee J. (1992). Four *Psychological Bulletin* articles in perspective. *Psychological Bulletin, 112*(3), 389–392.

Cross, Toni G. (1977). Mothers' speech adjustments: The contribution of selected child listener variables. In Snow, Catherine E. and Charles A. Ferguson (Eds.), *Talking to Children: Language Input and Acquisition*. Cambridge, UK: Cambridge University Press.

Crowder, Robert G. (1976). *Principles of Learning and Memory*. Hillsdale, NJ: Lawrence Erlbaum Associates.

Crowder, Robert G. and Richard K. Wagner (1991). *The Psychology of Reading: An Introduction*. New York: Oxford University Press.

Csikszentmihalyi, Mihaly (1990). *Flow—The Psychology of Optimal Experience*. New York: Harper & Row.

Culler, Jonathan (1981). *The Pursuit of Signs: Semiotics, Literature, Deconstruction*. Ithaca, NY: Cornell University Press.

Dale, Philip S. (1976). *Language Development: Structure and Function*. New York: Holt, Rinehart and Winston.

Davidson, J. J. (Ed.) (1988). *Counterpoint and Beyond: A Response to Becoming a Nation of Readers*. Urbana, IL: National Council of Teachers of English.

Davies, W. J. Frank (1973). *Teaching Reading in Early England*. London: Pitman.

Davis, Steven (Ed.) (1991). *Pragmatics: A Reader*. Oxford: Oxford University Press.

de Beaugrande, Robert (1981). Design criteria for process models of reading. *Reading Research Quarterly, 16*(2), 261–315.

de Beaugrande, Robert and P. Dressler (1981). *Introduction to Text Linguistics*. New York: Longman.

de Castell, Suzanne and Allan Luke (1986). Models of literacy in North American schools. Social and historical conditions and consequences. In de Castell, Suzanne, Allan Luke, and Kieran Egan (Eds.), *Literacy, Society and Schooling: A Reader*. New York: Cambridge University Press.

Deely, John (1982). *Introducing Semiotic*. Bloomington: Indiana University Press.

DeFord, Diane E. (1981). Literacy: Reading, writing and other essentials. *Language Arts, 58*(5), 652–658.

Delpit, Lisa D. (1988). The silenced dialogue: Power and pedagogy in educating other people's children. *Harvard Educational Review, 58*, 280–298.

Delpit, Lisa D. (1991). A conversation with Lisa Delpit. *Language Arts, 68*, 541–547.

den Buurman, Rudy, Theo Roersema, and Jack F. Gerrisen (1981). Eye movements and the perceptual span in reading. *Reading Research Quarterly, 16*(2), 227–235.

Derry, Sharon J. and Debra A. Murphy (1986). Designing systems that train learning ability: From theory to practice. *Review of Educational Research, 56*(1), 1–39.

Dickinson, David, Maryanne Wolf, and Sandra Stotsky (1989). Words move: The interwoven development of oral and written language. In Gleason, Jean Berko (Ed.), *The Development of Language* (2nd ed.). Columbus, OH: Merrill, pp. 225–273.

Doehring, Donald G. (1976). Acquisition of rapid reading responses. *Monographs of the Society for Research in Child Development. 41*(2), No. 165.

Doehring, Donald G. and Mark Aulls (1981). Implications of Neisser's cognitive theory for models of reading acquisition. *Reading/Canada/Lecture, 1*(1), 46–52.

Doggett, David and Larry G. Richards (1975). A reexamination of the effect of word length on recognition thresholds. *American Journal of Psychology, 88*, 583–594.

Dombey, Henriette (1988). Stories at home and at school. In Lightfoot, Martin and Nancy Martin (Eds.), *The Word for Teaching is Learning: Essays for James Britton*. London: Heinemann.

Donaldson, Margaret (1978). *Children's Minds*. Glasgow: Fontana/Collins.

Donaldson, Margaret and Jessie Reid (1982). Language skills and reading: A developmental perspective. In Hendry, A. (Ed.), *Teaching Reading: The Key Issues*. London: Heinemann.

Dorman, Casey (1985). Defining and diagnosing dyslexia: Are we putting the cart before the horse? *Reading Research Quarterly, 20*(4), 505–508.

Douglas, Mary (Ed.) (1968). *Rules and Meanings: The Anthropology of Everyday Knowledge*. Harmondsworth: Penguin.

Downing, John (1970). Children's concepts of language in learning to read. *Educational Research, 12*, 106–112.

Downing, John (Ed.) (1973). *Comparative Reading*. New York: Macmillan.

Downing, John (1977). How society creates reading disability. *Elementary School Journal, 77*, 274–279.

Downing, John (1979). *Reading and Reasoning*. New York: Springer-Verlag.

Downing, John (1985). Task-awareness in the development of reading skills. In Downing, John and Renate Valtin (Eds.), *Language Awareness and Learning to Read*. New York: Springer-Verlag.

Downing, John and Che Kan Leong (1982). *Psychology of Reading*. New York: Macmillan.

Downing, John and Peter Oliver (1973/1974). The child's conception of "a word." *Reading Research Quarterly, 9*(4), 568–582.

Downing, John, Lloyd Ollila, and Peter Oliver (1975). Cultural differences in children's concepts of reading and writing. *British Journal of Educational Psychology, 45*, 312–316.

Downing, John and Renate Valtin (Eds.) (1985). *Language Awareness and Learning to Read*. New York: Springer-Verlag.

Dreher, Mariam Jean and Sara D. Zenge (1990). Using metalinguistic awareness in first grade to predict reading achievement in third and fifth grades. *Journal of Educational Research, 84*(1), 13–21.

Dreyfus, Hubert L. and Stuart E. Dreyfus (1986). *Mind Over Machine*. New York: The Free Press.

Dudley-Marling, Curt and Don Dippo (1991). The language of whole language. *Language Arts, 68*, 548–554.

Dunn-Rankin, Peter (1968). The similarity of lower case letters of the English alphabet. *Journal of Verbal Learning and Verbal Behavior, 7*, 990–995.

Dunn-Rankin, Peter (1985). Perceptual characteristics of words. In Groner, R., G. W. McConkie, and C. Menz (Eds.), *Eye Movements and Human Information Processing*. North-Holland: Elsevier Science.

Durkin, Dolores (1966). *Children Who Read Early*. New York: Teachers College Press.

Durkin, Dolores (1981). What is the value of the new interest in reading comprehension? *Language Arts*, *58*(1), 23–43.

Durkin, Dolores (1984). Poor black children who are successful readers: An investigation. *Urban Education*, *19*, 53–76.

Eagleton, Terry (1983). *Literacy Theory: An Introduction*. Minneapolis, University of Minnesota Press.

Eckhoff, Barbara (1983). How reading affects children's writing. *Language Arts*, *60*(5), 607–616.

Eco, Umberto (1984). *Semiotics and the Philosophy of Language*. Bloomington: Indiana University Press.

Edelsky, Carole (1991). *With Literacy and Justice for All: Rethinking the Social in Language and Education*. Bristol, PA: Falmer.

Edfeldt, Ake W. (1960). *Silent Speech and Silent Reading*. Chicago: University of Chicago Press.

Ehri, Linnea C. (1985). How orthography alters spoken language competencies in children learning to read and spell. In Downing, John and Renate Valtin (Eds.), *Language Awareness and Learning to Read*. New York: Springer-Verlag.

Ehri, Linnea C. (1987). Learning to read and spell words. *Journal of Reading Behavior*, *19*, 5–31.

Ehri, Linnea C. (1992). Reconceptualizing the development of sight word reading and its relationship to recoding. In Gough, Philip B., Linnea C. Ehri, and Rebecca Treiman (Eds.), *Reading Acquisition*. Hillsdale, NJ: Lawrence Erlbaum Associates.

Ehri, Linnea C. and Claudia Robbins (1992). Beginners need some decoding skill to read words by analogy. *Reading Research Quarterly*, *27*(1), 12–27.

Ehri, Linnea C. and Lee S. Wilce (1985). Movement into reading: Is the first stage of printed word learning visual or phonetic? *Reading Research Quarterly*, *20*(2), 163–179.

Eisner, Elliot (1982). *Cognition and Curriculum: A Basis for Deciding What to Teach*. New York: Longman.

Eldredge, J. Lloyd (1990). Increasing the performance of poor readers in the third grade with a group-assisted strategy. *Journal of Educational Research*, *84*(2), 69–77.

Elley, Warwick (1989). Vocabulary acquisition from listening to stories. *Reading Research Quarterly*, *24*, 174–187.

Elley, Warwick and F. Mangubhai (1983). The impact of reading on second language learning. *Reading Research Quarterly*, *19*, 53–67.

Ellis, Andrew W. (1984). *Reading, Writing and Dyslexia: A Cognitive Analysis*. London: Lawrence Erlbaum Associates.

Erdmann, B. and R. Dodge (1898). *Psychologische Untersuchungen ueber das Lesen auf Experimenteller Grundlage*. Halle: Niemeyer.

Ericsson, K. Anders, William G. Chase, and Steve Falcon (1980). Acquisition of a memory skill. *Science*, *208*, 1181–1182.

Ewoldt, Carolyn (1981). A psycholinguistic description of selected deaf children reading in sign language. *Reading Research Quarterly*, *17*(1), 58–89.

Eysenck, Michael W. (1984). *A Handbook of Cognitive Psychology*. Hillsdale, NJ: Lawrence Erlbaum Associates.

Fantz, Robert L. (1964). Visual experience in infants: Decreased attention to familiar patterns relative to novel ones. *Science*, *146*, 668–670.

Ferreiro, Emilia (1978). What is written in a written sentence? A developmental answer. *Journal of Education*, *160*(4), 25–39.

Ferreiro, Emilia (1985). Literacy development: A psychogenetic perspective. In Olson, David R., Nancy Torrance, and Angela Hildyard (Eds.), *Literacy, Language and Learning: The Nature and Consequences of Reading and Writing.* Cambridge, UK: Cambridge University Press.

Ferreiro, Emelia and Ana Teberosky (1982). *Literacy Before Schooling.* Exeter, NH: Heinemann.

Feuerstein, Reuven, Mogens Jensen, Mildred B. Hoffman, and Yaacov Rand (1985). Instrumental enrichment: An intervention program for structural cognitive modifiability. In Segal, Judith W., Susan F. Chipman, and Robert Glaser (Eds.), *Thinking and Learning Skills, Vol. I: Relating Instruction to Research.* Hillsdale, NJ: Lawrence Erlbaum Associates.

Fillion, Bryant, Frank Smith, and Merrill Swain (1976). Language "basics" for language teachers: Towards a set of universal considerations. *Language Arts, 53*(7), 740–745.

Fiorito, Graziano and Pietro Scotto (1992). Observational learning in *octopus vulgaris. Science, 256,* 545–567.

Fiske, Donald W. and Donald T. Campbell (1992). Citations do not solve problems. *Psychological Bulletin, 112*(3), 393–395.

Flammer, August and Walter Kintsch (1982). *Discourse Processing.* Amsterdam: North Holland.

Flavell, John H. (1979). Metacognition and cognitive monitoring. *American Psychologist, 34*(10), 906–911.

Flavell, John H., James Ramsey Speer, Frances L. Green, and Diane L. August (1981). The development of comprehension monitoring and knowledge about communication. *Monographs of the Society for Research in Child Development, 46*(5), 192.

Flood, James (1984). Introduction to understanding reading comprehension. In Flood, James (Ed.), *Understanding Reading Comprehension.* Newark, DE: International Reading Association.

Fodor, Janet Dean (1977). *Semantics.* New York: Crowell.

Fodor, Jerry A. (1978). Tom Swift and his procedural grandmother. *Cognition, 6,* 229–247.

Fodor, Jerry A. (1979). *The Language of Thought.* Cambridge, MA: Harvard University Press.

Fodor, Jerry A. (Ed.) (1981). *Representations.* Cambridge, MA: MIT Press.

Fodor, Jerry A. (1983). *The Modularity of Mind.* Cambridge, MA: MIT Press.

Fodor, Jerry A. (1990). *A Theory of Content and Other Essays.* Cambridge, MA: MIT Press.

Fodor, Jerry A., Merrill F. Garrett, E. Walker, and C. H. Parkes (1980). Against definitions. *Cognition, 8,* 263–367.

Fodor, Jerry A. and Zenon W. Pylyshyn (1988). Connectionism and cognitive architecture: A critical analysis. *Cognition, 28,* 3–71.

Forester, Anne D. (1977). What teachers can learn from "natural readers." *The Reading Teacher, 31,* 160–166.

Forrest-Pressley, Donna-Lynn and T. Gary Waller (1984). *Cognition, Metacognition and Reading.* New York: Springer-Verlag.

Forster, Kenneth I. (1970). Visual perception of rapidly-presented word sequences of varying complexity. *Perception and Psychophysics, 8,* 215–221.

Fox, Mem (1993). Men who weep, boys who dance: The gender agenda between the lines in children's literature. *Language Arts, 70*(2), 84–88.

Fraisse, Paul (1984). Perceptual processing of words and drawings. In Sarris, Victor and Allen Parducci (Eds.), *Perspectives in Psychological Experimentation: Toward the Year 2000.* Hillsdale, NJ: Lawrence Erlbaum Associates.

Fredericksen, C. H. (1975). Representing logical and semantic structure of knowledge acquired from discourse. *Cognitive Psychology, 7,* 371–458.

Freebody, Peter and Richard C. Anderson (1983). Effects of vocabulary difficulty, text cohesion, and schema availability on reading comprehension. *Reading Research Quarterly, 18*(3), 277–294.

Freire, Paulo (1972). *Pedagogy of the Oppressed*. New York: Herder and Herder.
Friedman, Sarah L., Kenneth A. Klivington, and Rita W. Peterson (Eds.) (1986). *The Brain, Cognition and Education*. Orlando, FL: Academic Press.
Friendly, Michael L. (1977). In search of the M-gram: The structure of organization in free recall. *Cognitive Psychology*, *9*, 188–249.
Fries, Charles C. (1945). *Teaching and Learning English as a Foreign Language*. Ann Arbor: University of Michigan Press.
Fromkin, Victoria and Robert Rodman (1983). *An Introduction to Language*. New York: Holt, Rinehart and Winston.
Furness, David W. and Michael F. Graves (1980). Effects of stressing oral reading accuracy on comprehension. *Reading Psychology*, *2*(1), 8–14.

Gallistel, Charles R. (1990). *The Organization of Learning*. Cambridge, MA: MIT Press.
Gardner, Howard (1983). *Frames of Mind*. New York: Basic Books.
Gardner, Howard (1987). *The Mind's New Science*. New York: Basic Books.
Gardner, Howard (1991). *The Unschooled Mind: How Children Think and How Schools Should Teach*. New York: Basic Books.
Garner, Ruth (1992). Metacognition and self-monitoring strategies. In Samuels, S. Jay and Alan E. Farstrup (Eds.), *What Research has to Say about Reading Instruction* (Second edition). Newark, DE: International Reading Association.
Garner, Wendell R. (1962). *Uncertainty and Structure as Psychological Concepts*. New York: Wiley.
Garner, Wendell R. (1966). To perceive is to know. *American Psychologist*, *21*(1), 11–19.
Garner, Wendell R. (1974). *The Processing of Information and Structure*. Hillsdale, NJ: Lawrence Erlbaum Associates.
Gazzaniga, Michael S. (1970). *The Bisected Brain*. New York: Appleton.
Gelb, J. (1963). *A Study of Writing*. Chicago: University of Chicago Press.
Gellatly, Angus (Ed.) (1986). *The Skillful Mind*. Milton Keynes: Open University.
Gelman, Rochel (1979). Preschool thought. *American Psychologist*, *34*(10), 900–905
Gernsbacher, Morton Ann (1990). *Language Comprehension as Structure Building*. Hillsdale, NJ: Lawrence Erlbaum Associates.
Geyer, John J. (1968). Perceptual systems in reading: The prediction of a temporal eye-voice span constant. In Smith, H. K. (Ed.), *Perception and Reading*. Newark, DE: International Reading Association.
Gibbs, Raymond W. (1984). Literal meaning and psychological theory. *Cognitive Science*, *8*, 275–304.
Gibson, Eleanor J. (1965). Learning to read. *Science*, *148*, 1066–1072.
Gibson, Eleanor J. and Harry Levin (1975). *The Psychology of Reading*. Cambridge, MA: MIT Press.
Gibson, Roger F. Jr. (1988). *Enlightened Empiricism: An Examination of W. V. Quine's Theory of Knowledge*. Tampa: University of South Florida Press.
Gilhooly, K. J. (1982). *Thinking: Directed, Undirected and Creative*. London: Academic Press.
Gill, J. Thomas (1992). Development of word knowledge as it relates to reading, spelling and instruction. *Language Arts*, *69*, 444–453.
Gillooly, William B. (1973). The influence of writing system characteristics on learning to read. *Reading Research Quarterly*, *8*(2), 167–199.
Gilman, Sid and Sarah Winans Newman (1992). *Essentials of Clinical Neuroanatomy and Neurophysiology* (8th ed.). Philadelphia: Davis.
Giroux, Henry (1992). Educational leadership and the crisis of democratic government. *Educational Researcher*, *21*(4), 4–11.
Givón, T. (1989). *Mind, Code and Context*. Hillsdale, NJ: Lawrence Erlbaum Associates.

Gleason, Jean Berko (Ed.) (1989). *The Development of Language* (2nd ed.). Columbus, OH: Merrill.

Gleitman, Lila R. and Paul Rozin (1973a). Teaching reading by use of a syllabary. *Reading Research Quarterly, 8*(4), 447–483.

Gleitman, Lila R. and Paul Rozin (1973b). Phoenician go gome? (A response to Goodman). *Reading Research Quarterly, 8*(4), 494–501.

Glenn, Hugh W. (1975). The myth of the label "learning disabled child." *Elementary School Journal, 75*(6), 357–361.

Glucksberg, S. and J. H. Danks (1975). *Experimental Psycholinguistics: An Introduction.* Hillsdale, NJ: Lawrence Erlbaum Associates.

Glusko, Robert J. (1979). The organization and activation of orthographic knowledge in reading aloud. *Journal of Experimental Psychology: Human Perception and Performance, 5*, 674–691.

Glynn, Shawn M. and Frances J. DiVesta (1979). Control of prose processing via instructional and typographical cues. *Journal of Educational Psychology, 71*(5), 595–603.

Goelman, Hillel, Antoinette A. Oberg, and Frank Smith (Eds.) (1984). *Awakening to Literacy.* Portsmouth, NH: Heinemann.

Golden, Joanne M. and John T. Guthrie (1986). Convergence and divergence in reader response to literature. *Reading Research Quarterly, 21*(4), 408–421.

Golden, Richard M. (1986). A developmental neural model of visual word perception. *Cognitive Science, 10*(3), 241–276.

Goldenberg, Claude (1991). Learning to read in New Zealand: The balance of skills and meaning. *Language Arts, 68*, 555–562.

Goldsmith-Phillips, J. (1989). Word and context in reading development: A test of the interactive-compensatory hypothesis. *Journal of Educational Psychology, 81*, 299–305.

Goldstein, Ira and Seymour Papert (1977). Artificial intelligence, language and the study of knowledge. *Cognitive Science, 1*, 84–123.

Golinkoff, Roberta Michnick (1975/1976). A comparison of reading comprehension processes in good and poor readers. *Reading Research Quarterly, 11*, 623–659.

Golinkoff, Roberta Michnick (Ed.) (1983). *The Transition from Prelinguistic to Linguistic Communication.* Hillsdale, NJ: Lawrence Erlbaum Associates.

Goodman, Kenneth S. (1965). A linguistic study of cues and miscues in reading. *Elementary English, 42*, 639–643.

Goodman, Kenneth S. (1967). Reading: A psycholinguistic guessing game. *Journal of the Reading Specialist, 6*, 126–135.

Goodman, Kenneth S. (1969). Analysis of oral reading miscues: Applied psycholinguistics. *Reading Research Quarterly, 5*(1), 9–30.

Goodman, Kenneth S. (1970). Dialect rejection and reading: A response. *Reading Research Quarterly, 5*(4), 600–603.

Goodman, Kenneth S. (1973). The 13th easy way to make learning to read difficult. *Reading Research Quarterly, 8*(4), 484–493.

Goodman, Kenneth S. (1981). Letter to the editors. *Reading Research Quarterly, 16*(3), 477–478.

Goodman, Kenneth S. (1982). *Language and Literacy: The Selected Writings of Kenneth S. Goodman* (Frederick Gollasch, Ed.). *Vol. 1: Process, Theory, Research; Vol. 2: Reading, Language and the Classroom Teacher.* Boston: Routledge and Kegan Paul.

Goodman, Kenneth S. (1986). *What's Whole in Whole Language?* Richmond Hill, ON: Scholastic.

Goodman, Kenneth S. (1992). Why whole language is today's agenda in education. *Language Arts, 69*, 354–363.

Goodman, Kenneth S. (1992/1993). Gurus, professors, and the politics of phonics, in Point/Counterpoint, Whole language versus direct instruction models, *Reading Today, 10*(3), 8–10.

Goodman, Kenneth S., Patrick Shannon, Yvonne S. Freeman, and Sharon Murphy (1988). *Report Card on Basal Readers.* Katonah, NY: Richard C. Owen.

Goodman, Nelson (1990). Picture in the mind? In Barlow, Horace, Colin Blakemore, and Miranda Weston-Smith (Eds.), *Images and Understanding.* Cambridge, UK: Cambridge University Press.

Goodman, Yetta M. (1978). Kid watching: An alternative to testing. *National Elementary Principal, 57*(4), 41–45.

Goodman, Yetta M. (1980). The roots of literacy. In Douglass, Malcolm P. (Ed.), *Proceedings: Claremont Reading Conference, 44th Annual Yearbook.* Claremont, CA.

Goody, Jack and Ian Watt (1972). The consequences of literacy. In Gigliolo, P. P. (Ed.), *Language and Social Context.* London: Penguin.

Gorman, Tom, Dougal Hutchison, and John Trimble (1993). *Reading in Reform: The Avon Collaborative Reading Project.* Slough, UK: National Foundation for Educational Research in England and Wales.

Goswami, Usha C. (1986). Children's use of analogy in learning to read: A developmental study. *Journal of Experimental Child Psychology, 42,* 73–83.

Goswami, Usha C. (1990). Phonological priming and orthographic analogies in reading. *Journal of Experimental Child Psychology, 49,* 323–340.

Goswami, Usha C. and Peter Bryant (1990). *Phonological Skills and Learning to Read.* Hove, UK: Lawrence Erlbaum Associates.

Goswami, Usha C. and Peter Bryant (1992). Rhyme, analogy, and children's reading. In Gough, Philip B., Linnea C. Ehri and Rebecca Treiman (Eds.) *Reading Acquisition,* Hillsdale, NJ: Lawrence Erlbaum Associates.

Gough, Philip B., Linnea C. Ehri, and Rebecca Treiman (Eds.) (1992). *Reading Acquisition,* Hillsdale, NJ: Lawrence Erlbaum Associates.

Gough, Philip B. and M. L. Hillinger (1980). Learning to read: An unnatural act. *Bulletin of the Orton Society, 30,* 180–196.

Gough, Philip B. and Margaret A. Walsh (1991). Chinese, Phoenicians, and the orthographic cipher of English. In Brady, Susan A. and Donald P. Shankweiler (Eds.), *Phonological Processes in Literacy: A Tribute to Isabelle Y. Liberman.* Hillsdale, NJ: Lawrence Erlbaum Associates.

Gourley, Judith W. (1978). This basal is easy to read—or is it? *The Reading Teacher, 32,* 174–182.

Graff, Harvey J. (1986). The Legacies of Literacy: Continuities and Contradictions in Western Culture and Society. In de Castell, Suzanne, Allan Luke, and Kieran Egan (Eds.), *Literacy, Society and Schooling: A Reader.* New York: Cambridge University Press.

Graff, Harvey J. (1987a). *The Labyrinths of Literacy: Reflections on Literacy Past and Present.* Philadelphia: Falmer.

Graff, Harvey J. (1987b). *The Legacies of Literacy: Continuities and Contradictions in Western Culture and Society.* Bloomington: Indiana University Press.

Graham, Steven (1980). Word recognition skills of learning disabled children and average students. *Reading Psychology, 2*(1), 23–33.

Gray, William S. (1956). *The Teaching of Reading and Writing: An International Survey.* Paris: UNESCO.

Greeno, James G. (1974). Learning and comprehension. In Gregg, Lee W. (Ed.), *Knowledge and Cognition.* Hillsdale, NJ: Lawrence Erlbaum Associates.

Greenwood, John D. (Ed.) (1991). *The Future of Folk Psychology: Intentionality and Cognitive Science.* Cambridge, UK: Cambridge University Press.

Gregory, Michael and Susanne Carroll (1978). *Language and Situation.* London: Routledge and Kegan Paul.

Grimes, Joseph E. (1975). *The Thread of Discourse.* The Hague: Mouton.

Groner, R., George W. McConkie, and C. Menz (Eds.) (1985). *Eye Movements and Human Information Processing.* North-Holland: Elsevier Science.

Guthrie, John T. (1973). Models of reading and reading disability. *Journal of Educational Psychology, 65*, 9–18.

Haber, Ralph N. and Lyn R. Haber (1981). The shape of a word can specify its meaning. *Reading Research Quarterly, 16*(3), 334–345.

Haber, Lyn R., Ralph N. Haber, and Karen R. Furlin (1983). Word length and word shape as sources of information in reading. *Reading Research Quarterly, 18*(2), 165–189.

Hall, Nigel (1987). *The Emergence of Literacy.* Sevenoaks, Kent, UK: Hodder and Stoughton.

Hall, William S. and Larry F. Guthrie (1982). Situational differences in the use of language. In Langer, Judith A. and M. Trika Smith-Burke (Eds.), *Reader Meets Author/Bridging the Gap.* Newark, DE: International Reading Association.

Halliday, Michael A. K. (1973). *Explorations in the Functions of Language.* London: Arnold.

Halliday, Michael A. K. (1975). *Learning How to Mean: Explorations in the Development of Language.* London: Arnold.

Halliday, Michael A. K. (1985). *An Introduction to Functional Grammar.* Baltimore: Arnold.

Halliday, Michael A. K. and Ruqaya Hasan (1976). *Cohesion in English.* London: Longman.

Hamill, Donald D. and Gaye McNutt (1981). *The Correlates of Reading.* Austin, TX: Pro-Ed.

Hansen, Jane, Thomas Newkirk, and Donald Graves (1985). *Breaking Ground: Teachers Relate Reading and Writing in the Elementary School.* Portsmouth, NH: Heinemann.

Harding, Leonora M., John R. Beech, and William Sneddon (1985). The changing pattern of reading errors and reading style from 5 to 11 years of age. *British Journal of Educational Psychology, 55*, 45–52.

Hardyck, C. D. and L. F. Petrinovich (1970). Subvocal speech and comprehension level as a function of the difficulty level of reading material. *Journal of Verbal Learning and Verbal Behavior, 9*, 647–652.

Harper, Lawrence V. (1975). The scope of offspring effects: From caregiver to culture. *Psychological Bulletin, 82*(5), 784–801.

Harris, Roy (1981). *The Language Myth.* London: Duckworth.

Harris, Roy (1988). *Language, Saussure and Wittgenstein: How to Play Games with Words.* London: Routledge.

Harste, Jerome (1989). The basalization of American reading instruction. *Theory into Practice, 28*, 265–273.

Harste, Jerome C., Virginia A. Woodward, and Carolyn L. Burke (1984). *Language Stories and Literacy Lessons.* Portsmouth, NH: Heinemann.

Hart, Leslie A. (1976). Misconceptions about learning disabilities. *National Elementary Principal, 56*(1), 54–57.

Hartman, Maria and Robert E. Kretschmer (1992). Talking and writing: Deaf teenagers reading *Sarah, Plain and Tall, Journal of Reading, 36*(3), 174–180.

Hausman, Carl R. (1985). Can computers create? *Interchange, 16*(1), 27–37.

Havelock, Eric A. (1976). *Origins of Western Literacy.* Toronto: Ontario Institute for Studies in Education.

Haviland, Susan E. and Herbert H. Clark (1974). What's new? Acquiring new information as a process in comprehension. *Journal of Verbal Learning and Verbal Behavior, 13*, 512–521.

Heap, James (1980). What counts as reading: Limits to certainty in assessment. *Curriculum Inquiry, 10*, 265–292.

Heath, Shirley Brice (1982a). *Ways With Words.* Cambridge, UK: Cambridge University Press.

Heath, Shirley Brice (1982b). What no bedtime story means: Narrative skills at home and at school. *Language in Society, 11*, 49–76.

Heath, Shirley Brice (1983). Research currents: A lot of talk about nothing. *Language Arts, 60*(4), 999–1007.

Heath, Shirley Brice (1985). Being literate in America: A sociohistorical perspective. In Niles,

Jerome A. and Rosary V. Lalik (Eds.), *Issues in Literacy: A Research Perspective.* Rochester, NY: National Reading Conference, 34th Yearbook.

Heath, Shirley Brice (1986). The functions and uses of literacy. In de Castell, Suzanne, Allan Luke, and Kieran Egan (Eds.), *Literacy, Society and Schooling: A Reader.* New York: Cambridge University Press.

Heath, Shirley Brice, Leslie Mangiola, Sandra R. Schachter, and Glynda A. Hull (Eds.) (1991). *Children of Promise: Literate Activity in Linguistically and Culturally Diverse Classrooms.* Urbana, IL: National Council of Teachers of English.

Heath, Shirley Brice and Charlene Thomas (1984). The achievement of pre-school literacy for mother and child. In Goelman, Hillel, Antoinette A. Oberg, and Frank Smith (Eds.), *Awakening to Literacy.* Exeter, NH: Heinemann.

Heckenmueller, E. G. (1965). Stabilization of the retinal image: A review of method, effects and theory. *Psychological Review, 63,* 157–169.

Hedley, Carolyn and Anthony N. Baratta (Eds.) (1985). *Contexts of Reading.* Norwood, NJ: Ablex.

Henderson, John M. (1976). Learning to read: A case study of a deaf child. *American Annals of the Deaf, 121,* 502–506.

Henderson, Leslie (1984). Writing systems and reading processes. In Henderson, Leslie (Ed), *Orthographies and Reading: Perspectives from Cognitive Psychology, Neuropsychology, and Linguistics.* Hillsdale, NJ: Lawrence Erlbaum Associates.

Henderson, Leslie (1987). Word recognition: A tutorial review. In Coltheart, Max (Ed.), *Attention and Performance XIII: The Psychology of Reading.* Hove, UK: Lawrence Erlbaum Associates.

Herman, Patricia A., Richard C. Anderson, P. David Pearson, and William E. Nagy (1987). Incidental acquisition of word meaning from expositions with varied text features. *Reading Research Quarterly, 22*(3), 263–284.

Hidi, Suzanne, William Baird, and Angela Hildyard (1982). That's important but is it interesting? Two factors in text processing. In Flammer, August and Walter Kintsch (Eds.), *Discourse Processing.* Amsterdam: North Holland.

Hiebert, Elfrieda H. (1981). Developmental patterns and interrelationships of preschool children's print awareness. *Reading Research Quarterly, 16*(2), 236–260.

Hiebert, Elfrieda H. (1983). An examination of ability grouping for reading instruction. *Reading Research Quarterly, 18*(3), 231–255.

Hiebert, Elfrieda H. and Robert E. Calfee (1992). Assessing literacy: From standardized tests to portfolios and performances. In Samuels, S. Jay and Alan E. Farstrup (Eds.), *What Research Has to Say About Reading Instruction* (2nd ed.). Newark, DE: International Reading Association.

Hirst, William (Ed.) (1988). *The Making of Cognitive Science: Essays in Honor of George A. Miller.* Cambridge: Cambridge University Press.

Hochberg, Julian E. (1978). *Perception* (2nd ed.). Englewood Cliffs, NJ: Prentice-Hall.

Hochberg, Julian E. and Virginia Brooks (1976). Reading as intentional behavior. In Singer, Harry and Robert B. Ruddell (Eds.), *Theoretical Models and Processes of Reading* (2nd ed.). Newark, DE: International Reading Association.

Holdaway, Don. (1976). Self-evaluation and reading development. In Merritt, John (Ed.), *New Horizons in Reading.* Newark, DE: International Reading Association.

Hoosain, Rumjahn (1991). *Psycholinguistic Implications for Linguistic Relativity: A Case Study of Chinese.* Hillsdale, NJ: Lawrence Erlbaum Associates.

Howe, M. J. A. and Linda Singer (1975). Presentation variables and students' activities in meaningful learning. *British Journal of Educational Psychology, 45,* 52–61.

Howes, D. H. and R. L. Solomon (1951). Visual duration threshold as a function of word-probability. *Journal of Experimental Psychology, 41,* 401–410.

Huck, Charlotte S. (1992). Literacy and literature, *Language Arts, 69,* 520–526.

Hudson, Judith A. (1986). Memories are made of this. In Katherine Nelson (Ed.), *Event Knowledge*. Hillsdale, NJ: Lawrence Erlbaum Associates.

Huey, Edmund Burke (1908). *The Psychology and Pedagogy of Reading*. New York: Macmillan. Reprinted Cambridge, MA: MIT Press, (1968).

Hull, Robert (1985). *The Language Gap: How Classroom Dialogue Fails*. London: Methuen.

Hummel, John E. and Irving Biederman (1992). Dynamic binding in a neural network for shape recognition. *Psychological Review, 99*(3), 480–517.

Hunt, Earl and Franca Agnoli (1991). The Whorfian hypothesis: A cognitive psychology perspective. *Psychological Review, 98*(3), 377–389.

Huttenlocher, Janellen and Deborah Burke (1976). Why does memory span increase with age? *Cognitive Psychology, 8*(1), 1–31.

Intraub, Helen and James E. Hoffman (1992). Reading and visual memory: Remembering scenes that were never seen. *American Journal of Psychology, 105*(1), 101–114.

Iser, Wolfgang S. (1973). *The Act of Reading*. Baltimore: Johns Hopkins University Press.

Iser, Wolfgang (1978). *The Art of Reading: A Theory of Aesthetic Response*. London: Routledge and Kegan Paul.

Jaggar, Angela M. and M. Trika Smith-Burke (Eds.) (1985). *Observing the Language Learner*. Newark, DE: International Reading Association.

Jaggar, Angela M., Donna H. Carrara, and Sara E. Weiss (1986). The influence of reading on children's narrative writing (and vice versa). *Language Arts, 63*(3), 292–300.

Jakobson, Roman and Morris Halle (1956). *Fundamentals of Language*. The Hague: Mouton.

Jampole, Ellen S., Bonnie C. Konopak, John E. Readence, and E. Barry Moser (1991). Using mental imagery to enhance gifted elementary students' creative writing. *Reading Psychology, 12*, 183–197.

Jared, Debra and Mark S. Seidenberg (1991). Does word identification proceed from spelling to sound to meaning? *Journal of Experimental Psychology: General, 120*(4), 358–394.

Jaynes, Julian (1976). *The Origins of Consciousness in the Breakdown of the Bicameral Mind*. Boston: Houghton Mifflin.

Jaynes, Julian (1986). Consciousness and the voices of the mind. *Canadian Psychology, 27*(2), 128–140.

Jenkins, Joseph J. (1974). Remember that old theory of memory? Well, forget it! *American Psychologist, 29*(11), 785–795.

Jenkins, James R., R. B. Bausel, and L. M. Jenkins (1972). Comparison of letter name and letter sound training as transfer variables. *American Educational Research Journal, 9*, 75–86.

Jensen, Julie M. (Ed.) (1984). *Composing and Comprehending*. Urbana, IL: National Conference on Research in English.

Johnson, Neal S. (1975). On the function of letters in word identification: Some data and a preliminary model. *Journal of Verbal Learning and Verbal Behavior, 14*(1), 17–29.

Johnson-Laird, Philip N. (1982). Procedural semantics and mental models. In Mehler, Jacques, Edward C. T. Walker, and Merrill Garrett (Eds.), *Perspectives on Mental Representation*. Hillsdale, NJ: Lawrence Erlbaum Associates.

Johnson-Laird, Philip N. (1990). Human thinking and mental models. In Mohyeldin Said, K. A., W. H. Newton-Smith, R. Viale, and Kathleen V. Wilkes (Eds.), *Modeling the Mind*, Oxford, Clarendon.

Johnson-Laird, Philip N., Ruth M. J. Byrne, and Walter Schaeken (1992). Propositional reasoning by model. *Psychological Review, 99*(3), 418–439.

Johnston, Cathy (1989). Parents and reading: A U.K. perspective. *The Reading Teacher, 42*, 352–357.

Johnston, J. C. and James L. McClelland (1974). Perception of letters in words: Seek not and ye shall find. *Science, 184*, 1192–1193.

Johnston, Peter H. (1985). Understanding reading disability: A case-study approach. *Harvard Educational Review*, *55*(2), 153–177.

Jones, Edward E. (1986). Interpreting interpersonal behavior: The effects of expectancies. *Science*, *234*, 41–46.

Juel, Connie and Betty Holmes (1981). Oral and silent reading of sentences. *Reading Research Quarterly*, *15*, 545–568.

Juel, Connie and Diana Roper/Schneider (1985). The influence of basal readers on first grade reading. *Reading Research Quarterly*, *20*(2), 134–152.

Just, Marcel A. and Patricia A. Carpenter (Eds.) (1977). *Cognitive Processes in Comprehension*. Hillsdale, NJ: Lawrence Erlbaum Associates.

Just, Marcel A. and Patricia A. Carpenter (1980). A theory of reading, from eye fixations to comprehension. *Psychological Review*, *87*(6), 329–354.

Just, Marcel A. and Patricia A. Carpenter (1984). Using eye fixations to study reading comprehension. In Kieras, David E. and Marcel A. Just (Eds.), *New Methods in Reading Comprehension Research*. Hillsdale, NJ: Lawrence Erlbaum Associates.

Kagan, Jerome (1970). The determinants of attention in the infant. *American Scientist*, *58*, 298–306.

Kail, Robert (1979). *The Development of Memory in Children*. San Francisco: Freeman.

Kantor, Rebecca, Sandra M. Miller, and David E. Fernie (1992). Diverse paths to literacy in a preschool classroom: A sociocultural perspective. *Reading Research Quarterly*, *27*(3), 184–201.

Kieras, David E. and Marcel A. Just (Eds.) (1984). *New Methods in Reading Comprehension Research*. Hillsdale, NJ: Lawrence Erlbaum Associates.

Kimchi, Ruth (1992). Primacy of wholistic processing and global/local paradigm: A critical review. *Psychological Bulletin*, *112*(1), 24–38.

Kimmel, Susan and Walter H. MacGinitie (1984). Identifying children who use a perseverative text processing strategy. *Reading Research Quarterly*, *19*(2), 162–172.

Kintsch, Walter (1982). Memory for text. In Flammer, August and Walter Kintsch. *Discourse Processing*. Amsterdam: North Holland.

Kintsch, Walter (1988). The use of knowledge in discourse processing: A construction-integration model. *Psychological Review*, *95*, 163–182.

Kintsch, Walter and Teun A. van Dijk (1975). Recalling and summarizing stories. *Language*, *40*, 98–116.

Kintsch, Walter and Teun A. van Dijk (1978). Towards a model of text comprehension and production. *Psychological Review*, *85*, 363–394.

Klahr, D., W. G. Chase, and E. A. Lovelace (1983). Structure and process in alphabetic retrieval. *Journal of Experimental Psychology: Learning, Memory and Cognition*, *9*, 462–477.

Klatzky, Roberta L. (1980) *Human Memory: Structures and Processes* (2nd ed.). San Francisco: Freeman.

Kleiman, Gary M. (1975). Speech recoding in reading. *Journal of Verbal Learning and Verbal Behavior*, *14*, 323–339.

Klein, Gary A. and Helen Altman Klein (1973). Word identification as a function of contextual information. *American Journal of Psychology*, *86*(2), 399–406.

Klein, Helen Altman, Gary A. Klein, and Mary Bertino (1974). Utilization of context for word identification in children. *Journal of Experimental Psychology*, *17*, 79–86.

Kluender, Keith R., Randy L. Diehl, and Peter R. Killeen (1987). Japanese quail can learn phonetic categories. *Science*, *237*, 1195–1197.

Kolers, Paul A. (1966). Reading and talking bilingually. *American Journal of Psychology*, *79*, 357–376.

Kolers, Paul A. (1967). Reading is only incidentally visual. In Goodman, Kenneth S. and James

T. Fleming (Eds.), *Psycholinguistics and the Teaching of Reading*. Newark, DE: International Reading Association.

Kolers, Paul A. (1970). Three stages of reading. In Levin, Harry and Joanna P. Williams (Eds.), *Basic Studies on Reading*. New York: Basic Books.

Kolers, Paul A. (1975). Specificity of operations in sentence recognition. *Cognitive Psychology, 7*, 289–306.

Kolers, Paul A. (1976). Buswell's discoveries. In Money, R. A. and J. W. Senders (Eds.), *Eye Movements and Psychological Processes*. Hillsdale, NJ: Lawrence Erlbaum Associates.

Kolers, Paul A. and M. T. Katzman (1966). Naming sequentially presented letters and words. *Language and Speech, 9*(2), 84–95.

Kolers, Paul A. and Henry L. Roediger (1984). Procedures of mind. *Journal of Verbal Learning and Verbal Behavior, 23*, 425–449.

Komatsu, Lloyd K. (1992). Recent views of conceptual structure. *Psychological Bulletin, 112*(3), 500–526.

Korkeamäki, Riitta-Liisa, and Mariam Jean Dreher (1993). Finland, phonics, and whole language: Beginning reading in a regular letter-sound correspondence language. *Language Arts, 70*, 475–482.

Kosslyn, Stephen M. (1980). *Image and Mind*. Cambridge, MA: Harvard University Press.

Krashen, Stephen D. (1976). Formal and informal linguistic environments in language acquisition and language learning. *TESOL Quarterly, 10*(2), 157–168.

Krashen, Stephen D. (1985). *Inquiries and Insights*. Hayward, CA: Alemany Press.

Krashen, Stephen D. (1987). *Comic Book Reading and Language Development*. Victoria, BC: Abel Press.

Krashen, Stephen D. (1991). *Fundamentals of Language Education*. Torrance, CA: Laredo.

Krashen, Stephen D. (1993). *The Power of Reading: Insights from the Research*. Englewood, CO: Libraries Unlimited.

Krueger, Lester E. (1975). Familiarity effects in visual information processing. *Psychological Bulletin, 82*(6), 949–974.

Krueger, Lester E., Robert H. Keen, and Bella Rublevich (1974). Letter search through words and nonwords by adults and fourth-grade children. *Journal of Experimental Psychology, 102*(5), 845–849.

Kuhn, Thomas (1970). *The Structure of Scientific Revolutions*. Chicago: University of Chicago Press.

Kutas, Marta and Steven A. Hillyard (1980). Reading senseless sentences: Brain potentials reflect semantic anomaly. *Science, 207*, 203–204.

Kutz, Eleanor (1992). Teacher research: Myths and realities. *Language Arts, 69*, 193–197.

Lakoff, George (1987). *Women, Fire, and Dangerous Things: What Categories Reveal About the Mind*. Chicago: University of Chicago Press.

Langer, Judith A. (1982a). Facilitating text processing: The elaboration of prior knowledge. In Langer, Judith A. and M. Trika Smith-Burke (Eds.), *Reader Meets Author/Bridging the Gap*. Newark, DE: International Reading Association.

Langer, Judith A. (1982b). Reading, thinking, writing . . . and teaching. *Language Arts, 59*(4), 336–341.

Langer, Judith A. and M. Trika Smith-Burke (Eds.) (1982). *Reader Meets Author/Bridging the Gap*. Newark, DE: International Reading Association.

Langer, Suzanne K. (1951). *Philosophy in a New Key*. Cambridge, MA: Harvard University Press.

Larsen, Steen F. (1986). Procedural thinking, programming and computer use. In Hollnagel, E., G. Mancini, and D. Woods (Eds.), *Intelligent Decision Aids in Process Environments*. Berlin: Springer-Verlag.

Laufer, Batia (1992). Reading in a foreign language: How does L2 lexical knowledge interact with the reader's general academic ability? *Journal of Research in Reading, 15*(2), 95–103.

Lawler, R. W. and M. Yazdani (Eds.) (1987). *Artificial intelligence and Education (Vol. 1): Learning Environments and Tutoring Systems.* Norwood, NJ: Ablex.

Lenneberg, Eric H. and Elizabeth Lenneberg (Eds.) (1975). *Foundations of Language Development: A Multidisciplinary Approach* (2 vols.). New York: Academic Press.

Levin, Beth and Steven Pinker (1991). Introduction to special issue of *Cognition* on lexical and conceptual semantics. *Cognition, 41,* 1–7.

Levin, Harry (1987). Successions in psychology (review of Baars, Bernard J. *The Cognitive Revolution in Psychology*). *Science, 236,* 1683–1684.

Levine, K. (1986). *The Social Context of Literacy.* London: Routledge and Kegan Paul.

Levy, Betty Ann (1978). Speech analysis during sentence processing: Reading and listening. *Visible Language, 12,* 81–102.

Lewis, Donald J. (1979). Psychobiology of active and inactive memory. *Psychological Bulletin, 86,* 1054–1083.

Liben, Lynn S. (1983). *Piaget and the Foundations of Knowledge.* Hillsdale, NJ: Lawrence Erlbaum Associates.

Liberman, Alvin M., Franklin S. Cooper, Donald P. Shankweiler, and M. Studdert-Kennedy (1957). Perception of the speech code. *Psychological Review, 54,* 358–368.

Liberman, Alvin M. and Ignatius G. Mattingly (1989). A specialization for speech perception. *Science, 243,* 489–494.

Liberman, Isabelle Y. and Alvin M. Liberman (1992). Whole language versus code emphasis: Underlying assumptions and their implications for reading instruction. In Gough, Philip B., Linnea C. Ehri and Rebecca Treiman (Eds.) *Reading Acquisition*, Hillsdale, NJ: Lawrence Erlbaum Associates.

Liberman, Isabelle Y. and Donald P. Shankweiler (1979). Speech, the alphabet and teaching to read. In Resnick, Lauren B. and Phyllis A. Weaver (Eds.), *Theory and Practice of Early Reading* (Vol. 2). Hillsdale, NJ: Lawrence Erlbaum Associates.

Lieberman, Philip (1984). *The Biology and Evolution of Language.* Cambridge, MA: Harvard University Press.

Lindsay, Peter H. and Donald A. Norman (1977). *Human Information Processing* (2nd ed.). New York: Academic Press.

Lipson, Marjorie Y. (1983). The influence of religious affiliation on children's memory for text information. *Reading Research Quarterly, 18*(4), 448–457.

Lipson, Marjorie Y. (1984). Some unexpected issues in prior knowledge and comprehension. *The Reading Teacher, 37,* 760–764.

Lipson, Marjorie Y. and Karen K. Wixson (1986). Reading disability research: An interactionist perspective. *Review of Educational Research, 56*(1), 111–136.

Littlefair, Alison B. (1991). *Reading All Types of Writing: The Importance of Genre and Register for Reading Development.* Milton Keynes: Open University.

Llewellyn-Thomas E. (1962). Eye movements in speed reading. In *Speed Reading: Practices and Procedures, No. 10.* Newark, DE: University of Delaware Reading Study Center.

Lodge, David (1990). *After Bakhtin: Essays on Fiction and Criticism.* London: Routledge.

Long, Shirley A., Peter N. Winograd, and Connie A. Bridge (1989). The effects of reader and text characteristics on imagery reported during and after reading. *Reading Research Quarterly, 24*(3), 353–372.

Lott, Deborah and Frank Smith (1970). Knowledge of intra-word redundancy by beginning readers. *Psychonomic Science, 19*(6), 343–344.

Lucas, Margery M. (1991). Semantic representation of meaning: A defense. *Psychological Bulletin, 2,* 254–263.

Lyons, John (1977). *Semantics* (2 vols.). Cambridge, UK: Cambridge University Press.

MacGinitie, Walter (1984). Readability as a solution adds to the problem. In Anderson, Richard C., Jean Osborn, and Robert J. Tierney (Eds.), *Learning to Read in American Schools: Basal Readers and Content Texts*. Hillsdale, NJ: Lawrence Erlbaum Associates.

MacGinitie, Walter and Ruth K. MacGinitie (1986). Teaching students not to read. In de Castell, Suzanne, A. Luke, and Kieran Egan (Eds.), *Literacy, Society and Schooling: A Reader*. New York: Cambridge University Press.

Mackworth, Norman H. (1965). Visual noise causes tunnel vision. *Psychonomic Science, 3*, 67–68.

Macnamara, John (1972). Cognitive basis of language learning in infants. *Psychological Review, 79*(1), 1–13.

MacWhinney, Brian and Jared Leinbach (1991). Implementations are not conceptualizations: Revising the verb-learning model. *Cognition, 40*, 121–157.

Magee, Bryan (1973). *Popper*. London: Fontana.

Makita, Kiyoshi (1968). The rarity of reading disability in Japanese children. *American Journal of Orthopsychiatry, 38*(4), 599–614.

Makita, Kiyoshi (1976). Reading disability and the writing system. In Merritt, John E. (Ed.), *New Horizons in Reading*. Newark, DE: International Reading Association.

Mandler, George (1967). Organization and memory. In Spence, Kenneth W. and Janet T. Spence (Eds.), *The Psychology of Learning and Motivation* (Vol. 1). New York: Academic Press.

Mandler, George (1980). Recognizing: The judgment of previous occurrence. *Psychological Review, 87*(3), 252–271.

Mandler, George (1985). *Cognitive Psychology: An Essay in Cognitive Science*. Hillsdale, NJ: Lawrence Erlbaum Associates.

Mandler, Jean Matter (1978). A code in the node: The use of a story schema in retrieval. *Discourse Processes, 1*, 14–35.

Mandler, Jean Matter (1984). *Stories, Script, and Scenes: Aspects of Schema Theory*. Hillsdale, NJ: Lawrence Erlbaum Associates.

Mandler, Jean Matter (1992). How to build a baby: II Conceptual primitives. *Psychological Review, 99*(4), 587–604.

Mandler, Jean Matter and Marsha S. Goodman (1982). On the psychological validity of story structure. *Journal of Verbal Learning and Verbal Behavior, 21*, 507–523.

Mandler, Jean Matter and Neal S. Johnson (1977). Remembrance of things parsed: Story structure and recall. *Cognitive Psychology, 9*, 111–151.

Maratsos, Michael (1992). Constraints, modules and specificity. In Gunnar, Megan R. and Michael Maratsos (Eds.), *Modularity and Constraints in Language and Cognition* (The Minnesota Symposia on Child Psychology, Vol. 25). Hillsdale, NJ: Lawrence Erlbaum Associates.

Marcel, Tony (1978). Unconscious reading: Experiments on people who do not know that they are reading. *Visible Language, 12*(4), 391–404.

Marchbanks, Gabrielle and Harry Levin (1965). Cues by which children recognize words. *Journal of Educational Psychology, 56*(2), 57–61.

Margolis, Howard (1987). *Patterns, Thinking and Cognition: A Theory of Judgment*. Chicago: University of Chicago Press.

Markman, Ellen M. (1992). Constraints on word learning: Speculations about their nature, origins and domain specificity. In Gunnar, Megan R. and Michael Maratsos (Eds.), *Modularity and Constraints in Language and Cognition* (The Minnesota Symposia on Child Psychology, Vol. 25). Hillsdale, NJ: Lawrence Erlbaum Associates.

Marr, David (1982). *Vision*. San Francisco: Freeman.

Marshall, John C. and F. Newcombe (1966). Syntactic and semantic errors in paralexia. *Neuropsychologia, 4*, 169–176.

Martin, Maryanne (1979). Top-down processing and target search in reading. *Perceptual and Motor Skills, 48*, 467–470.

Mason, Jana M. (1980). When do children begin to read?: An exploration of four-year-old children's letter and word reading competencies. *Reading Research Quarterly, 15*(2), 203–227.

Mason, Jana M. (Ed). (1989). *Reading and Writing Connections.* Boston: Allyn and Bacon.

Massaro, Dominic W. (1975). *Experimental Psychology and Information Processing.* Skokie, IL: Rand McNally.

Massaro, Dominic W. and David Klitzke (1977). Letters are functional in word identification. *Memory and Cognition, 5*, 292–298.

Masson, Michael E. J. and Linda S. Sala (1978). Interactive processes in sentence comprehension and recognition. *Cognitive Psychology, 10*, 244–270.

Mathews, M. M. (1966). *Teaching to Read: Historically Considered.* Chicago: University of Chicago Press.

Mattingly, Ignatius G. (1985). Reading, linguistic awareness, and language acquisition. In Downing, John and Renate Valtin (Eds.), *Language Awareness and Learning to Read.* New York: Springer-Verlag.

Mayher, John S. and Rita S. Brause (1986). Is your classroom like your grandmother's? *Language Arts, 63*(6), 617–620.

Mayor, Barbara M. and Anthony K. Pugh (Eds.) (1987). *Language, Communication and Education.* London: Croom Helm.

McCabe, Viki (1986). Epilogue: Cognition and ethics. In McCabe, Viki and Gerald J. Balzano (Eds.), *Event Cognition: An Ecological Perspective.* Hillsdale, NJ: Lawrence Erlbaum Associates.

McCabe, Viki and Gerald J. Balzano (Eds.) (1986). *Event Cognition: An Ecological Perspective.* Hillsdale, NJ: Lawrence Erlbaum Associates.

McCartney, K. and Katherine Nelson (1981). Children's use of scripts in story recall. *Discourse Processes, 4*, 59–70.

McCawley, James D. (1968). The role of semantics in a grammar. In Eamon Bach and R. T. Harms (Eds.), *Universals in Linguistic Theory.* New York: Holt, Rinehart and Winston.

McClelland, James L. (1985). Putting knowledge in its place: A scheme for programming parallel processing structures on the fly. *Cognitive Science, 9*(1), 113–146.

McClelland, James L. and David E. Rumelhart (1981). An interactive activation model of context effects in letter perception: Part I: An account of basic findings. *Psychological Review, 88*, 375–407.

McConkie, George W. and Keith Rayner (1975). The span of the effective stimulus during a fixation in reading. *Perception and Psychophysics, 17*, 578–586.

McFarland, Carl E. and Deborah H. Rhodes (1978). Memory for meaning in skilled and unskilled readers. *Journal of Experimental Child Psychology, 25*, 199–207.

McGee, Lea M. (1982). Awareness of text structure: Effects on children's recall of expository text. *Reading Research Quarterly, 17*(4), 581–590.

McGee, Lea M. (1992). Exploring the literature-based reading revolution. *Language Arts, 69*, 529–537.

McKeown, Margaret G. (1985). The acquisition of word meaning from context by children of high and low ability. *Reading Research Quarterly, 20*(4), 482–496.

McKeown, Margaret G. (1993). Creating effecting definitions for young word learners. *Reading Research Quarterly, 28*(1), 16–31.

McLaughlin, Barry (1977). Second-language learning in children. *Psychological Review, 84*(3), 438–459.

McMahon, Margaret L. (1983). Development of reading-while-listening skills in the primary grades. *Reading Research Quarterly, 19*(1), 38–52.

McMahon, Susan I. (1992). Book club: A case study of a group of fifth graders as they participate in a literature based reading program. (IRA Outstanding Dissertation Award for 1991–1992). *Reading Research Quarterly, 27*(4), 292–293.

McNamara, Timothy P., Diane I. Miller, and John D. Bransford (1991). Mental models and reading comprehension. In Barr, Rebecca, Michael L. Kamil, Peter Mosenthal, and P. David Pearson (Eds.), *Handbook of Reading Research*. New York: Longman.

McNeill, David (1967). Developmental psycholinguistics. In Smith, Frank and George A. Miller (Eds.), *The Genesis of Language*. Cambridge, MA: MIT Press.

McNeill, David (1985). So you think gestures are nonverbal? *Psychological Review, 92*(3), 350–371.

McNeill, David and Karen Lindig (1973). The perceptual reality of phonemes, syllables, words and sentences. *Journal of Verbal Learning and Verbal Behavior, 12*(4), 419–430.

McPeck, John E. (1981). *Critical Thinking and Education*. Oxford: Martin Robertson.

Medin, D. L. (1989). Concepts and conceptual structures. *American Psychologist, 44*, 1469–1481.

Meek, Margaret (1982). *Learning to Read*. London: Bodley Head.

Meek, Margaret (1984). Speaking of shifters. In Meek, Margaret and Jane Miller (Eds.), *Changing English: Essays for Harold Rosen*. London: Heinemann.

Meek, Margaret (1988). How texts teach what readers learn. In Lightfoot, Martin and Nancy Martin (Eds.), *The Word for Teaching is Learning: Essays for James Britton*. London: Heinemann.

Meek, Margaret, Stephen Armstrong, Vicky Austerfield, Judith Graham, and Elizabeth Plackett (1983). *Achieving Literacy: Longitudinal Studies of Adolescents Learning to Read*. London: Routledge and Kegan Paul.

Menyuk, Paula (1971). *The Acquisition and Development of Language*. Englewood Cliffs, NJ: Prentice-Hall.

Merritt, John E. (Ed.) (1976). *New Horizons in Reading*. Newark, DE: International Reading Association.

Meyer, Bonnie J. F. (1985). Prose analysis: Purposes, procedures and problems. In Britton, B. K. and J. B. Black (Eds.), *Understanding Expository Text*. Hillsdale, NJ: Lawrence Erlbaum Associates.

Meyer, David E. and Roger W. Schvaneveldt (1971). Facilitation in recognizing pairs of words: Evidence of a dependence between retrieval operations. *Journal of Experimental Psychology, 90*, 227–234.

Michotte, A. (1946). *La Perception de la Causalité*. Louvain: Institut Supérieur de Philosophie.

Mikulecky, Larry (1982). Job literacy: The relationship between school preparation and workplace actuality. *Reading Research Quarterly, 17*(3), 400–419.

Miller, George A. (1951). *Language and Communication*. New York: McGraw-Hill.

Miller, George A. (1956). The magical number seven, plus or minus two: Some limits on our capacity for processing information. *Psychological Review, 63*, 81–92.

Miller, George A. (1964). *Mathematics and Psychology*. New York: Wiley.

Miller, George A. (1965). Some preliminaries to psycholinguistics. *American Psychologist, 20*, 15–20.

Miller, George A. (1977). *Spontaneous Apprentices: Children and Language*. New York: Seabury.

Miller, George A., Jerome S. Bruner, and Leo Postman (1954). Familiarity of letter sequences and tachistoscopic identification. *Journal of Genetic Psychology, 50*, 129–139.

Miller, George A. and Christine Fellbaum (1991). Semantic networks of English. *Cognition, 41*, 197–229.

Miller, George A., G. A. Heise, and W. Lichten (1951). The intelligibility of speech as a function of the context of the test materials. *Journal of Experimental Psychology, 41*, 329–335.

Miller, George A. and Philip N. Johnson-Laird (1976). *Language and Perception*. Cambridge, MA: Belknap Press.

Miller, George A. and Patricia E. Nicely (1955). An analysis of perceptual confusions among some English consonants. *Journal of the Acoustical Society of America, 27*, 338–353.

Miller, Larry (1991). The whole language path: Postholes and signposts. *Reflections on Canadian Literacy*, 9(2), 123–127.

Minsky, Marvin (1980). K-lines: A theory of memory. *Cognitive Science*, 4, 117–133.

Moerk, Ernest L. (1977). *Pragmatic and Semantic Aspects of Early Language Development.* Baltimore: University Park Press.

Mohyeldin Said, K. A., W. H. Newton-Smith, R. Viale, and Kathleen V. Wilkes (Eds.) (1990). *Modelling the Mind.* Oxford: Clarendon.

Moll, Luis C. (Ed.) (1990). *Vygotsky and Education: Instructional Implications and Applications of Sociohistorical Psychology.* Cambridge, UK: Cambridge University Press.

Moore, David W. (1983). A case for naturalistic assessment of reading comprehension. *Language Arts, 60*(4), 957–969.

Moore, Timothy E. (Ed.) (1973). *Cognitive Development and the Acquisition of Language.* New York: Academic Press.

Moorman, Gary B., William E. Blanton, and Thomas M. McLaughlin (1992). The rhetoric of whole language, Parts 1 and 2. *Reading Psychology, 13*(2) iii-xiv and *13*(3) iii-xiv.

Morris, Charles (1946). *Signs, Language and Behavior.* New York: Prentice-Hall.

Morris, P. E. (1988). Expertise and everyday memory. In Gruneberg, M. M., P. E. Morris, and R. N. Sykes (Eds.), *Practical Aspects of Memory: Current Research and Issues, Vol. I: Memory in Everyday Life.* Chichester, UK: Wiley.

Morrow, Lesley Mandel (1992). The impact of a literature-based program on literacy achievement, use of literature, and attitudes of children from minority backgrounds. *Reading Research Quarterly*, 27(3), 251–275.

Morrow, Lesley Mandel and Carol Simon Weinstein (1986). Encouraging voluntary reading: The impact of a literature program on children's use of library centers. *Reading Research Quarterly, 21*(3), 330–346.

Morton, John (1969). Interaction of information in word recognition. *Psychological Review*, 76(2), 165–178.

Morton, John (1982). Disintegrating the lexicon: An information-processing approach. In Mehler, Jacques, Edward C. T. Walker, and Merrill Garrett (Eds.), *Perspectives on Mental Representation.* Hillsdale, NJ: Lawrence Erlbaum Associates.

Mosberg, Ludwig (1978). A response: Comments on *Language by Ear and by Eye* (eds. James S. Kavanagh and Ignatius G. Mattingly). In Murray, Frank B. and John J. Pukulski (Eds.), *The Acquisition of Reading: Cognitive, Linguistic and Perceptual Prerequisites.* Baltimore: University Park Press.

Mosenthal, Peter (1976/1977). Psycholinguistic properties of aural and visual comprehension as determined by children's abilities to comprehend syllogisms. *Reading Research Quarterly, 12*(1), 55–92.

Mosenthal, Peter (1983). The influence of social situation on children's classroom comprehension of text. *Elementary School Journal, 8*(5), 537–547.

Moskowitz, Breyne Arlene (1978). The acquisition of language. *Scientific American, 12*, 92–108.

Moyer, Sandra B. and Phillis L. Newcomer (1977). Reversals in reading diagnosis and remediation. *Exceptional Children, 43*, 424–429.

Myers, Jamie (1992). The social contexts of school and personal literacy. *Reading Research Quarterly*, 27(4), 296–333.

Nagy, William E. and Richard C. Anderson (1984). The number of words in printed school English. *Reading Research Quarterly, 19*(2), 304–330.

Nagy, William E. and Patricia A. Herman (1987). Breadth and depth of vocabulary knowledge: Implications for acquisition and instruction. In McKeown, Margaret G. and M. E. Curtis (Eds.), *The Nature of Vocabulary Acquisition.* Hillside, NJ: Lawrence Erlbaum Associates.

Nagy, William E., Patricia A. Herman, and Richard C. Anderson (1985). Learning words from context. *Reading Research Quarterly, 20*(2), 233–253.

Navon, David (1977). Forest before trees: The precedence of global features in visual perception. *Cognitive Psychology, 9*, 353–385.

Naylor, Hilary (1980). Reading disability and lateral asymmetry: An information-processing analysis. *Psychological Bulletin, 87*(3), 531–545.

Neilsen, Lorri (1993). Response to Ridgeway, Dunston and Qian: Authoring the questions: Research as an ethical enterprise. *Reading Research Quarterly, 28*(4), 349–353.

Neisser, Ulric (1967). *Cognitive Psychology*. New York: Appleton.

Neisser, Ulric (1977). *Cognition and Reality*. San Francisco: Freeman.

Neisser, Ulric (1983). Components in intelligence or steps in routine procedures? *Cognition, 15*, 189–197.

Neisser, Ulric and H. K. Beller (1965). Searching through word lists. *British Journal of Psychology, 56*, 349–358.

Nell, Victor (1988). The psychology of reading for pleasure: Needs and gratifications. *Reading Research Quarterly, 23*(1), 6–50.

Nelson, Katherine (1973). Structure and strategy in learning to talk. *Monographs of the Society for Research in Child Development, 38*, 149.

Nelson, Katherine (1974). Concept, word and sentence: Interrelations in acquisition and development. *Psychological Review, 81*(4), 267–285.

Nelson, Katherine (1985). *Making Sense: Development of Meaning in Early Childhood*. New York: Academic Press.

Nelson, Katherine (1986). *Event Knowledge*. Hillsdale, NJ: Lawrence Erlbaum Associates.

Newell, Allen (1990). *Unified Theories of Cognition*. Cambridge, MA: Harvard University Press.

Newman, Edwin B. (1966). Speed of reading when the span of letters is restricted. *American Journal of Psychology, 79*, 272–278.

Newman, Judith M. (Ed.) (1985). *Whole Language: Theory and Use*. Portsmouth, NH: Heinemann.

Newson, John and Elizabeth Newson (1975). Intersubjectivity and the transmission of culture: On the social origins of symbolic functioning. *Bulletin of the British Psychological Society, 28*, 437–446.

Nicholson, Tom and Robert Imlach (1981). Where do their answers come from? A study of the inferences which children make when answering questions about narrative stories. *Journal of Reading Behavior, 13*(2), 111–129.

Ninio, A. and Jerome S. Bruner (1978). The achievement and antecedents of labelling. *Journal of Child Language, 5*, 5–15.

Nisbett, Richard E. and Timothy DeCamp Wilson (1977). Telling more than we can know: Verbal reports on mental processes. *Psychological Review, 84*(3), 231–259.

Norman, Donald A. (1969). *Memory and Attention: An Introduction to Human Information Processing*. New York: Wiley.

Norman, Donald A. (1976). *Memory and Attention: An Introduction to Human Information Processing* (2nd ed.). New York: Wiley.

Norman, Donald A. (1993). Cognition in the head and in the world: An introduction to the special issue on situated action. *Cognition, 17*(1), 1–6.

Norman, Donald A. and Daniel G. Bobrow (1979). Descriptions: An intermediate stage in memory retrieval. *Cognitive Psychology, 11*, 107–123.

Norman, Donald A. and David E. Rumelhart (1975). *Explorations in Cognition*. San Francisco: Freeman.

Nystrand, Martin (1986). *The Structure of Written Communication*. Orlando, FL: Academic Press.

Nystrand, Martin and Jeffrey Wiemelt (1991). When is a text explicit? Formalist and dialogical conceptions. *Text, 11*(1), 25–41.

Oatley, Keith (1978). *Perceptions and Representations: The Theoretical Bases of Brain Research and Psychology*. New York: The Free Press.

O'Brien, Edward J. and Jerome L. Myers (1985). When comprehension difficulty improves memory for text. *Journal of Experimental Psychology: Learning, Memory and Cognition*, *11*(1), 12–21.

Ollila, Lloyd O. and Margie I. Mayfield (1992). Home and school together: Helping beginning readers succeed. In Samuels, S. Jay and Alan E. Farstrup (Eds.), *What Research Has to Say About Reading Instruction* (2nd ed.). Newark, DE: International Reading Association.

Olson, David R. (1970). Language and thought: Aspects of a cognitive theory of semantics. *Psychological Review, 77*, 257–273.

Olson, David R. (1975). Review of *Towards a Literate Society* (Carroll, John B. and Jeanne Chall, Eds.). In *Proceedings of the National Academy of Education, 2*, 109–178.

Olson, David R. (1977). From utterance to text: The bias of language in speech and writing. *Harvard Educational Review, 47*(3), 257–281.

Olson, David R. (Ed.) (1980). *The Social Foundations of Language and Thought*. New York: Norton.

Olson, David R. and Nancy Torrance (Eds.) (1991). *Literacy and Orality*. Cambridge, UK: Cambridge University Press.

Olson, David R., Nancy Torrance, and Angela Hildyard (Eds.) (1985). *Literacy, Language and Learning: The Nature and Consequences of Reading and Writing*. Cambridge, UK: Cambridge University Press.

Olson, Gary M. (1973). Memory development and language acquisition. In Moore, Timothy E. (Ed.), *Cognitive Development and the Acquisition of Language*. New York: Academic Press.

Olson, Gary M., Susan A. Duffy, and R. L. Mack (1984). Thinking-out-loud as a method for studying real-time comprehension processes. In Kieras, David E. and Marcel A. Just (Eds.), *New Methods in Reading Comprehension Research*. Hillsdale, NJ: Lawrence Erlbaum Associates.

Ong, Walter J. (1982). *Orality and Literacy: The Technologizing of the Word*. London: Methuen.

Ortony, Andrew (Ed.) (1979). *Metaphor and Thought*. Cambridge, UK: Cambridge University Press.

O'Shea, Lawrence J., Paul T. Sindelar, and Dorothy J. O'Shea (1985). The effects of repeated readings and attentional cues on reading fluency and comprehension. *Journal of Reading Behavior, 17*(2), 129–142.

Otto, Wayne (1992). The role of research in reading instruction. In Samuels, S. Jay and Alan E. Farstrup (Eds.), *What Research has to Say about Reading Instruction* (2nd ed.). Newark, DE: International Reading Association.

Paivio, Allan (1971). *Imagery and Verbal Processes*. New York: Holt, Rinehart and Winston.

Paris, S. G. and A. Y. Carter (1973). Semantic and constructive aspects of sentence memory in children. *Developmental Psychology, 9*, 109–113.

Park, Soji and Tannis Y. Arbuckle (1977). Ideograms vs alphabets: Effects of script on memory in 'biscriptal' Korean subjects. *Journal of Experimental Psychology: Human Learning and Memory, 3*, 631–642.

Pastore, R. E. and C. J. Scheirer (1974). Signal detection theory: Considerations for general application. *Psychological Bulletin, 81*(12), 945–958.

Pattanayak, D. P. (1991). Literacy: An instrument of oppression. In Olson, David R. and Nancy Torrance (Eds.), *Literacy and Orality*. Cambridge, UK: Cambridge University Press.

Patterson, Karalyn E. (1981). Neuropsychological approaches to the study of reading. *British Journal of Psychology, 72*, 151–174.

Pearson, P. David (1974/1975). The effects of grammatical complexity on children's comprehension, recall and conception of certain semantic relations. *Reading Research Quarterly, 10*, 155–192.

Pearson, P. David (1993). Teaching and learning reading: A research perspective. *Language Arts, 70*, 502–511.

Pearson, P. David, Laurel R. Roehler, Janice A. Dole, and Gerald G. Duffy (1992). Developing expertise in reading comprehension. In Samuels, S. Jay and Alan E. Farstrup (Eds.), *What Research has to Say about Reading Instruction* (2nd ed.). Newark, DE: International Reading Association.

Pearson, P. David and Alice Studt (1975). Effects of word frequency and contextual richness on children's word identification abilities. *Journal of Educational Psychology, 67*(1), 89–95.

Peirce, Charles A. (1931, 1958). *Collected Papers*. Cambridge, MA: Harvard University Press.

Perfetti, Charles A. (1985). *Reading Ability*. New York: Oxford University Press.

Perfetti, Charles A. (1991). The psychology, pedagogy, and politics of reading. *Psychological Review, 2*, 70–76.

Perfetti, Charles A., S. R. Goldman, and T. W. Hogaboam (1979). Reading skill and the identification of words in discourse context. *Memory and Cognition, 4*, 273–282.

Perfetti, Charles A. and S. Roth (1981). Some of the interactive processes in reading and their role in reading skill. In Lesgold, Alan M. and Charles A. Perfetti (Eds.), *Interactive Processes in Reading*. Hillsdale, NJ: Lawrence Erlbaum Associates.

Petersen, Steven E., Peter T. Fox, Michael L. Posner, Mark Mintun *et al.* (1989). Positron emission tomographic studies of the processing of single words. *Journal of Cognitive Neuroscience, 1*(2), 153–170.

Phillips, John L. (1981). *Piaget's Theory: A Primer*. San Francisco: Freeman.

Piaget, Jean (1954). *The Construction of Reality in the Child*. New York: Basic Books.

Piaget, Jean and Barbel Inhelder (1969). *The Psychology of the Child*. New York: Basic Books.

Piattelli-Palmarini, Massimo (Ed.) (1980). *Language and Learning: The Debate Between Jean Piaget and Noam Chomsky*. Cambridge, MA: Harvard University Press.

Pierce, J. R. (1961). *Signs, Signals and Noise: The Nature and Process of Communication*. New York: Harper and Row.

Pierce, J. R. and J. E. Karlin (1957). Reading rates and the information rate of a human channel. *Bell Systems Technical Journal, 36*, 497–516.

Pillsbury, W. B. (1897). A study in apperception. *American Journal of Psychology, 8*, 315–393.

Pinker, Steven (1984). Visual cognition: An introduction. *Cognition, 18*, 1–63.

Pinnell, Gay-Su (1989). Success for at-risk children in a program that combines reading and writing. In Mason, Jana M. (Ed.), *Reading and Writing Connections*. Boston: Allyn and Bacon.

Piper, David (1987). Teaching story grammar: Some reasons for caution. *Canadian Journal of English Language Arts, 10*(1), 30–37.

Polanyi, Michael (1966). *The Tacit Dimension*. Garden City, NY: Doubleday.

Pomerantz, James R. (1983). Global and local precedence: Selective attention in form and motion perception. *Journal of Experimental Psychology: General, 112*, 511–535.

Popper, Karl R. (1973). *Objective Knowledge: An Evolutionary Approach*. Oxford: Clarendon.

Popper, Karl R. (1976). *Unended Quest: An Intellectual Autobiography*. London: Fontana/Collins.

Posner, Michael I. and Thomas H. Carr (1992). Lexical access and the brain: Anatomical constraints on cognitive models of word recognition. *American Journal of Psychology, 195*(1), 1–26.

Potter, Mary C. (1975). Meaning in visual search. *Science, 187*, 965–966.

Potter, Mary C. (1984). Rapid serial visual presentation (RSVP): A method for studying language processing. In Kieras, David E. and Marcel A. Just (Eds.), *New Methods in Reading Comprehension Research*. Hillsdale, NJ: Lawrence Erlbaum Associates.

Potter, Mary C., J. F. Kroll, B. Yachzel, and C. Harris (1980). Comprehension and memory in rapid sequential reading. In Nickerson, R. (Ed.), *Attention and Performance VIII*. Hillsdale, NJ: Lawrence Erlbaum Associates.

Pribram, Karl H. (1971). *Languages of the Brain*. Englewood Cliffs, NJ: Prentice-Hall.

Pritchard, R. M. (1961). Stabilized images on the retina. *Scientific American, 204*(6), 72–78.

Puff, Richard C. (Ed.) (1977). *Memory Organization and Structures*. New York: Academic Press.

Pugh, Anthony K. (1978). *Silent Reading*. London: Heinemann.

Pylyshyn, Zenon W. (1973). What the mind's eye tells the mind's brain: A critique of mental imagery. *Psychological Bulletin, 80*, 1–24.

Pylyshyn, Zenon W. (1979). Imagery theory: Not mysterious, just wrong. *Behavioral and Brain Sciences, 2*, 561–563.

Quastler, Henry (1956). Studies of human channel capacity. In Cherry, Colin (Ed.), *Information Theory*. London: Butterworths.

Rack, John P., Margaret J. Snowling, and Richard K. Olson (1992). The nonword reading deficit in developmental dyslexia: A review. *Reading Research Quarterly, 27*(1), 28–53.

Raichle, Marcus (1990). Images of the functioning human brain. In Barlow, Horace, Colin Blakemore, and Miranda Weston-Smith (Eds.), *Images and Understanding*. Cambridge, UK: Cambridge University Press.

Raphael, Taffy E. (Ed.) (1986). *The Contexts of School Based Literacy*. New York: Random House.

Rayner, Keith (1977). Visual attention in reading: Eye movements reflect cognitive processes. *Memory and Cognition, 5*, 443–449.

Rayner, Keith (1978). Eye movements in reading and information processing. *Psychological Bulletin, 85*, 618–660.

Rayner, Keith (ed.) 1983. *Eye Movements in Reading*. New York: Academic Press.

Rayner, Keith (1992). *Eye Movements and Visual Cognition: Scene Perception and Reading*, New York: Springer-Verlag.

Rayner, Keith and Robin K. Morris (1992). Eye movement control in reading: Evidence against semantic preprocessing. *Journal of Experimental Psychology: Human Perception and Performance, 18*(1), 163–172.

Rayner, Keith and Alexander Pollatsek (1987). Eye movements in reading: A tutorial review. In Coltheart, Max (Ed.), *Attention and Performance XIII: The Psychology of Reading*. Hove, UK: Lawrence Erlbaum Associates.

Rayner, Keith and Alexander Pollatsek (1989), *The Psychology of Reading*. Englewood Cliffs, NJ: Prentice-Hall.

Read, Charles (1971). Pre-school children's knowledge of English phonology. *Harvard Educational Review, 41*(1), 1–34.

Read, Charles, Zhang Yun-Fei, Nie Hong-Yin, and Ding Bao-Qing (1986). The ability to manipulate speech sounds depends on knowing alphabetic writing. *Cognition, 24*, 31–44.

Reber, Arthur S. (1989). Implicit Learning and tacit knowledge. *Journal of Experimental Psychology: General, 118*, 219–235.

Reder, Lynne M. (1980). The role of elaboration in the comprehension and retention of prose: A critical review. *Review of Educational Research, 50*(1), 5–53.

Reichardt, Konrad W. (1977). Playing dead or running away: Defense mechanisms during reading. *Journal of Reading, 20*, 706–711.

Reicher, G. M. (1969). Perceptual recognition as a function of meaningfulness of stimulus material. *Journal of Experimental Psychology, 81*, 275–280.

Reid, L. Starling (1974). Towards a grammar of the image. *Psychological Review, 81*(6), 319–334.

Reilly, Ronan G., and Noel E. Sharkey (1992). *Connectionist Approaches to Natural Language Processing*. Hove, UK: Lawrence Erlbaum Associates.

Resnick, Lauren B. and Phyllis A. Weaver (Eds.) (1979). *Theory and Practice of Early Reading* (3 vols.). Hillsdale, NJ: Lawrence Erlbaum Associates.

Restle, F. (1970). Theory of serial pattern learning. *Psychological Review, 77*, 481–495.

Rhode, Mary and Bruce Cronnell (1977). *Compilation of a Communication Skills Lexicon Coded with Linguistic Information*. Los Alamitos, CA: Southwest Regional Laboratory for Educational Research and Development, Technical Report No. 58.

Rice, Mabel L. (1990). Preschoolers' QUIL: Quick Incidental Learning of Words. In Conti-Ramsden, Gina and Catherine E. Snow (Eds.), *Children's Language (Vol. Seven)*. Hillsdale, NJ: Lawrence Erlbaum Associates.

Rieben, Laurence and Charles A. Perfetti (1991). *Learning to Read: Basic Research and Its Implications*. Hillsdale, NJ: Lawrence Erlbaum Associates.

Robinson, H. Alan, Vincent Faraone, Daniel R. Hittelman, and Elizabeth Unrah (1990). *Reading Comprehension Instruction 1783–1987: A Review of Trends and Research*. Newark, DE: International Reading Association.

Robinson, Ian (1975). *The New Grammarians' Funeral*. Cambridge, UK: Cambridge University Press.

Robinson, Richard (1991). Leaders in reading research and instruction: An interview with Dr. Marilyn Adams. *Reading Psychology, 12*, 159–164.

Rock, Irvin (1983). *The Logic of Perception*. Cambridge, MA: MIT Press.

Rosch, Eleanor and B. B. Lloyd (1978). *Cognition and Categorization*. Hillsdale, NJ: Lawrence Erlbaum Associates.

Rosen, Harold (1986). The importance of story. *Language Arts, 63*(3), 226–237.

Rosen, Harold (1988). Stories of stories: Footnotes on sly gossipy practices. In Lightfoot, Martin and Nancy Martin (Eds.), *The Word for Teaching is Learning: Essays for James Britton*. London: Heinemann.

Rosenberg, Steven and Herbert A. Simon (1977). Modelling semantic memory: Effects of presenting semantic information in different modalities. *Cognitive Psychology, 9*, 293–325.

Rosenblatt, Louise M. (1978). *The Reader: The Text: The Poem*. Carbondale: Southern Illinois University Press.

Rosenblatt, Louise M. (1980). What facts does this poem teach you? *Language Arts, 57*(4), 386–394.

Rosinski, Richard R., Roberta Michnick Golinkoff, and Karen S. Kukish (1975). Automatic semantic processing in a picture-word interference task. *Child Development, 46*(1), 247–253.

Rothkopf, Ernst Z. and M. J. Billington (1974). Indirect review and priming through questions. *Journal of Educational Psychology, 66*(5), 669–679.

Rothkopf, Ernst Z. and Richard P. Coatney (1974). Effects of readability of context passages on subsequent inspection rates. *Journal of Applied Psychology, 59*(6), 679–682.

Rottenberg, Claire J. and Lyndon W. Searfoss (1992). Becoming literate in a preschool class: Literacy development of hearing-impaired children. *Journal of Reading Behavior, 24*(4), 463–479.

Rozin, Paul, Susan Poritsky, and Raina Sotsky (1971). American children with reading problems can easily learn to read English represented by Chinese characters. *Science, 171*, 1264–1267.

Rumelhart, David E. (1980). Schemata: The building blocks of cognition. In Spiro, Rand C., Bertram C. Bruce, and William F. Brewer (Eds.), *Theoretical Issues in Reading Comprehension: Perspectives from Cognitive Psychology, Linguistics, Artificial Intelligence, and Education*. Hillsdale, NJ: Lawrence Erlbaum Associates.

Rumelhart, David E. and James L. McClelland (1981). An interactive activation model of context effects in letter perception: Part II: The contextual enhancement effect and some tests and extensions of the model. *Psychological Review, 89*, 60–94.

Rumelhart, David E., and James L. McClelland (1987). Learning the past tenses of English verbs: Implicit rules or parallel distributed processing. In Brian MacWhinney (Ed.), *Mechanisms of Language Acquisition*, Hillsdale, NJ: Lawrence Erlbaum Associates.

Rumelhart, David E., James L. McClelland, and the "PDP Research Group" (1986). *Parallel Distributed Processing* (2 vols.), Cambridge, MA: MIT Press.

Rumelhart, David E. and Andrew Ortony (1977). The representation of knowledge in memory. In Anderson, Richard C., Rand J. Spiro, and William E. Montague (Eds.), *Schooling and the Acquisition of Knowledge*. Hillsdale, NJ: Lawrence Erlbaum Associates.

Rumelhart, David E. and Elizabeth Siple (1974). Process of recognizing tachistoscopically presented vowels. *Psychological Review, 81*, 99–118.

Sachs, Jacqueline S. (1974). Memory in reading and listening to discourse. *Memory and Cognition, 2*(1A), 95–100.

Sacks, Oliver (1989). *Seeing Voices: A Journey Into the World of the Deaf*. Berkeley: University of California Press.

Sadoski, Mark (1983). An exploratory study of the relationships between reported imagery and the comprehension and recall of a story. *Reading Research Quarterly, 19*(1), 110–121.

Sadoski, Mark, Ernest M. Goetz, and S. Kansinger (1988). Imagination in story response: Relationships between imagery, affect and structural importance. *Reading Research Quarterly, 23*, 320–336.

Saenger, Paul (1991). The separation of words and the physiology of reading. In Olson, David R. and Nancy Torrance (Eds.), *Literacy and Orality*. Cambridge, UK: Cambridge University Press.

Sakamoto, Takahiko (1976). Writing systems in Japan. In Merritt, John E. (Ed.), *New Horizons in Reading*. Newark, DE: International Reading Association.

Salmon, Phillida (1985). *Living in Time: A New Look at Personal Development*. London: Dent.

Salmon, Phillida (1988). *Psychology for Teachers*. London: Hutchinson.

Salmon, Phillida and Hilary Claire (1984). *Classroom Collaboration*. London: Routledge and Kegan Paul.

Sampson, Geoffrey (1985). *Writing Systems: A Linguistic Introduction*. London: Hutchinson.

Samuels, S. Jay (1971). Letter-name versus letter-sound knowledge in learning to read. *The Reading Teacher, 24*, 604–608.

Samuels, S. Jay (1979). The method of repeated readings. *The Reading Teacher, 32*, 403–408.

Samuels, S. Jay, Gerald Begy, and Chau Ching Chen (1975/1976). Comparison of word recognition speed and strategies of less skilled and more highly skilled readers. *Reading Research Quarterly, 11*(1), 72–86.

Santa, John L., Carol Santa, and Edward E. Smith (1977). Units of word recognition: Evidence for the use of multiple units. *Perception and Psychophysics, 22*, 285–291.

Scarfe, M. and Jerome S. Bruner (1975). The capacity for joint visual attention in the infant. *Nature, 25*, 265–266.

Schank, Roger C. (1980). What's a schema anyway? [Review of Freedle, Roy O. (Ed.) (1979). *New Directions in Discourse Processing* (Vol. 2). Norwood, NJ: Ablex]. *Contemporary Psychology, 25*(10), 814–816.

Schank, Roger C. (1982). *Reading and Understanding: Teaching from the Perspective of Artificial Intelligence*. Hillsdale, NJ: Lawrence Erlbaum Associates.

Schank, Roger C. and Robert Abelson (1977). *Scripts, Plans, Goals, and Understanding*. Hillsdale, NJ: Lawrence Erlbaum Associates.

Schatz, Elinore Kress and R. Scott Baldwin (1986). Context cues are unreliable predictors of word meanings. *Reading Research Quarterly, 21*(4), 439–454.

Schneider, Walter and Richard M. Shiffrin (1977). Controlled and automatic human information processing: I. Detection, search and attention. *Psychological Review, 84*(1), 1–66.

Scholes, Robert J. and Brenda J. Willis (1991). Linguists, literacy and the intensionality of Marshall McLuhan's Western man. In Olson, David R. and Nancy Torrance (Eds.), *Literacy and Orality*. Cambridge, UK: Cambridge University Press.

Schwab, Eileen C. and Howard C. Nussbaum (Eds.) (1986). *Pattern Recognition by Humans and Machines* (Vol. 2: Visual Perception). Orlando: Academic Press.

Schwanenflugel, Paula J. (Ed). (1991). *The Psychology of Word Meanings.* Hillsdale, NJ: Lawrence Erlbaum Associates.

Scribner, Sylvia and Michael Cole (1978). Literacy without schooling: Testing for intellectual effects. *Harvard Educational Review, 48*(4), 448–461.

Searle, John R. (1980). The intentionality of intention and action. *Cognitive Science, 4,* 47–70.

Sebasta, Sam (1981). Why Rudolph can't read. *Language Arts, 5,* 545–548.

Seidenberg, Mark S. (1985). The time course of phonological code activation in two writing systems. *Cognition, 19,* 1–30.

Seidenberg, Mark S. and James L. McClelland (1989). A distributed, developmental model of word recognition and naming. *Psychological Review, 96,* 523–568.

Seligman, Martin E. P. (1975). *Helplessness: On Depression, Development and Death.* San Francisco: Freeman.

Senner, Wayne M. (Ed.) (1989). *The Origins of Writing.* Lincoln: University of Nebraska.

Serafica, F. C. and I. E. Sigel (1970). Styles of categorization and reading disability. *Journal of Reading Behavior, 2,* 105–115.

Shallice, Tim and Elizabeth K. Warrington (1975). Word recognition in a phonemic dyslexic patient. *Quarterly Journal of Experimental Psychology, 27,* 187–199.

Shanahan, T. (Ed.) (1990). *Reading and Writing Together: New Perspectives for the Classroom.* Norwood, MA: Christopher-Gordon.

Shannon, Claude E. (1951). Prediction and entropy of printed English. *Bell Systems Technical Journal, 30,* 50–64.

Shannon, Patrick (1983). The use of commercial reading materials in American elementary schools. *Reading Research Quarterly, 19*(1), 68–85.

Shannon, Patrick (1984). Mastery learning in reading and the control of teachers and students. *Language Arts, 61*(5), 484–493.

Shannon, Patrick (1985). Reading instruction and social class. *Language Arts, 62*(6), 604–613.

Shannon, Patrick (1986). Teachers' and administrators' thoughts on changes in reading instruction within a merit pay program based on test scores. *Reading Research Quarterly, 21*(1), 20–35.

Shannon, Patrick (1989). *Broken Promises: Reading Instruction in Twentieth Century America.* Granby, MA: Bergin and Garvey.

Shannon, Patrick (1993). Critique of false generosity: A response to Baumann. *Reading Research Quarterly, 28*(1), 8–14.

Shanon, Benny (1991). The representational view of mind in perspective: A response to Lucas. *Psychological Bulletin, 2,* 264–267.

Sharkey, Noel E. and D. C. Mitchell (1985). Word recognition in a functional context: The use of scripts in reading. *Journal of Memory and Language, 24*(2), 253–270.

Shatz, Marilyn (1978). On the development of communicative understandings: An early strategy for interpreting and responding to messages. *Cognitive Psychology, 10,* 271–301.

Shuy, Roger W. (1981). Four misconceptions about clarity and simplicity. *Language Arts, 58*(3), 557–561.

Silverman, Wayne P. (1976). Can "words" be processed as integrated units? *Perception and Psychophysics, 20*(2), 143–152.

Simon, Herbert A. (1974). How big is a chunk? *Science, 183,* 482–488.

Simon, Herbert A. (1980). Cognitive science: The newest science of the artificial. *Cognitive Science, 4,* 33–46.

Simonton, Dean Keith (1988). *Scientific Genius: A Psychology of Science.* Cambridge, UK: Cambridge University Press.

Sinclair, Hermine (1970). The transition from sensory-motor behavior to symbolic activity. *Interchange*, *1*(3), 119–126.

Sinclair-de Zwart, Hermine (1973). Language acquisition and cognitive development. In Moore, Timothy E. (Ed.), *Cognitive Development and the Acquisition of Language*. New York: Academic Press.

Singer, Harry and Robert B. Ruddell (Eds.) (1976). *Theoretical Models and Processes of Reading* (2nd ed.). Newark, DE: International Reading Association.

Skinner, B. F. (1985). Cognitive science and behaviorism. *British Journal of Psychology*, *76*(3), 291–301.

Slater, Wayne H. (1985). Revising inconsiderate elementary school expository text: Effects on comprehension and recall. In Niles, Jerome A. and Rosary V. Lalik (Eds.), *Issues in Literacy: A Research Perspective*. Rochester, NY: National Reading Conference, 34th Yearbook.

Slobin, Dan I. (1979). *Psycholinguistics* (2nd ed.). Glenview, IL: Scott Foresman.

Slobin, Dan I. and C. A. Welsh (1973). Elicited imitation as a research tool in developmental psycholinguistics. In Ferguson, Charles A. and Dan I. Slobin (Eds.), *Readings in Child Language Acquisition*. New York: Holt, Rinehart and Winston.

Smith, Edward E. and Glenn M. Kleiman (1979). Word recognition: Theoretical issues and instructional hints. In Resnick, Lauren B. and Phyllis A. Weaver (Eds.), *Theory and Practice of Early Reading* (Vol. 2). Hillsdale, NJ: Lawrence Erlbaum Associates.

Smith, Edward E. and Kathryn T. Spoehr (1974). The perception of printed English: A theoretical perspective. In Kantowitz, B. H. (Ed.), *Human Information Processing: Tutorials in Performance and Cognition*. Hillsdale, NJ: Lawrence Erlbaum Associates.

Smith, Frank (1969). The use of featural dependencies across letters in the visual identification of words. *Journal of Verbal Learning and Verbal Behavior*, *8*, 215–218.

Smith, Frank (1976). Learning to read by reading: A brief case study. *Language Arts*, *53*(3), 297–299.

Smith, Frank (1977a). Making sense of reading—and of reading instruction. *Harvard Educational Review*, *47*(3), 386–395.

Smith, Frank (1977b). The uses of language. *Language Arts*, *54*(6), 638–644.

Smith, Frank (1979). Conflicting approaches to reading research and instruction. In Resnick, Lauren B. and Phyllis A. Weaver (Eds.), *Theory and Practice of Early Reading* (Vol. 2). Hillsdale, NJ: Lawrence Erlbaum Associates.

Smith, Frank (1981a). Demonstrations, engagement and sensitivity: A revised approach to language learning. *Language Arts*, *58*(1), 103–112.

Smith, Frank (1981b). Demonstrations, engagement and sensitivity (2): The choice between people and programs. *Language Arts*, *58*(6), 634–642.

Smith, Frank (1983a). *Essays into Literacy*. Portsmouth, NH: Heinemann.

Smith, Frank (1983b). Reading like a writer. *Language Arts*, *60*(5), 558–567.

Smith, Frank (1986). *Insult to Intelligence*. New York: Arbor House.

Smith, Frank (1988). *Joining the Literacy Club*. Portsmouth, NH: Heinemann.

Smith, Frank (1989). Overselling literacy. *Phi Delta Kappan*, *70*(5), 352–359.

Smith, Frank (1990). *to think*. New York: Teachers College Press.

Smith, Frank (1992). Learning to read: The never-ending debate. *Phi Delta Kappan*, *73*(6), 432–441.

Smith, Frank (1993). *Whose Language? What Power?* New York: Teachers College Press.

Smith, Frank (1994). *Writing and the Writer* (2nd ed.). Hillsdale, NJ: Lawrence Erlbaum Associates.

Smith, Frank and Peter Carey (1966). Temporal factors in visual information processing. *Canadian Journal of Psychology*, *20*(3), 337–342.

Smith, Frank and Deborah Lott Holmes (1971). The independence of letter, word and meaning identification in reading. *Reading Research Quarterly*, *6*(3), 394–415.

Smith, Frank, Deborah Lott, and Bruce Cronnell (1969). Effect of type size and case alternation on word identification. *American Journal of Psychology, 82*(2), 248–253.

Smith, Frank and George A. Miller (Eds.) (1966). *The Genesis of Language.* Cambridge, MA: MIT Press.

Smith, Mary K. (1941). Measurement of the size of general English vocabulary through the elementary grades and high school. *Genetic Psychology Monographs, 24,* 311–345.

Snow, Catherine E. (1977). Mothers' speech research: From input to interaction. In Snow, Catherine E. and Charles A. Ferguson (Eds.), *Talking to Children: Language Input and Acquisition.* Cambridge, UK: Cambridge University Press.

Snow, Catherine E. and Charles A. Ferguson (Eds.) (1977). *Talking to Children: Language Input and Acquisition.* Cambridge, UK: Cambridge University Press.

Spencer, Margaret Meek (1987). *How Texts Teach What Readers Learn.* Victoria, BC: Abel Press.

Sperling, George (1960). The information available in brief visual presentations. *Psychological Monographs, 74*(11), Whole No. 498.

Sperry, R. W. (1968). Hemisphere disconnection and unity in conscious awareness. *American Psychologist, 23,* 723–733.

Spiro, Rand J., Bertram C. Bruce, and William F. Brewer (Eds.) (1980). *Theoretical Issues in Reading Comprehension: Perspectives from Cognitive Psychology, Linguistics, Artificial Intelligence, and Education.* Hillsdale, NJ: Lawrence Erlbaum Associates.

Spoehr, Kathryn T. and S. W. Lehmkuhle (1982). *Visual Information Processing.* San Francisco: Freeman.

Spragins, Anne B., Lester A. Lefton, and Dennis F. Fisher (1976). Eye movements while reading and searching spatially transformed text: A developmental examination. *Memory and Cognition, 4*(1), 36–42.

Squire, James R. (Ed.) (1987). *The Dynamics of Language Learning.* Urbana, IL: National Conference on Research in English.

Squire, Larry S. (1986). Mechanisms of memory. *Science, 232,* 1612–1619.

Staller, Joshua (1982). Neurological correlates of reading failure. In Singer, Martin H. (Ed.), *Competent Reader, Disabled Reader: Research and Application.* Hillsdale, NJ: Lawrence Erlbaum Associates.

Stanovich, Keith E. (1980). Toward an interactive-compensatory model of individual differences in the development of reading fluency. *Reading Research Quarterly, 15,* 32–71.

Stanovich, Keith E. (1981). Attentional and automatic context effects in reading. In Lesgold, Alan M. and Charles A. Perfetti (Eds.), *Interactive Processes in Reading.* Hillsdale, NJ: Lawrence Erlbaum Associates.

Stanovich, Keith E. (1982a). Individual differences in the cognitive processes of reading: I. Word decoding. *Journal of Learning Disabilities, 15,* 485–493.

Stanovich, Keith E. (1982b). Individual differences in the cognitive processes of reading: II. Text-level processes, *Journal of Learning Disabilities, 15,* 549–554.

Stanovich, Keith E. (1986). Matthew effects in reading: Some consequences of individual differences in the acquisition of literacy. *Reading Research Quarterly, 21*(4), 360–407.

Stanovich, Keith E. (1991). Cognitive science meets beginning reading. *Psychological Science, 2*(70), 77–81.

Stanovich, Keith E. (1992). Speculations on the causes and consequences of individual differences in early reading acquisition. In Gough, Philip B., Linnea C. Ehri, and Rebecca Treiman (Eds.) *Reading Acquisition,* Hillsdale, NJ: Lawrence Erlbaum Associates.

Stanovich, Keith E., Anne E. Cunningham, and Dorothy J. Feeman (1984). Intelligence, cognitive skills, and early reading progress. *Reading Research Quarterly, 19*(3), 278–303.

Stein, Dieter (Ed.) (1992). *Cooperating with Written Texts: The Pragmatics and Comprehension of Written Texts.* Berlin: Mouton de Gruyter.

Stein, Nancy L. and Christine G. Glenn (1979). An analysis of story comprehension in elementary school children. In Freedle, Roy O. (Ed.), *New Directions in Discourse Processing* (Vol. 2). Norwood, NJ: Ablex.

Steinberg, Danny (1982). *Language, Mind and the World*. New York: Longman.

Steinberg, Danny, M. Harada, M. Tashiro, and H. Harper (1980). Acquiring written language as a first language by deaf children. *Working Papers in Linguistics* (University of Hawaii), *12*, 3.

Steinberg, Danny and Jun Yamada (1978/1979). Are whole word *kanji* easier to learn than syllable *kana*? *Reading Research Quarterly, 14*(4), 88–89.

Sternberg, Robert J. (1983). Components of human intelligence. *Cognition, 15*, 1–48.

Sternberg, Robert J. (1985). Human intelligence: The model is the message. *Science, 230*(4730), 1111–1118.

Stevenson, V. (Ed.) (1983). *Words: The Evolution of Written Languages*. London: Methuen.

Stich, Stephen P. (1983). *From Folk Psychology to Cognitive Science: The Case Against Belief*. Cambridge, MA: MIT Press.

Sticht, Thomas G., Frederick R. Chang, and Suzanne Wood (Eds.) (1986). *Advances in Reading/Language Research (Vol. 4): Cognitive Science and Human Resources Management*. Greenwich, CT: JAI.

Stotsky, Sandra (1983). Research on reading/writing relationships: A synthesis and suggested directions. *Language Arts, 60*, 627–642.

Stotsky, Sandra (1986). On learning to write about ideas. *College Composition and Communication, 37*, 276–293.

Strickland, Dorothy S. and Lesley Mandel Morrow (1989). *Emerging Literacy: Young Children Learn to Read and Write*. Newark, DE: International Reading Association.

Stuart, M. and Coltheart, M. (1988). Does reading develop in a sequence of stages? *Cognition, 30*, 139–181.

Stubbs, Michael (1982). *Discourse Analysis: The Sociolinguistic Analysis of Natural Language*. Oxford: Blackwell.

Suhor, Charles (1992). Semiotics and the English language arts. *Language Arts, 69*, 228–230.

Sulzby, Elizabeth (1985). Children's emergent reading of favorite story books: A developmental study. *Reading Research Quarterly, 20*(4), 458–481.

Swanson, H. Lee (1984). Phonological recoding and suppression effects in children's sentence comprehension. *Reading Research Quarterly, 19*(4), 393–403.

Swets, John A. (1973). The receiver operating characteristic in psychology. *Science, 182*, 990–1000.

Swets, John A., W. P. Tanner, and T. G. Birdsall (1961). Decision processes in perception. *Psychological Review, 68*, 301–320.

Tannen, Deborah (1982a). Oral and literate strategies in spoken and written narrative. *Language, 58*, 1–21.

Tannen, Deborah (1982b). *Spoken and Written Language: Exploring Orality and Literacy*. Norwood, NJ: Ablex.

Taylor, Barbara M. (1992). Text structure, comprehension and recall. In Samuels, S. Jay and Alan E. Farstrup (Eds.), *What Research Has to Say About Reading Instruction* (2nd ed.). Newark, DE: International Reading Association.

Taylor, Denny (1983). *Family Literacy: Young Children Learning to Read and Write*. Exeter, NH: Heinemann.

Taylor, Denny (1991). *Learning Denied*. Portsmouth, NH: Heinemann.

Taylor, Denny and Dorothy S. Strickland (1986). *Family Storybook Reading*, Portsmouth, NH: Heinemann.

Taylor, Insup (1976). *Introduction to Psycholinguistics*. New York: Holt, Rinehart and Winston.

Taylor, Nancy E., Irene H. Blum, and David M. Logsdon (1986). The development of written language awareness: Environmental aspects and program characteristics. *Reading Research Quarterly, 21*(2), 132–149.

Taylor, Stanford E. (1971). *The Dynamic Activity of Reading: A Model of the Process*. Huntington, NY: Educational Development Laboratories, Inc., Bulletin No. 9.

Taylor, Stanford E., Helen Frackenpohl, and James L. Pettee (1960). *Grade Level Norms for the Components of the Fundamental Reading Skill*. Huntington, NY: Educational Development Laboratories, Inc., Bulletin No. 6.

Teale, William H. (1981). Parents reading to their children: What we know and need to know. *Language Arts, 58*(8), 902–912.

Teale, William H. (1982). Toward a theory of how children learn to read and write naturally. *Language Arts, 59*(6), 555–570.

Teale, William H. and Elizabeth Sulzby (Eds.) (1986). *Emergent Literacy: Reading and Writing*. Norwood, NJ: Ablex.

Templeton, Shane (1991). New trends in an historical perspective: The "what" and "why" of skills instruction in literacy. *Language Arts, 68*, 590–595.

Templin, Mildred C. (1957). *Certain Language Skills in Children*. Minneapolis: University of Minnesota Press.

Thompson, G. Brian. (1981). Toward a theoretical account of individual differences in the acquisition of reading skill. *Reading Research Quarterly, 15*(4), 596–599.

Thompson, Richard A. (1992). A critical perspective on whole language. *Reading Psychology, 13*(2), 131–155.

Thorndike, E. (1977). Reading as reasoning: A study of mistakes in paragraph reading. *Journal of Educational Psychology, 9*, 77–110.

Thorndike, E. L. and I. Lorge (1944). *The Teacher's Word Book of 30,000 Words*. New York: Teachers College.

Tierney, Robert J. and J. W. Cunningham (1984). Research on teaching reading comprehension. In Pearson, P. David (Ed.), *The Handbook of Reading Research*. New York: Longman.

Tierney, Robert J. and Jill LaZansky (1980). The rights and responsibilities of readers and writers: A contractual agreement. *Language Arts, 57*(6), 606–613.

Tierney, Robert J. and James Mosenthal (1982). Discourse comprehension and production: Analyzing text structure and cohesion. In Langer, Judith A. and M. Trika Smith-Burke (Eds.), *Reader Meets Author/Bridging the Gap*. Newark, DE: International Reading Association.

Tierney, Robert J. and P. David Pearson (1983). Toward a composing model of reading. *Language Arts, 60*(5), 568–580.

Tierney, Robert J. and T. Shanahan (1991). Research on the reading-writing relationships: Interactions, transactions and outcomes. In Barr, Rebecca, Michael L. Kamil, Peter Mosenthal, and P. David Pearson (Eds.), *Handbook of Reading Research*. New York: Longman.

Tinker, Miles A. (1951). Fixation pause duration in reading. *Journal of Educational Research, 44*, 471–479.

Tinker, Miles A. (1958). Recent studies of eye movements in reading. *Psychological Bulletin, 54*, 215–231.

Tinker, Miles A. (1965). *Bases for Effective Reading*. Minneapolis: University of Minnesota Press.

Torrance, Nancy A. and David R. Olson (1985). Oral and literate competencies in early school years. In David R. Olson, Nancy A. Torrance, and Angela Hildyard (Eds.), *Literacy, Language and Learning: The Nature and Consequences of Reading and Writing*. Cambridge, UK: Cambridge University Press.

Torrey, Jane W. (1969). Learning to read without a teacher: A case study. *Elementary English, 46*, 550–556.

Torrey, Jane W. (1979). Reading that comes naturally: The early reader. In Walker, T. G. and

G. E. Mackinnon (Eds.), *Reading Research: Advances in Theory and Practice* (Vol. 1). New York: Academic Press.

Tough, Joan (1974). Children's use of language. *Educational Review* (Birmingham University, UK), *26*(3), 166–179.

Treiman, Rebecca (1992). The role of intrasyllabic units in learning to read and spell. In Gough, Philip B., Linnea C. Ehri, and Rebecca Treiman (Eds.), *Reading Acquisition*, Hillsdale, NJ: Lawrence Erlbaum Associates.

Treiman, Rebecca, Usha C. Goswami, and Maggie Bruck (1990). Not all nonwords are alike. Implications for reading development and theory. *Memory and Cognition, 18*, 559–567.

Treisman, Anne M. (1969). Strategies and models of selective attention. *Psychological Review*, *76*(3), 282–299.

Truax, Roberta R. and Richard R. Kretschmer, Jr. (1993). Finding new voices in the process of meeting all the needs of children. *Language Arts, 70*(7), 592–601.

Tulving, Endel (1985a). How many memory systems are there? *American Psychologist, 40*, 385–398.

Tulving, Endel (1985b). Memory and consciousness. *Canadian Journal of Psychology, 25*, 1–12.

Tulving, Endel and Donald M. Thomson (1973). Encoding specificity and retrieval processes in episodic memory. *Psychological Review, 80*(5), 352–373.

Tulving, Endel and Michael J. Watkins (1975). Structure of memory traces. *Psychological Review, 82*(4), 261–275.

Tuman, Myron C. (1987). *A Preface to Literacy: An Inquiry into Pedagogy, Practice, and Progress*. Tuscaloosa: University of Alabama Press.

Underwood, Geoffrey (Ed.) (1978). *Strategies of Information Processing*. London: Academic Press.

Underwood, Geoffrey (1992). Review of M. C. Robeck and R. R. Wallace (1990). *The Psychology of Reading: An Interdisciplinary Approach*. (Hillsdale, NJ: Lawrence Erlbaum Associates.) *Journal of Research in Reading, 15*(2), 139–140.

Urwin, Cathy (1982). The contribution of nonvisual information systems and language to knowing oneself. In Beveridge, Michael (Ed.), *Children Thinking Through Language*. London: Arnold.

Vachek, J. (1973). *Written Language*. The Hague: Mouton.

Vallar, Guiseppe and Tim Shallice (1990). *Neuropsychological Impairments of Short-Term Memory*. Cambridge, UK: Cambridge University Press.

van Dijk, Teun A. (1980). *Macrostructures: An Interdisciplinary Study of Global Structures in Discourse, Interaction and Cognition*. Hillsdale, NJ: Lawrence Erlbaum Associates.

van Dongen, Richard (1987). Children's narrative thought, at home and at school. *Language Arts, 64*(1), 79–87.

Van Orden, Guy C., J. C. Johnson, and B. L. Hale (1988). Word identification in reading proceeds from spelling to sound to meaning. *Journal of Experimental Psychology: Learning, Memory and Cognition, 14*, 371–385.

Van Orden, Guy C., Bruce F. Pennington, and Gregory D. Stone (1990). Word identification in reading and the promise of subsymbolic psychlinguistics. *Psychological Review, 97*(4), 488–522.

VanLeirsburg, Peggy (1993). Standardized reading tests: Then and now. In Johns, Jerry L. (Ed.), *Literacy: Celebration and Challenge*. Bloomington: Illinois Reading Council.

Vellutino, F. R. (1991). Has basic research in reading increased our understanding of developmental reading and how to teach reading? *Psychological Science, 2*(70), 81–83.

Vellutino, Frank R. (1987). Dyslexia. *Scientific American, 256*(3), 34–41.

Venezky, Richard L. (1967). English orthography: Its graphical structure and its relation to sound. *Reading Research Quarterly*, *2*, 75–106.

Venezky, Richard L. (1970). *The Structure of English Orthography*. The Hague: Mouton.

Venezky, Richard L. (1977). Research on reading processes: A historical perspective. *American Psychologist*, *32*, 339–345.

Vincente, Kim J. and William F. Brewer (1993). Reconstructive remembering of the scientific literature. *Cognition*, *46*, 101–128.

Vygotsky, Lev S. (1962). *Language and Thought*. Cambridge, MA: MIT Press.

Vygotsky, Lev S. (1978). *Mind in Society: The Development of Higher Psychological Processes*. Cambridge, MA: Harvard University Press.

Walker, Carol H. and Bonnie J. F. Meyer (1980). Integrating information from text: An evaluation of current theories. *Review of Educational Research*, *50*, 421–437.

Walkerdine, Valerie (1982). From context to text: A psychosemiotic approach to abstract thought. In Beveridge, Michael (Ed.), *Children Thinking Through Language*. London: Arnold.

Walters, Gloria S., Melvin K. Komoda, and Tannis Y. Arbuckle (1985). The effects of concurrent tasks on reading: Implications for phonological recoding. *Journal of Memory and Language*, *24*(1), 27–45.

Wanner, Eric and Lila Gleitman (Eds.) (1982). *Language Acquisition: The State of the Art*. Cambridge, UK: Cambridge University Press.

Warrington, Elizabeth K. and Tim Shallice (1979). Semantic access dyslexia. *Brain*, *102*, 43–63.

Wasik, Barbara A. and Robert E. Slavin (1993). Preventing early reading failure with one-to-one tutoring: A review of five programs. *Reading Research Quarterly*, *28*(2), 178–200.

Waterland, Liz (1988). *Read With Me: An Apprenticeship Approach*. South Woodchester, UK: Thimble Press.

Weaver, Constance (1988). *Reading Process and Practice: From Socio-Psycholinguistics to Whole Language*. Portsmouth, NH: Heinemann.

Weaver, Phyllis and Fredi Shonkoff (1978). *Research Within Reach*. Washington, DC: National Institute of Education.

Weber, Rose-Marie (1968). The study of oral reading errors: A survey of the literature. *Reading Research Quarterly*, *4*, 96–119.

Weintraub, Sam (1986). The fuzzy area of literature reviews. In Weintraub, Sam, Helen K. Smith, Nancy L. Roser, Walter J. Moore, Michael W. Kibby, Kathleen S. Jongsma, and Peter L. Fisher (Eds.), *Summary of Investigations Relating to Reading: July 1, 1984 to June 30, 1985*. Newark, DE: International Reading Association.

Weir, Ruth H. (1962). *Language in the Crib*. The Hague: Mouton.

Wells, Gordon (1981). *Learning Through Interaction: The Study of Language Development*. Cambridge, UK: Cambridge University Press.

Wells, Gordon (1985). Preschool literacy-related activities and success in school. In Olson, D. R., Nancy Torrance and Angela Hildyard (Eds.), *Literacy, Language and Learning: The Nature and Consequences of Reading and Writing*. Cambridge, UK: Cambridge University Press.

Wells, Gordon (1986). *The Meaning Makers*. Portsmouth, NH: Heinemann.

Wells, Gordon and Jane Nicholls (1985). *Language and Learning: An Interactional Perspective*. Lewes, UK: Falmer.

West, Richard F., Keith E. Stanovich, and Harold R. Mitchell (1993). Reading in the real world and its correlates. *Reading Research Quarterly*, *28*(1), 34–50.

Wheeler, D. D. (1970). Processes in word recognition. *Cognitive Psychology, 1*, 59–85.

White, Thomas G., Michael F. Graves, and Wayne H. Slater (1990). Growth of reading vocabulary in diverse elementary schools: Decoding and word meaning. *Journal of Educational Psychology*, *82*(2), 281–290.

Whorf, Benjamin Lee (1956). *Language, Thought and Reality.* Cambridge, MA: MIT Press.

Wildman, Daniel and Martin Kling (1978/1979). Semantic, syntactic and spatial anticipation in reading. *Reading Research Quarterly, 14*(2), 128–164.

Wilkinson, Andrew M. (Ed.) (1971). The context of language. *Educational Review* (Birmingham University, UK), *23*(3).

Willinsky, John (1990). *The New Literacy: Redefining Reading and Writing in the Schools.* London: Routledge.

Willows, Dale M., Richard S. Kruk, and Evelyne Corcos (Eds.) (1993). *Visual Processes in Reading and Reading Disabilities.* Hillsdale, NJ: Lawrence Erlbaum Associates.

Wilson, Stephanie Gray, Mike Rinck, Timothy P. McNamara, Gordon H. Bower, and Daniel G. Morrow (1993). Mental models and narrative comprehension: Some qualifications. *Journal of Memory and Language, 32,* 141–154.

Wimmer, Heinz, Karin Landerl, Renate Linortner, and Peter Hummer (1991). The relationship of phonemic awareness to reading acquisition: More consequence than precondition, but still important. *Cognition, 40,* 219–249.

Winograd, Terry (1982). What does it mean to understand language? In Norman, Donald A. (Ed.), *Perspectives on Cognitive Science,* Norwood, NJ: Ablex.

Wolf, Maryanne (1991). Naming speed and reading: The contribution of the cognitive neurosciences. *Reading Research Quarterly, 26*(2), 123–141.

Wong, Bernice Y. L. (1982). Understanding learning disabled students' reading problems: Contributions from cognitive psychology. *Topics in Learning and Learning Disabilities,* 43–50.

Wood, Barbara S. (1981). *Children and Communication.* Englewood Cliffs, NJ: Prentice Hall.

Woodworth, Robert S. (1938). *Experimental Psychology.* New York: Holt.

Woodworth, Robert S. and Harold Schlosberg (1954). *Experimental Pscyhology.* New York: Holt, Rinehart & Winston.

Wray, David and Maureen Lewis (1992). Primary children's use of information books. *Reading, 26*(3), 19–24.

Yates, Jack (1985). The content of awareness is a model of the world. *Psychological Review, 92*(2), 249–284.

Yatvin, Joanne (1982). Learning to read at forty-eight. *Language Arts, 59*(8), 822–828.

Ylisto, Ingrid P. (1977). Early reading responses of young Finnish children. *The Reading Teacher, 31,* 167–172.

Young, Andrew W. and Andrew W. Ellis (1981). Asymmetry of cerebral hemispheric functioning in normal and poor readers. *Psychological Bulletin, 89*(1), 183–190.

Zipf, Paul (1960). *Semantic Analysis.* Ithaca, NY: Cornell University Press.

Author Index

Subject Index

(See also Glossary)